PLANNING ETHICS

PLANNING ETHICS

A Reader in Planning Theory
Practice
and Education

edited by

SUE HENDLER

CENTER
FOR URBAN
POLICY RESEARCH

New Brunswick
New Jersey

Published by the Center for Urban Policy Research
New Brunswick, New Jersey 08903

Printed in the United States of America

Cover design: Helene Berinsky

Library of Congress Cataloging-in-Publication Data

Planning ethics : a reader in planning theory, practice, and education
 /   edited by Sue Hendler.
      p.   cm.
    Includes bibliographical references and index.
    ISBN 0-88285-151-9

    1. City planning—Moral and ethical aspects.   2. Urban policy—
Moral and ethical aspects.   3. Professional ethics.   I. Hendler, Sue.
HT167.P53   1995
307.1'216—dc20   94–17143
                                                                  CIP

To Mortimer, Lewina, and Celia Hendler

Contents

PART I
Ethical Theory and Planning Theory

Acknowledgments

This book would not have been completed without the support of the School of Urban and Regional Planning at Queen's University in Kingston, Ontario, Canada. It has benefited from discussions with many, if not all, of the contributors as to its structure, content, and use. The students in my planning ethics courses, too, helped me to formulate the idea for the book and envision its potential role in planning education. I appreciated the encouragement, patience, and industry of Robert W. Lake at the Center for Urban Policy Research at Rutgers, the State University of New Jersey, his editorial staff, and all of the contributors. Thanks also to Jo-Anne Williamson, Jackie Bell, and Terry Busse, who typed, edited, and generally assisted with the manuscript. Kim Flick, Sherilyn MacGregor, and Catherine Nash helped to locate references and draw figures; they were a great help with the myriad of glitches I encountered in getting a pile of paper to the manuscript stage. Thanks also to all who have asked ad nauseam the question, "How's the book going?" Thank you for your prodding.

Finally, I owe a special word of appreciation to Martin Wachs, who started it all and who encouraged me to keep it going.

MARTIN WACHS

Foreword

Over the past two decades our collective understanding of planning has changed markedly. Having in the past described planning primarily as a technical activity involving data collection, analysis, and synthesis of physical plans and supporting policies, we have gradually come to see planning as a much broader set of human activities, encompassing the physical world and also the realm of public and social services. While retaining technical analytical and design components, planning has come to be seen also as intensely political and value laden. Not surprisingly, planners' discussions of ethics within the realm of their profession have evolved in reflection of our changing conception of the field. "Professional ethics" was—and to an extent is still—regarded by many planners to be limited to a set of rules of behavior regarding interactions with the public, with sources of data, with government officials, and with one another.

However, planners are gradually becoming comfortable with a more global conception of planning ethics in which the content of plans and their indirect as well as direct impacts are seen as having ethical as well as technical dimensions. This shift is symbolized by the evolution of the labels by which we discuss ethics: from a circumscribed view of "professional ethics" two decades ago to a broader concept of "ethics in planning" a decade ago, we have evolved to discussions of "planning ethics" in this book. The latest term adopted here by Sue Hendler symbolizes that, as an intellectual and professional community, planners recognize that every act of planning pursues certain human values and that planning is in many fundamental ways a series of statements about what we take to be right or wrong and what we take to represent the highest priorities of the society in which the planning is undertaken.

This book deals with the intersection of planning theory, practice, and education. In so doing, it perfectly encapsulates the status of planning ethics as we approach the new century. In many ways, planning rests on these three foundation stones, and in order to understand planning ethics we must understand its connection to each of them.

Planning is among the most self-conscious of professions, and the growing body of literature produced under the rubric of planning theory deals with the roles of planners and the functions of planning, particularly in democratic societies. It is especially within the realm of planning theory that the growing significance of moral theory and concerns for social equity are addressed by planners. Drawing upon the works of important social theorists and ethicists, planning theorists have focused increasingly on the ethical dimensions of planning. The fit between planning theory and moral philosophy is a natural one because the concerns of the two fields so plainly intersect. The pressing question for me is not whether planning theory and ethics can be integrated, for the answer is obvious in the scholarly activity that has established that they can and must be joined. Rather, the more challenging question for me is whether planning practice can or will usefully apply the insights of either planning theory or moral philosophy.

The institutions of government and the practices of consultants are amazingly resistant to abstract theorizing by academics. Nevertheless, since the Watergate scandal in the United States and perhaps as a reflection of concerns over widespread corruption throughout government, and partly in response to the moral imperatives being raised by a worldwide environmental movement, American planning practitioners have also paid increasing attention to the ethical and moral dimensions of their daily work. The American Planning Association (APA), for example, has adopted a statement of ethical principles that, though advisory and hortatory rather than formal or binding, is taken to apply to all participants in the planning process and not just to "professional" planners. The American Institute of Certified Planners (AICP) has amended its ethical code and published several new "ethical advisory rulings," and both APA and AICP have sponsored workshops and formal sessions on ethics topics at their annual conferences. Still, while espousing high standards and asserting that planning in the world must be directly concerned with the social equity of its outcomes and with preservation of the natural environment, ethics in planning practice barely scratches the surface of the rich and varied terrain of moral concerns raised within the realm of planning theory.

The role of educators with respect to planning ethics is a demanding one. Educators are the bridge between planning theory and practice. They draw upon the rich literature of planning theory and upon insights from planning practice in order to prepare the next generation of professional practitioners. Planners learn much of their art through practice, and professional education really prepares planners to learn on the job to a greater extent than it directly trains them to practice. Still, the inclusion of ethical concerns in planning curricula is critically important. Only if planning education sensitizes neophytes to the moral dimensions of their work are they likely to carry that sensitivity throughout their careers. Only if the connection is made in school will practitioners over time make the practice of planning more amenable to the incorporation of rich moral insights from theory. If planning education is devoid of ethical content, the practice of planning will be sadly deficient in ethical content and planning theory will consequently fail to be enriched by insights from practice. Since it is in practice that planning truly influences society, this loss would indeed be terribly unfortunate.

This book's singular contribution to planning, then, is in the clarity with which it addresses the connections between theory, practice, and education. The many contributors have helped to clarify the relationship among them for the next generation of students, educators, and practitioners.

SUE HENDLER

Introduction

Planning ethics is often thought to have begun formally with the publication of Peter Marcuse's 1976 journal article, "Professional Ethics and Beyond: Values in Planning." This was quickly followed by Elizabeth Howe and Jerome L. Kaufman's trilogy of articles on planners' ethics, roles, and values (Howe and Kaufman 1979, 1980, and 1981). Since the mid-1970s to the early 1990s, there have been literally dozens of journal articles, book chapters, conference presentations, and graduate theses on the subject of the integration of ethics with planning. Martin Wachs's 1985 volume, *Ethics in Planning,* documented the early years of this trend. In the ensuing several years, however, there has been much written and much said on the role of moral philosophy or ethics with respect to defining the mandate of planning, discussing issues encountered by planners in their daily work, and, more generally, defining the nature of the planning profession in our contemporary society. Accordingly, the purpose of this book is to document this new work, to provide sources for readers to consult if they wish to go beyond the confines of the contents of this volume, and to indicate potential directions for further work in the area of planning ethics.

Planning Ethics was selected as the title for this book because I wished to connote the integration of planning and ethics as opposed to the application of ethics to planning or, indeed, the application of planning to ethics. It has been a theme of my work, as well as many other writers, that we can learn the most from each other in a mutualistic fashion as opposed to a manner in which one discipline assumes a position of superiority. Therefore, this book is intended to be a resource for both planners and philosophers, as well as for professional ethicists in general.

The contents illustrate the depth, diversity, and scope of discussing the professional ethics of one particular discipline, that of planning. However, the kinds of arguments and discussions that the reader will find in the ensuing pages can well represent directions and trends in other professions as well. Having said this, what can planners and ethicists expect to learn from this collection of essays? Planners, it is hoped, will see that, first, their discipline is fraught with ethical questions. These questions include the usual issues of professional etiquette, such as conflict of interest, as well as the more complex issues of fairness, social justice, and equity. In addition, planners will see that the dilemmas and challenges they face in their professional practice are more than merely questions of so-called subjective values and personal preferences. Instead, the contributors' thoughts on ethics and ethical theory should indicate that many of the questions encountered by professional planners are ones that have permeated discussions of ethics for hundreds of years. Thus, they are not easily resolved nor should they be relegated to back-room politics only because they do not fit the "rational" process advocated by many planners and many planning textbooks.

Conversely, scholars in the area of moral philosophy will be able to see how their theories and perspectives actually work on the ground. They will learn the difficulties professionals have in trying to be ethical and, accordingly, will see how hard it is to apply contemporary ethical theory in the professional arena. Perhaps such recognition will play a role in philosophical discussions regarding the merits of various ethical theories.

With these thoughts in mind, the goal of this book is to contribute to the development of planning ethics as both a scholarly endeavor and a professional area of competence. More specifically, the objectives of this book are: (1) to document current thinking in the application of ethics or the integration of ethics to planning theory; (2) to show how some of these ideas have been applied to planning practice; (3) to give examples of how professors in planning schools have attempted to teach these ideas to planning students; and, finally, (4) to contribute to the state of the art of planning ethics in, primarily, North America and Great Britain through the synthesis of these three areas. These objectives form the basis for the structure and content of this book. It was my aim from the outset to develop a text that could be useful to planning practitioners, planning students, and planning educators, as well as to those of us who have been working in the area of planning ethics and planning philosophy for some time. In this regard, it was important to identify and include some of the more interesting or important papers that have been published in this area recently but also to ask individuals to develop new arguments and new insights especially for this volume. It is a matter of fact that planning ethicists are scattered throughout the United States, Canada, Europe, and other parts of the world. An international sampling of these works was thought to be the best route to provide for a timely, interesting, and relevant presentation of current ideas. This book, though, is necessarily a compromise between selectivity and comprehensiveness. The section on ethics and planning theory, for instance, does not contain chapters explicitly on such things as pragmatism, relativism, or intuitionism. These are only three examples of ethical perspectives that were not included although they, and others, are referred to by various contributors. Other sections, and indeed individual chapters, may also be accused of omitting ideas undoubtedly thought by some readers to be important. However, I hope that readers will be able to glean something of value from the following pages and be stimulated to pursue further work in this area.

While this book begins with theory and proceeds to discuss practice and education, readers should be able to begin in, or sample from, any one of the three parts. This was intentional; while it means that some ideas are repeated in places throughout the text, it enables readers to browse in a fashion most conducive to their own work. Having said that, though, a rationale for my selection of the three parts might be useful.

First, the part on planning theory/ethical theory provides arguments as to the nature and role of planning, according to different perspectives in moral philosophy. This part introduces various ethical theories and also presents a language or form of discourse that is common to most, if not all, of the chapters in this book. Thus, while it is not necessary, many individuals who are unfamiliar with philosophical terms, philosophers' names, or philosophical concepts may wish to begin with this part so as to facilitate their reading of parts II and III.

The second part includes discussions of the application of ethical ideas such as equity, rights, and fairness to contemporary planning issues. "Substantive" issues such as waste management, agricultural land preservation, and education planning were selected; this focus can be compared to ethical aspects of planning techniques, such as forecasting (Wachs 1989) and evaluation (Smith 1985). While the latter certainly merits attention, it is part of a vast, multidisciplinary literature that was thought to be beyond the desired scope of this book. Having said that, however, a reader on ethics and planning techniques would be a useful supplement to the discussions presented here.

Finally, the third part pertains to ethics and planning education. The purpose of this part is to stimulate thought on how best to teach the ideas discussed in the preceding chapters. While this part may be most useful to educators, students, too, may well find it interesting to discover how their colleagues in other programs learn about particular material. Lively interactions between students and their teachers will hopefully be the result.

Each of the three parts begins with an introduction that discusses some of the central themes of the chapters in that part. Some readers may wish to read these introductions and gain an overview prior to reading the individual chapters; others may prefer to wait and form their own ideas regarding contributors' arguments and then confirm or contrast their interpretations with those offered in the introduction. Again, it is up to the reader and her or his objectives.

Planning ethics has reached a level of sophistication and what seems like no less than exponential growth. Keeping up with the theoretical, professional, and pedagogical developments in this area has become increasingly challenging. The chapters collected here represent a touchstone between the rich history and future growth of ethics, planning, and the integration thereof. Discourse resulting from the reading of these chapters will, I hope, stimulate the critical, imaginative, and synthetic perspectives of planners of all sorts. That is the future of planning ethics.

Bibliography

Howe, E. 1980. Role choices of urban planners. *Journal of the American Planning Association* 46, 398–409.

Howe, E. and Kaufman, J. 1979. The ethics of contemporary American planners. *Journal of the American Planning Association* 45, 243–255.

———. 1981. The values of contemporary American planners. *Journal of the American Planning Association* 47, 266–278.

Marcuse, P. 1976. Professional ethics and beyond: values in planning. *Journal of the American Institute of Planners* 42, 264–275.

Smith, N. 1985. Some characteristics of moral problems in evaluation practice. *Evaluation and Program Planning* 8, 5–11.

Wachs, M. 1989. When planners lie with numbers. *Journal of the American Planning Association* 55, 476–479.

———, ed. 1985. *Ethics in planning.* New Brunswick, NJ: Center for Urban Policy Research, Rutgers—The State University of New Jersey.

PLANNING
ETHICS

Ethical Theory
and
Planning Theory

SUE HENDLER

Introduction

Planning theory has been part of planning texts and planning curricula for decades. It has evolved, and definitions of its scope, intent, and substance have changed. Instead of attempting to develop consensus on a single approach to planning theory, many writers have advocated the delineation of different types of planning theory. Shean McConnell (1981), for example, follows Andreas Faludi (1973), among others, and speaks of theory *in, of,* and *for* planning. Theory *in* planning includes ideas developed in other disciplines that may be used by planners and planning theorists. Theories developed by ecologists, for instance, have contributed to both planners' understanding of urban systems and the incorporation of such understanding in theories of how planning functions within these systems. Theories in planning are, therefore, those that come from outside the planning field and help us to explain or direct planning efforts in particular directions given this information.

Theories *of* planning are those ideas concerning planning processes that pertain to the ways planners and planning work. How planners make decisions, how planning organizations function, and how these fit together are the kinds of issues discussed here. Procedural theories of planning constitute what could be called the conventional scope of theories of planning. Incrementalism, mixed scanning, comprehensive rationality, and other models of how planning decisions are made fit into this segment of planning theory (Faludi 1973). While

3

comprehensive rationality has, until recently, easily been named the "winner" among competing theories, it now has many detractors and faces strong competition from strategic planning and other variations of procedural thought.

Theories *for* planning have to do with the role of planning in society. They unify, uphold, and justify planning values in the form of a conceptual foundation for the field and profession. The six chapters in this first part of *Planning Ethics* are concerned primarily with these sorts of theories. They are searching for answers to questions pertaining to the direction of planning—its stated purpose, impacts, and the congruence thereof. Each of the following chapters posits a particular point of view in attempting to address the norms that, the authors argue, should govern the planning profession. In so doing, the contributors discuss planning theory in terms of ethics or moral theory, where the latter provides moral guidance helping to define what planning can and cannot or should and should not do for us in contemporary Western society.

Theories in, of, and for planning have both descriptive/explanatory and prescriptive/normative content. We can talk about what planners do as well as what they should do. We can explain how cities function or we can propose ways in which they ought to function. As just outlined, we can argue that planning does perform a particular role or we can present premises supporting conclusions that planning should fulfill yet another set of societal expectations. Contributors to the first part of this collection of essays fall primarily into the last of these categories; they present ideas about what planning should be like and how planners should behave. In this regard, they prescribe roles for planning and provide answers to questions such as "Why plan?" and "What is planning for?" (Alexander 1992).

Answers to these kinds of questions can be found throughout the planning theory literature. Do we plan to preserve the integrity of the natural environment? To uphold the rights of disadvantaged members of communities? To ensure that the value of property is maintained or increased? To define and strengthen communities? To respond to the wishes of the majority of municipal residents? To balance "efficiency" and "effectiveness"? Some writers in planning theory have chosen to come out clearly on the side of one or another of these orientations. Others have preferred to maintain a position but to do so implicitly, almost passively.

Paul Davidoff (1978, pp. 69–70) has given us one of the most decisive perspectives in terms of an explicit and clearly articulated position. He states:

> If a planner is not working directly for the objective of eradicating poverty and racial and sexual discrimination, then she or he is counter-productive. If the work is not specific in its redistributive aims, then it is at best inefficient. If the work is not aimed at redistribution, then a *presumption* stands that it is amoral. These are strong words. They must be. So long as poverty and racism exist in our society, there is an ethical imperative for a single direction in planning (emphasis added).

His argument, however, is not based explicitly on any sort of underlying ethical theory and thus does not have the philosophical rigor demanded by at least some planning theorists. He himself *presumes* that his stance is appropriate; while Davidoff's statements are passionate and persuasive, there is no analysis leading skeptics to his conclusion.

On the other end of the continuum is Guy Benveniste. His book, *Mastering the Politics of Planning* (1989, pp. 48–49), is an example of an ethical stance that is taken quietly, with little discussion or articulation. He says, for example:

> I would argue that planners should not be afraid to use secrecy when appropriate. Nor should they worry if they do not consult with everyone or if they step on a few toes. Ethical behavior matters, but we should also remember the old saying that one cannot make an omelette without breaking some eggs.

Benveniste seems to be saying that secrecy is a bad thing; all things being equal, planners should be honest and inclusive. However, he appears to believe, too, that making an omelet (that is, getting plans implemented, for example) is more important than these ethical norms (Hendler 1993). This position is taken, though, with few clear premises or arguments. It is up to the reader to find the underlying ideas and choose to refute or support them.

The kinds of arguments presented by the contributors to this part seek to avoid these criticisms. They endeavor to present clear, structured positions as to the role(s) they believe planners should play or, alternatively, background material underlying the subsequent development of such positions. The authors' arguments can be seen as having a number of objectives: to persuade, to explain, to enjoy the challenge of developing logically coherent positions, and to provide the intellectual backdrop against which planners can choose their normative orientations.

While most anthologies of writings on planning theory contain at least some reference to ethics and the kinds of questions and answers posed above (Burchell and Sternlieb 1978; Faludi 1973; Healey et al. 1982; Paris 1982), none provide the basis for sustained debate on planning ethics/theory as do the following chapters. They progress from discussions of traditional liberal conceptions of ethics and planning through to more radical perspectives of planning rooted in environmentalism and feminism. While some writers attempt to refute some aspects of their colleagues' work, for the most part, they leave it up to the reader to decide where she or he stands. This first part thus acts as a springboard from which should arise new ideas and new questions on the part of planning students, educators, and practitioners alike.

The Arguments

In chapter 1, Thomas L. Harper and Stanley M. Stein present a liberal or, more specifically, libertarian perspective of planning. This approach is based on values such as equality, liberty, tolerance, fairness, and impartiality. A view of planning that flows from these values and related concepts is one that is conservative, relatively noninterventionist, and focused on the negative rights of individuals. Planning should remedy past wrongs and can protect citizens from other citizens' actions but should do little in the way of what is often called "proactive" decision making.

Shean McConnell takes another view of liberalism in chapter 2. Here he discusses the contributions John Rawls's theory of justice can make to planning theory. Rawls's central idea of justice as fairness, as well as his accompanying principles and priority rules, leads McConnell to develop an approach to planning and planning theory that emphasizes meeting the needs of disadvantaged individuals. He cites practical planning examples in this regard, such as the equity planning practices of Norman Krumholz's planning department in Cleveland, Ohio, during the 1970s, as well as similar cases in Great Britain. McConnell sees Rawls's theory as a route for planning our way out of an era characterized by inequities, environmental degradation, and political strife.

In chapter 3, Harper and Stein again team up to present a third perspective of a liberal approach to planning theory. Their position here is one focused on procedural elements of planning theory. How planners and planning organizations should make normative decisions is discussed. John Rawls's notion of a Wide Reflective Equilibrium, Jürgen Habermas's quest for liberation from ideological distortion, and Michael Walzer's critical interpretation are provided as liberal-based reasoning processes relevant to the planning endeavor. Harper and Stein conclude by connecting these methods of decision making with trends in planning theory (for example, advocacy, radical, equity, and so on). They maintain that even within the framework of liberalism, the planner should be committed to critical thinking and freedom from oppression.

Communitarianism, often seen as an opponent of liberalism, is the focus of chapter 4. Hilda Blanco identifies four "jewels" of planning: reason, democratic process, nature, and community. Community is seen as the goal of planning—an antidote to Western trends toward ever-increasing individualism. Blanco discusses philosophers' contributions to communitarian thinking (such as Alasdair MacIntyre, Michael J. Sandel, and Michael Walzer) and argues that such thinking should be at the heart of the theory and practice of planning.

Nature, one of Blanco's four jewels, is the subject of chapter 5. Here Harvey M. Jacobs presents several strands of environmental ethics or environmental philosophy and weaves these strands into a planning theory tapestry. This tapestry is comprised of philosophical thought from deep ecology, bioregionalism, and ecological feminism, as well as planning notions of both substance and process. Environmental philosophy, Jacobs argues, leads to a context-rich, relevant, and sustainable planning effort that does not play social goals against environmental ones.

In chapter 6, a final perspective presented is that of feminist thinking. Marsha Ritzdorf discusses gender and planning theory and, while recognizing the diversity inherent in feminist work, identifies themes common to most such endeavors. The eradication of women's oppression, the commitment of feminist researchers to changing the circumstances they study, and the meshing of theory and practice are examples of such themes. Five American and Canadian planning theorists who incorporate these ideas into their work are discussed; their efforts are seen as pioneering attempts at making planning and planning theory more responsive to the gendered nature of the field.

Toward a Planning Ethics

The six chapters in this part provide insight into how ethical and planning theory can be integrated to give new direction to planning thought and work. Clearly, the integration is not complete. One can point to areas of moral philosophy that are not represented here (such as relativism), as well as facets of chapters that could benefit from further elaboration. Examples include coverage of conventional environmental ethics theories in Jacobs's discussion of environmental philosophy (such as Peter Singer's animal liberation, Tom Regan's animal rights, Paul Taylor's respect for nature, Albert Schweitzer's reverence for life) and more detailed material on feminist ethics in Ritzdorf's chapter on feminist planning theory (for example, ethic of care, maternal ethics, relational ethics, and lesbian ethics; Hendler 1994). Suffice it to say, however, that the discussions presented paint a rather colorful mural of planning ethics in which some shades are complementary (contemporary liberalism and Rawlsian thought, for instance) and others contrasting or even clashing (such as some views of feminism with most liberal approaches).

The diverse positions taken by contributors in this part of the book illustrate the lack of consensus as to the role of planning in contemporary society. The degree of intervention and the justification for this intervention vary tremendously depending upon the ethical stance one assumes to be appropriate. While it is not surprising that planning ethicists cannot agree on a single moral position (philosophers have been trying for centuries!), it makes the delineation of planning functions and processes difficult. It also raises the eyebrows of skeptics who question the professional status of planning and wonder whether any field that cannot clearly identify its reason for being should be seen as a profession. Clearly, though, one cannot wait for unanimity before proceeding with professional work. Other professions, too, such as medical or bioethics, are rife with internal conflict regarding the nature of professional-client relationships, whether professionals should take on advocacy roles, and so on. Planning is not alone in having difficulty selecting a normative theory guiding its present and future direction. So what do the arguments presented here tell us about the next steps in theorizing for planning?

An emphasis on participation, democratic decision making, equity, and facilitated consensus building seems to be alluded to by most, or at least many, of the contributors. In fact, this appears to be a theme running through contemporary discussions in both philosophy and planning. An example from philosophy is Seyla Benhabib (1992), who develops a communicative ethics based on discourse that is fair, empathetic, inclusive, and self-reflective. Corresponding examples from planning theory are many but include John Forester, Patsy Healey, and several others. It seems that a focus on a reasonable and equitable process is the vehicle destined to bring together current developments in ethical and planning theory. Perhaps, given our Western emphasis on pluralism, this is to be expected. Perhaps, even, this is sufficient to forge new roles and functions for planners and planning that are relevant, needed, and appropriate in today's uncertain and turbulent environment. Perhaps this is, indeed, the route forward—a route leading to an agreed-upon role for planners, one complete with ethical justification.

While intuitively and maybe practically attractive, a system of planning ethics based on notions of inclusiveness, communication, and equity is not easy to live up to. It requires skills that are often not part of planning education—skills such as dispute resolution, listening, cross-cultural communication, working in small groups, and so on. Further, it means attracting individuals and groups to the planning table, a table currently rendered invisible or irrelevant in the eyes of many disillusioned publics. In a related sense, it also means identifying and then finding voices that have been quiet or even absent in planning, as well as philosophy. Finally, planning ethics founded on these norms must be reformulated as a basis for evaluating planners' behavior. How might we codify values of inclusiveness, equitable discourse, and consensus?

The translation of theories for planning into sets of guiding principles for planners is a challenge faced by professional planning bodies, as well as academics. Martin Wachs (1985) presents some of the results of planners facing this challenge; professional codes represent the application of the kinds of theories discussed in this part. Until recently, such codes emphasized issues of professional etiquette, including conflict of interest, advertising, and everyday behavior. Now, however, it is common for codes to address the "big" questions of social responsibility and professional roles. Extant codes list environmental integrity, the rights of the disadvantaged, some form of the "public interest," and other equally plausible values as being central to the work of planners. It is rare, though, to find mention of priorities and potential contradictions or conflicts that may arise in trying to fulfill all of the obligations articulated in a code.

The commonalities among the chapters in this part may provide some help in this regard. A model of planning has emerged in which inclusive and meaningful discursive participation is thought by many to be central to the profession. Such a model enables us to discuss, argue, and potentially reach consensus on the issues we believe to be central to our work. A communicative planning ethics may thus have a role within planning circles as well as the larger professional/societal realm. While not without its problems (for example, what if a "bad" consensus emerges from the process?), a communicative process can help us to structure the codes that guide our behavior, as well as articulate that behavior (Hendler 1990). In other words, inclusive discourse becomes both the process and substance leading to a theoretical and practice-oriented planning ethics.

Parts II and III of this book, which discuss the practice and pedagogy of planning, respectively, provide a basis for evaluating or comparing existing conditions within planning to the kinds of ideas expressed here. Readers may wish to ask themselves whether examples of planning practice live up to the kinds of norms suggested in this part, as well as whether those of us teaching planning ethics are including in our syllabi the skills indicated in this discussion as being of critical importance. Where there are gaps it becomes a challenge for all of us to, in a manner reminiscent of Harper and Stein's discussion of Rawls's Wide Reflective Equilibrium, come to an agreement as to whether it is our practice or our theory that requires revision.

Bibliography

Alexander, E. 1992. *Approaches to planning.* 2d ed. Philadelphia: Gordon and Breach.
Benhabib, S. 1992. *Situating the self.* New York: Routledge.
Benveniste, G. 1989. *Mastering the politics of planning.* San Francisco: Jossey-Bass.
Burchell, R. and Sternlieb, G., eds. 1978. *Planning theory in the 1980s.* New Brunswick, NJ: Center for Urban Policy Research, Rutgers—The State University of New Jersey.
Davidoff, P. 1978. The redistributive function in planning: creating greater equity among citizens of communities. In Burchell, R. and Sternlieb, G., eds. *Planning theory in the 1980s.* New Brunswick, NJ: Center for Urban Policy Research, Rutgers—The State University of New Jersey, 69–72.
Faludi, A., ed. 1973. *A reader in planning theory.* New York: Pergamon Press.
Healey, P., McDougall, G., and Thomas, M. J., eds. 1982. *Planning theory: prospects for the 1980s.* New York: Pergamon Press.
Hendler, S. 1990. Professional codes as bridges between planning and ethics: a case study. *Plan Canada* 30, 22–29.
———. 1993. The three e's of planning: effectiveness, efficiency, ethics. *Planning Theory* 9, 49–54.
———. 1994. Feminist/planning ethics. *Journal of Planning Literature* 9(2), 115–127.
McConnell, S. 1981. *Theories for planning: an introduction.* London: Heinemann.
Paris, C., ed. 1982. *Critical readings in planning theory.* New York: Pergamon Press.
Wachs, M., ed. 1985. *Ethics in planning.* New Brunswick, NJ: Center for Urban Policy Research, Rutgers—The State University of New Jersey.

THOMAS L. HARPER AND STANLEY M. STEIN

1   *A Classical Liberal (Libertarian) Approach to Planning Theory*

The Liberal Perspective

"Liberal" is a very broad term that can encompass a variety of political and moral philosophies (such as that of Isaiah Berlin, Ronald Dworkin, Jürgen Habermas, William Kymlicka, Kai Nielsen, Robert Nozick, John Rawls, and Richard Rorty) and planning theories (such as that of John Forester and Norman Krumholz, along with John Friedmann's Social Learning). Depending on the definition used, the liberal perspective often appears to underlie many of the policies of every mainstream political party, such as the Republican, Democrat, Conservative, Liberal, New Democrat, or Labour parties. To a significant degree, it might be seen as the dominant perspective of our North American culture; as such, it may have some negative overtones to those who are critical of this culture. Our moral commitment to the basic liberal values, which will be described below, does not mean that we necessarily endorse

This is a substantially revised version of the authors' 1983 article, "The Justification of Urban Intervention," that was originally published in *Environments, A Journal of Interdisciplinary Studies* 15(1), published by the Faculty of Environmental Studies, University of Waterloo, Ontario, Canada.

11

the actual functioning of the institutions of any particular liberal democratic society.

The basic fundamental common value shared by the liberal positions that concern us here is their focus on the free, equal, and autonomous individual person as the basic unit of society—the ultimate object of moral concern and the ultimate source of value. Specific liberal values include (1) equality of persons—each is entitled to inalienable individual rights and to fair, impartial treatment; (2) liberty—autonomy or freedom of choice to live a good life, that is, a life worth living; (3) tolerance—acceptance and respect for a plurality of conflicting conceptions of the good life; (4) rational, reflective choice—critical evaluation of life conceptions; (5) society as a fair system of cooperation between free and equal persons; (6) the rule of law—the impartial application of law to all persons; (7) a primary government role in protection of liberty; and (8) restrictions on the coercive powers of government.[1] Many of these values lead to an emphasis on procedural justice, a focus on the design of legal and political procedures, rather than just substantive conditions or outcomes. The more pluralistic the society and the more diverse the differing conceptions of the good life, the more important are the procedural aspects of its social institutions.

The liberal perspective arises out of the period of intellectual, social, and cultural change known as the Enlightenment in the ideas of John Locke (1632–1704), Jean-Jacques Rousseau (1712–1778), and Thomas Jefferson (1743–1826). The Enlightenment was the beginning of what is now known as "Modernism." Thus, the liberal perspective has come under recent attack from Postmodernists. While a full examination is beyond the scope of this chapter, it is important to understand the relationship between liberalism and the assumptions of Modernism.

The liberal valuing of the person is often related (by its critics) to a metaphysical, or Kantian, notion of the person. It is important to recognize that one can accept a critique of the Enlightenment's metaphysical notion of the person (as a floating atom or a monad of consciousness) without giving up the Enlightenment's moral and political view of the individual as the ultimate object of ethical concern (Kymlicka 1989; Rawls 1985; Rorty 1990).[2] We believe that the moral and political notion does not require a metaphysical foundation.

Critics may argue that the philosophical notion of the autonomous "free-floating individual" unrelated to the social context in which one develops is an empty one. It may be that one's initial choice of the goals that one considers worthy is largely socially determined. Liberals can concede such communitarian (see chapter 4) claims and can reject the metaphysical "autonomous person" without in any way weakening the moral and political conception of the "autonomous person." It does not follow from the social origin of our initial goals that we should switch from the individual to the community as the proper object of moral concern. To argue that it does presupposes an absolute dualism between person and community, that is, an implicit acceptance of the absolute foundationalism of Modernism.[3]

The individual has the right, obligation, and capacity to critically evaluate and modify these community-based goals and values, so when John Rawls (1971, p. 31) speaks of "the priority of the right over the good" and says that "the self is prior to the ends which are affirmed by it" (ibid., p. 560), it is meant in this sense: of persons being able to critically evaluate and modify their ends in the light of moral values. In this sense, an appeal to the autonomous individual is necessary for critical rationality.

The notion of the person that is required for liberalism is someone who is able to play an individualistic and critical "role in social life, and hence exercise and respect its various rights and duties" (Rawls 1985, p. 233); that is, a creature who has the properties reflected in liberal values: one who is free, rational, and autonomous, with a capacity for a sense of justice, and one who is capable of making choices, of formulating a conception of a good life, and of critically evaluating and modifying this concept. Entities generally seen as lacking these properties—groups of people (such as nations or ethnic groups), states, objects, or the natural environment—do not have intrinsic moral value. If they have a moral value, it is instrumental, stemming from their value to persons.[4]

Views that most clearly contrast with liberalism are those that reject the liberal focus on the autonomous person—statists, fascists, deep ecologists, radical feminists, Friedmann's radical planners, some Marxists, some Postmodernists, some conservatives, many utilitarians, and most communitarians, among others. Because we view the valuing of the autonomous person as so key to the liberal worldview, we do not include perspectives that reject this basic value within our account of the liberal perspective.

Utilitarianism and Liberalism

Until recently, many moral justifications of government and of planning and the dominant planning methodology (that is, the Rational Comprehensive Model[5]) rested on the normative ethical theory[6] of utilitarianism. Although some utilitarians are generally regarded as liberals, we argue that utilitarianism violates what we hold to be the fundamental liberal value.

Utilitarian ethical theory holds that the best act (whether rule, plan, policy, system, or intervention) is the one that maximizes the sum total of whatever is intrinsically good—usually happiness or well-being.[7] There are numerous variants of utilitarianism. Unitary utilitarian theories (when applied to the public policy realm) tend to be expressed in terms of one single "public interest" that can be maximized. Economic utilitarian theories hold that an approximation of this single total can be derived by translating individual utilities into a commensurable unit (such as a monetary unit) and then summed to give a total measure (or at least a proxy measure) of well-being. This requires some assumptions[8] that many people (at least noneconomists) might view as dubious.[9] Pluralistic utilitarian theories hold that individual utilities cannot be measured and summed but that an open political process will yield the best approximation of maximum well-being.[10]

A key attraction of utilitarianism to the scientistic[11] mind-set is that, in principle, moral issues can be resolved by the empirical calculation of consequences. Moral thought can be reduced to the empirical, and public policy questions can be determined by social science. Moral obscurity arises only from technical limitations. A further attraction is that utilitarianism provides a common currency of moral thought: the concerns of different parties and the different claims on one party can all be translated (in principle) into a common commensurable unit—happiness. Thus, it is impossible to have a moral conflict between two claims that are both valid and irreconcilable (Williams 1972).

Utilitarianism provides the normative rationale for the Rational Comprehensive Method in planning. Utilitarians seek a planning process that determines the best means to maximize the "good." The choice of "good" or ends should come from a political process beyond the scope of the "planner-as-scientist"; only the choice of *means* is a technical/ social scientific matter. It is assumed that the gathering and analysis of data, the construction of explanatory models, and the evaluation of alternative means to achieve public ends can be divorced from any consideration of the appropriateness of these public ends. The planner is seen as a "value-free means technician" who deals with " 'factual' data but avoids the 'value' questions of defining these objectives" (Klosterman 1978, p. 52). While unitary utilitarians will most strongly favor the Rational Comprehensive Method, even pluralistic utilitarians (and more pluralistic versions of the Rational Comprehensive Method) retain the foundational idea that only the ends are moral and the means strictly practical and technical (Harper and Stein 1992).

Many recent writers in normative ethical theory have given preeminence to the individual and are very critical of utilitarianism. (Utilitarianism is rejected by all of the ethical theorists we discuss here and in chapter 3, including Robert Nozick, John Rawls, Jürgen Habermas, and Michael Walzer.) Bernard Williams's *Morality* (1972) is one of the best general critiques. Alasdair MacIntyre (1977) and others criticize the economic utilitarian version, as embodied in cost-benefit analysis.

The most relevant critique for our purpose here is that (although it developed out of the Enlightenment) utilitarianism allows for overriding the autonomy of the individual by focusing on one end state, property, or attribute (such as happiness) of all individuals and then seeking to maximize the *total* of that attribute, with no concern about the distribution of costs and benefits. Thus, value is placed on an attribute of individuals (or even of other creatures[12]) rather than on the autonomy of the individual person (that is, on his or her freedom to choose a life worth living). This can "justify" overriding the interests or rights of some individuals (even inflicting great suffering on them) "in the public interest" to achieve some greater good. A common example of a utilitarian perspective being applied is the justification of a new rapid transit line as having benefits (which go to many more people— that is, the commuters) exceeding costs (such as the harm to nearby and displaced residents, who are relatively few in number).

In planning theory, we believe the widespread rejection of the Rational Comprehensive Method reflects in part a rejection of its underlying utilitarian basis and its violation of liberal values. C. W. Anderson (1979) and John Friedmann (1987, chapter 4) both argue that the flaws of the Rational Comprehensive Method reflect, and flow from, its basis in utilitarianism.

Utilitarians may advocate liberal values, such as freedom or pluralism, and institutions but only as a means to achieve their goal. For example, John Stuart Mill asserted the "individual's absolute right to liberty with respect to acts which do not harm others" but did so because the "general well-being is always on balance maximized if this right is respected" (Day 1964, p. 360). Thus, his advocacy of rights is contingent on their resulting in the best outcome. In contrast, liberals believe that these values are inherently good, independent of any good consequences. Although Mill is generally regarded as a liberal, his primary concern is not for autonomy. Our conception of liberalism is that the autonomy of the individual person is essential. Therefore, our account of liberalism excludes Mill, along with other utilitarians, and (for similar reasons) liberal communitarians such as Michael J. Sandel (1982).[13]

Classical Liberalism versus Contemporary Liberalism

Even within the kind of liberalism that does focus on the autonomous individual person as the ultimate object of moral concern, this shared value points in different directions for two schools of thought. Classical liberals, or libertarians—ironically often referred to today as conservatives—adhere fairly closely to the original ideas of John Locke (1967). Contemporary liberals, or social democrats—often referred to today simply as liberals—have modified the position, giving a much greater role to government and a much greater scope for (public) planning.

For the classical liberal, equality refers to equality of opportunity and impartiality of treatment by the state. To the contemporary liberal, fairness requires some redistribution of wealth to correct inequalities resulting from attributes and capacities seen as "morally arbitrary." There is thus some tension between fulfilling the ideals of liberty and of equality.

Classical liberals emphasize negative rights and do not recognize positive rights (unless they can be derived from negative rights). Where the John Rawls quote (1985, p. 233: The notion of the person that is required for liberalism is someone who is able to play an individualistic and critical "role in social life, and hence exercise and respect its various rights and duties") refers to duties as well as to rights, the only individual duty recognized is respect for the negative rights of others. Contemporary liberals recognize some positive rights; this creates more extensive duties toward other individuals and leads to some restriction of negative rights.

The distinction between positive and negative rights is intuitively simple. Positive rights are rights *to* something tangible, often a good or a service. In contrast, there is really only one basic negative right—the right to be free. It is not a right *to* anything. Rather, it can be expressed only negatively; it is the right not to be interfered with, to be free from interference with the pursuit of one's goals. In practice, the distinction between the two kinds of rights is clearest with regard to the implementation and adjudication process.

Negative rights are enshrined in constitutions, charters of right, and criminal law. In general, these documents specify what *cannot* be done to individual persons. Changing any of these provisions usually requires a high degree of consensus (for example, passing two legislative houses; agreement by two levels of government; or adoption by plebiscite). This is because these rights are regarded by liberal democratic societies as very fundamental and not to be changed arbitrarily. The remedy for the violation of negative rights is judicial action by the state, often implemented in planning via quasi-judicial local bodies.

In contrast, positive rights are usually enacted by ordinary legislation and implemented administratively; the remedy for alleged violations of positive rights is usually political or administrative. If people do go to the courts for a remedy, they must show that they were treated unfairly or partially and that they were denied something that other persons in relevantly similar circumstances were given.[14]

In this chapter, we present one interpretation of the classical liberal perspective and outline some of its implications for planning. We try to give a systematic account of this important view, which has many more adherents (and more validity) than generally recognized by planning theory. However, we do believe classical liberalism has some significant weaknesses, which we point out. These weaknesses lead us toward contemporary liberalism. In chapter 2, Shean McConnell discusses some substantive aspects of contemporary liberalism; in chapter 3, we examine some of its procedural implications.

Nozick and Negative Rights[15]

Classical liberal positions argue that a respect for the equal and ultimate worth of the individual person as a source of value leads to the adoption of a "negative rights" approach to morality. Negative rights are "natural rights" in that all persons have the rights discussed simply by virtue of being persons.[16]

One of the most forceful contemporary advocates of this position is Robert Nozick (1974).[17] However, because Nozick himself avoids any explicit statement of his basic principles, the principles we present are our interpretations of Nozick or, in some cases, our modifications (that is, what we think is consistent with the classical liberal perspective).

A negative rights approach begins with a basic rights principle something like the following, which is adapted from Nozick (1974, pp. 28–35):

P1 Each individual person has the right to freely act in any way he or she chooses, provided that choice recognizes the same right for every other person.

This principle is intended to be an operationalization of Kant's dictum that each person should be treated "never simply as a means, but always at the same time as an end" (Kant 1956, p. 96). Thus, the only limitation on rights should be the recognition that every other person has the same rights. This recognition places (negative) side constraints on our behavior. These side constraints express the inviolability of each person; "there is no justified sacrifice of some of us for others" (Nozick 1974, p. 33).

One way of viewing *P1* is that it recognizes what G. A. Cohen (1986, p. 77) calls self-ownership: the notion that "each person is the morally rightful owner of his own person and powers." Although some contemporary liberals (notably Rawls[18]) would take issue with the notion of self-ownership, most classical liberals would find it acceptable. What is controversial for classical liberals is how it relates to the ownership of objects, particularly in the economic realm.

Suppose we begin with all persons owned by themselves and all objects unowned. Nozick (1974, pp. 150–153) argues that:

P2a A person who acquires anything without violating the rights of any other person is entitled to that holding;

P2b A person who acquires anything (without violating anyone's rights) from another person who is entitled to it is also entitled to that holding; and

P2c No one is entitled to a holding except (1) by (repeated) application of (a) and (b) or (2) in rectification of violations of (a) or (b).

His rationale is that there is no reason to interfere with any acquisition unless it threatens someone's freedom, that is, self-ownership. A state based on *P2*(a–c) would be characterized by the free operation of markets, in other words, a laissez-faire economic system. The free market is the economic expression of the classical liberal approach; free people freely contract to exchange goods and services in order to achieve their own goals. Under this approach, the only moral grounds for government intervention in such exchanges would be the violation of negative rights; indeed, the very raison d'être of the state is to protect individual rights. This involves laws to preserve individual freedom, protect property rights (such as patents or land titles), prevent fraud, enforce contracts, and so on (Harper 1987). According to some interpretations of these principles of *P1* and *P2*, the sole legitimate role for the state is to provide this system of laws, a judicial system to adjudicate conflicts, a police force to enforce the laws, and an army to defend against outside intrusion.[19]

Natural Resources: A Lockean Proviso

The real crunch comes on the issue of the ownership of natural resources.[20] If your acquisition affects other people, then they should have a voice. Cohen (1986) identifies two ways of dealing with natural resources: common ownership and joint ownership.

Nozick advocates a form of common ownership. He claims that any individual should be free to appropriate any natural resource (that is, claim ownership to it), as long as this appropriation does not violate anyone else's right to be free (that is, to be self-owned). Nozick (1974) claims that this condition is fulfilled as long as there is, in Locke's (1964) terms, "enough, and as good left in common for others" (p. 306). If this "Lockean Proviso," as Nozick dubs it, is not met, then

> a process giving rise to a permanent bequeathable property right in a previously unowned thing will not do so if the position of others no longer at liberty to *use* the thing is thereby *worsened* (Nozick 1974, p. 178).[21]

Nozick acknowledges that titles to many natural resources do include "the historical shadow of the Lockean Proviso" (1974, p.179) on their appropriation but believes that the operation of a free market system "will not actually run afoul of the Lockean proviso" and thus it "will not provide a significant opportunity for future state action" (Nozick 1974, p. 182). His claim rests on his belief that the free market produces such an abundance of goods that anyone whose rights under the Lockean Proviso have been violated is more than compensated, that is, they are better off because of the existence of the free market system (Nozick 1974).

This claim seems to us to be the greatest weakness in Nozick's argument. In order to justify a free market system, he has to define "better off" in free market, or economic, terms. Other definitions of well-being could lead to a different conclusion. Not everyone who has lost their autonomy would view themselves as adequately compensated because they are materially better off.

Cohen's (1986) argument against a Nozickian view is to advocate joint ownership of natural resources: each person has an equal interest in each and every molecule of each and every natural resource. This gives each a complete veto over every other individual's economic acts. Cohen postulates that this would result in a system opposite to what Nozick advocates, an egalitarian one in which all wealth is equally distributed since this is the only system that could command the 100 percent consensus required by joint ownership.[22]

We agree with Cohen that Nozick's Lockean Proviso is too weak, in that it permits acquisitions of natural resources that destroy options for others, thus (in our view) violating their rights.[23] However, joint ownership seems far too strong a constraint on individuals—one that would violate their rights by prohibiting actions that really do not infringe on anyone else's rights. The following is a Lockean Proviso that we view as consistent with classical liberalism:

P3a   A natural resource may be appropriated (that is, become privately owned) as long as the resource is not scarce.

P3b   An entitlement to a natural resource is contingent on that resource not being scarce.

When is a resource scarce? A crude test[24] is the economist's: something is scarce when its price is greater than zero. When a resource becomes scarce, ownership of it starts to become "common." The claims of owners of that natural resource then become limited, perhaps ultimately extinguished altogether. The reason for this is that their ownership now violates others' rights to pursue their goals.

If the natural resource has no value[25] added by human endeavor (for example, uncleared pastureland), then the government may simply take some of it away from existing owners and give it to others. If division of the resource among everyone who values it would result in units too small to be useful (for instance, wilderness), then the government may legitimately hold enough of it in common that it is no longer scarce. A farsighted government might reserve some of a natural resource in common before it actually becomes scarce (for example, future urban open space or roads). However, in many situations, the owner will have added significant value to the natural resource, such as by clearing and cultivating the land. Here the only fair and feasible approach may be to collect a royalty on the natural resource component and redistribute it to all persons as reimbursement for their common ownership. Other natural resources may have no value without the application of human effort, ingenuity, and risk-taking, such as with petroleum or minerals. This could be recognized by a government auction (as agent for the common owners) of the right to explore for the natural resource, subject to a royalty when the resource is actually extracted.[26]

The existence of other persons, and of society in general, may also limit the individual's ability to pursue his or her goals. Nozick's device for applying the Lockean Proviso to this situation is a hypothetical "state of nature." It is assumed that any person in a state of nature (that is, with no other persons nearby and with unconstrained use of natural resources) could obtain adequate food, clothing, and shelter. Thus,

> *P3c* If the social, political, and economic institutions of a society, or its technical complexity, render any person unable to obtain adequate food, clothing, and shelter, then they should be compensated so that they can obtain same.

So a negative rights approach may recognize certain limited positive rights. The nature of such positive rights is contingent on the particular society and environment. For example, in a complex technological society, quite a bit of education may be required while in a cold climate, shelter would be necessary for survival. Exactly what baseline level is "adequate" will always be controversial. Nozick (1974) believes that the baseline would be so low that it would seldom be relevant to society with private appropriation. Our principle—*P3c*—clearly provides for some positive planning for the redistribution of economic resources to provide a minimum living standard.

The Regulation of Negative Externalities

Some of the most significant urban planning implications of a classical liberal approach arise out of its application to negative externalities. An externality is the unintended side effect of any action on a person (or persons) not directly involved in an original action. These effects may be on the persons themselves, on their holdings, or on unowned things, such as natural resources.

Some activities intrinsically involve side effects. It is in the nature of any competition that the entry (or exit) of any one contestant unavoidably affects other contestants, as does the performance of each contestant. For instance, the entry of an applicant for a job or an educational program alters the prospects of other applicants; the entry of a buyer or seller in the housing market affects all other buyers and sellers of housing; and the development of a new shopping center decreases the profits of other shopping centers nearby. Economists refer to such intrinsic, or price, effects as "pecuniary externalities" (Bish and Nourse 1975, p. 111).

Negative rights approaches are not concerned with regulating pecuniary externalities because no rights are violated. Individuals should have the right to pursue their goals but not necessarily have the right to *achieve* them; the new entrant does not normally alter the ability of other competitors to pursue the job, the educational admission, or the profits. The outcome may be altered, but there is no general right to outcomes. Thus, our use of "externality" will exclude such intrinsic effects; we are here referring to "nonpecuniary externalities."

Although the justification for regulating the effects of externalities is usually couched in utilitarian terms, the concept of externality can be intimately linked to notions of individual rights. The general principle regarding negative, or nonpecuniary, externalities flows directly from the basic rights principle in *P1*:

> *P4*   Each person has a right not to suffer from significant nega-
> tive externalities.

Negative externalities are a direct violation of the right to pursue one's goals without (unjustified) interference, goals such as health, movement, privacy, material comforts, and so on. Negative externalities decrease real noncreated options for the individual.

The tricky part of implementing a principle such as *P4* is that it requires some criterion for eliminating immaterial or insignificant complaints. We would view as "insignificant" those effects that a reasonable person would regard as not important enough to take any action to avoid or mitigate. In contrast, the economic utilitarian would not regulate a negative externality unless it was "Pareto-relevant." A negative externality is "Pareto-relevant" if sufferers are willing to pay enough to completely cover the cost of elimination or amelioration of it (Bish and Nourse 1975, p. 112), whereas it is "relevant" if there is anyone willing to pay anything to eliminate it.[27] Our *P4* would regulate most "relevant" externalities even if they are not "Pareto-relevant" (that is, it would regulate if any sufferers are willing to take action to prevent it, even when they are not willing to pay enough to cover the cost of elimination). Although Nozick (1974) appears to accept the Pareto criterion, we cannot see any negative rights–based argument for it.

Also note that the right in *P4*, unless it is justifiably overridden, gives the sufferer a *veto* over the infliction of the negative externality. In some instances, this may effectively be a veto over the externality-generating activity itself! A homeowner who would suffer significant negative externalities from the construction of a new rapid transit line, a freeway, or an apartment building would be able to veto these activities. Of course, those who favored the activity could compensate or buy out the homeowner, but they could not force the person to accept compensation. Here again, not every loss can be compensated by an increase in material well-being.

There are many urban issues to which the notion of negative externality is relevant, including land use; air, water, and noise pollution; sunlight access; and transportation. The attempt to apply *P4* to complex urban problems results in many situations where prima facie rights are in conflict. In order to adjudicate, subsidiary principles are required. We have devised the following principles that attempt to "unpack" some of the notions implicit in a negative rights approach:

P5   The right not to suffer from significant negative externalities—*P4*—does not override any (voluntary and informed) surrender of any rights as part of any contractual relationship to which the sufferer is a party.

P6   If any hierarchy of rights or goals can be established, then the right to be free from serious impairment of the pursuit of a higher (ranked) goal should override the right to be free from impairment of the pursuit of a lower (ranked) goal.

P7   The right not to suffer from significant negative externalities—*P4*—does not give one person the right to prevent another from inflicting a reciprocal negative externality on him or her.[28]

P8   The right to continue an activity, or maintain a condition, without suffering from new negative externalities should take precedence over the right to initiate new activity.

P9   In situations where bona fide rights remain in conflict, the person who would suffer the more substantial harm should have the overriding right.[29]

P10   In situations where the bona fide right not to suffer from a negative externality is overridden by the principle of relative harm—*P9*—there should be just compensation.[30]

Of course, the exact nature of each principle would have to be the subject of both a political and a legal debate. The priority order in which the principles should be applied would also be debated, as this would be key to the outcome in many conflicts. A process such as Rawls's Wide Reflective Equilibrium (see chapter 3) would be invaluable in seeking consensus as to what reasonable persons should be expected to tolerate in an urban environment.

Although there would be a legislative framework, the public decision-making mechanism would also involve judicial or quasi-judicial bodies that would evaluate an objection to a proposed action (for instance, a building or a rapid transit line) by applying each principle (starting with *P4*) in turn until one was found that gave clear grounds for either permitting or prohibiting an activity. For example, if *P5, P6,* and *P7* did not resolve the dispute,[31] the occupants of a house could block a new apartment building next door that would inflict the new negative externalities of noise, loss of privacy, traffic congestion, and so on, as violating *P8* by interfering with their quiet enjoyment of their home.

With regard to the means used to implement these principles, many of the considerations discussed by economic utilitarians will be relevant because a government carrying out justifiable interventions has an obligation to do so in an efficient way. In situations where the transaction costs of private agreements are low (that is, a small number of inflicters and sufferers), it may be sufficient to clearly define personal and property rights and then to provide a judicial (or quasi-judicial) process to adjudicate disputes (Bish and Nourse 1975).[32] However, in the many urban situations where the number of sufferers (or inflicters) is large, transaction costs become so high that private negotiations and court actions would likely be inadequate. Although the possibility of group or class-action suits (Nozick 1974) would help, direct government regulation seems unavoidable.

Implications for Planning

We have already mentioned some implications of this approach for resource conservation, wealth redistribution, and pollution control. While these concerns do have local relevance, it is the application of the above principles concerning negative externalities to zoning and to transportation that would have the most direct consequences for planning and for urban form.

These principles applied to planning would tend to be very conserving of the existing physical form of the city. Once an urban area was developed, it would be quite difficult to change land uses (for example, from residential to commercial or from low-density residential to a higher density) or to construct major transportation "improvements," such as an urban highway or a rapid transit line. Conversely, these principles could be very permissive with regard to new development; developers would have a great deal of freedom internally (say with regard to density, layout, circulation, and so on), although they would be limited by negative externality effects outside their own developments (such as "downstream" transportation and utility impacts) and by requirements to reserve land for future transportation and other public uses (Harper 1987). Of course, the more macro-level impacts of new development could lead to restrictions on population, density, or usage or even on the outright prohibition of development.

The difficulties in changing developed areas would likely result in smaller cities, with employment decentralized to the edges and further development occurring along radial axes formed by major highways out of the city (or any other transportation corridors that had been reserved as the city developed). The shape of the city would thus be greatly dependent on how farsighted public authorities had been in reserving land for future anticipated uses.

Our interpretation of a classical liberal approach to planning obviously bears some resemblance to current North American planning practices. Some aspects of current practice do evidence a great deal of respect for individual rights, such as the preservation of residential areas and attempts to control pollution. Other aspects, such as transportation improvements and urban redevelopment, seem utilitarian based.

One interesting divergence is that the approach we have outlined here probably would be less respectful of the "sanctity" of private property rights in land than current North American institutions. It is ironic that the ownership of land is not a clear-cut case of a negative right to private property; in fact, in our view, it may be quite difficult to justify without making an appeal to utilitarian considerations. In *P3*, both (a) and (b) are likely to restrict the ownership of agricultural land and to justify the conservation of natural resources, including agricultural land, which could involve limiting urban expansion. The *P1* to *P10* principles outlined are unlikely to limit the ownership of urban land because its scarcity often arises out of its location relative to other urban activities, not out of any natural attribute. Still, these principles would not permit the unlimited development that might be expected from a "libertarian" perspective. The right to change land use (or intensity of use) could be quite restricted out of respect for the interests and autonomy of other persons.

Conclusion

The classical liberal emphasis on equality of opportunity, impartiality of treatment, and the negative rights of individuals points to a relatively minimalist role for the state and thus for planning. However, contemporary recognition of certain problems (for example, present and potential natural resource scarcity as populations increase and the problems arising from negative externalities as more of us live in close proximity to each other) leads to a much more substantial regulatory role for planning. Therefore, under contemporary circumstances, we would argue that this approach could be somewhat more interventionist—and less "antiplanning"—than is often supposed.[33]

Notes

1. Our outline of these values is adapted from Rawls (1985).

2. Contrary to Sandel's (1982) claim, liberalism does *not* require that we have a conception of the person that is essentially presupposed in all judgments and prior to all experience.

3. With regard to dualism, we have argued elsewhere for a more pragmatic approach to dichotomies—as endpoints of continuua that are useful for particular practical social purposes (Harper and Stein 1992).

4. Even if it were acknowledged that nonpersons had some intrinsic moral value, this would never justify overriding the moral value of persons or violating their rights.

5. John Friedmann (1987) refers to this approach as "Policy Analysis"; Richard E. Klosterman (1978) calls it "instrumental planning."

6. We are using "normative" to refer to what ought to be as opposed to what is (that is, the descriptive/predictive). In ethical theory, "normative" is also contrasted with "metaethical" theory, which analyzes the meaning of ethical concepts but avoids making normative/prescriptive statements. We are using "ethical theory" very loosely to encompass any systematic, coherent account of ethical behavior. We are emphatically not restricting "theory" to any scientistic conception that attempts to reduce all questions of meaning, norms, and normative ethics to matters of empirical science.

7. This recommendation may be viewed as either procedural or substantive. If "good" is defined as, say, "pleasure," then it is a substantive principle; if the definition is open, then it is a procedural one (that is, "decide what is good, then maximize it").

8. These assumptions are (1) that the value of goods and services exchanged in the marketplace is an approximate measure of well-being and (2) that each monetary unit of consumption gives equal well-being regardless of its distribution. These assumptions are implicit in the "compensation principle" of traditional welfare economics, as presented in such works as M. W. Reder (1947, p. 17). Modern welfare economics theorists often reject these assumptions; see E. S. Phelps (1973) for a brief discussion. However, they still seem to underlie most practical economic policy analysis.

9. It should be noted that our use of the label "economic" does not imply that all economists adopt this ethical perspective.

10. We have elsewhere applied the label "political utilitarian" to those who advocate applying the utilitarian principle but advocate "measuring" the well-being created by any act or plan or intervention by the number of persons who benefit from the act less the number of persons who suffer as a result (Harper 1987). Those supporters and objectors who express their views through the political process may be counted as a proxy for benefiters and sufferers.

11. "Scientism" is defined in our discussion of Jürgen Habermas in chapter 3.

12. Hedonistic utilitarianism, which values pleasure, should encompass nonpersons; other versions of utilitarianism, which place value on the achievement of reflectively selected goals, include only the happiness of persons.

13. As we discuss in chapter 3, Michael Walzer is a communitarian whose recent ideas come very close to our conception of liberalism.

14. Note that this is essentially a negative rights argument in that it appeals to the notion of impartiality. If there are to be positive rights, they must be allocated fairly.

15. Substantial portions of the remaining sections of this chapter are drawn from our previous papers (Harper and Stein 1984, 1986).

16. In more technical terms, this normative ethical theory is deontological (involving rules or norms that should be obeyed because of their *inherent* rightness) and monistic (all of its principles are derived from a single basic underlying principle, such as *P1*).

17. This position is also advocated by David Gauthier (1978). His "Mutual Advantage" theory is superficially similar to Nozick's in that both begin with individuals in a state of nature and attempt to derive a society. The difference is that Nozick begins with a moral principle based on the liberal valuing of the inherent worth of the person; Gauthier assumes only self-interest.

18. Rawls argues that other people may have a claim on a person's wealth if this wealth results from personal powers, or attributes, that are morally arbitrary, even though acquisition of the wealth has not violated anyone's rights.

19. Even this "minimal state" appears to violate the rights of those individuals who do not wish to be protected. However, Nozick's (1974, chapters 4 and 5) justification of this apparent violation is that those who reject the minimal state (desiring to protect their own rights and arbitrate their own disputes) pose a substantial threat to the rights of others.

20. Nozick actually speaks of "unowned objects" in the quote below (1974, p. 178). We are applying his analysis to "natural resources," that is, objects that are part of the natural environment rather than the result of any human endeavor. Economists refer to "natural resources" in contrast to (human-created) capital, (human) labor, and (human) management or entrepreneurship.

21. Emphasis added. Nozick notes that this provision would not preclude acquisitions that worsen others' situations in *other* ways; for example, worsening due to a more limited opportunity to appropriate or worsening a seller's position

by acquiring some of the materials to make whatever she or he is selling and then competing with her or him.

22. Cohen also argues that Nozick's Lockean Proviso would allow someone to acquire all of a natural resource under certain conditions (specifically, if the acquisition makes no one worse off and it makes some people better off than they would have been if it had not been acquired).

23. The persons denied the options may be better off than if the natural resources had not been acquired (thus satisfying Nozick's Lockean Proviso) but still be worse off than if they had been able to acquire some of the natural resource.

24. This test is crude because it assumes the existing distribution of wealth.

25. When we speak of value being added in this discussion, we mean value to persons. Value to persons may be approximated by economic value as measured in the marketplace, but it is not identical. As we discussed above, "better off" should not be viewed solely in economic terms.

26. The process we have described is followed by many governments, such as in the province of Alberta, Canada, with regard to petroleum exploration.

27. Since time is also a cost, the willingness of anyone to take action to prevent it makes a negative externality "relevant."

28. We define "reciprocal negative externalities" as those that can reasonably be expected (and are normally accepted) as a result of an activity in which both parties (the inflicter and the sufferer) are engaged. If person X and I have similar effects on each other because we are engaged in similar activities, then this "mutual violation" of each other's rights entails a surrender of part of our rights to each other (without altering our rights vis-à-vis other parties).

29. One way to view this notion of substantial harm is as a measure of the intensity (or degree) of the violation of one's freedom; a second way is as a measure of the degree to which each person's real options are decreased; a third way to view it is as a utilitarian criterion that is subordinate to rights criteria.

30. Although principles *P9* and *P10* are not based on the economist's Pareto criterion, note that those negative externalities that have "survived" (that is, not been prohibited by) prior principles (*P5* to *P8*) will be eliminated (or restricted) by *P9* and *P10* only if they are Pareto-relevant.

31. This means there has been no contractual surrender of the relevant rights, the relevant goals are at an equal level of any goal hierarchy, and the negative externalities are not reciprocal.

32. Of course, a rights-based approach will be concerned with the correctness of the assignment of rights, an issue to which utilitarians would be indifferent.

33. Some of the ideas in this chapter appeared originally in Harper and Stein (1983).

Bibliography

Anderson, C. W. 1979. The place of principles in policy analysis. *American Political Science Review* 73, 711–723.

Bish, R. L. and Nourse, II. O. 1975. *Urban economics and public policy*. New York: Oxford University Press.

Cohen, G. A. 1986. Self-ownership, world ownership and equality: part II. *Social Philosophy and Policy* 3, 77.

Day, J. P. 1964. John Stuart Mill. In O'Connor, D. J., ed. *A critical history of Western philosophy*. New York: The Free Press, 341–364.

Friedmann, J. 1987. *Planning in the public domain: from knowledge to action*. Princeton, NJ: Princeton University Press.

Gauthier, D. 1978. The social contract as ideology. *Philosophy and Public Affairs* 6, 130–164.

Harper, T.L. 1987. Economists vs planners? A framework for zoning debates. *Plan Canada* 27, 180–191.

Harper, T. L. and Stein, S. M. 1983. The justification of urban intervention: a moral framework. *Environments* 15, 39–47.

————. 1984. A rights approach to urban externalities. Paper delivered at the annual meeting of the Association of Collegiate Schools of Planning, New York.

————. 1986. Positive rights: the only justification for positive planning? Paper delivered at the annual meeting of the Association of Collegiate Schools of Planning, Milwaukee.

————. 1992. Out of the post-modern abyss: preserving the rationale for liberal planning. Paper delivered at the annual meeting of the Association of Collegiate Schools of Planning, Columbus, Ohio.

Kant, I. 1956. *Groundwork of the metaphysic of morals*. Translated by H. J. Paton as *The moral law*. London: Hutchison.

Klosterman, R. E. 1978. Foundations for normative planning. *Journal of the American Institute of Planners* 44, 51–69.

Kymlicka, W. 1989. *Liberalism, community and culture*. Oxford: Clarendon Press.

Locke, J. 1964. Second treatise. In Laslett, P., ed. *Two treatises of government*. New York: Cambridge University Press, Section 27.

MacIntyre, A. 1977. Utilitarianism and the presuppositions of cost-benefit analysis: an essay on the relevance of moral philosophy to the theory of bureaucracy. In Sayre, K., ed. *Values in the electric power industry*. Notre Dame, IN: University of Notre Dame Press, 217–237.

Nozick, R. 1974. *Anarchy, state and utopia*. New York: Basic Books.

Phelps, E. S., ed. 1973. *Economic justice*. Baltimore: Penguin Books.

Rawls, J. 1971. *A theory of justice*. Cambridge: Harvard University Press.

————. 1985. Justice as fairness: political not metaphysical. *Philosophy and Public Affairs* 14, 223–251.

Reder, M. 1947. *Studies in the theory of welfare economics*. New York: Columbia University Press.

Rorty, R. 1990. The priority of democracy to philosophy. In Malachowski, A., ed. *Reading Rorty*. Oxford: Basil Blackwell, 279.

Sandel, M. J. 1982. *Liberalism and the limits of justice*. Cambridge: Cambridge University Press.

Williams, B. 1972. *Morality: an introduction to ethics*. New York: Harper and Row.

SHEAN McCONNELL

2 *Rawlsian Planning Theory*

Those who make decisions in any branch of public planning are part of an activity that is political, sometimes with ethical aspects (Klosterman 1985; McConnell 1981), and the politically motivated decisions may not be the ethically acceptable ones. Arguments about what is a moral decision are eternal. People have evolved codes of behavior—cognitive ethical rules (Oppenheim 1976)—but it requires political agreement to enforce such rules, one of the concerns of which may be justice. For John Rawls (1971, p. 586) "justice is the first virtue of social institutions":

> to respect persons is to recognise that they possess an inviolability founded on justice that even the welfare of society as a whole cannot override. It is to affirm that the loss of freedom for some is not made right by a greater welfare enjoyed by others.

The purpose of this chapter is to discuss Rawls's perspective of justice as fairness and to apply his ideas to the discipline and profession of urban and regional planning. In *A Theory of Justice* (1971), Rawls explained that in much modern moral philosophy "the predominant systematic theory has been some form of Utilitarianism" (p. vii),[1] which can be said to be concerned with the greatest good or the greatest happiness, sometimes for the greatest number (Allison 1975; Brown 1986; MacIntyre 1985; Sillence 1986; see chapter 1). However, Rawls's objection to this approach to decision making is that it does not take seriously the distinction between persons (p. 27). Individuals are considered as being equal in utilitarianism, whereas manifestly human beings are unequal and only some are born with qualities that enable them to compete successfully under free market conditions. Furthermore, the interests of minority groups tend to be outnumbered in a utilitarian approach to decision making.

Rawls explained that a decision may be based on what is considered, by intuition, to cause more good than any other decision (Moore 1903 [1968]; Warnock 1967), but in such an approach there are "no higher-order constructive criteria for determining the proper emphasis for the competing principles of justice" (p. 34). In other words, there is no standard to assign relative weights to competing principles. For instance, among those who make important planning decisions there is likely to be disagreement as to the overriding principles to be used in making a decision. There will be "a plurality of first principles which may conflict to give contrary directives in particular types of cases" (p. 34); there will be no explicit methods and no priority rules for weighting selected principles against one another. However, a pluralistic approach to decision making can proceed without intuition—but instead by use of priority rules. The rules that Rawls recommended are based on the theory of social contract (Popper 1966; Rousseau 1954). Although Rawls does not refer to the application of his principles to planning, they can provide a rational, cognitive, fair approach to making the often difficult decisions that are needed to be made in urban, regional, or other branches of public planning. They apply particularly to the major, strategic decisions. Before examining what Rawls wrote, though, it is appropriate to review some of the philosophical ideas with which he dealt.

Justice and Distributive Principles: Rights, Needs, Equality, and Liberty

Justice, it is often said, is an idea and an ideal. Like law and morality, it rests on the tension or contradiction between what is and what at least some men think ought to be. It represents or presupposes a criticism of an existing reality or state of affairs allegedly in the light of principles or an ideal end-state; it is in that sense said to be both transcendent and a guide to action and evaluation (Kamenka 1979, p. 1).

The word "justice," like equality and liberty, represents a normative idea, which philosophers have discussed for more than two thousand years and people with different cultural backgrounds and values explain differently. A problem is to know exactly what is meant. For John Stuart Mill (1806–1873), justice was "a name for certain classes of moral rules which concerned the essentials of well-being more nearly, and was therefore of more moral obligation, than any other rules for the guidance of life" (Mill 1973, p. 465). In the ethical usage justice may be considered as *social justice* or as *economic justice* (Miller 1976; Phelps 1973) and is concerned with distributive principles or with who is to get how much of some benefit that will contribute to well-being. Many of the critics of urban planning argue that planning is, in fact, a distributive mechanism with a redistributive potential that may be unrecognized (Harvey 1973; Pahl 1982; Simmie 1974). A difficulty is to decide which principles of distribution should be operative. It is a matter of political preference and can be relative (Miller 1976; Pitkin 1972), but an aim is to find some nonarbitrary principles. For example, there may be compensation for those whose resources are "redistributed" to others; those prohibited from realizing potential resources, like the development value of land; or the "inarticulate and unaware, or otherwise . . . powerless segments of the community" whose environment will be harmed by some traffic scheme being implemented (Marlin 1989, p. 39).

Distributive principles of justice have been formulated in various ways, using the criteria of desert, or merit, in which one receives what one deserves, or rights, needs, or equality (Feinberg 1973). Rawls cites all these criteria except for desert, which he did not accept as a first principle.

Concerning *rights,* in the seventeenth century, natural rights included rights to life, inheritance, freedom, and the use of possessions— bounded by the rights of others to life, health, liberty, and possessions. It can be argued that planning does not undermine natural rights since one of its purposes is to ensure a healthy environment for everyone. Although a person's right to do as he or she may wish may be prevented because of the environmental harm that might be caused to others, such persons are reciprocally protected from harmful behavior by their neighbors. Another way of expressing this situation is that a person's freedom to act, or his or her liberty to act, is constrained to protect the freedom of others to enjoy what they have.

Need is another criterion of distribution, but a major difficulty is that its assessment is based on values that vary among peoples, cultures, and nations (Raphael 1976). At best, perhaps, people can agree on a minimum level of need for nutrition, shelter, health, security, and education that may have universal acceptance. More controversial is the need for employment and surplus income. The yardstick of need may be linked with the criterion of relative *equality* within a community; for example, in space standards or in relative access to open spaces, transport, retail, community, and other facilities. A positive approach to planning for equality is that of Rawls (1971, pp. 100–101):

> [U]ndeserved inequalities call for redress; and since inequalities of birth and natural endowment are undeserved, these inequalities are to be somehow compensated for. Thus the principle holds that in order to treat all persons equally, to provide genuine equality of opportunity, society must give more attention to those with fewer native assets and to those born into the less favorable social positions. The idea is to redress the bias of contingencies in the direction of equality.

It is a question as to whether recognition of individual rights and different satisfaction of needs can be reconciled with the aim of equality in distribution or through redistribution. These are philosophical problems at the kernel of the idea of justice in society. The application of redistributive justice involves taking from some people—if only through the taxation system—to give to others who are unequally disadvantaged often through no negligence of their own. The requirement to keep a balance between redressing inequalities without unreasonably infringing liberties underlies Rawls's work. The analysis of negative and positive forms of freedom is important in philosophy (Berlin 1969; Hart 1963; Mannheim 1964; Quinton 1967) and relates to how justice should be achieved.

A Contractual Theory of Justice

John Rawls's *A Theory of Justice* (1971) contains a set of distributive principles that brought together a weighing of considerations relating to equality and distribution and liberty. He offered his theory of "justice as fairness" as an alternative to the utilitarian view. Although Rawls did not refer to urban or related forms of planning, his principles are directly applicable to the illumination of the sorts of value-laden decisions that planners have to make. Rawls's ethical theory of justice can be adapted as an ethical theory *for* planning, and the moral question "Who would gain and who lose?" can be refined by asking "Would social justice result from a particular decision?" Rawls (1971, pp. 3–4) states:

> Justice denies that the loss of freedom for some is made right by a greater good shared by others. It does not allow that the sacrifices

imposed on a few are outweighed by the larger sum of advantages
enjoyed by many.

Rawls's concept of justice thereby conflicts with the utilitarian
notion that a doubt in decision making can be settled by reference to
the greatest amount of pleasure or happiness. Even the use of the
preferable negative-utilitarian yardstick (O'Hear 1980; Popper 1966) to
assess the least suffering can still leave the problem of a residual
disadvantaged minority. Instead, in a Rawlsian approach, rational choice
is to be based on criteria of justice. Rawls's (1971, pp. 302–303) two
principles of justice are:

- *First Principle:* Each person is to have an equal right to the most
  extensive total system of equal basic liberties compatible with a
  similar system of liberty for all.
- *Second Principle:* Social and economic inequalities are to be
  arranged . . . to the greatest benefit of the least advantaged,
  consistent with the just savings principle.

The second principle, as presented, is shorter than in the original,
which, in its extended form, is less clear and less applicable to the
purpose of this chapter. The background to Rawls's theory is, however,
difficult for some to accept. His principles are based on what he believed
people would choose if they were in a certain situation, such as amnesia.
The assumption made by Rawls is that if people were behind a "Veil of
Ignorance" about their own attributes and advantages or disadvantages,
they would choose an ethical balancing of rights and equalities in society
that would protect them if their natural and economic attributes were
meager. They would want protection of their freedom as well as protection from the disadvantages of great inequality. This hypothetical situation he termed "the original position of equality" (p. 12). Since there is
a tendency for the redressing of inequality for some persons to be
undertaken in a way that infringes some personal freedom or liberty of
others, and since the people behind the Veil of Ignorance also want to
protect any liberties that they might enjoy if they were fortunate enough
to be advantaged, Rawls recognized the requirement to establish an
order of priority between his principles. Therefore, he established rules
of priority. In the game of life, there should be fairness. He considered
that people should agree on the rules of the game before they know
how well they are likely to succeed or fail in it, thus accepting the
uncertainties that cloud any vision of the shape of the future:

- *First Priority Rule (The Priority of Liberty):* The principles of justice are to be ranked in lexical order[2] and therefore liberty can be restricted only for the sake of liberty. There are two cases:
    1. A less extensive liberty must strengthen the total system of liberty shared by all; and
    2. A less than equal liberty must be acceptable to those with the lesser liberty.
- *Second Priority Rule (The Priority of Justice over Efficiency and Welfare):* The second principle of justice is lexically prior to the principle of efficiency and to that of maximizing the sum of advantages; and fair opportunity is prior to the difference principle. There are two cases:
    1. An inequality of opportunity must enhance the opportunities of those with the lesser opportunity; and
    2. An excessive rate of saving must on balance mitigate the burden of those bearing this hardship.
- *General Conception:* All social primary goods—liberty and opportunity, income and wealth, and the bases of self-respect—are to be distributed equally unless an unequal distribution of any or all of these goods is to the advantage of the least favored (Rawls 1971, pp. 302–303).

These principles and rules were developed over many years as Rawls refined his approach in response to criticisms. They provide a set of ethical ideas that can philosophically support the ethical approaches accepted in many planning offices in the last quarter of the twentieth century. However, before explaining their relationship to planning, it is proper to summarize some of the main criticisms of Rawls's approach so that the reader may determine her or his degree of acceptance of the Rawlsian approach.

Criticisms of Rawls's Theory

Philosophers have reacted to the Rawlsian approach in analytical and in political terms. Moreover, he has written additional presentations of his approach in an attempt to clear up some aspects in which he may have been misunderstood (Rawls 1985, 1989). For many philosophers, Rawls's idea of a neutral ethical position based on the mythical Veil of Ignorance, thereby preventing one knowing one's own state of advantage or disadvantage, has been found to be an unconvincing one.[3]

Ronald Dworkin (1958, pp. 151, 166) has called principles of justice thus selected "compromises with infirmity," which will change in detailed application as the conditions of people change, and, more fundamentally, he describes a contract made behind a veil as a hypothetical contract and therefore not a contract at all. Rawls has emphasized that his approach, "justice as fairness," is "intended as a political conception of justice"—an alternative to utilitarianism (Rawls 1985, p. 224). To be implemented, it would have to be given the force of political backing. Only those of Rawls's own implied centralist/liberal political position, though, may wish to accept his principles.

Rawls has also been criticized from the political "Right" because his principles imply too much interference in the free market as the distributive agency for resources (Hayek 1967, 1976) and from the political "Left" because he did not adequately consider the materialist facts as to who owns the systems of production and distribution; the theory is thus alleged to be too abstract. A different criticism of Rawls is of the egalitarian liberalism in his principles. Some critics believe that his version of liberalism is too egalitarian; others believe it to be insufficiently so. Still others argue that he has not paid enough attention to merit as a criterion for just distributive processes or to entitlement (Nozick 1974). Robert Paul Wolff (1977, pp. 132, 195, 210) stated that Rawls had "commitment to an Idealist conception of the harmonious and organic society" and that he failed to do justice to the traditions of Marx and Freud. Wolff, in view of the facts of inequality in wealth distribution in the United States, characterized Rawls's view as an ideology or as a "prescription masquerading as value-neutral analysis"; he thus placed A *Theory of Justice* in the tradition of "the utopian liberal political economy of the late 19th and early 20th centuries." Wolff concluded his criticisms by stating that Rawls's failure grew inevitably out of:

> his uncritical acceptance of the socio-political presuppositions and associated modes of analysis of classical and neo-classical liberal political economy. By focusing exclusively on distribution rather than on production Rawls obscures the real roots of that distribution.

Liberty and Planning

Rawls's principles provide a careful relationship between the redressing of inequalities without infringing on liberty with the proviso that liberty can be restricted for the sake of liberty. Insofar as his rules can be applied to the liberty or rights associated with property ownership, Rawls's concept is useful as a contribution to planning theory. However, when applied to personal liberties in a wider sense, it has been argued that there are flaws in his reasoning (Hart 1975). Certain groups can and do use their socioeconomic advantages to lobby their representatives more easily than can disadvantaged groups from, say, inner-urban ghettos. This constitutes an inequality of opportunity or, expressed differently, an inequality in the value of citizenship liberties (Daniels 1975).[4]

One reason for the careful qualifications in Rawls's approach is that he was attempting to reconcile liberty, equality, and justice. To obtain collective justice and equality, there is an inevitable restriction of some freedom for self-determination. Redistribution means that some lose so that others may gain. Intervention of the public sector in compulsorily acquiring land for development for public purposes usually means that landowners have no choice except to sell at a price that is settled at arbitration. Land-use planning is an alternative decision-making mechanism to one in which individuals make decisions regarding the use and development of land through free market processes. One of the purposes—and, hopefully, one of the results—of planning is to ensure a better and also a more just use of the natural resource of space. However, another inevitable result is the denial of some individual freedom of choice for people to do as they wish with the space that they control. Isaiah Berlin (1969) noted the incompatibility between political equality, efficient organization—which public planning seeks to achieve—and social justice with individual liberty or freedom. His preference was for pluralism as a way of getting a measure of "negative" liberty, but that would not necessarily be of assistance to disadvantaged minority groups.

Application of Rawlsian-Type Ideas to Planning

Rawls's basic liberties include voting or standing for election. Thus, people have a right to influence planning processes either by being elected to serve on councils or by electing people to represent their views. They also have the right to lobby elected representatives. Another liberty is that of property owning. In Rawls's "First Priority Rule," outlined above, liberty can be restricted only for the sake of liberty. In his first case, the *less* extensive liberty for two people to do what they want with their property (for example, to be unable to develop it as an automobile repair yard) is justified because they have the guarantee of freedom or liberty from a worse nuisance, say, glue manufacturing from horses' hooves on their neighbor's property. The loss of liberty by those who wish to develop their land for unneighborly uses strengthens the total system of liberty to enjoy property quietly, with no environmental intrusion, which is shared by all. Whether those whose rights to develop a repair yard accept their loss of liberty to do so (cited in Rawls's second case) will vary from person to person. Most people, though, do tend to accept general regulatory or zoning policies until, perhaps, the day when they are refused permission to do what they want.

Rawls's idea of inequalities arranged for the greatest benefit of the least advantaged can be related to allocation of priorities in implementing plans so that projects for the most disadvantaged are completed first. This may be inferred from the *Code of Ethics* of the American Institute of Certified Planners (1981), of which Principle A5, "A planner must strive to expand advice and opportunity for all persons, recognizing a special responsibility to plan for the needs of disadvantaged groups and persons," uneasily follows the statement, later qualified, that "A planner's primary obligation is to serve the public interest." The term "public interest" is usually interpreted in a utilitarian way as the greater happiness of the greater number—to reflect the wishes and advantages of the majority. Principle A5 also follows the exhortation in A4 concerning participation, which is another device that tends to favor local majority preference and not necessarily the best interests of disadvantaged minority groups.

Another way to relate Rawls's idea, as expressed in his "Second Priority Rule," is that "inequality of opportunity must enhance the opportunities of those with the lesser opportunity." Thus, the opportunity for access to regional parks should be provided for those without the opportunity to use their own vehicles, in particular, the poorest and, especially, oldest people in a community. As in Rawls's "General Conception," opportunities should be distributed equally unless an unequal distribution, made necessary because of a lack of resources, is to the advantage of the least favored.

The former part of the second principle is supported in the "Second Priority Rule" and in the concluding "General Conception." An illustration from public planning would be that when there are inadequate resources, an authority should first rehouse those who are worse off—something that has not been the rule in most countries because the worse off may not be able to afford even the minimum rental for low-income public housing. However, in several South American countries that dilemma has been tackled by providing sites for the poorest people to build their own homes. Another example of providing for the least advantaged is to provide work for the unemployed and least skilled before providing more technologically based jobs in well-equipped new factories for skilled workers. Hopefully, a ripple effect from such examples would result in those in need being housed and those who were unemployed getting work.

There are or have been plans with politically and morally explicit goals and objectives. A famous example was the American *Cleveland Policy Planning Report 1975:*

> In a context of limited resources and pervasive inequalities, priority attention must be given to the task of promoting a wider range of choices for those who have few, if any, choices (Vol. 1, p. 48).

Objectives under the headings of "Income," "Housing," and "Transportation" were specific interpretations of this goal, but consequent political and financial power realities in Cleveland meant that the outcome was very different (Krumholz 1982). In the United Kingdom, despite the Conservative government's post-1979 insistence that town planning was principally concerned with land uses, a number of Labour-controlled authorities prepared plans with explicit social goals. Some, like the London Borough of Greenwich, specifically referred to the need to plan for categories of people disadvantaged by reasons of gender, age, ethnicity, infirmity, and sexual orientation (*The Greenwich Borough Plan,* "The People's Plan," adopted by the council in 1989). The Unitary Development Plan for the London Borough of Ealing (*Draft "Plan for the Environment,"* June 1991) has a section on "Equal Opportunity":

> The Council will ensure that the needs of all sections of the community are taken into account in the implementation of planning policies. Particular regard will be paid to the needs of, and implications of any proposals for elderly people, women, people with disabilities, people of ethnic minorities, and people on low incomes (Policy A1).

These goals are reflected in proposals for sheltered housing (H17); shop fronts "should enable ease of access . . . by people with disabilities" (S29); positive encouragement to leisure and cultural activities, including those "preferred by women . . . including women-only projects" (CF14); and parking spaces for drivers with disabilities (T48). The London Borough of Bexley Unitary Development Plan (September 1991 draft) policies H13 and H14 are also concerned with "Special Needs Housing" and "Sheltered Dwellings." Such policies have a goal of social justice.

Just Savings

Rawls's idea of "just savings" is that there is a duty on one generation to uphold institutions and resources generally for future generations, including each nation's heritage. The "just savings" principle arises from the concept that each generation should make a contribution to forthcoming generations just as it has benefited from its predecessors—just as parents who have received some help from earlier generations in terms of knowledge, culture, skills, and maybe in possessions save something for their children, grandchildren, and successive generations. However, when children have inherited nothing, it is part of the ethic of justice that they should be especially well compensated so that their children receive legacies that will sustain future generations. In physical planning terms, the ethic of "just savings" justifies the preservation of old buildings and parts of the built environment and countryside for future generations, thus justifying conservation and preservation policies. For example, those alive in the world today have a duty not to allow the world's water, air, and land systems to become incurably polluted or overpopulated if that will damage the interests of future generations. Rawls's "just savings" principle thus provides a foundation for an ecological ethic—despite some criticisms (Partridge 1985; see also chapter 5).

The Criterion of Need

It is accepted that there is difficulty in accurately defining need. Nevertheless, need is the sort of yardstick likely to be acceptable to politicians of all shades of opinion. Rawls (1971, p. 277) states:

> Since the market is not suited to answer the claims of needs, these should be met by a separate arrangement. Whether the principles of justice are satisfied, then, turns on whether the total income of the least advantaged (wages plus transfers) is such as to maximize their long-run expectations (consistent with the constraints of equal liberty and fair equality of opportunity).

Rawls believed that what he termed the "transfer" branch of government would guarantee people a certain level of well-being and satisfaction of their needs in a way that the market does not. Toward such ends, a government imposes taxes. The revenue it obtains is transferred to those in need through a range of schemes of assistance, including subsidies and grants, not least sometimes to help create new employment and housing. The effect is redistributive. The principles of justice provide a standard whereby the distributive principles used by branches of government can be assessed, and justice is defined by the role of its principles in assigning rights and duties and in defining the appropriate division of social advantages.

Using need as a yardstick by which to measure relative disadvantage at local levels, planners can assess such criteria as the need for open spaces for recreation in urban areas by different age groups based on the maximum distances people of different ages can be expected to walk. The need for schools, shops, community centers, and the like can also be measured. By contrast with need, the measurement of demand for facilities can be assessed through the market.

There may be unexpected consequences from plans that are supposed to satisfy needs, and other needs may be created. For example, the relocation of families from inner to outer urban areas, unless they are offered equally attractive local employment and other facilities and services, may result in members of the family having to travel back to the urban area to work, with the additional burden of transport costs. Thus, the families may be worse off, in greater financial need, than before they were rehoused. The goods in the shops in the new suburban areas may also be more expensive than in the old inner-urban locality. The rents and local taxes may also be considerably greater than with the old housing. A conclusion is that the provision of new homes for those in housing need may have resulted in an increase in financial costs and therefore in greater economic need. The people affected may in some ways be worse off as a result of enlightened planning based on the satisfaction of one sort of need.

The measuring of this sort of "comparative financial balances" is concerned with people's "real income," which is made up of all the benefits that increase an individual's or family's access to or use of a society's resources (Titmuss 1962). It may be argued that the major aim of planning should be the increase of real income and its distribution in accordance with need. In the example above, a loss of real income can occur when a family is rehoused from an inner-urban area to an estate on the periphery of a sprawling city, necessitating an expensive journey to work or to shop. Another example is when new industrial parks are constructed without associated residential areas and related facilities and services, so that the workers have to commute so far to their new jobs that any increase in wages is negated by the traveling costs. David Harvey (1972, p. 309) argues:

A general tenet of location theory and spatial interaction theory is that the local price of a resource is a function of its accessibility and proximity to the user. If accessibility or proximity changes (as it must do every time there is a locational shift) then the local price changes and, by extension, there is an implied change in the real income of the individual. Command over resources, which is our general definition of real income, is, therefore, a function of locational accessibility and proximity. Therefore, the changing spatial form of the city and the continuous process of run-down, renewal and creation of resources within it, will affect the distribution of incomes and it may form a major mechanism for the redistribution of real income.

Real income is also affected by the value of property rights (Harvey 1972, 1973). Those who own their own homes have capital assets that may eventually increase in value with inflation, although such capital appreciation is realized only by selling and by not spending the sales price on another house of equal value. By contrast, tenants enjoy no such capital appreciation. Their subsidized rental (if any) in a discussion on relative equities in society has to be compared against tax rebates given to those paying mortgage payments secured on a house, whose environment may also be bettered through the means of spatial planning.

Planning to increase real income means that *either* homes, jobs, schools, and shops with recreation and social facilities need to be close together *or* transportation and other costs must be minimized through subsidies. Thus, accepting that some form of redistribution of spatial advantages is needed to achieve justice, what remedies lie in public planning? One answer is that the spatial imbalance between employment and residential areas should be corrected in spatial terms (which may be an expensive and long-term solution in developed countries) or in fiscal policies, so that the costs of movement between jobs and home cease to penalize those in need. One problem in such an answer is that those who make the spatial planning decisions are seldom the same people who make the fiscal decisions.

Transportation offers an example of a service that is basic to satisfying people's needs and to increasing their real income. Transportation policies are closely linked to other policy areas, such as land-use strategies for the location of employment and residential areas, including policies for residential density. For example, it is difficult to have adequate transportation in a low-density area because the cost of providing for relatively few passengers is prohibitive. A solution may be high-density development along the transport routes, but this sort of development may not be suitable for families. The critical social problem is that the cost of transport can be one of the "break" items in the budget of a poor family. Therefore, the amount of subsidy needed by a family for transportation and housing costs is related to the spatial relationships of residential areas and transportation networks. Moreover, policies for land use and transportation should not be determined separately if the demands of effectiveness and of justice are to be satisfied. However, it is difficult to be sanguine about easy solutions because of the serious problems resulting from the separation of decision-making networks in government—for example, between those who make decisions for land use, for transportation, for allocation of financial resources between new capital investments, for the maintenance of existing services, and for subsidies, social benefits, and allowances. It is no simple matter to plan for increases in real income. Nevertheless, a goal of planning from Rawls's perspective would be to increase real income and to distribute it in accordance with need. Planning decisions should thus be made in response to the preferences and the needs of disadvantaged people despite the fact that others living in the area that is affected may have other preferences.

In effect, the residents of the community will have had their rights to freedom from governmental decisions, which affect their way of life, "trumped" by the rights of more disadvantaged people to have freedom to have a home and/or work that satisfies their needs. It may be asked whether Rawls's priority of liberty has been safeguarded adequately. The answer is that the total system of liberty for all to have adequate shelter, space, and work means that some "advantaged" people may lose the liberty to enjoy any exceptionally favorable unequal advantages. They may receive compensation for some of their losses.

Planning for Justice

The principles of planning for justice should, where practicable, form the decision-making criteria in planning and in the implementation of plans. Admittedly, the application of this ethical theory will often be very difficult and not always successful, as it was in Cleveland. Nevertheless, accepting the principle of liberty, the aim will be to follow Rawls's second principle so that *planning decisions should be to the greatest benefit of the least advantaged, consistent with the just savings principle.* This should also be an aim with public sector development and redevelopment projects. The application of the principles of justice will mean that restructuring of urban areas in the subregional context should be for the advantage of the most disadvantaged first. The only caveats may be

the long-term effects of the "just savings" principle of protecting resources for the future. There is always a tension between the requirements for the amelioration of short-term needs and the "just saving" of
resources for the future, which necessitates a longer view for priorities.
In the wider context of planning for justice, Harvey's (1973, pp. 116–
117) set of planning principles, based on the goal of justice, are relevant:

1. The distribution of income should be such that (a) the needs
    of the population within each territory are met, (b) resources
    are so allocated to maximize interterritorial multiplier ef-
    fects, and (c) extra resources are allocated to help overcome
    special difficulties stemming from the physical and social
    environment.
2. The mechanisms (institutional, organizational, political and
    economic) should be such that the prospects of the least
    advantaged territory are as great as they possibly can be.

A caveat is that it is essential to balance national economic prospects
against regional because if the nation does not have economic growth
then it will be less able to have a surplus from which to distribute to the
most disadvantaged—usually the most remote—regions. The "correct"
balance between national and regional interests is a most sensitive
political matter in any country.

Harvey's principles do not depart from Rawls's concepts, but Harvey (1973) asked some questions as to how such principles might be met
and warned that not to answer them would tacitly be to endorse the
status quo. The questions included how need would be specified and
what sort of allocative mechanisms would ensure that the prospects of
the poorest region are maximized. The answers given to such questions depend on the political views of the decision makers. Values are
the basis of policy-making and may determine whether proposals are
implemented.

In the sharing of resources in every society, there are injustices that
are unacceptable. No person should lack adequate nutrition, adequate
space in dry, warm, and safe shelter, or access to appropriate educational, health, recreational, and work facilities or adequate surplus
income. To achieve such a just society, and to redress any inequalities
that leave any groups of persons permanently in want, as above, there
should be continued redistribution of existing resources through taxes,
as well as more equitable distribution in the future. Moreover, the aim
of "just savings" may justify use of resources to explain birth control to

people. The essence of the recommended ethic of justice, following
Rawls (1985, p. 224), is that decisions should be made:

1. For the greatest benefit of the least advantaged—that is, for
   those who are most handicapped in physical, mental, racial,
   economic, social, political or environmental terms; provided
   that
2. The "just savings" principle is safeguarded, and thus that any
   resource which will be of benefit in the future is protected
   within reason.
3. Any one person's liberty is restricted only for the sake of the
   liberty of others, and that
4. Any future distribution or redistribution of spatial resources,
   facilities, services and opportunities is made equally, with the
   exception that an unequal distribution or availability is to the
   advantage of the least advantaged in regard to their future
   opportunities.
5. In the event of a conflict between responsiveness based on
   representative democracy and justice, the ethic of justice
   should prevail.

The world's opposing political systems, those based on the "free"
market and those theoretically based on Marxism-Leninism, erroneously
termed communist, have failed to provide both freedom of choice and
social justice. The USSR (now the Commonwealth of Independent
States) failed in economic terms as well as in providing individual liberty.
The United States (as well as Canada, to a lesser extent) has continuing
great inequalities among its peoples. The United Kingdom, after a
decade of "right-wing" government (1979 to 1990), has rising unemployment, a declined manufacturing base, and a greater gap between
the "advantaged" and the "disadvantaged." The planet's ecosystems are
under dire threat, and the differences between rich and poor nations
multiply. Nowhere has planning had many successes. There is in nearly
every nation in the world a need for a "fairer" system on which to base
planning decisions. Despite the reservations of many philosophers,
Rawls (1985, p. 244) has offered such a system: "justice as fairness," a
"political conception of justice . . . a moral conception worked out . . .
for political, social and economic institutions." It is within such institutions that planners recommend and politicians make planning decisions.
The Rawlsian approach realizes the values of liberty and equality.
Rawls (1985, pp. 244–246) has tried to get away from philosophical
controversy; to conceive of society as a "fair system of social cooperation

in which the fair terms of cooperation are agreed upon by citizens. . . ."
In such a society, "justice as fairness seeks to identify the kernel of an
overlapping consensus. . . ." In such a society, planners might be able to
believe that what they were doing was just, right, and good.[5]

Notes

1. All page references, unless indicated otherwise, are from Rawls (1971).

2. A lexical order "requires us to satisfy the first principle in the ordering
before we can move on to the second, the second before we consider the third
and so on" (p. 43).

3. These include both R. M. Hare and J. Feinberg in N. Daniels (1975).
People, it is argued, are often risk-takers, gamblers, who would assume that they
are not disadvantaged, relatively. Compare A. Brown (1986) with D. Meyers
(1987) and W. Sadurski (1990).

4. However, see Rawls (1971, p. 204).

5. This chapter is a revised and reduced version of chapter 6 of McConnell (1981). Its attempt to relate ideas from Karl Popper and John Rawls was not
entirely successful, and its treatment of critical theory was inadequate. It went
out of print once Heinemann was taken over by a larger company. Copies,
though, are available for sale from the author.

Bibliography

Allison, L. 1975. *Environmental planning: a political and philosophical analysis.*
    London: Allen and Unwin.
American Institute of Certified Planners. 1981. *Code of ethics and professional
    conduct.* Washington, DC: American Institute of Certified Planners.
Berlin, I. 1969. *Four essays on liberty.* Oxford: Oxford University Press.
Brown, A. 1986. *Modern political philosophy.* London: Penguin Books.
Cleveland City Planning Commission. 1975. *Policy planning report.* Cleveland:
    City Planning Commission.
Daniels, N., ed. 1975. *Reading Rawls.* New York: Basic Books.
Dworkin, R. 1958. *Taking rights seriously.* London: Duckworth.
Feinberg, J. 1973. *Social philosophy.* Englewood Cliffs, NJ: Prentice Hall.
Hart, H. L. A. 1963. *Law, liberty, and morality.* Oxford: Oxford University Press.
———. 1975. Rawls on liberty and its priority. In Daniels, N., ed. *Reading Rawls.*
    New York: Basic Books, 169–205.
Harvey, D. 1972. Social processes. In Stewart, M., ed. *The city: problems of
    planning.* Harmondsworth: Penguin Books.
———. 1973. *Social justice and the city.* London: Edward Arnold.
Hayek, F. A. 1967. *Studies in philosophy and politics and economics.* London:
    Routledge and Kegan Paul.

————. 1976. *The road to serfdom.* Chicago: University of Chicago Press.

Kamenka, E. 1979. What is justice? In Kamenka, E. and Erb-Soon Taya, A., eds. *Justice.* London: Edward Arnold, 1–24.

Klosterman, R. E. 1985. Foundations for normative planning. In Wachs, M., ed. *Ethics in planning.* New Brunswick, NJ: Center for Urban Policy Research, Rutgers—The State University of New Jersey, 51–69.

Krumholz, N. 1982. A retrospective view of equity planning, Cleveland 1969–1979. *Journal of the American Planning Association* 48, 163–175.

McConnell, S. 1981. *Theories for planning: an introduction.* London: Heinemann.

MacIntyre, A. 1985. Utilitarianism and the presuppositions of cost-benefit analysis: an essay on the relevance of moral philosophy to the theory of bureaucracy. In Wachs, M., ed. *Ethics in planning.* New Brunswick, NJ: Center for Urban Policy Research, Rutgers—The State University of New Jersey, 216–232.

Mannheim, K. 1964. Planning for freedom. In Etzioni, A. and Etzioni, E., eds. *Social change.* New York: Basic Books, 463–470.

Marlin, R. 1989. Rawlsian justice and community planning. *International Journal of Applied Philosophy* 4, 36–44.

Meyers, D. 1987. The socialized individual and individual autonomy: an intersection between philosophy and psychology. In Kittay, E. and Meyers, D., eds. *Women and moral theory.* Totowa, NJ: Rowman and Littlefield, 139–153.

Mill, J. S. 1973. On liberty *and* Utilitarianism. In Bentham, J., *The Utilitarians: an introduction to the principles of morals and legislation.* Garden City, NY: Anchor Press/Doubleday, p. 465. Mill's "Utilitarianism" was originally published in 1863.

Miller, D. 1976. *Social justice.* London: Clarendon.

Moore, G. E. 1903 (1968 edition). *Principia ethica.* Cambridge: Cambridge University Press.

Nozick, R. 1974. *Anarchy, state and utopia.* New York: Basic Books.

O'Hear, A. 1980. *Karl Popper.* London: Routledge and Kegan Paul, 157–158.

Oppenheim, F. E. 1976. *Moral principles in political philosophy.* New York: Random House.

Pahl, R. 1982. Urban managerialism reconsidered. In Paris, C., ed. *Critical readings in planning theory.* Oxford: Pergamon Press, 47–67.

Partridge, E. 1985. Are we ready for an ecological morality? In Wachs, M., ed. *Ethics in planning.* New Brunswick, NJ: Center for Urban Policy Research, Rutgers—The State University of New Jersey, 318–334.

Phelps, E. S., ed. 1973. *Economic justice.* Harmondsworth: Penguin Books.

Pitkin, H. F. 1972. *Wittgenstein and justice.* Berkeley: University of California Press.

Popper, K. R. 1966. *The open society and its enemies.* London: Routledge and Kegan Paul.

Quinton, A., ed. 1967. *Political philosophy.* Oxford: Oxford University Press.

Raphael, D. D. 1976. *Problems of political philosophy.* London: Macmillan.

Rawls, J. 1971. *A theory of justice.* Cambridge: Harvard University Press.

————. 1985. Justice as fairness: political not metaphysical. *Philosophy and Public Affairs* 14, 223–241.

————. 1989. The priorities of right and ideas of the good. *Philosophy and Public Affairs* 17, 251–275.

Rousseau, J.-J. 1954. *The social contract.* Translated by W. Kendall. Chicago: H. Regnery.

Sadurski, W. 1990. *Moral plurism and legal neutrality.* Boston: Kluwer Academic Publishers.

Sillence, J. 1986. *A theory of planning.* Aldershot: Gower.

Simmie, J. M. 1974. *Citizens in conflict.* London: Hutchinson.

Titmuss, R. 1962. *Income distribution and social change.* London: Allen and Unwin.

Warnock, G. J. 1967. *Contemporary moral philosophy.* New York: St. Martin's.

Wolff, R. P. 1977. *Understanding Rawls.* Princeton, NJ: Princeton University Press.

THOMAS L. HARPER AND STANLEY M. STEIN

3 Contemporary Procedural Ethical Theory and Planning Theory

The Contemporary Liberal Approach

In chapter 1, we outlined the essential elements of the liberal perspective and presented a classical liberal, or libertarian, variant of this perspective. We also indicated some of the key differences between the classical and contemporary approaches to liberalism. Two sets of considerations move contemporary liberals (social democrats) away from the classical liberal position toward one advocating additional roles for government and, therefore, public planning. The first is a substantive concern for autonomy and equality of condition; the second is to provide an institutional framework or structure—political, legal, or economic—that satisfies a procedural concern for full, free, uncoerced, undistorted communication in democratic public decision making.

Although contemporary liberals share the classical liberals' concern

Permission is granted by *Plan Canada* for publication of the portion of material contained in this chapter that was originally published in the authors' article "Normative ethical theory: is it relevant to contemporary planning practice?", *Plan Canada* (September 1993), 6–12.

for impartiality and equality, they feel that equality of opportunity is insufficient to guarantee autonomy, that the formal notion of freedom fails to reflect a true valuing of the autonomous individual. An individual cannot lead a meaningful life, a life worth living, without access to some level of resources (Nielsen 1981). This emphasis on the importance of being able to lead a life worth living leads the contemporary liberal to advocate significant government intervention to correct oppressive inequalities of power and to create a social framework that offsets certain conditions and attributes (seen as arbitrary from a moral point of view) affecting the possibility of autonomy. In addition to the traditional negative rights (such as freedom of speech, assembly, movement, religion, and so on), the contemporary liberal espouses some positive rights to education, social services, health care, housing, and some level of minimum income. This form of liberalism is probably best expressed by John Rawls's two principles of justice (presented in chapter 2), which, for example, explicitly underlie Norman Krumholz's Equity Planning (Krumholz and Forester 1990).

Rawls's two principles (like Robert Nozick's [1974] theory) are substantive. Substantive ethical theory advocates actual normative ethical principles and judgments. These principles are meant to be applied to judge the rightness or wrongness of specific social institutions, actions, plans, policies, and so on. Procedural ethical theory is a level "above" substantive theory. It makes recommendations about the process that should be followed in deriving and justifying substantive ethical principles and in arriving at ethical conclusions. In this chapter, we focus on the procedural aspects of contemporary liberal ethical theory and on their application to planning.

Rawls and Wide Reflective Equilibrium

Rawls's (1971, 1985, 1987) normative ethical theory is an unusually comprehensive one; it offers both a procedure for arriving at the ethical principles that should govern a society and the substantive principles of justice that (he argues) would arise out of such a procedure and that best embody the moral ideals of liberty and equality for a constitutional liberal democracy, giving fair terms of social cooperation between free and equal persons. A fundamental part of Rawls's (1971) procedural ethical theory is the notion of "Wide Reflective Equilibrium"[1] (WRE). This term refers to a process that attempts to objectively devise the structure or rules for particular types of situations, within a particular set of value commitments.

A WRE position is a coherent set of beliefs, including:

1. A set of considered moral judgments (which may be intuitive);
2. A set of normative substantive and/or procedural ethical principles (which could constitute a normative ethical theory); and
3. A set of background theories that are used to show that the set of normative ethical principles are more acceptable than alternative normative ethical principles. These background theories may incorporate (a) ethical notions (but they should be different from those in the normative ethical principles held, such as fairness or impartiality), and (b) empirical theories and observations (Daniels 1985).

The process involves seeking coherence among the above elements, that is, reflecting on one's own ethical principles, judgments, and intuitions; correcting intuitions by reference to principles; generating and correcting principles that reflect intuitions; and using background theories to justify both judgments and principles.[2] In contrast, a narrow (or partial) reflective equilibrium process (the procedure followed by intuitionists) would attempt to match only (1) considered moral judgments and (2) generalized moral principles, without reference to (3) background theories of either kind (Nielsen 1991).

The goal is a reflective equilibrium where all of these factors are coherent and consistent, giving as much sense as possible to our shared moral life. Thus, WRE does not merely reflect/discover existing moral values, it offers a way to interpret them critically. One of the crucial features of this approach lies in the idea that progress and legitimation of ethical judgments depend on procedures and do not require an appeal to an absolute outside foundation that is independent of our social framework.

Issues in the Application of WRE

Is WRE Modernist? WRE gives us a procedure for providing a justification for moral judgments and commitments (for example, to the rights of individuals) without presupposing an absolute foundation or an absolute transcendent perspective. This position is neither absolutist nor relativist. Thus, it avoids the pitfalls of both Modernism and Postmodernism. It provides all the justification we need for morality. The moral notions central to liberalism—respect for the individual as a moral and political concept—can be derived via this methodology without the

Enlightenment/Modernist notion of absolute foundations presupposed by Kant.

Is WRE conservative?[3] The answer depends on what is meant by "conservative." WRE is philosophically and methodologically conservative. A complete break with tradition (what we already accept morally, socially, and scientifically) is impossible; even a radical break is incoherent. We argue below (in the sections on Michael Walzer and effective criticism) that we must begin within our own context and tradition. If we hope to resolve our differences, they must be publicly debated within a shared context, appealing to an overlapping consensus of shared beliefs and values. However, WRE is not inherently conservative in either a moral or political sense. It can tolerate a wide spectrum of views, including those of G. A. Cohen, John Friedmann, David Gauthier, Jürgen Habermas, Kai Nielsen, Robert Nozick, John Rawls, and Michael Walzer. Which view comes out best in a particular context depends on the way the dialogue goes. The best position is the one that is consistent with the best reflective equilibrium. The debate continues. For example, social democrats interpret Rawls's second principle as justifying inequality of economic condition if it yields sufficient prosperity to make everyone better off; egalitarians argue that such inequality cannot be justified because it leads to a loss of individual autonomy (Nielsen 1985). Either position might call for the overthrow of a government that seriously violates individual autonomy.

Is WRE ethnocentric? No; it does not follow from the fact that our WRE will have a particular context that it is relativistic or that it cannot be justified. WRE would be ethnocentric only if communities were incommensurable, that is, if language is culturally determined. We have elsewhere argued against this claim (Harper and Stein forthcoming; Stein 1994.) Once we acknowledge that translation, communication, and dialogue within and between communities is possible, then different sorts of questions arise. We might conceive of a continuum concerning the possibility of agreement between people or communities, where one extreme is incommensurability and the other is complete consensus on social, political, and economic institutions, policies, and specific actions. The question, then, is how do we move toward the "consensus" end? When different communities or cultures dialogue, the liberal hope is that each will affect the other in reasonable ways, with each widening its own perspective and perhaps changing some of its beliefs.

WRE Applied to Planning

How would the process of WRE be applied to planning?[4] Planners might begin by consciously attempting to be objective, that is, putting aside (as much as possible) self-interest and feelings about particular persons. They would consider (1) a set of judgments about particular situations (for example, it is wrong that worst-off groups have no political power; development should not be allowed to destroy inner-city neighborhoods; and car commuting should be limited to reduce air pollution) and select (2) a normative ethical theory or set of normative ethical principles, such as Rawls's or Nozick's principles, that conforms to these judgments and probably modify some of them to achieve some level of consistency. They would then apply (3) background theories (for instance, does my normative ethical theory respect personhood, does it treat all persons impartially, does it protect the innocent, is it realistic in its assumptions about behavior, and so on). They would then work back and forth, revising the judgments, the normative ethical theory, and the background theories until an equilibrium was reached (that is, until these comparisons no longer resulted in any changes). Any of these comparisons can lead to the recognition of ideological distortion.

The same process then also structures debates with others. The starting point would be to seek agreement on an "overlapping consensus" (concerning shared moral principles, general and specific liberal democratic values, empirical facts, and specific judgments) and work from there. Rawls's "overlapping consensus" (1971, 1987), including the liberal values that we listed in chapter 1, which he believes is shared within Western liberal democracies, may provide an explicit framework for planning debates. As different situations are experienced, judgments or normative ethical theories may change. Even when the result of this kind of dialogue is that others hold a different normative ethical theory, there will be some institutions, policies, proposals, and principles that can be supported by arguments from more than one normative ethical theory. It will, however, usually be the case that "morality . . . is something we have to argue about" (Walzer 1987, p. 32).

Experience in conducting this sort of ethical argument and analysis can be utilized by planners in many different situations: with individuals, groups, meetings, and even public hearings. The procedure could be adapted at all levels of planning debate, from a planner interacting with individual citizens to a provincial government devising a new planning act. Of course, there is no guarantee of achieving complete agreement, but it is likely that there will be some agreement on issues that require a decision, and it will be much more solid than merely a compromise of initial positions.

An example of a position that is not in narrow equilibrium (that is, there are inconsistencies between judgments) might be someone who is both pro nonhuman animal rights and pro abortion. Here, normative ethical theory would help with an analysis of the nature of rights. In order to establish that a nonhuman animal has rights and a fetus does not, then it would have to be shown that a fetus is lacking some property of nonhuman animals that is morally relevant (to whatever theory of rights is being used). Otherwise, the two views are inconsistent.

Another example of an appeal to the notion of narrow equilibrium is found in some feminist arguments. They hold that the "persons" for whom we plan are not neutral but are, in fact, "male" (see chapter 6). Their arguments appeal to our shared beliefs in the equal rights of *all* persons and hold that they have not been consistently applied. They have succeeded in persuading us to change our language; whether the underlying concepts have yet changed is still open to question. Thus, this position does not ask us to change our normative ethical theories but to apply them more consistently and vigorously.[5] In contrast, our moral views would have to change if we could find properties of nonhuman animals that give us reasons to include them as objects of moral concern, perhaps even as persons (for example, if dolphin language were translated). This would be an example of expanding our beliefs on their periphery.

An example of a shift that required changes to all components of a WRE is the shift from urban renewal to urban preservation. It involved not only a change in considered judgments and intuitions (from "urban renewal is good" to "preservation is good") but also a switch from a utilitarian moral perspective to something more like a Rawlsian one, concerned with individual rights and with the well-being of the worst off (that is, the existing residents). It also involved the abandonment of supporting normative theories (such as a positivistic physical determinism) and empirical (such as social science) theories, like the "trickledown" theory of housing (which held that the best way to increase housing for the poor was to build new housing for the more affluent and then let their old housing "trickle down" to the poor), as well as a critical awareness of the actual distribution of costs and benefits of urban renewal.

An example of a position that would require a much more profound shift in all components of WRE is "deep ecology" (see chapter 5), which holds that the environment has moral value that is inherent (that is, in and of itself) rather than instrumental (that is, due to its value to persons). This shift in perspective would involve a conversion, abandoning some of our very deeply held moral notions and their relation to our conception of persons. This would be an extremely radical change, with very little link to current frameworks.[6]

Habermas and Ideological Distortion

Other contemporary liberals focus more on critique of society's institutions and their actual functioning. Some liberal thinkers go further than Rawls in arguing that another factor that interferes with autonomy is that of ideological distortion. In his wide-ranging critical communicative theory of society, Jürgen Habermas (1984) has forcefully argued that individuals in our liberal democratic society suffer from "ideological distortion"—they fail to recognize that their true interests are not being served by the existing institutional structure. Thus, the goal of autonomy requires a critique of our contemporary liberal institutional structure.

As a leading critical theorist,[7] Habermas might not appear to be a liberal since he is so critical of how liberal institutions function. We include Habermas because of his adherence to basic liberal values and because he works within the framework of WRE—he is philosophically conservative in the sense of accepting critical dialogue within our culture. "Critical liberals" (Harper and Stein 1992) who apply his critique might be regarded as a subset of contemporary liberalism.

Habermas (1971) is critical of "scientism"—another underpinning of the Rational Comprehensive Method. Scientism is the notion that all action, thought, and knowledge can be reduced to the "objective" scientific paradigm. It claims that the only valid form of knowledge is the instrumental (scientific/technical) kind, that is, an action is "rational" only if it is an efficient means to whatever ends have been chosen. In the scientistic view, ends cannot be evaluated as rational or irrational, as better or worse. Ends are just chosen, and one is as good as another.

Habermas views scientism as a distorting and reductionistic ideology that prevents us from reaching self-knowledge and emancipation because all our communication is systematically distorted. Acceptance of this ideology leads to oppression of the individual because it makes effective critique of oppressive institutions difficult (though not impossible). It is a mechanism for a hierarchical, authoritarian, power elite to maintain its control of society behind a veil of technocratic knowledge. This is exemplified by the organizational form of bureaucracy, which is explicitly based on the scientific fallacy. It serves as a tool for controlling people as if they were objects (Schaar 1984), for example, by applying the Rational Comprehensive Method to planning.

In addition to instrumental rationality (which, at least in part, serves the human interest of controlling nature), Habermas postulates two other forms of rationality. Communicative rationality serves the human interest of understanding within community; critical rationality serves the interest of emancipation from (unrecognized) oppression (Habermas 1984).

In order to achieve liberation from ideological distortion, Habermas says we need (1) an ideological critique of present social institutions; (2) a social science that is both explanatory and critical; and (3) an "ideal-speech" situation, allowing for undistorted communication (genuine dialogue and debate), where we can come to a constraint-free consensus. The ideal speech situation is a regulative ideal that requires the first two conditions. Until we achieve undistorted communication, Habermas argues, we will not yet be in a position to finally decide whether principles such as Rawls's are the ideal ones. He does believe that, under certain ideal conditions, we could come to a consensus concerning our moral, political, and social disagreements.

Habermas's "ideal speech situation" has been widely criticized as a naive, unrealistic fantasy. We view it as a heuristic, a regulative ideal. (This does not imply that we expect to attain it nor even that we can conceive of what it would be like to attain it—such a conception would require an outside "God's eye" view.) All it means, in particular concrete situations, is that we should attempt to identify and eliminate communicative and ideological distortions through dialogue. It has also been criticized as too Kantian and foundationalist. Our interpretation and use of Habermas would be entirely consistent with the coherentist or nonfoundational approach to procedural ethical theory. We believe that WRE is a feasible way of conducting the kind of dialogue that Habermas recommends.[8]

Another important aspect of Habermas that qualifies him as a liberal is his commitment to rational dialogue for resolving disputes. He recommends that we work toward making our political decision-making processes into dialogues where we can gain a less distorted view of ourselves and the functioning of the system we live in. His focus would be on approximating the "ideal speech" situation, in which all participants in dialogue are free from ideological distortions.

Acceptance of the possibility of ideological distortions has implications for planning. The goals that individuals express politically should not be accepted uncritically. The individual requires a critical awareness of the nature of our social institutions; this may lead to a revision of their goals. A crucial part of the planner's role, then, is "conscious-raising," that is, helping the people they are planning with to recognize their own unconscious distortions and to arrive at goals that reflect these true interests.

Walzer and Critical Interpretation

Michael Walzer is a noted communitarian philosopher who is not generally regarded as a liberal. Most communitarians believe that normative values both arise out of the community and are legitimized by the community's acceptance (see chapter 4). In contrast, Walzer allows for effective criticism while warning that it cannot be too far "outside" the community, that is, it cannot be too radical philosophically and morally.

Most social institutions—including ours—have embedded within them the potential for ethical critique. Walzer makes this point concerning the French philosopher Jean-Paul Sartre's opposition to the Algerian War. Though Sartre described himself as an enemy of French ideas, Walzer points out,

> the principles he applied were well-known in France . . . the idea of self-determination . . . was already there, they had only . . . to extend its application to Algeria (Walzer 1987, p. 59).

In other words, he appealed to the ideals of the French revolution— liberty, equality, and fraternity. Thus, effective social criticism must appeal to ethical positions already held (perhaps in an intuitive or nontheoretical form) within that moral culture. Otherwise, the critic cannot give good reasons for change.

Walzer argues that there is a middle ground between uncritical acceptance of the status quo and seeking to radically change, or revolutionize, social institutions via what he calls "critical interpretation." The effective social critics must be "inside" the society. They must stand "a little to the side, but not outside: critical distance is measured in inches." The critic "is not a detached observer . . . not an enemy . . ." because he or she finds a "warrant for critical engagement in the idealism . . . of the actually existing moral world" (Walzer 1987, p. 61). Few institutions are completely static; there is always disagreement over how they should be interpreted and applied. Learning to apply the concepts of the institution necessarily involves a critical element.

Changes in our social institutions emerge from a critical dialogue, usually in an incremental fashion. This dialogue requires a background of shared values and presuppositions about human nature and society. Walzer draws a parallel between changes in a society's public morality and Thomas Kuhn's (1962) notion of a scientific revolution paradigm shift (except that the social changes are generally gradual and less

dramatic). In many ways, this is exemplified by the process of change
in law. All in all, most change occurs within a broader framework
of sameness.

Effective Critique

It is important to recognize that many radical planning theories
share important assumptions with the established social institutions that
they are criticizing and in this sense are philosophically and methodologically conservative. (Even when they challenge our basic social institutions, they often appeal to similar normative ethical theories.) Planning
that is too radical (in a philosophical and methodological sense) will be
ineffective, unable to communicate with and persuade other planners,
politicians, and the public. If there is too radical a break and no (or too
little) common ground between the position rejected and the position
advocated, then the dialogue and debate, necessary for the elimination
of ideological distortion and necessary for persuasion and consensus,
will be impossible. At best, one might produce something akin to a
religious conversion.[9] There must be some common framework that is
shared in order for the planner's arguments to be persuasive. Thus,
Norman Krumholz justifies his equity planning as

> serving tradition by affirming what has been advocated consistently
> throughout history: that equity in the social, economic, and political
> relationships among people is a requisite condition for a just and lasting
> society (Krumholz and Forester 1990, pp. 50–51).

He quotes Plato, Jesus, Thomas Jefferson, and Franklin Delano Roose-
velt as supportive of "freedom, liberty and justice." This led Hoch (1988,
cited in Krumholz and Forester 1990, p. 250) to comment that

> you were not really advocate planners . . . you advocated for a more
> politically inclusive system. You . . . pointed to the lack of fairness. . . .
> Your effort was therefore conservative instead of radical: restoring a
> fair balance, rather than inciting a revolution.

Thus, the critical planners are "outside" the framework of conventional
planning practice (in that they are critiquing it) but must remain "inside"
it (in the sense of sharing many of its basic liberal values) in order to be
able to effectively critique it and to communicate their critique to other
planners, politicians, and the public.

Of course, the existing power structures use our institutions for their own ends, but this can be fought within the paradigm. It is the domination that must be opposed:

> Criticism does not require us to step back from society as a whole but only to step away from certain sorts of power relationships within society. It is not connection but authority and domination from which we must distance ourselves (Walzer 1987, p. 60).

Marx criticized capitalism using its own notion of equality (Walzer 1987, p. 43); he argued the hypocrisy of the dominating elite. This is what he meant by "capitalism carries the seeds of its own destruction." In order to persuade people to accept domination or oppression, ideology must appeal to ideas that have genuine moral force. This gives social criticism its inside starting point (Walzer 1987).

Planning Paradigms[10]

As already suggested, although its practitioners often regarded themselves as liberals, the Rational Comprehensive Method is *not* an exemplification of liberalism. It is disqualified on the basis of its roots in utilitarianism and scientism (that is, positivism).

John Friedmann (1973) proposed a social learning approach to planning (originally called Transactive Planning) as an alternative to the scientism and elitism of the rational comprehensive approach. Social learning focuses on integrating knowledge and action. Knowledge is "derived from experience and validated in practice" (Friedmann 1987, chapter 5); it emerges from an ongoing process of mutual learning (a "transactive" process between professional and client) in which the emphasis is on application. Rather than being set at the beginning of the planning process, objectives emerge during the process from ongoing action. In Habermas's terms, social learning recognized that instrumental rationality was an inadequate basis for planning and emphasized communicative rationality. However, by 1987, Friedmann had become pessimistic about the potential of the social learning paradigm to achieve emancipation.

Friedmann now critiques U.S. society on grounds very similar to Habermas. He has argued (1987, pp. 9, 13, 299) that because we are in a time of crisis, effective planners must be "radical."[11] The more fundamental, core, or deeply embedded are the objects of the challenge, the more "radical" will be the planning responses advocated and the more obvious it is that normative and ethical issues are at stake. The term "radical" can be ambiguous. A practical crisis may suggest the need for radical political change, but it does not necessarily imply the need for a radical methodological and philosophical break with tradition nor for a different conceptual framework.

Friedmann (1987, p. 30) presents his "radical planner," who seeks societal transformation from below (rather than societal guidance from above), as the extreme endpoint on a sort of continuum. He seems, though, to feel that there is a major discontinuity (almost an absolute dualism) between planning for societal guidance and planning for societal transformation.[12] We would argue that it is much more of a real continuum, that the difference between Krumholz working for incremental change within a government bureaucracy and Friedmann's radical planner seeking systemic change may be only a matter of degree.

While Friedmann's social learning is strong on communicative action, we believe that John Forester's progressive planning paradigm best expresses the ideals of contemporary liberalism. It is explicitly based on Habermas's work, attempting to incorporate both communicative and critical rationality. It is also a "refinement of traditional advocacy planning" (Forester 1989, p. 46). Advocacy planning (Davidoff 1965) sought to extend traditional institutional planning processes to incorporate the interests of disadvantaged groups in a pluralistic society (thus better fulfilling liberal ideals); the role of the planner was to represent these groups in the political process. Forester seeks to advance the interests of these excluded groups by providing them with information, technical resources, and critical analysis. This includes the attempt to anticipate and correct "systematic sources of misinformation" (Forester 1989, p. 46) and the obligation to direct public attention toward distortions and injustices.

Forester is not "radical" philosophically or politically, in the sense that he accepts the basic structure of Western (and particularly U.S.) liberal democracy; he seeks a "genuinely democratic planning process" that works for all its citizens (Forester 1989, p. 28). Thus, Forester is consistent with Walzer in appealing to existing liberal values as a basis for change toward a more just society.

While Forester's procedural approach reflects Habermas, his substantive positions, particularly his endorsement of Krumholz's "Equity Planning" (Krumholz and Forester 1990), seem to us to implicitly reflect Rawls's substantive principles. His advocacy aims would be well served by the WRE method.

We have elsewhere (Harper and Stein 1990) extended Forester's paradigm to more explicitly incorporate both liberal values and Rawls's substantive principles of justice. Within such a paradigm, the planner could legitimately play a number of roles, such as the mediator, reflective critical interpreter, advocate (of resistance to injustice), or agent of (incremental) change. Planners must be committed. They are no longer value-neutral technicians; they require "skills embedded in critical thinking and in a moral commitment to . . . the possibility of a non-oppressive society" (Friedmann 1987, p. 306).

Contemporary liberalism's focus on the procedural is particularly important in pluralistic societies where conceptions of the good life vary widely, making consensus on substantive matters more difficult to achieve. We have drawn on Rawls, Habermas, and Walzer in our outline of how contemporary liberalism ideals can be expressed in plannng procedures. It is crucial that these procedures are structured such that they are both seen to be fair and that they maximize the chances of reaching consensus.

Conclusion: The Postmodern Abyss[13]

Contemporary planning is seen by many as being in a state of crisis, both practical and intellectual (Friedmann 1987, 1992). Planning theory seems suspended between Modernism and Postmodernism (Beauregard 1989). Planning practice is still largely wedded to Modernism (Dalton 1986) and is seen as ineffectual, unable to achieve even modest aims. Postmodernism has created a crisis in planning because it undermines and rejects Modernist bases of planning, yet it provides no substitute rationale.

Much of the Postmodernist critique of Modernism is valid. In addition to its liberal tenet (and sometimes in contradiction to it), Modernism also holds a scientistic tenet: that science is the only source of valid knowledge. Most of what we believe should be rejected in Modernism flows from this tenet: foundationalism, absolutism, positivism, and absolute dualism. To the extent that Postmodernists are opposing these aspects of planning, we agree with their critique.

However, "full-blown" Postmodernism cannot provide an adequate basis for planning. It is fatally flawed by an inconsistent retention of the metaphysics of Modernism. Postmodernist arguments for relativism presuppose foundationalism in requiring an outside perspective (a "God's eye" view) that could tell us that competing views are both right. Postmodernist arguments against rationality presuppose an absolute dichotomy[14] between acceptance of the narrow Modernist conception of rationality and rejection of rationality altogether.[15] Thus, Postmodernism is still infected by the very foundationalism and absolute dualism that it purports to reject. Even worse, Postmodernism flirts with giving up the Modernist notions of consistency and rational argument. This rejection means that no reasons can be given for accepting (or rejecting) Postmodernism or Modernism.

Robert A. Beauregard notes that while "the intellectual base of the modern planning project" has been undermined, the Postmodernist alternative threatens to reduce planners to "authors of texts," forced to eschew "authoritative positions in public debates" and to remain "politically silent" when confronted by "inequality, oppression, ignorance, and greed" (Beauregard 1991, p. 193). In spite of this, Beauregard proceeds to challenge planners not to succumb to pessimism. In the face of the Postmodern abyss, he asserts that "people can struggle successfully to improve their lives" and that planners "do have something to contribute" (Beauregard 1991, p. 193). He seems here to draw on Forester (1989) for inspiration, but this "third way" is advanced as a blind leap of faith, devoid of any rationale, argument, or justification. It stands in apparent contradiction (if one may use such a dualistic term) to the Postmodernist position he seems to espouse.

We have elsewhere (Harper and Stein 1992) argued that it is possible to reject the scientistic aspects of Modernism and yet still retain normative liberal ideals that can be justified, ideals that are (in an important sense) objective, ideals that allow for a liberating critique of society. By rejecting the Postmodern notion that the stories of diverse communities are incommensurable, plurality and diversity can be recognized while retaining optimism concerning the potential for consensus-seeking dialogue. In philosophy, this view might be labeled "neopragmatism"; it is associated with the works of Richard J. Bernstein (1992), Donald Davidson (1985), W. V. Quine (1969), Richard Rorty (1991), and (on some interpretations) L. Wittgenstein (1958). In planning, Freidmann now seems to be taking a similar view. While critical of the ". . . attempt to totalize the idea of modernity," he has expressed admiration for parts of the "legacy of the Enlightenment," including "respect for the individual and [for] human rights" and the "legal-political order of liberal democracy" (Friedmann 1989, pp. 218–219). We believe a neopragmatic approach can incorporate everything that is useful in Postmodernism, that is, it can effectively critique and correct the errors of Modernism while avoiding the contradictions, absurdities, nihilism, and impotence of Postmodernism.

Contemporary liberalism (particularly what we call "critical liberalism") can provide a rationale for the sort of planning that Beauregard ends up advocating, an alternative approach to planning—one that is neither Modernist nor Postmodernist and one that eliminates the scientistic features of Modernism but retains its positive aspects. This approach preserves the rationale for Friedmann's social learning and his non-Euclidean planning, Forester's progressive planning, and Krumholz's equity planning—providing a moral basis for such approaches without appealing to the metaphysical foundationalism of Modernism.

Notes

1. John Rawls (1971) originally spoke of "reflective equilibrium"; Norman Daniels (1985) coined the term "wide reflective equilibrium" to distinguish the procedure from that of the narrow reflective equilibrium of ethical intuitionists (Nielsen 1991).

2. For a very detailed account, see Kai Nielsen (1991, chapters 9 to 11).

3. Jürgen Habermas is critical of WRE as being too context dependent, that is, assuming liberal democratic values. We feel that it can have more general application.

4. This discussion is drawn from our paper (Harper and Stein 1993).

5. This might be called a "liberal feminist" view; it would be rejected by many "radical feminists."

6. This is aside from its incoherence; it cannot be literally practiced.

7. Critical theory refers to the work of the Frankfurt School. Jürgen Habermas is probably the most influential contemporary critical theorist. John Forester (1989) drew on Habermas and critical theory in formulating his "progressive planning" approach; his book contains extensive references to Habermas and his interpreters.

8. There are still some important differences between John Rawls and Jürgen Habermas, but they do not have implications for the sort of planning procedure we are recommending.

9. The problem with conversion is that there is no justification, no reason for the change, no way of evaluating it as good or bad. It might be right, but all we can judge is whether or not there are good reasons to accept it.

10. This section is based on our paper (Harper and Stein 1990).

11. In John Freidmann's most recent work (1992), he refers to his ideal as "non-Euclidean" planning, indicating he may not have intended to invoke the connotations of "radical."

12. This reflects his orientation of dividing society into two classes: the powerful and the powerless.

13. This section is drawn from our paper (Harper and Stein 1992).

14. With regard to dualism, we have provided a rationale for a more pragmatic approach to dichotomies—as continuua that are useful for particular practical social purposes. What needs to be eliminated is the notion of *absolute* dualism.

15. In our discussion of John Rawls, we put forward a pragmatic notion

of rationality that is broad enough to encompass communicative, critical, and emancipatory conceptions.

Bibliography

Beauregard, R. A. 1989. Between modernity and postmodernity: the ambiguous position of US planning. *Environment and Planning D: Society and Space* 7, 381–395.
————. 1991. Without a net: modernist planning and the postmodern abyss. *Journal of Planning Education and Research* 10, 189–194.
Bernstein, R. J. 1992. *The new constellation: the ethical-political horizons of modernity/postmodernity*. Cambridge: MIT Press.
Dalton, L. C. 1986. Why the rational model persists—the resistance of professional education and practice to alternative forms of planning. *Journal of Planning Education and Research* 5, 147–153.
Daniels, N. 1985. Two approaches to theory acceptance in ethics. In Copp, D. and Zimmerman D., eds. *Morality, reason and truth*. Totowa, NJ: Rowman and Allanheld, 120–140.
Davidoff, P. 1965. Advocacy and pluralism in planning. *Journal of the American Institute of Planning* 31, 331–337.
Davidson, D. 1985. On the very idea of a conceptual scheme. In Rajchman, J. and West, C., eds. *Post-analytic philosophy*. New York: Columbia University Press, 129–143.
Forester, J. 1989. *Planning in the face of power*. Berkeley: University of California Press.
Friedmann, J. 1973. *Retracking America*. Garden City, NY: Anchor Press.
————. 1987. *Planning in the public domain: from knowledge to action*. Princeton, NJ: Princeton University Press.
————. 1989. The dialectic of reason. *International Journal of Urban and Regional Research* 13, 218–219.
————. 1992. Educating the next generation of planners. Paper delivered at the annual meeting of the Association of Collegiate Schools of Planning, Columbus, Ohio.
Habermas, J. 1971. *Knowledge and human interests*. Translated by J. S. Shapiro. Boston: Beacon Press.
————. 1984. *The theory of communicative action*. Boston: Beacon Press.
Harper, T. L. and Stein, S. M. 1990. A framework for an integrated planning paradigm. Paper delivered at the annual meeting of the Association of Collegiate Schools of Planning, Austin, Texas.
————. 1992. Out of the post-modern abyss: preserving the rationale for liberal planning. Paper delivered at the annual meeting of the Association of Collegiate Schools of Planning, Columbus, Ohio.
————. 1993. Normative ethical theory: is it relevant to contemporary planning practice? *Plan Canada* (September), 6–12.

————. Forthcoming 1995. Post-modern planning theory: the incommensurability premise. In Mandelbaum, S.; Mazza, L.; and Burchell, R., eds. *Explorations in planning theory*. New Brunswick, NJ: Center for Urban Policy Research, Rutgers University.

Hoch, C. 1988. Letter to Krumholz. In Krumholz, H. and Forester, J. 1990. *Making equity planning work: leadership in the public sector.* Philadelphia: Temple University Press, p. 250.

Krumholz, N. and Forester, J. 1990. *Making equity planning work: leadership in the public sector.* Philadelphia: Temple University Press.

Kuhn, T. 1962. *The structure of scientific revolutions.* Chicago: University of Chicago Press.

Nielsen, K. 1981. A rationale for egalitarianism. *Social Research* 48, 2.

————. 1985. *Equality and liberty: A defense of radical egalitarianism.* Totowa, NJ: Rowman and Allanheld.

————. 1991. *After the demise of the tradition: Rorty, critical theory, and the fate of philosophy.* Boulder, CO: Westview Press.

Nozick, R. 1974. *Anarchy, state and utopia.* New York: Basic Books.

Quine, W. V. 1969. *Ontological relativity and other essays.* New York: Columbia University Press.

Rawls, J. 1971. *A theory of justice.* Cambridge: Harvard University Press.

————. 1985. Justice as fairness: political not metaphysical. *Philosophy and Public Affairs* 14, 223–251.

————. 1987. The idea of an overlapping consensus. *Oxford Journal of Legal Studies* 7, 1–25.

Rorty, R. 1991. *Objectivity, relativism and truth.* Cambridge: Cambridge University Press.

Schaar, J. H. 1984. Legitimacy and the modern state. In Connolly, W., ed. *Legitimacy and the state.* New York: New York University Press, 104–133.

Stein, S. M. 1994. Wittgenstein, Davidson and the myth of incommensurability. In Couture, J. and Nielsen, K., eds. *Reconstruction in philosophy: new essays in metaphilosophy.* Calgary, Alberta, Canada: University of Calgary Press, 181–221.

Walzer, M. 1987. *Interpretation and social criticism.* Cambridge: Harvard University Press.

Wittgenstein, L. 1958. *Philosophical investigations.* Oxford: Basil Blackwell.

HILDA BLANCO

4   *Community and the Four Jewels of Planning*

The title of this chapter refers to a Buddhist metaphor, and by the four jewels, I mean four core values. A novice in a number of Buddhist traditions is asked to do five exercises 100,000 times. The first exercise involves a ritual in which the novice takes refuge in the Three Jewels of Buddhism, which are the Buddha, the Dharma (the teaching), and the Sangh (the community). In the same way I see four concepts as constituting the jewels of planning—guiding concepts that provide justification for our work, subjects of study and reflection from which we can obtain inspiration. The four jewels of planning, I suggest, are *reason, democratic process, community,* and *nature.* I believe these four are not ordinary values or principles but core values, and thus I turned to the Buddhist concept of jewels.[1]

The purpose of this chapter is to present a largely communitarian view of planning. I do so in the first part of this essay in a similar way that John Udy (1980) presented the eternal Western values of Truth, Goodness, and Beauty, to which he added Love as the justification or the "why" of planning. After setting out the proposed core values for planning, I focus on the intrinsic value of community and briefly review the role the concept has played in planning and the recent development of a communitarian ethical perspective in philosophy, sociology, and economics. In conclusion, I turn back to the jewels and indicate the communitarian aspects of my approach.

Before examining each of them, I would like to stress how each jewel adds and completes the others. I see the jewels as forming a synergistic system. Most philosophers concerned with ethics spend much effort trying to arrive at ultimate principles of ethics and to show how these principles or values are independent from each other. Instead, I believe that values in a human practice or way of life are inextricably interdependent. They form a web of values that form a culture. The task in ethics is as much to articulate the interrelations among values as to explore their distinctness.

The Four Jewels of Planning

REASON

Notice first that it is reason I claim is the jewel—not knowledge and not rationality. Knowledge is not the jewel because knowledge is a product of reason. Reason is the process through which we acquire knowledge. Reason is also the process that enables us to apply knowledge. In John Friedmann's well-known definition of planning as the linkage between knowledge and action, the operative word is "linkage" (Friedmann 1987). The linkage is reason. Certainly, planning is to be grounded in the best available knowledge, but our allegiance should not be to this or that particular finding or theory but to a process of reasoning that produces and corrects such knowledge.

This jewel is expressed in planning in the rational process model, a normative model aimed at guiding planning practice, not at explaining actual decision making. Although this model has been commonly interpreted under the concept of rationality—finding the efficient means to carry out given ends or objectives—I interpret this model under a broader concept than rationality, that of reason. The process of reasoning, or reason, is an interpretive, richly imaginative process that evaluates both means and ends and not the narrow, technical problem-solving concept we have come to associate with rationality. There has been much criticism of the rational process model in the literature of planning, so much so that some theorists believe the model to be intellectually defunct. The title of Ernest Alexander's 1984 review article "After Rationality, What?" expresses this point of view quite well. The critics of the model clearly establish that there are institutional, political, and broader social aspects of the planning process beyond the cognitive aspect expressed in the model. These aspects are important; they provide the context for reason, but they do not offer a true alternative to reason. There is nothing beyond rationality except a broader concept of reason.

Before turning away from this jewel, let me emphasize that the concept of reason I advocate is not individual reason. I argue for a view of reason, as developed by pragmatic philosophy, that is thoroughly social. Truth and reality, under this viewpoint, are defined as ultimate products of an ongoing, ever-inclusive community of interpretation, inquiry, and practice. This is important to remember because this interpretation reconciles the traditional opposition between reason and community that arises when reason is interpreted as functioning apart from a community.

Under this interpretation, communities provide the ground for reason not merely in that their members are the agents of reason but also literally, in that the material and social conditions of a community enable reason and determine it to a great extent. This responds to the charges some theorists have made about the abstract nature of the rational process model. Marxist theorists, in particular, in their objections to the separation of process theory from substantive theory in planning, argue that it is wrong to discuss a reasoning process (the rational model) apart from political and material conditions. I believe that for purposes of analysis, process and substance can be separated; but if reason is to be productive, then it must be situated within the complex of relations of a community.

DEMOCRATIC PROCESS

Notice that the jewel is not democracy. Our jewel is broader; it does not refer only to the way we elect our top government officials. By democratic process, I mean a way of planning, making decisions, and acting so as to include all those affected within these processes. All the public doings of a community are the subject matter of democratic process. Its place is in the classroom, the boardroom, the factory, the office, the home and not only in the town hall.

Here the synergistic systemic nature of the jewels becomes evident. Reason, in itself, has validity, but the imposition of reason through force, legal or otherwise, defeats reason, undermines it—for reason is *the* alternative to force. Reason imposed through force is a falling short, a travesty of reason. To fully empower or actualize reason, the rational process must be inclusive, must incorporate more and more of the public within it. In the planning process, this means opening all the stages, including information gathering, decision making, implementing, and evaluating, to public participation. Here again, we are dealing with an ideal, one that the social learning theorists first brought to our attention (Friedmann 1987).

COMMUNITY

Reason and democratic process are not complete in and of themselves. They are process values. They require a ground and a goal. The concept of community provides the goal.

Notice that the jewel is not the public interest but community. This is because the concept of the public interest refers to a balance or resultant of conflicting private interests and as such is context bound. That is, one has to spell out the context of various interests before one can arrive at "the public interest." The context of all interests is community.

What do I mean by community? I find most insightful and useful Josiah Royce's (1913) definition of community—a group of individuals that shares a common past, that is, a memory; a group that shares a common practice through communication, decision making, and action and thus shares a common present; and a group that shares hopes and plans for a common future infused with values and ideals. To form a community is to develop a public, collective entity—a public mind. This public mind is that part of individual consciousness that is shared, that bridges individual experience, that establishes solidarity among individuals.

Such a definition leaves open whether the community involved is a community of place or of interest, but most communities with which planners deal share a territory, are communities of place. The rootedness of communities that planners deal with makes these communities the ground from which arises a great array of substantive ends. Substantive goals or values refer to relations among people, things, and processes within a grounded community. Take, for example, the concept of distributive justice, of such concern to planners. Justice is embedded in the concept of community. Like the concept of the public interest, it takes on meaning from the social and material relations within a community. How just a community is is not just a matter of income distribution but also of access to education, housing, transportation, child care, health care. An investigation into the status of justice in a community would require an examination of the full panoply of the community's social and physical systems and its interactions with the natural environment. Community is thus the ground, the receptacle for all the substantive values of a community, whether these ends concern economic vitality, fiscal health, justice, or a good quality of life.

If the meaning and evaluation of substantive ends depend on community, is not their value relative to the community in which they are found? How can this value of community provide guidance when we know that the values of some communities are better than others and that some communities are destructive? Is community such an intrinsic value that we should foster all communities? Clearly not, and part of the value of this jewel of community is that it enfolds an ideal of community. Part of what we mean by community is an ideal community. We may not be able to adequately describe the ideal community but we know its outlines. It is the inclusive community, the learning community, the sustainable community, the just community, the liberating community. It is the Beloved Community, as Royce (1913) called it. When we work as planners in communities, we should work to approximate this ideal.

In community, we have, as it were, a three-pronged value: the concrete ground of existing, substantive ends with a local habitation and a name; the ideal community, which gives us something to strive for; and the means to foster it, to give it momentum so that it can move toward its full expression—a common memory, a shared practice, and shared values that project a common future.

NATURE

If community is the goal of planning, nature is its framework. There is no community without a place where air, water, and energy are exchanged and where flora and fauna sustain and delight. Nature provides the opportunities and constraints around which a community evolves a way of life. In its exchanges with the local ecology, a community establishes *mores* that provide an objective ground for reason and ethics.

Nature sets the framework for language, thought, and reason. It underlies our deepest metaphors. As the poet Richard Wilbur puts it, nature is the glass through which we see and speak ourselves: ". . . What should we be without/The dolphin's arc, the dove's return,/These things in which we have seen ourselves and spoken?' (Wilbur 1988, pp. 182–183). Or consider Gerald Manley Hopkins's strikingly beautiful metaphor: ". . . we are wound/With mercy round and round/As if with air." (1953, p. 55) This metaphor works because, although seldom celebrated, air *is* the fundamental mercy. Without it, there is not life.

Nature is the objective ground for all cultures. Until this century, it set the distinctive regional character of cultures. The landscape, weather, water bodies, energy sources, flora and fauna of a region, to varying degrees, are reflected in the language, the economy, the mores of a people. Today, technology and global markets have eroded the sustaining links between local cultures and nature, resulting in the widespread destruction and impoverishment of nature and the eventual decline of local cultures.

Notice that nature is the jewel and not the environment. What we have come to mean by the environment is the functional aspect of nature, its narrow instrumental value to us—the biological necessity to breathe clean air, drink clean water, grow food, and live on safe land. The concept of nature goes back to the Greek concept of *physics,* the constitution, the foundation that surrounds us, sustains us, gives us our natures.

Mind and nature, nature and community have been throughout history interdependent, continuously interacting. In the past, community was the more receptive partner. Nature set the dance in which communities evolved. Today, the challenge is to evolve communities that will act as guardians of their local ecologies. For us, the challenge is to extend the realm of ethics beyond communities to nature. (See chapter 5 for a fuller discussion of ethics and nature.)

THE VALUE OF THE JEWELS

What is the use, the value of these jewels? For one, they justify the practice of planning to ourselves and others. They identify the areas of excellence in the practice of planning. They provide standards for practice since values can be actualized. To what extent are we incorporating reason in this social process in which we are involved? How are we incorporating more and more people in this reasoning-deciding-and-acting process called planning that we lead? How are our efforts furthering the actualization of the ideal community with respect to inclusiveness or social justice? How are our efforts enabling existing communities by enriching their common memory, enhancing their practice, actualizing their values and their visions of desirable futures? How are we facilitating that change in community consciousness where nature becomes an active focus of concern in every physical and social action we entertain? How are we guarding nature, enhancing nature in our plans for transportation, housing, industrial development, garbage, sewage, waterworks, and not just mitigating environmental impacts? How do we reweave nature into existing communities to create stronger and more sustainable communities?

The Concept of Community in Planning

THE IMPORTANCE AND NEGLECT OF COMMUNITY IN PLANNING

The concept of community has been important in planning history. The loss of community in the industrial city at the turn of the century motivated, to a large extent, the Garden Cities movement to reject existing cities and turn to a smaller town scale where the sense of community could be regained. Underlying Clarence Perry's neighborhood unit plan is an attempt to create manageable communities within the larger framework of the city by facilitating a sense of belonging and participation (Perry 1929). For Lewis Mumford (1970), the concept of community was central. Jane Jacobs's influential (yet frequently ignored in planning schools) *The Death and Life of Great American Cities* (Jacobs 1961) argued for street-oriented, mixed-use neighborhoods because they achieve a lively sense of community, even in large, impersonal cities. Lawrence Haworth, in *The Good City* (1963), comes closer to suggesting community as a goal for urban planning. He articulates the concept of a good city in terms of three leading ideas: power, freedom, and community. Haworth makes a strong argument for restoring community to the city while maintaining the diversity of opportunity that characterizes city life. John Friedmann's influential work (1973, 1979, 1987) has been motivated by the search for the good society. In his *Planning in the Public Domain* (1987), Friedmann charts a course for planners to "recenter political power in civil society" by mobilizing social units—the household, regional networks of work and play, the peasant periphery (in the Third World), and the global community. Finally, urban planning has a field of practice called "community development," although this term is often narrowly applied to efforts to revitalize inner-city neighborhoods devastated by poverty and disinvestment.

Despite the significance of the concept of community for planning, the concept, as an end in itself, has not been a prominent part of either the practice or rhetoric of the profession. This is partly explained by the fact that most planners share the dominant individualistic model of social reality common to the social sciences, where community, if valued at all, is conceived as a derivative, aggregate, or instrumental value and is often identified as the public interest. Also, since the late 1960s, the profession has been reluctant to link social values, such as community, to physical strategies. This reluctance stems from the grueling internal and external criticisms of the profession's assumption of physical determinism—a belief that supported the contested policy of urban renewal. During that period, numerous empirical studies of suburbia and slum communities pointed to nonphysical causes of human behavior (Fried 1963; Gans 1962, 1963; Marris 1962, 1963). An even more devastating criticism of physical determinism, and a more important explanation for the recent lack of attention to the concept of community, was Melvin Webber's argument (1963, 1964) along with his and Carolyn Webber's argument (1967). Webber argued that owing to modern developments in transportation and communication, and the values and opportunities associated with social mobility, communities of place and their characteristics were losing their importance while communities of interest were assuming a greater role in our lives. The full response to these arguments cannot be provided in this chapter. It is important to point out, however, that (1) although the strong thesis of physical determinism is false, the new discipline of environmental psychology provides ample evidence to support the assumption that physical form can facilitate or hinder behavior; and (2) the sprawl of suburban development from the 1960s through the 1980s has brought about a variety of problems, including traffic congestion, loss of open space, local financial stress, placeless and ugly landscapes, and unabated social segregation and alienation. These problems have prompted a revaluing of communities of place.[2]

The profession is concerned on a day-to-day basis with one major means to strengthen communities—community or public participation or involvement in planning. The rationale and rhetoric for these efforts, though, has been, typically, either procedural or instrumental. Community participation is often perceived as a set of legal or procedural requirements involving due notice, ensuring that meetings are open to the public, or providing forums for public comments; or community participation is seen as an instrumental value, as a means of empowering certain groups so they can obtain a fair share of public benefits.

THE RISE OF COMMUNITARIANISM IN THE WEST

That the concept of community has not been pursued as an intrinsic value in planning practice should not be surprising. The profession of planning typically follows and does not lead intellectual trends. The dominant individualism of American and British culture has resulted in neglect of the concept of community. However, following a Hegelian dialectic, while the "me" decade was raging in President Ronald W. Reagan's America and Prime Minister Margaret Thatcher's Britain and communist regimes in the Soviet Union and Eastern Europe proceeded to their demise, American and British philosophers were reviving the concept of community (Rasmussen 1990).

Alasdair MacIntyre, through his original and profound essay, *After Virtue* (1981), must be credited with reviving a communitarian ethical approach. MacIntyre argues that the problem with Western ethics since the Renaissance is that when Western philosophy turned to a radical individualism, it lost the ground in community and life practices of an earlier ethical tradition. Western philosophy, MacIntyre argues, continues to use concepts from earlier communitarian traditions. This results in the incoherencies and dead ends that characterize modern ethical thought and that may culminate in emotivism—the belief that fundamental ethical conflicts are not subject to reason but are ultimately expressions of individual feelings. MacIntyre argues that in order to bring coherency back to our *mores,* we need to acknowledge their rootedness in social practices and character within particular communities.

In the same vein as MacIntyre, Michael Sandel aimed his communitarian critique on the foremost formulation of individualistic liberalism of our time, John Rawls's (1971) theory of justice (see chapter 2). In *Liberalism and the Limits of Justice* (1982), Sandel challenges the primacy of the principle of justice in Western ethics. Of particular interest to a communitarian ethics is his persuasive argument that Rawls's theory requires for its coherence a conception of community where community is not merely valued by the individual for its instrumental sentimental value but also as constitutive of a person's identity. He concludes that the principle of justice, in Rawls's recent and elaborate formulation—the vision quest of a deontological ethical approach since Kant's theory—is flawed in its own terms and fails to account for important aspects of moral experience, such as character, self-knowledge, and friendship. With respect to character, for example, Sandel points out that the ethical self does not merely weigh preferences from an impersonal, characterless vacuum, as deontological theory would have us believe, but when the self weighs preferences, it does this in terms of their intensity, as well as in terms of "how they suit the person I (already) am" (Sandel 1982, p. 180). Ethical deliberation involves "who I really am" as well as "what I want." Ethics is not only a question of figuring out preferences but also of establishing character.

Michael Walzer, conversely, instead of a negative critique offers a communitarian theory of distributive justice. In *Spheres of Justice* (1983),

Walzer starts with the position that the notion of justice should be developed in a concrete sociohistorical setting, and he proceeds to do so for today's United States. Further, for Walzer, each community imparts certain meanings and values on goods; thus, all goods are socially constituted goods. He emphasizes how: "Justice is relative to social meanings. . . . Every substantive account of distributive justice is a local account" (Walzer 1983, p. 312). The task of the philosopher is, then, to understand what the good is, what it means in a particular community, and out of this understanding can be inferred this particular community's notion of distributive justice for this specific good.

For Walzer, each type of good has a distinctive meaning and value, and from this arises the central notion of his book, that is, that justice is not a unitary concept but rather that it stands for a plurality of standards applied to different types of goods. He thus eschews the idea of simple equality and proposes his concept of "complex equality," wherein "spheres" of goods should be kept separate. For example, if through investigation we establish that the good of money or income in our society is distributed according to a standard of free exchange while the good of higher education or political office is distributed according to a standard of merit, then, according to Walzer's theory of complex equality, it would be unjust to distribute higher education or political office on the basis of money or income.

In *Habits of the Heart* (1985), Robert Bellah and his associates have applied MacIntyre's thesis to modern American culture. Based on hundreds of in-depth interviews with middle-class Americans, they argue that individualism is the first language of American society. Bellah and his colleagues show convincingly how when middle-class Americans, including public professionals such as planners and policy analysts, are pressed to understand and explain their commitments beyond self-interest or expression, they become incoherent or confused or reach for earlier communitarian traditions, such as the biblical or the political traditions of the Founding Fathers.

In their sequel, *The Good Society* (Bellah et al. 1991), the authors provide an insightful attempt to develop a coherent public philosophy for our times drawing on progressive American thought, including the writings of Herbert Croly, John Dewey, and Walter Lippmann. Countering the individualistic strain in American culture, they emphasize the importance of a critical understanding of, and sustained attention to, the mediating institutions (for example, the family, school, or private corporation) in our lives. Bellah and his associates provide a sociohistorical examination of the major institutions in contemporary American life, uncovering their moral and mythic aspects, and convincingly demonstrate the divergence between current social conditions and the conditions that originally gave rise to these institutions. Furthermore, they employ strands in American progressive thought to suggest needed changes. Thus, their criticism of American institutions has more moral force, and is likely to be more effective, than that of the radical left, much of which is drawn from a neo-Marxist tradition.

As we have seen, for MacIntyre and other communitarians, the concept of a tradition—a way of life and the paradigmatic characters and institutions that exemplify the virtues or values of a community—is central to ethical understanding. Ethics is not, as modern philosophy has held, the abstract quest for ultimate moral principles and their consistent application in life. Instead, ethics is concerned with concrete social practices, institutions, and character.

Perhaps most important for planning is Amitai Etzioni's attempt to spearhead a communitarian social movement in the United States; Etzioni in the past few years has published two books that have laid the groundwork for the movement, *The Moral Dimension. Toward a New Economics* (1988) and *A Responsive Society* (1991). In addition, in 1991 he founded a journal, *The Responsive Community*, which he edits and publishes out of George Washington University. The movement has enlisted various well-known people, is affiliated with People for the American Way, has conducted a number of teach-ins around the country, and subscribes to both conservative and liberal thinkers.

Much like his methodological synthesis (Etzioni 1967, 1968) of the rational model of decision making and disjointed incrementalism, in *The Moral Dimension* (1988) Etzioni attempts a synthesis of two competing socioeconomic models, that of the dominant utilitarian/rational-individual/neoclassical model and its social-conservative challenger, where the individual is conceived as deficient, a cell within the body of a community, "who must be inoculated with values to develop moral character, and authority is needed to keep on the lid of social order" (Etzioni 1988, p. 7). Etzioni's third position sees individuals as capable of acting rationally for their own ends but firmly connected to a community and supported by a moral and emotional personal framework. Individuals under Etzioni's new socioeconomic model are involved in communities that they perceive as theirs, as "we" rather than an imposed restraining "they." He refers to his synthesizing paradigm as the "I&We" (Etzioni 1988, pp. 1–19).

Under the "I&We" paradigm, actors pursue two types of goals, moral commitments as well as self-interest. The choices actors make, according to the model, are influenced by values and emotions as well as constrained by their limited intellectual capacities; hence, most choices are subrational.

The "I&We" paradigm becomes the basis for a new approach to economics—socioeconomics (see Granovetter 1985; Swedberg 1987; and Swedberg et al. 1985 for other work in socioeconomics). In socioeconomics, the economy is treated as a subsystem, "embedded" in the social system; the social system is the "capsule" in which the economy lies (Etzioni 1988, p. 204). Given the character of the "I&We" model, group rationality, the encapsulated economy, and various strands of supporting evidence, socioeconomics arrives at a number of conclusions counter to neoclassical economics: competition is not self-sustaining and does not result in harmony—it requires ongoing intervention from society (Etzioni 1988, pp. 202–213); transactions in the market are never among equals; power is part and parcel of every economic transaction, thus price + power = cost (Etzioni 1988, pp. 213–236); and (the most striking conclusion), the more people accept the neoclassical paradigm, the more their ability to sustain the market economy is undermined (Etzioni 1988, pp. 237–251).

A Responsive Society (1991) is a collection of Etzioni's essays written over the past three decades that brings together different aspects of his theory of social guidance, including his mixed scanning model of the planning process and his more recent communitarian work. Of particular interest to planners is his essay, "Liberals and Communitarians" (Etzioni 1991, pp. 127–152), in which he casts his "I&We" socioeconomic model as a mediating third between liberal (such as John Rawls, Ronald Dworkin, and Robert Nozick) and communitarian philosophical positions (such as those of Alasdair MacIntyre, Michael J. Sandel, and Michael Walzer). For Etzioni, communitarian philosophers lack a way of securing individual rights, especially the ability of an individual to disagree with or criticize his or her communities (Etzioni 1991, pp. 134–137). His "I&We" paradigm is crafted to deal with this shortcoming.

Etzioni's position recognizes both individuals and communities as having "a basic moral standing; neither is secondary or derivative" (Etzioni 1991, p. 137). He stresses the interlocking, interdependent relationship between individuals and communities.

The distinction Etzioni makes between his position and the communitarian philosophers is worth stressing. Communitarian philosophers have developed insights and arguments to counter individualism and argue for communitarian values. Their positions are moderate when compared to earlier collectivist philosophies. However, they still stumble on the problem of legitimating individual rights in potentially

destructive communities. For the sake of clarity, I suggest we follow
Etzioni's lead (1991, p. 131) and refer to the communitarian philosophical positions as "moderate communitarianism." The communitarianism
of Etzioni, on the one hand, and Bellah and his associates, on the other
hand, is mixed in nature, seeking a synthesis between individualism and
its attendant liberal political philosophy and philosophical communitarianism. Their alignment with moderate communitarianism, evident in
their adoption of the term "communitarianism," stems from the historical dominance of individualism in our society and the need to recognize
and stress the other side of the equation. To keep in mind this important
difference, I suggest we refer to the communitarian works that spring
from the social disciplines and have a practical interest as "pragmatic
communitarianism." Bellah and his associates draw deeply from pragmatic philosophy; thus, for them, this term would be doubly appropriate. Although I am not aware that Etzioni has been significantly
influenced by American pragmatism, many of his positions reveal a
strong affinity with pragmatic themes.[3]

Pragmatic communitarianism will hopefully generate a creative
tension between individual and community rights and responsibilities.
This position calls for greater articulation of individual obligations to a
community through public dialogue and deliberation. Under Etzioni's
leadership, communitarian teach-ins have occurred in various parts of
the country. These teach-ins have the dual and related objectives of
exposing concerned citizens to communitarian concepts and of initiating
fresh dialogue on issues currently deadlocked under the liberal, individual rights approach. For example, the issue of pornography under this
approach pits advocates of pornography and opponents, such as feminist groups, in an irreconcilable battle since both parties rely on the
protection of individual rights to make their case. Advocates of pornography and civil libertarians claim that the right to distribute and use
pornography is protected by the American Constitution under the First
Amendment. Feminists claim that the rights of women to human dignity,
especially the rights of those individuals displayed in pornography
materials, are violated by pornography. Therefore, under a framework
of individual rights, the issue of pornography is locked between two
interest groups in a zero-sum game. A communitarian response indicates the impasse and argues that a community also has rights, specifically, "the power to regulate and curb open and visible assaults on
human dignity" (Elshtain 1984, p. 20; quoted in Etzioni 1991, p. 141).

This lively interest in the concept of community found today in
philosophy and the social sciences is very promising for planning theory.
In particular, the work of the pragmatic communitarians may provide

the theory and arguments that planning requires to effectively counter the various interest group conflicts that riddle planning practice. This work may also help to advance social and environmental welfare against the dominant ideology of market economics.

The Coda

The four core values I proposed in the first part of this chapter follow a communitarian approach in the following ways. Just as MacIntyre argues that virtues are grounded in a practice and represent the excellencies potential in a practice, the four values are proposed as values or virtues of a practice—the practice of planning. Moreover, the values are grounded in and interlinked with the concept of community. Finally, community itself is held as an intrinsic value, fully recognized as constitutive of a person's identity.

I began with an Eastern metaphor but will conclude with a thoroughly Western one. The ultimate end in Buddhism is compassion. Taking refuge in the Buddha, the teaching, and the community is meant to lead to the achievement of compassion. We have a parallel concept in the West—the concept of love (Udy 1980). I believe that the core of love is beneficence—the principle of not merely willing but of doing good. I suggest that this is also the ultimate end of planning and that the four values I propose can assure this end. The four values respond to hard lessons experience has taught us this century: that attempts to do good based on a narrow rationality without democratic process backfire; that support for caring acts is hindered by a narrow sense of self and furthered by incorporating our communities into our very identities (Etzioni's "I & We"); and that nature, so vulnerable to our technology and industry, must become a new subject for caring acts.

Charles Sanders Peirce (1839–1914), the great American philosopher, in his first public oration in 1863, decried how civilization thus far had used knowledge and technology only minimally to improve social conditions. He argued that the true ends of science and technology are to liberate humanity from material want and to enable the full development of human capacities. He noted how little his age had moved to achieve these ends. In one of the passages in the oration, Peirce used the Archimedean metaphor: "The fulcrum has yet to be found that will enable the lever of love to move the world" (Wiener 1958).

Notes

1. Except for the addition of the fourth jewel, nature, the first part of this chapter was presented at the Association of Collegiate Schools of Planning's conference in Portland, Oregon, October 4–7, 1989.

2. See, for example, the State of New Jersey's first Development and Redevelopment Plan (New Jersey State Planning Commission 1992), which is entitled *Communities of Place* and has an explicit policy to foster community at different urban and suburban scales through a variety of strategies. I resurrected the concept of communities of place while working on the New Jersey plan in 1987–88, fully aware of the 1960s controversy concerning the importance of communities of place and communities of interest. The many arguments for reviving the concept and fostering such places are made explicit in the rationale for the plan (Blanco et al. 1988). Also, see the work of the neotraditional movement. The movement, especially the work of Andres Duany and Elizabeth Plater-Zyberk (1992; Bookout 1992), is vitally concerned with reviving a tradition of public life and with advancing the formation of community. This is evident in their update and promotion of Clarence Perry's neighborhood planning unit for our times, which they entitle the "Traditional Neighborhood District," and other planning strategies.

3. For example, Amitai Etzioni's focus on societal guidance, emphasis on process, continuing attention to changes in the situation, and feedback learning processes in his mixed-scanning model have strong parallels to John Dewey's theory of inquiry.

Bibliography

Alexander, E. 1984. After rationality, what? *Journal of the American Planning Association* 50, 62–69.

Bellah, R., Madsen, R., Sullivan, W., Swidler, A., and Tipton, S. 1985. *Habits of the heart: individualism and commitment in American life.* Berkeley: University of California Press.

———. 1991. *The good society.* New York: Knopf.

Blanco, H.; Strum, C.; Neuman, M.; and Newman, L. 1988. Strategy for developing and redeveloping communities of place. Draft concept paper. Trenton: New Jersey Office of State Planing.

Bookout, L. W. 1992. Neotraditional town planning: a new vision for the suburbs? *Urban Land* January, 20–26.

Duany, A. and Plater-Zyberk, E. 1992. The second coming of the American small town. *The Wilson Quarterly* 16 (Winter), 19–48.

Elshtain, J. B. 1984. The new porn wars: the indecent choice between censorship and civil libertarianism. *The New Republic* 190, 15–20.

Etzioni, A. 1967. Mixed scanning: a "third" approach to decision-making. *Public Administration Review* 27, 385–392

————. 1968. *The active society.* New York: Free Press.

————. 1988. *The moral dimension: toward a new economics.* New York: Free Press.

————. 1991. *A responsive society.* San Francisco: Jossey-Bass.

Fried, M. 1963. Grieving for a lost home. In Duhl, L., ed. *The urban condition.* New York: Basic Books, 151–171.

Friedmann, J. 1973. *Retracking America.* Garden City, NY: Anchor Press.

————. 1979. *The good society.* Cambridge: MIT Press.

————. 1987. *Planning in the public domain: from knowledge to action.* Princeton, NJ: Princeton University Press, 38.

Gans, H. 1962. *The urban villagers.* New York: Free Press of Glencoe.

————. 1963. Effects of the move from city to suburb. In Duhl, L., ed. *The urban condition.* New York: Basic Books, 184–198.

Granovetter, M. 1985. Economic action and social structure: a theory of embeddedness. *American Journal of Sociology* 91, 481–510.

Haworth, L. 1963. *The good city.* Bloomington: Indiana University Press.

Hopkins, G. M. 1953. *Poems and prose of Gerald Manley Hopkins.* Selected by W. H. Gardner. Baltimore: Penguin Books.

Jacobs, J. 1961. *The death and life of great American cities.* New York: Random House.

MacIntyre, A. 1981. *After virtue.* Notre Dame, IN: Notre Dame University Press.

Marris, P. 1962. The social implications of urban redevelopment. *Journal of the American Institute of Planning,* 28, 180–186.

————. 1963. A report on urban renewal in the United States. In Duhl, L., ed. *The urban condition.* New York: Basic Books, 113–134.

Mumford, Lewis. 1970. *The culture of cities.* New York: Harcourt Brace Jovanovich.

New Jersey State Planning Commission. 1992. *Communities of place: state of New Jersey development and redevelopment plan.* Trenton: New Jersey State Planning Commission.

Perry, Clarence A. 1929. The neighborhood unit. *The regional survey of New York and its environs.* vol. 7. New York: Regional Plan Association, 34–60.

Rasmussen, D., ed. 1990. *Universalism vs. communitarianism.* Cambridge: MIT Press.

Rawls, J. 1971. *The theory of justice.* Cambridge: Harvard University Press.

Royce, J. 1913. *The problem of Christianity.* Vol. 2. New York: Macmillan.

Sandel, M. J. 1982. *Liberalism and the limits of justice.* Cambridge: Cambridge University Press.

Swedberg, R. 1987. Economic sociology. *Current Sociology* 35, 1–221.

Swedberg, R., Himmelstrand, U., and Brulin, G. 1985. The paradigm of economic sociology: premises and promises. *Research Reports from the Department of Sociology, Uppsala University* 1, 1–62.

Udy, J. 1980. Why plan? Planning and the eternal values. *Plan Canada* 20, 176–183.

Walzer, M. 1983. *Spheres of justice.* New York: Basic Books.

Webber, M. 1963. Order in diversity: community without propinquity. In Wingo, L., Jr., ed. *Cities and space.* Baltimore: Johns Hopkins Press.

————. 1964. The urban place and the nonplace urban realm. In Webber, M.;
    Dyckman, J. W.; Foley, D. L.; Guttenberg, A. Z.; Wheaton, W. L. C.; and
    Wurster, C. B. *Explorations into urban structure*. Philadelphia: University of
    Pennsylvania Press, 79–153.
Webber, M. and Webber, C. 1967. Culture, territoriality and the elastic mile. In
    Eldredge, H. W., ed. *Taming megalopolis*. Vol. 1. New York: Praeger, 35–53.
Wiener, P. P. 1958. *Charles S. Peirce: collected writings*. New York: Dover Paper-
    back Edition.
Wilbur, R. 1988. *New and collected poems*. San Diego: Harcourt Brace Jovanovich.

HARVEY M. JACOBS

5 *Contemporary Environmental Philosophy and Its Challenge to Planning Theory*

Introduction

The subject of the environment seems to be everywhere these days: in the news (in all media), in popular culture (in songs, videos, books, and films), through the birth of so-called green consumerism, and via the concern about the long-term global aftermath of international political events, such as the Persian Gulf War and the Chernobyl nuclear disaster. Issues such as the destruction of the global rain forests, acid rain, desertification, the thinning of the ozone layer, groundwater pollution, the availability of landfill space, recycling, and the safety of the world's beaches are only some of the environmental concerns that confront us daily as we go about our lives, listening, watching, and shopping.

To some extent, all of this attention, interest, and concern can be understood as an evolution that follows from the publication of Rachel Carson's *Silent Spring* (1962), the first Earth Day in 1970, and the popular and legislative events of that period (Borelli 1987; Faber and

O'Connor 1989). As environmentalism has grown so has the environmental movement, and with it has evolved and grown the companion
area of environmental philosophy and ethics.

Environmental ethics is a branch of philosophy intended to raise a
set of fundamental questions about the relationships among people and
the natural world. Many of these questions are long-standing ethical
issues that are now recast in the context of new scientific knowledge and
popular consciousness. These include, for instance, issues of intergenerational equity, the rights of natural objects, and ways of living in
harmony with natural systems. Issues pertaining to, and, in fact, the
rights of, the future nonhuman sentient beings (that is, animals) and
nonhuman, seemingly nonsentient beings (that is, trees and the earth
itself) are the grist of this literature.

As a relatively new field, and one tied to a seemingly constant array
of ever new and complex environmental problems, environmental ethics
covers broad terrain, so it is not always clear what are and are not
appropriate areas of ethical discourse and deliberation. However, even
though it is new, the field does have some accepted guideposts for
organizing itself internally (Hargrove 1989; Rolston 1988; Taylor 1986).

Timothy Beatley (1989) has provided one categorization of the
field and literature of environmental ethics for planners. He notes that
much of the discussion in the field can be understood as echoing the
long-standing debate over the so-called "conservation versus preservation" perspective that structured the rise of early forest management
practices in North America. Embedded in this debate is the issue of
whether environmental resources exist for human use—and our primary moral responsibilities are to each other (both in present time and
future time)—or whether environmental resources can claim existence
on their own bases. Viewpoints on this fundamental issue are played out
into debates about utilitarianism and market efficiency and how to assess
risk in making resource management decisions. Beatley further notes
that a concern within the field is whether environmental ethics is viewed
primarily as a human to resource relationship or if it also encompasses
a social, or human to human, ethic.

Perhaps more popularly, the field of environmental ethics is known
for what Beatley (1989, p. 14) calls efforts at "expanding the moral
community." The animal rights/animal liberation theoretical literature
and activist experience is one of the best examples of this component of
the field (Regan 1983); its adherents and detractors fill the academic
journals and popular magazines that discuss environmental ethics.
While the moral community Beatley refers to covers other aspects of
nature in addition to animals, it is this aspect that seems to have made

the easiest translation to popular consciousness. The field has also rejuvenated discussion about how to think critically about responsibilities to future generations and whether non-Western notions of resources and property (Booth and Jacobs 1990; Devall 1980) or indigenous but radically different Western ones, such as Aldo Leopold's land ethic (Leopold 1949), are essential to the creation of a sustainable planet.

The rise of environmental ethics has spawned its own, respected academic journal, *Environmental Ethics,* though as with many new intellectual fields, and especially one whose field of focus is so present in the "real world," discourse is in no way restricted to this journal. In colleges and universities, courses in environmental ethics are taught in curricula as diverse as philosophy, law, urban and regional planning, and integrative environmental sciences and environmental studies programs.

However, one other thing is important in understanding the development of environmental ethics. This is the fact that it has developed in the same period that there has been a virtual revolution in social and political theory. Critical reexaminations of old ideas and the articulation of new frameworks have fed into the development of contemporary environmental ethics. The invention and refinement of feminist theory, the recasting of Marxist theory, and the critical reexamination of concepts such as dualism, modern scientific thought, and contemporary Western religion are all intellectual movements that have contributed to a new environmental ethics.

Curiously, though, until very recently there seems to have been little direct impact from this field of inquiry into planning education and theory.[1] While many planning schools have courses in environmental planning—analysis, technique, and policy—evidence of connections to environmental ethics is less prominent, albeit increasing (Martin and Beatley 1993). The evidence of any connection of the issues raised in environmental ethics to courses in planning theory is even less strong. So far, only one major paper has appeared on this subject, and this paper largely takes up "classical" environmental ethics and says little about its relationship to planning theory (Beatley 1989).

There are thus two purposes to this chapter. The first is to outline, discuss, and explore three of the more provocative strains within contemporary environmental ethics, those being deep ecology, ecological feminism (or ecofeminists) and bioregionalism. The objective here is to make planners and planning scholars aware of these streams and how they are impacting upon environmental movements and environmentalism. Second, and more importantly, though, the exploration of these streams is undertaken so as to speculate on their relationship to that body of literature known as planning theory and to determine how a serious engagement of these aspects of environmental ethics might reflect, reshape, and inform the development of such theory.[2]

The results of this exploration reflect upon planning theory and its internal dialogues in a number of ways. Contemporary environmental philosophy[3] partially affirms the position taken by self-described progressive planners, the position that argues that in order to successfully plan one needs to articulate and engage a set of deeper, more fundamental issues and questions about the root causes of the current situation (Beauregard 1978; Kraushaar 1988; Kravitz 1970). Yet contemporary environmental philosophy does more than this; it points toward the concept of a critical comprehensive planning.

Certain aspects of this exploration (most prominently that of ecofeminists) speak quite directly to concerns of certain so-called "introverted" theorists about the importance of interpersonal communication, the relationship of process to outcome, and means to ends (Forester 1989, 1990; Simmie 1989). Other aspects (those most prominently explored by bioregionalists) can serve to reawaken long-standing but now relatively dormant debates about the actual substance and focus of planning activity, issues raised by Lewis Mumford (1938), H. W. Odum and H. E. Moore (1938), and the Regional Planning Association of America (Sussman 1976). These aspects challenge the structure of contemporary urban and regional form, particularly the inevitable domination of large cities and urban culture existing in counterpoint with a depopulated countryside and deflated rural social structures.

Like planning theory, contemporary environmental philosophy originates in concerns about action. As philosophy, it argues that root questions must be posed if an action is going to be effective, equitable, and sustainable. This is its principal challenge.

Contemporary Environmental Philosophy

DEEP ECOLOGY

Deep ecology is a phrase coined by the Norwegian philosopher Arne Naess (1973). In his brief introductory article on the subject, Naess used the term to contrast it with a concept he termed "shallow ecology." Shallow ecology is what would be popularly thought of as the legislative-management orientation of the mainstream environmental movement. Naess argued that this orientation was fundamentally flawed in concept and asserted that as long as environmentalism and the environmental movement focused upon reforms and at-the-margin tinkering with an industrial-technological society in which people related to nature in a utilitarian and anthropocentric fashion, society could never truly fashion a sustainable way of living with the earth. For Naess, and those who have worked to further develop his initial conceptualizations, the problem is not one of a particular law or management approach but rather the *attitude* people bring to their relationship with the natural world.

Naess's views have been elaborated upon most prominently by a set of U.S. and Australian scholars and activists into one of the most pronounced strands of environmental ethics (Devall 1980; Devall and Sessions 1985; Fox 1990; Sessions 1987). Building upon Naess, they argue that to achieve an environmentally sustainable world, people have to acknowledge and afford equality (that is, equal rights) to all living creatures, whether animals, plants, landscapes, or even the earth itself. Their argument is that until we stop seeing humans as separate, above, and better than other parts of the natural world, environmental justice cannot be achieved.

This general axiom of "biospherical egalitarianism" (Naess 1973, p. 95) is tied to several other key working principles. Among these is the idea that the richest and most just form of life on earth is a broad state of species and social organization diversity and complexity. Drawing from a position that values all life on its own terms, deep ecology sees a natural wisdom to the organization and functioning of ecological systems that have not been disrupted by human activity. Thus, deep ecology urges us to learn from wild nature, generally to place high value on the preservation and protection of wild nature areas, and also to afford more credibility to the lessons that can be learned from more nature-based human societies. The dual focus on a diverse and complex social organization and more nature-based human societies leads deep ecologists to be strongly supportive of local autonomy and decentralized forms of social and political organization. In terms of social design, deep ecology urges a perspective in which quality of life is the measure used. Its proponents are thus strongly skeptical about growth per se and an uncritical acceptance of the benefits of a technological-industrial society. They urge upon us a society in which people work less and where the spiritual side of human nature (broadly defined) is given freer rein.

To some extent, the biospherical egalitarian axiom of the deep ecological viewpoint has a basis in new scientific research, particularly that of James Lovelock (1979). Lovelock formulated a concept that he termed the Gaia Hypothesis. What he argues is that according to many widely accepted definitions of biological life, the earth, with one exception (that being possession of the ability to reproduce), can be understood as itself fully alive. This is important to ponder—Lovelock and those who take his work seriously are arguing that the earth is not just a platform upon which life occurs in its various forms but that the earth is itself a living, breathing, stability-seeking organism.

The real impact of this philosophical discourse is in the realm of action. So-called radical environmental groups—such as Earth First!, the Sea Shepherds, Greenpeace, and the Greens—often justify their obstructionist and sometimes destructionist actions on a deep ecological analysis (Russell 1987). For these radical environmentalists, the acquisition of rights by nature is a natural evolution of the acquisition of rights by other oppressed groups, such as women, children, minorities, the elderly, and the disabled. Strong, radical action is justified in the defense of nature, whether it be endangered species, objects, or landscapes, in the same way society will now condone (but did not always) such action against slavery, wife or child abuse, racism, or discrimination based on age or physical ability.

In terms familiar to those who know the early-twentieth-century history of resource management and policy debates in the United States, deep ecology represents the resurrection and reassertion of the classical debate between John Muir (representing the preservationist position of the then nascent Sierra Club) and Gifford Pinchot (representing the utilitarian-conservationist position of the then nascent U.S. Forest Service) about the bases and terms upon which resources will be "used." This time, however, the academic debate and the action of the radical activists appear to favor Muir's position.

ECOLOGICAL FEMINISM

Like deep ecology, ecofeminism starts with a concern with the ability of the "shallow" environmental movement to solve environmental problems, and, like deep ecology, it pushes for a deeper analysis and understanding (Salleh 1984). As the name implies, ecofeminism evolves out of the feminist movement of the 1970s, which itself spawned a tremendous growth in feminist theory and philosophy (Warren 1987, 1990).[4]

In many ways, the theme of ecofeminism is quite simple. Ecofeminists argue that the roots of oppression of nature—be it the oppression of animals, plants, landscapes, or places—and the roots of oppression of women are inextricably linked (King 1983). These two modes of oppression originate in a patriarchal culture that validates male-associated values and denigrates that which is nonmale. The values that are identified as particularly problematic include, for example, an excessive reliance on rationalism and rationalistic ways of reasoning; dualistic forms of intellectual organization; hierarchy as a mode of conceptualization and organization; and rule-based modes of management. Ecofeminists see that the subjugation of women and nature comes from their being viewed as, for instance, wild and irrational. Thus, it is the validation and predominance of these male-associated values that result in the domination of both women and nature.

From an ecofeminist point of view, the roots of liberation of women and the roots of liberation of nature are likewise linked by a need to reform how we understand, think about, and conceptualize the world around us. From an ecofeminist point of view, it is this internal, conceptual reorganization and reorientation that is the truly revolutionary environmental work. As a beginning, they seek a validation of alternative concepts of knowledge and management. These include concepts that stress intuition, interconnected and systems forms of organizations, nonhierarchical forms of organization, and process and substantive equity ways of management (see the collections by Diamond and Drenstein 1990 and Plant 1989). Women's (and nature's) ways of knowing are not to be viewed as less valid than men's; rather, they are to be seen (at least) as equally valid and perhaps even more insightful from living in a complex and dynamic world. From an ecofeminist perspective, the issue is not to seek control over but rather to learn to live with. Together these are values and ideas that are tagged, sometimes problematically, as more female associated.

The impact of ecofeminism is likewise in action. It, too, influences the new environmental radicals by encouraging a challenge to the process of how things are done—the equity of administrative hearings, environmental impact statements, and judicial proceedings—as being able to afford an appropriate forum for true dialogue about "environmental management."

Deep ecology and ecofeminism share a great deal in common, though there are also important differences between them (Fox 1989; Zimmerman 1987). They both argue, in their own ways, that it is people's attitudes that are the key to the construction of a sustainable world. Together they represent a rejuvenation of discourse about the underlying principles of environmental management. They both recognize that how you view the world is critical to the type of action you will take toward it and that the long-accepted ways of viewing the world in which we live—as encompassed in the standard scientific–technological–industrial paradigms—are open for serious intellectual and activist challenge.

However, these areas of agreement should not overshadow the

real areas of difference between these two strains of environmental philosophy. In fact, the debate between these two schools of thought has dominated the environmental philosophy journals as much as their individual developments (see, for example, Biehl 1988; Bradford 1989; and Salleh 1984). It has largely been launched by ecofeminists, whose arguments are twofold. On the one hand, they find fault with deep ecology. They point out that it is an approach to environmental philosophy that is quite abstract in its origins (meaning that it comes from thinking about the environmental problem rather than reflecting upon the experience of it) and that in offering an alternative framework, deep ecology seeks to universalize human experience (an approach that feminists of various persuasions find objection to). On the other hand, from an ecofeminist point of view, the focus of deep ecology seems to be on the utility of lessons to be learned from Eastern religions and Native American philosophy; social theory and political theory seem to have little place in this discourse. Also, ecofeminists note that in its presentation, deep ecology tends to be quite romantic in content, often urging adherents to lose themselves to the experience of nature.

In contrast, ecofeminism is, for many of its adherents, an approach to finding oneself. It is a process of discovery of the place of women (and other oppressed groups) relative to the oppression of nature and in contrast to that which is oppressing. Even though ecofeminism itself has many strains (two of the most significant fault lines have to do with the necessary centrality of women-based spirituality to ecofeminism and the issue of whether women are inherently closer to nature than men), as a whole it is founded on the need for a wide-ranging and deep social, cultural, and political critique of historical and contemporary social structures. Ecofeminism seeks to be explicitly critical in its examination of the sources of women's and nature's oppression. As such, ecofeminism explicitly recognizes the influence of race, class, and culture in the development of contemporary social systems and how action on these issues is linked to ecological liberation.

While the debate between these two groups has often been acrimonious, a number of scholars and activists have striven to derive the commonalities in these strains of environmental philosophy and to emphasize how they can be understood as mutually reinforcing in the development of a new environmental ethic (Devall 1988; Fox 1989; Zimmerman 1987).

BIOREGIONALISM

Bioregionalism is distinguished from deep ecology and ecofeminism in several ways. Perhaps most importantly, it does not originate as an approach to environmental philosophy by posing abstract or philosophical questions. That is, it did not come about by asking questions about the relationship of people to the natural world and from that concluding that changes in a worldview were necessary to facilitate long-term environmental change. Rather, bioregionalism originates through observation of the earth, its patterns, and the ways people accommodate and become part of those patterns. Bioregionalism is concerned with how people live in a place and learn from living in that place (Andruss et al. 1990). It is from this practical basis that it develops a set of philosophical positions about human–earth relationships.

Bioregionalism starts with the concept of bioregion. Two of the leading proponents of bioregionalism have said that the term bioregion "refers to a geographical terrain and a terrain of consciousness—to a place and the ideas that have developed about how to live in a place. Within a bioregion the conditions that influence life are similar and these in turn have influenced human occupancy" (Berg and Dasmann 1978, p. 218). Similarly, another author has defined a bioregion as "any part of the earth's surface whose rough boundaries are determined by natural characteristics rather than human dictates, distinguishable from other areas by particular attributes of flora, fauna, water, climate, soils, landforms and by the human settlements and cultures those attributes have given rise to" (Sale 1985, p. 55). The key factors here are that a bioregion is a distinct ecospace, distinguishable from other ecospaces (even though the exact boundaries between ecospaces may be difficult to precisely delineate) and that the bioregion gives rise to distinct human use, which reflects the influence, the power, of the land.

How does a systems-ecological definition give rise to a strain of ecological philosophy (Alexander 1990)? Bioregionalism is not just about thinking about the environment or just acting to prevent environmentally destructive behaviors but instead involves living in such a way as to know your place and to be profoundly affected by it (Berg 1990). Peter Berg and Raymond Dasmann (1978, p. 218) say it means ". . . applying for membership in a biotic community and ceasing to be its exploiter." The notion is that by being fully alive in and with a place, people will cease to cause such profound damage to it. By developing sensitivities to the ecosocial carrying capacities of different bioregions, people will learn how to more fully use land without abusing it.

One obvious implication of the bioregional perspective is that people should not live the same everywhere. From a bioregional viewpoint, the fact that urban and regional form is, with minor trappings, largely the same throughout North America is exactly the problem. We are isolated and insulated from the places in which we live. We protect ourselves from the land; we protect it from speaking to us, affecting us, and because we do, the quality of our lives is diminished. As our lives are diminished, the quality of the environment is likewise diminished. If we want the environment to be rich, diverse, and sustainable in fully ecological terms, we need to promote and mirror those conditions in human society. One way to do this is to live with the land.[5]

Like many deep ecologists, bioregionalists take great solace from Lovelock's Gaia Hypothesis. The aliveness of the earth provides the opportunity for a mutual relationship, the same as we can have with any other living creature. However, in contrast to many deep ecologists, who are focused on the preservation of unique ecological areas and threatened species, bioregionalists seek to understand how to actively and appropriately use the land. The bioregional project is a long-term one—Peter Berg is known to comment that it is a multicentury effort—but bioregionalists do not despair. On the whole, they have great faith in the human species and see that through life-styles—our individual acts of living—we can make significant impact upon the earth.

Comparing bioregionalism with the two other strands of contemporary environmental philosophy is instructive. In addition to building a philosophy from the ground up, bioregionalists have to date afforded little attention to the social and economic roots of the contemporary environmental crisis. While they agree with both the deep ecologists and ecofeminists that a change in the concept we hold of ourselves and our relationship with life on the planet is at the root of solving environmental problems, bioregionalism has afforded little discourse into issues such as gender, race, or class and how these affect the bioregional vision. Not unlike the ecofeminist critique of deep ecology, bioregionalism is open to the criticism that it treats all people the same and assumes that all types of people in all places both want and have the capacity to achieve the changes that are advocated. In other ways, bioregionalism shares important tenets with both deep ecology and ecofeminism. Like deep ecology, bioregionalism stresses the importance of local autonomy and decentralization and admires the wisdom of more nature-based human societies. Like ecofeminism, bioregionalism is antihierarchical. Like both (or at least one strand of ecofeminism), bioregionalism emphasizes the need to reintegrate aspects of spirituality back into everyday life.

The Challenge to Planning Theory

A BRIEF REVIEW OF PLANNING THEORY

To speak of the relationship of any body of literature or thought to planning theory is itself difficult, if only because of the internal debate as to what constitutes planning theory and how to classify it.[6] For the purpose of this chapter, I use a conventional and simplistic typology of the field. This typology characterizes planning theory into three parts: comprehensive-rational, incremental, and advocate-progressive. I will briefly describe the essential elements of each, emphasizing their differences from each other and then highlighting the particular challenges to planning theory in its parts and as a whole offered by the developments in contemporary environmental philosophy.

Comprehensive-rational planning is understood to be the foundational paradigm in planning. It is an approach that argues that in order to plan effectively it is necessary to be comprehensive with regard to both the types of functions within a geographic area (planning should cover all functions) and relative to the area itself (one needs to plan for the entire city, county, state, province, and so on). Because of the effort that goes into this type of planning, it is necessary that it be both general in its content and long-range in its time frame; Kent (1964) is a classic statement of this approach. The type of planner who uses this approach is often characterized as a neutral technician, whose method is the systematic application of scientific-rational techniques, such as in population and economic forecasting and land use and environmental analysis (see, for example, Chapin and Kaiser 1979). The position of neutrality originates from the planners' perspective that they are working for the greater public interest and therefore their planning is of benefit to all.

Incremental planning arose in response to the perceived failure in the practice and theory of comprehensive-rational planning. Largely beginning with Martin Meyerson and Edward C. Banfield's (1955) classic study of the Chicago Housing Authority, incremental planning is an approach that argues that there are major obstacles to the implementation of the ideal of comprehensive-rational planning. Some of these are practical in nature, such as the politics of planning and organizations; some of them are more theoretical, such as the rationality, from a decision maker's point of view, of taking a low-risk small step rather than a high-risk large step (Altshuler 1973; Banfield 1973; Lindblom 1973).

The alternative model put forth by incrementalists is almost the opposite to that of comprehensive-rational planners. Incrementalists argue that planning should be limited in scope and area, specific in its content, and short-range in its time frame (Lindblom 1973 is the classic statement of this position). Yet, for very different reasons, the definition of the planner's role is the same—the argument is that the planner should be a neutral technician. The reasoning for neutrality is that it is functionally impossible to define a greater public interest, and therefore planners end up using their own values, or their sense of what the public interest should be, as the basis for planning. Planners have no legitimacy to impose their values upon a planning situation; this is a right reserved to politicians and citizens (Altshuler 1973). The best planners can do is act as technical advisers, providing focused analysis to decision makers that assists in the understanding of planning problems (Lindblom 1973).

The third major school or paradigm of planning theory—advocate-progressive—emerged in the 1960s and is largely associated with Paul Davidoff's (1973) seminal article on advocacy. Emphasizing the issue of how a planner should function, rather than how a plan should be prepared and what it should consist of, Davidoff offered up a very different notion of the practitioner. Rather than the role of a neutral technician, Davidoff argued for the necessity and functionality of a politicized planner. Starting with the same conclusions as the incrementalists about the inability to identify an overriding public interest, Davidoff argued for planners to work with multiple, focused public interests and to promote a highly participatory, plural planning process.

Davidoff's work provided a wedge that opened an approach to planning theory emphasizing the need to put the act of planning into a larger structural context. Questions such as "Whose interests are served by planning?" "How are the good intentions of planning misused?" and "How does planning as a profession and a social action relate to other social and economic forces in society and history?" have come to characterize the so-called progressive paradigm (see, for example, Beauregard 1978; Kraushaar 1988; and Kravitz 1970). Progressive planning, though, is not just a critical examination of planning practice but also a search for how to promote a more socially equitable planning (Clavel 1985; Krumholz 1982). Progressive planners in general seem less concerned with the issues of what constitutes the plan (comprehensive or limited) and how to plan (general or specific, long-range or short-range) as with the workings of planning itself—particularly the empowerment of citizens, especially from oppressed groups, into the planning process and the design of planning programs that not only redress and prevent social injustice but also promote social justice.

AN ECOVIEW OF PLANNING THEORY

How do the contemporary environmental philosophies inform the planning theory debate? While different strands of each environmental philosophy perspective have particular implications for planning and planning theory, some general direct observations and indirect speculations can be made.

Most directly, it seems that the environmental philosophy literature presses the invalidity of the incrementalist's claim relative to perspective and process. Incrementalists seek to narrow the scope of planning; a common thrust in the environmental philosophies discussed here is that long-term, substantive success will come only from a broadening of the scope of analysis and recommendation. In planners' terms, the message of environmental philosophy is that it is not useful to make little plans. Not only will they not stir people's souls, ultimately they will be counterproductive by delaying an examination of the underlying and fundamental causes of problems. It is within this examination that lies the basis of long-lasting, sustainable solutions.

Also directly, environmental philosophy can lend validity to the positions of *both* comprehensive-rational and progressive planning. As noted above, an environmental philosophy perspective suggests the need to pose a set of questions that exposes the structural origins of the conditions that underlay the world, so these conditions are understood in their long-term systemic context, *and* to think about responding to these conditions with a comprehensive (though not solely rational) strategy. Drawing as it does from ecological science, environmental philosophy has a natural tendency to place issues into a systems context, a context that in planning terms is comprehensive. Ecology is a perspective that starts with the premise that everything is connected to everything else, and you cannot affect one element of a system without causing some correlative change in another part of it. Therefore, analysis tends toward being comprehensive in both area and function—one strives to examine an entire ecosystem and all of its parts. The implication of all this for planning theory is to suggest that environmental philosophy establishes the basis for a critical comprehensiveness. This critical comprehensiveness will differ from both comprehensive-rational planning and progressive planning in two ways: first, by drawing upon the critical perspective of progressive planning as the basis for comprehensiveness analysis; and, second, by utilizing the rational mode of analysis that is the explicit foundation of comprehensive-rational planning, and the barely guised basis of progressive planning, as only one of several systems of informing and knowing.

Indirectly, the environmental philosophy literature presses a number of points upon planning theory, including the legitimacy of an abstract or contextless planning theory, the general anthropocentric orientation of planning theory and practice, the relationship of means (or process) and ends (or outcomes), and the loss of "place" as a specific basis for planning.

A common theme in planning theory is the debate about whether the field is, in and of itself, legitimate enough. That is, planning theory grew out of the idea that you could have a body of literature about how to plan that need not be tied to the actual object of this planning.[7] In this way, the body of literature that is commonly identified as planning theory is described as abstract and general—it exhibits one set of characteristics that identifies a theory. Environmental philosophy, while it is philosophy and thus by its very nature often abstract and theoretical, originates from the actual conditions of environmental degradation and the consequent need for environmental management. It is the very question "How do we go about managing the environment?" (or "How do we achieve environmental sustainability?") that serves as an origin of the various strains of environmental philosophy. While they may come to different answers to this question, it is the real conditions of acid rain, rain forest destruction, species extinction, water pollution, and so on, that drive the inquiry. From this basis, planning theory seems context-less—that is, it is a discourse absent a subject. Environmental philosophy presses the question "What is the actual object of planning theory?" From an environmental philosophy point of view, it seems untenable that one can have a discourse on how to plan (or manage) without knowing what one was planning for. To put it another way, environmental philosophy might suggest that the validity of a planning approach would be contingent on the object of planning—whether it be landscape management, species protection, housing, or social services provision.

The points discussed so far in this section refer to elements of environmental philosophy that are common to the three strains profiled. However, there are specific points about planning theory that are alluded to by the individual perspectives.

From the perspective of deep ecology, planning is disturbingly utilitarian and anthropocentric in its orientation. It is a literature and a practice focused upon the needs and concerns of humans. In a more pronounced way than the other perspectives, deep ecology stresses the rights[8] of the "nonhuman." The rights of natural objects—the rights of these objects to exist for their own purpose rather than for how they serve a human need—have been a subject of debate since the early days of the contemporary environmental movement (Stone 1974). Just as advocacy and progressive planning have stressed the need to expand the types of human constituencies involved in and served by planning, deep ecology raises the issue of how to structure planning so that the nonhuman species (not just the intergenerational human species) receives a voice.

If deep ecology promotes an alternative, supplementary object orientation for planning, then ecofeminism advances an alternative process agenda, though one that is not dissimilar to that raised by planning theorists such as John Forester (1989). From an ecofeminist perspective, the relationship of means and ends is absolutely critical. A just end cannot be achieved through unjust means. The very nature of means permeates the quality of the solution that results. Specifically, ecofeminism recognizes that the very process of how we do things—the words we use to communicate, the forums we provide for communication, the individuals who are empowered to act as representatives in discourse, the types of knowledge bases that are legitimate for representing what one "knows" to be true—is intimately connected to the types of solutions that are crafted for problems. Processes that are more encompassing and empowering will generate solutions that are more enduring, for several reasons. The participants will be more vested in them, and they will be because they will have been treated more equally in the process of problem identification and solving. Also, solutions will endure because through a multiparty communicative process all of the participants will be changed by their participation.

The implication of all this for planning theory and practice has to do with how planners conceive of their own roles and the place that is afforded to citizen participation and communication. An ecofeminist perspective suggests a more democratic conception of knowledge and expertise. Planners would need to acknowledge the necessary broad basis for understanding the nature of a problem and seek to solicit and incorporate, on its own terms, alternative conceptions. Thus, planners would move into active roles as facilitators and legitimators. To some extent this is analogous to the type of activity that occurred in the 1960s with community planning centers, following from the type of pluralistic planning Davidoff (1973) originally called for; but to a significant extent, it is quite different. It is different because ecofeminist planners would not seek to be experts, to impose their expertise and/or to be neutral in the application of their knowledge and analysis. An ecofeminist-informed planning would strive for a politically critical and astute facilitative process.

Bioregionalism is concerned with learning to live in place and then how to be affected by the uniqueness of place so that a life pattern evolves that fits with the particular ecological conditions of the place. Bioregionalism stresses the importance of intimate knowledge about place and the utilization of that knowledge in the design of all of the aspects of everyday life—the economy, the architecture, the art.

From a bioregional point of view, planning theory seems too abstract, a point similar to that made above that planning theory, from the point of view of environmental philosophy in general, seems contextless. However, bioregionalism is much more specific and can serve to reawaken a debate central and long-standing in planning. The bioregional argument about place is analogous to that raised by Mumford (1938), Odum and Moore (1938), and the Regional Planning Association of America (Sussman 1976). Mumford, along with Odum and Moore, publishing in the same year, explored different aspects of regionalism, with Mumford emphasizing physical regionalism and Odum and Moore emphasizing sociocultural regionalism. Both sets of authors, though, advanced a similar thesis—that planning needed to be based on the integrity of these regions and, conversely, planning that was not fully cognizant of these regional realities would necessarily fall short of effectiveness and success. In many ways, a bioregional position is not very far from the vision of Patrick Geddes that served as the inspiration for Mumford's own perspective, a vision that a people can be understood only in the context of their place and can find themselves only by knowing their place (Sussman 1976).

Thus, a bioregional perspective on planning theory stresses (1) the imperative of bringing into all planning analysis a specific spatial element, that of the region, and (2) using this element to both ground planning theory and to free it.

Conclusions

The mirror that environmental philosophy holds up to planning theory ends up making a number of significant challenges to the internal structure of the planning theory literature. As outlined above, some of these are challenges offered by environmental philosophy as a whole body of literature, irrespective of its internal differences, and some of these challenges derive from the particular strains of environmental philosophy. These challenges have to do with planning theory's internal debates, where environmental philosophy may offer a way to recast and reformulate some long-held positions, and with specific issues within planning theory, some of which are the focus of contemporary theorists, some of which have faded from the theory agenda, and some of which have never even been addressed.

These challenges should not be dismissed and, in fact, should be taken quite seriously. Not only are the points raised by environmental philosophy insightful in and of themselves (to illuminate what planning does and does not take up and perhaps should) but more fundamentally the challenges raised by environmental philosophy must be addressed because the root of contemporary environmental philosophy and the root of planning theory are the same—both are born from concerns about how to act in the world. While the spheres from which they originate are ostensibly different—the so-called natural environment for environmental philosophy and the person-constructed city and its impact on a surrounding region for planning—both are concerned with how to organize human action so as to achieve desired ends. If planning theory is the basis for planning action, then the challenges offered by environmental philosophy must be engaged because they confront base notions of effective action.

Finally, and perhaps most fundamentally, it seems that the challenges brought forth by environmental philosophy echo the speculations of Michael P. Brooks (1988). As Brooks sees it, the transformation of planning in the twentieth century has been a continuing search for relevance and influence in the decision-making process. What has been lost in this search is a connection to the visionary tradition of planning that asked questions and posed issues about the nature of the good life—what it is we are planning for. Brooks wonders whether in our search we have achieved any more influence (he thinks not) and, if not, whether we have lost something important (he thinks we have). A parallel to Brooks's argument in the environmental literature is a strident article by Kirkpatrick Sale (1986). Here he accuses the mainstream environmental movement and its lead organizations of being so enamored of the potential for influence within the corridors of power that they no longer pose fundamental questions and challenges to the power structure itself, a structure that Sale argues is at the root of environmental problems.

Contemporary environmental philosophy wants us, implores us, challenges us, not to be afraid to ask fundamental questions. Contemporary environmental philosophy argues that to the extent we do not pose these underlying questions and then act upon their implications, our planning deeds may be irrelevant at best and counterproductive at worst. This is not the easy path; contemporary environmental philosophy would have us believe, though, that there is no other if our goal is an effective, long-term, sustainable, and equitable planning.

Notes

1. It is perhaps not unlike the lag we have experienced in integrating the discourses about Postmodernism into our dialogues; the notable exception is the 1991 issue of the *Journal of Planning Education and Research* (volume 10, number 3) that contains a five-article symposium.

2. A cautionary note, though. Given the nature of this chapter, it is possible to make only a rudimentary and cursory presentation of these respective strains of environmental philosophy. Since my interest is presenting the essence of what is contained in this literature and then exploring its connections with planning theory, I necessarily have to slight many of the nuances within the philosophical discussions themselves. My goal has been to extract those elements that most clearly identify and explain these tendencies and to highlight those factors that most clearly illustrate the challenge they present to planning theory and practice.

3. Environmental ethics, environmental philosophy, earth ethics, and other terms are often regarded as synonyms (Martin and Beatley 1993). I use environmental ethics and environmental philosophy interchangeably in this chapter.

4. Feminist theory is a subject, like Postmodernism, that planning academics and planners have been slow to take up. For two recent treatments, see Beth Moore Milroy (1991) and Leonie Sandercock and Ann Forsyth (1992).

5. A very similar point is made in Native American thinking; see Annie L. Booth and Harvey Jacobs (1990) for a review of this perspective.

6. The literature on what constitutes and how to classify planning theory is itself quite large. See John Forester (1984), John Friedmann (1987), Patsy Healey et al. (1982), and Barclay M. Hudson (1979) for only some examples.

7. Andreas Faludi (1973) discusses this in his distinction of the difference between a theory *of* planning versus a theory *in* planning; James Simmie (1989) and Robert A. Beauregard (1990) are two recent expressions of this debate, siding for a theory *in* planning.

8. However, many deep ecologists might well be reluctant to use the word "rights," in that the concept of rights may not be consistent with their philosophical and spiritual orientation.

Bibliography

Alexander, D. 1990. Bioregionalism: science or sensibility? *Environmental Ethics* 12, 161–173.

Altshuler, A. A. 1973. The goals of comprehensive planning. In Faludi, A., ed. *A reader in planning theory.* New York: Pergamon Press, 193–210.

Andruss, V.; Plant, C.; Plant, J.; and Wright, E., eds. 1990. *Home! A bioregional reader.* Philadelphia: New Society Publishers.

Banfield, E. C. 1973. Ends and means in planning. In Faludi, A., ed. *A reader in planning theory*. New York: Pergamon Press, 139–150.

Beatley, T. 1989. Environmental ethics and planning theory. *Journal of Planning Literature* 4, 1–32.

Beauregard, R. A. 1978. Planning in an advanced capitalist state. In Burchell, R. W. and Sternlieb, G., eds. *Planning theory in the 1980's*. New Brunswick, NJ: Center for Urban Policy Research, Rutgers—The State University of New Jersey, 235–254.

———. 1990. Bringing the city back in. *Journal of the American Planning Association* 56, 210–215.

Berg, P. 1990. Growing a life-place politics. In Andruss, V.; Plant, C.; Plant, J.; and Wright, E., eds. *Home! A bioregional reader*. Philadelphia: New Society Publishers, 137–143.

Berg, P. and Dasmann, R. 1978. Reinhabiting California. In Berg, P., ed. *Reinhabiting a separate country*. San Francisco: Planet Drum Foundation, 217–220.

Biehl, J. 1988. Ecofeminism and deep ecology: unresolvable conflict? *Our Generation* 19, 19–31.

Booth, A. L. and Jacobs, H. M. 1990. Ties that bind: Native American beliefs as a foundation for environmental consciousness. *Environmental Ethics* 12, 27–43.

Borelli, P. 1987. Environmentalism at a crossroads. *The Amicus Journal* 9, 24–37.

Bradford, G. 1989. *How deep is deep ecology?* Ojai, CA: Times Change Press.

Brooks, M. P. 1988. Four critical junctures in the history of the urban planning profession: an exercise in hindsight. *Journal of the American Planning Association* 54, 241–248.

Carson, R. 1962. *Silent spring*. Boston: Houghton Mifflin.

Chapin, F. S., Jr. and Kaiser, E. J. 1979. *Urban land use planning*. Urbana: University of Illinois Press.

Clavel, P. 1985. *The progressive city: planning and participation, 1969–1984*. New Brunswick, NJ: Rutgers University Press.

Davidoff, P. 1973. Advocacy and pluralism in planning. In Faludi, A., ed. *A reader in planning theory*. New York: Pergamon Press, 277–296.

Devall, B. 1980. The deep ecology movement. *Natural Resources Journal* 20, 299–322.

———. 1988. Deep ecology and its critics. *Trumpeter* 5, 55–64.

Devall, B. and Sessions, G. 1985. *Deep ecology: living as if nature mattered*. Salt Lake City: Gibbs M. Smith.

Diamond, I. and Drenstein, G., eds. 1990. *Reweaving the world: the emergence of ecofeminism*. San Francisco: Sierra Club Books.

Faber, D. and O'Connor, J. 1989. The struggle for nature: environmental crisis and the crisis of environmentalism in the United States. *Capitalism, Nature, Socialism* 2, 12–39.

Faludi, A. 1973. What is planning theory? In Faludi, A., ed. *A reader in planning theory*. New York: Pergamon Press, 1–10.

Forester, J. 1984. Bounded rationality and the politics of muddling through. *Public Administration Review* 44, 23–31.

———. 1989. *Planning in the face of power.* Berkeley: University of California Press.

———. 1990. Comment on Simmie. *Planning Theory Newsletter* 3, 65–67.

Fox, W. 1989. The deep ecology–ecofeminism debate and its parallels. *Environmental Ethics* 11, 5–25.

———. 1990. *Toward a transpersonal ecology: developing new foundations for environmentalism.* Boston: Shambhala Press.

Friedmann, J. 1987. *Planning in the public domain: from knowledge to action.* Princeton, NJ: Princeton University Press.

Hargrove, E. C. 1989. *Fundamentals of environmental ethics.* Englewood Cliffs, NJ: Prentice Hall.

Healey, P., McDougall, G., and Thomas, M. J. 1982. Theoretical debates in planning: towards a coherent dialogue. In Healey, P., McDougall, G., and Thomas, M. J., eds. *Planning theory: prospects for the 1980s.* New York: Pergamon Press, 5–22.

Hudson, B. 1979. Comparison of current planning theories. *Journal of the American Planning Association* 45, 387–398.

Joy, C. 1952. *Albert Schweitzer, an anthology.* London: Adam and Charles Black.

Kent, T. J. 1964. *The urban general plan.* San Francisco: Chandler Publishing.

King, Y. 1983. Toward an ecological feminism and a feminist ecology. In Rothschild, J., ed. *Machina ex dea: feminist perspectives on technology.* New York: Pergamon Press, 118–129.

Kraushaar, R. 1988. Outside the whale: progressive planning and the dilemma of radical reform. *Journal of the American Planning Association* 54, 91–100.

Kravitz, A. S. 1970. Mandarinism: planning as handmaiden to conservative politics. In Beyle, T. L. and Lathrop, G. T., eds. *Planning and politics: uneasy partnership.* New York: Odyssey Press, 240–267.

Krumholz, N. 1982. A retrospective view of equity planning, Cleveland 1969–1979. *Journal of the American Planning Association* 48, 163–174.

Leopold, A. 1949. *A Sand County almanac.* Oxford: Oxford University Press.

Lindblom, C. E. 1973. The science of muddling through. In Faludi, A., ed. *A reader in planning theory.* New York: Pergamon Press, 151–170.

Lovelock, J. E. 1979. *Gaia: a new look at life on earth.* New York: Oxford University Press.

Martin, E. and Beatley, T. 1993. Our relationship with the earth: environmental ethics in planning education. *Journal of Planning Education and Research* 12, 117–126.

Meyerson, M. and Banfield, E. C. 1955. *Politics, planning and the public interest.* New York: The Free Press.

Milroy, B. M. 1991. Taking stock of planning, space and gender. *Journal of Planning Literature* 6, 3–15.

Mumford, L. 1938. *The culture of cities.* New York: Harcourt, Brace and Company.

Naess, A. 1973. The shallow and the deep, long range ecology movement, summary. *Inquiry* 16, 95–100.

Odum, H. W. and Moore, H. E. 1938. *American regionalism: a cultural-historical approach to national integration.* New York: Henry Holt.

Plant, J., ed. 1989. *Healing the wounds: the promise of ecofeminism.* Philadelphia: New Society Publishers.

Regan, T. 1983. *The case for animal rights.* Berkeley: University of California Press.

Rolston, H., III. 1988. *Environmental ethics: duties to and values in the natural world.* Philadelphia: Temple University Press.

Russell, D. 1987. The monkeywrenchers. *The Amicus Journal* 9, 28–42.

Sale, K. 1985. *Dwellers in the land: the bioregional vision.* San Francisco: Sierra Club Books.

———. 1986. The forest for the trees: can today's environmentalists tell the difference? *Mother Jones* November, 25–26, 28–29, 32–33, and 58.

Salleh, A. K. 1984. Deeper than deep ecology: the eco-feminist connection. *Environmental Ethics* 6, 339–345.

Sandercock, L. and Forsyth, A. 1992. A gender agenda: new directions for planning theory. *Journal of the American Planning Association* 58, 49–59.

Sessions, G. 1987. The deep ecology movement: a review. *Environmental Review* 9, 105–125.

Simmie, J. 1989. A preliminary sketch of a non-introverted planning theory. *Planning Theory Newsletter* 2, 38–54.

Singer, P. 1975. *Animal liberation.* New York: Random House.

Stone, C. D. 1974. *Should trees have standing? Toward legal rights for natural objects.* Los Altos, CA: W. Kaufmann.

Sussman, C., ed. 1976. *Planning the fourth migration: the neglected vision of the Regional Planning Association of America.* Cambridge: MIT Press.

Taylor, P. W. 1986. *Respect for nature: a theory of environmental ethics.* Princeton, NJ: Princeton University Press.

Warren, K. J. 1987. Feminism and ecology: making connections. *Environmental Ethics* 9, 3–20.

———. 1990. The power and promise of ecological feminism. *Environmental Ethics* 12, 125–146.

Zimmerman, M. E. 1987. Feminism, deep ecology, and environmental ethics. *Environmental Ethics* 9, 21–44.

MARSHA RITZDORF

6 *Feminist Contributions to Ethics and Planning Theory*

Introduction

High on the list of popular nonfiction books during 1990 was Professor Deborah Tannen's *You Just Don't Understand: Women and Men in Conversation*. Tannen, a sociolinguist, decided to enter the dialogue on gender and language "because the risk of ignoring differences is greater than the danger of naming them. Sweeping something big under the rug doesn't make it go away; it trips you up and sends you sprawling when you venture across the room" (Tannen 1990, p. 16).

Gender is a significant aspect of the cultural, social, economic, and political construction of reality. When theory is put forth in general categorical language, as "gender blind," it denies that the analysis is most often based on the experience of white, middle- or upper-class men in Western societies (Forsyth 1990). Humankind is not a generic mass of undifferentiated people. While gender is not the only possible category of analysis (certainly class and race are highly significant), it is a category that has been virtually invisible in planning theory and practice. As Susan Moller Okin sums up in her book on women in Western political thought, "It is by no means a simple matter to integrate the female half of the human race into a tradition of political theory which has defined them and intra familial relationships as outside the scope of the political" (Okin 1979, p. 286).

What is "feminist theory"? Sherry Boland Ahrentzen (1990, p. 12) writes: "Perhaps the most agreed upon view of feminist research is that there is no single or agreed upon model." However, at the heart of all feminist work is a unifying idea: that gender is a significant aspect of the cultural, social, political, and economic construction of reality. Feminist thought rejects the facile explanation that theory can be or is "neutral" (that is, gender blind).

Whether or not gender is explicitly mentioned in a theoretical construct, there is an implicit if not explicit set of values and attitudes about the role of women that frames the analysis. Prevailing values render the epistemological search across many fields of inquiry as "male." Feminist theory rejects the pretense of value-free research in favor of consciously partial thought, arguing that the supposedly value-free, neutral science model is actually a male-defined and male-centered model (Hess and Ferree 1987).

There are three root assumptions in feminist work. While all three may not be present in an individual piece of work, at least one of them will frame the inquiry. They are:

1. The position that women are exploited, oppressed, or devalued by society;
2. An interest on the part of the feminist thinker in helping to change the conditions of women's lives; and
3. The assertion that traditional, and still dominant, theory, research, and practice ignore or justify inappropriate and/or exploitative treatment of women (adapted from Acker et al. 1983).

In feminist inquiry, the split between theory and practice and between the object of the research and the researcher is not a desirable goal. Many feminists assert that the best research ideas are those that bridge the gap between theory and practice (Hess and Ferree 1987) and that acknowledge that personal experience and grounded research are valuable theory building and research tools (Cook and Fonow 1986). The selection of research focus is often tied to emotional and volatile life experiences, focused on the immediate environment and driven by a goal to have the theorizing or research results lead to explicit political action for change (Fonow and Cook 1991).

Planning Theory and Feminist Planning

Planning theory, as pointed out by Leonie Sandercock and Ann Forsyth (1990), remains a male bastion. "Of all the fields within planning, that of theory remains arguably the most male dominated, the least influenced by any awareness of the importance of gender" (Sandercock and Forsyth 1990, p. 3).

Planning theorists, like feminist theorists, do not agree on any one theory. Instead, competing theoretical perspectives are used to explain their respective fields. Regardless of which theory or theories of planning are under discussion, it is fair to say that their differential meaning to and impact upon men and women have not been explored in the literature. Sandercock and Forsyth suggest that there are diverse intersections where the analysis of gender is relevant:

> The economic status of women, how women are located in and move through space, the connection between capitalist production and patriarchal relationships and between "public" and "domestic" life, how women know about the world and about what is good, what forms of communication women are most comfortable with or most threatened by, and more (Sandercock and Forsyth 1990, p. 4).

In the 1970s and 1980s, literature about women and planning flourished. This literature primarily focuses on policy and practice. Gerda Wekerle, Rebecca Peterson, and David Morley's 1980 edited volume *New Spaces for Women* was instrumental in helping define women and environments research. A special edition of *Signs* (the highly regarded feminist journal) devoted to women and the city appeared the same year. These collections addressed women's activities in the urban environment. The pieces acknowledged that women have different daily life activities and patterns than men and therefore make different use of the environment and may encounter different problems than their male counterparts. The authors asserted that understanding and responding to these differences are important in developing the community. Their analyses of urban and suburban structures and the policy-making process from a feminist perspective took into account the totality of people's lives and the ways in which men and women are treated and situated differently in political, social, economic, and physical space.

Writing about feminist advocacy theory in 1986, Jacqueline Leavitt asserts: "Planners assume a value set that is inherently and historically masculine . . . the overriding goals and objectives are more likely to be shaped by men than women politicians, male corporate heads rather than female" (Leavitt 1986, p. 187). However, in addition to the growing body of literature, demographic changes during these two decades made it almost impossible for planning practitioners to continue to ignore the differences between men's and women's lives in the community. For example, it is estimated that 80 percent of American mothers of children under the age of eighteen will be in the work force by the year 2000. A recent census report in the United States indicates that 49 percent of mothers of one-year-old babies are currently working outside their homes. Policy and planning decisions need to take these phenomena into account.

A growing body of feminist planning academicians see to it that these issues are discussed in the literature, at conferences, and in their classrooms. While much of their work contains important theoretical statements and is widely quoted in other feminists' research, their papers are rarely presented on theory panels at the conferences or cited in traditional planning theorists' work.

Contemporary planning theory, according to Robert A. Beauregard, is anchored in values and perspectives that emphasize a "belief in the transferability of knowledge across time, space and social groups" and "an authoritarian stance that assumes an Archimedean position from which to speak" (Beauregard 1990, p. 2). In simple language, this means that it is strongly committed to functional rationality as the basis of human action and to the use of abstract "principles and rights as the criteria for decision making" (Beauregard 1990, p. 2).

Only a small number of planning theorists are beginning to question the notions of objectivity, neutrality, and the maintenance of a critical distance. It is little wonder that most feminist planners have steered clear of theory as their primary field of discourse in planning education. However, planning theory and practice should be concerned with the implicit and explicit exclusion of women from full participation as practitioners, teachers, citizens, and students of the art of planning.

Feminist political theorists debate the scope and meaning of citizenship and the nature of political action for women in contemporary society. Writing about the meaning of feminist citizenship, Kathleen B. Jones (1988) suggests that the following themes are important to understanding women's citizenship: Expanding the Meaning of Political Action, Personal Commitment and Connection, and the Search for New Forms of Organization. Planning theory and practice need to attend to this debate as well.

Since planning is inherently political, it is important to understand that the boundaries between the personal and the political are merged for women. Women are generally interested in expanding the range, intensity, and modes of action in planning. They are often interested in holistic approaches to problems and cooperative problem solving. They see issues impacting their bodies, their families, and their neighbor-hoods as both political and personal (Ritzdorf 1993).

Landmark research into male and female moral development by Carol Gilligan found that caring about others and protecting them from harm are prominent features of women's worldview and that this view profoundly impacts their resolution of moral dilemmas (Gilligan 1982). Patricia Hill Collins (1989) argues that black feminist thought creates the convergence of Afrocentric and feminist values through the creation of an alternative epistemology based on an ethic of caring. Other feminist researchers question whether feminist research is or should be framed by such an ethic.

For planners and policy analysts, though, this is a cogent question since it is inevitable in any public decision-making process that "Who gets?" and "Who pays and how?" are the framing questions of the cost-benefit analysis of a decision. Who an individual or a society cares about will definitively affect decision making.

Since economic productivity is at the heart of policy decision making in a capitalist society, it is important to understand that for women reproductive and domestic activities are inextricably bound up with traditional economic production in their assessments of policy and their analysis of needed change. The issues and language of family life are highly significant to most women. So are matters of personal safety. As a result, the issues they see as most important to them in the public policy arena are far removed from the issues that are identified or weighed as highly significant for most men. For example, issues related to an urban parking structure for women will focus on the safety of such a building. If it is poorly lit or designed or too heavily landscaped it becomes, for women, a possible matter of life or death, not simply a matter of good urban design, aesthetics, or the economic viability of downtown. Whether or not they clearly articulate these concerns is irrelevant to the fact that they will not use the structure if they are scared and may curtail their travel to the part of town where it is located as a result. For instance, a survey found that the majority of female faculty members at the University of Oregon refused to teach at night because of perceived safety problems on and around the campus pri-marily related to lighting and design (Ritzdorf 1990).

While the above is true for most women whether or not they are feminists in their orientation, female planners and planning scholars have to make a conscious choice about their "identity." If one chooses to approach planning from a feminist perspective, she (or rarely he) must be ready to be labeled and have her or his professional credibility, intelligence, or research methodology questioned by hostile or, at best, indifferent colleagues. After all, if planners admit they have a perspective, they are denying the myth of neutral, technological rationality on which many planners depend for their identity. "In the planning profession, to be a feminist or interested in women's issues is to reject explicitly much of the professional socialization of one's training" (Leavitt 1986, p. 185). While Leavitt was referring to planning practitioners, the same pressures to conform exist in the world of academia as well.

For feminist thought and feminist ethics to truly impact planning theory will require an acceptance, at a minimum, of the notions of pluralistic thought and personal connection. It will mean a rejection of the rational model in favor of a model that acknowledges that there are different ways of "knowing" the world and constructing answers to problems. It means a model based on flexibility rather than immutable principles of the "right" and "wrong" decision.

The new emphasis on negotiation and mediation as essential tools of the practitioner's trade is an indication that the notion of flexibility is becoming more important in planning decision making. Feminist social scientists are suggesting that a combination of qualitative and quantitative studies is one way to achieve flexibility, offset the shortcomings of using only one or the other method, and produce a more powerful product that more effectively tests theory (Jayaratne and Stewart 1991). Within planning, narrative research is becoming more popular and several male and female academicians are at work on pieces that use narrative methodologies.[1]

Through their life experiences, women have learned the end result of an action always reflects the personal experiences of those involved in the decision making. A simple example of this is the overwhelming relationship between child battering (and spouse battering) and the childhood experiences of the batterers, who often were battered themselves.

Women are highly sensitive to the potentials of the misuse of power and of arbitrary claims of rational or correct behavior or answers. Process is extremely important. More and more frequently, the importance of process is acknowledged in many contemporary planning theorists' work. I doubt, though, that by process they are thinking about the totality of life experiences that the planner/theorist brings to his/her work.

However, it is important to the development of the knowledge, skills, and attitudes that will be necessary for planning in the twenty-first century that feminist sensibilities be incorporated into planning theory.

The dramatic shifts in women's roles and the attendant ways in which families, economies, and communities will have to reorganize themselves demand conscious attention in theory as well as in practice.

Planning theory is grounded in many of the principles that feminist theorists reject outright, making it difficult to find a common ground. In addition to the feminist acceptance of a relationship between research subject and object, feminist theorists question the existence of universally applicable principles and do not necessarily regard rationality as the basis of most human action. They are generally uninterested in knowledge for its own sake and want to see how it will be applicable to real world problems. Caroline Andrew and Beth Moore Milroy comment:

> The debate about theorizing in the research community at large reminds us to think about why we do research in the social sciences in the first place. Is it purely to acquire knowledge for its own sake? Or is it to change and improve something? Feminist researchers who are acutely aware of the pervasive androcentricity that has influenced the shape of urban environments cannot be disinterested inquirers removed from the prospect of creating a non-sexist environment. For that half of humankind which feels isolated from the social science explanations of its own experience, it would be shooting itself in the foot to settle simply for understanding. Acknowledging purposefulness in the research experience, in both researcher and researched, creates a dialectic between understanding and changing (Andrew and Moore Milroy 1988, p. 177).

Sandercock and Forsyth (1990) suggest several substantive areas in which feminist thought has contributed, or could contribute, to planning theories. They are: the organization of space; the economics of reproduction and social relationships; language and communication; methodology and epistemology; morality in planning; and a better understanding of the public domain.

In developing their ideas, they identify the work of women and a small number of men who as planning educators are beginning to create a corpus of work that connects feminist ideology with planning thought and practice. They address the need for a serious reform of planning education and the need for good theoretical work that:

> starts with the need for the production and maintenance of life rather than the production and consumption of goods and services. Life sustaining work by women is labor intensive and not rewarded economically. It fits badly in materially based theories, including much econom-

ics which ignores or devalues it. And yet, it is important work, and a theory which does not encompass it is extremely narrow (Sandercock and Forsyth 1990, p. 41).

Five Feminist Thinkers

The work of the five women profiled here exemplifies the bridging of feminist theory, ethics, and practice. In each case, the woman is known for both her academic and practical contributions to the world of planning. This is exemplified by the fact that three of them (Dolores Hayden, Jacqueline Leavitt, and Marsha Ritzdorf) have won the Diana Donald Award from the American Planning Association (APA), an award given for contributions to the advancement of women in planning practice in the United States. All their work is linked by a common commitment to a vision of a better built environment that acknowledges the needs of the diverse residents of the planet by race, class, and gender.

DOLORES HAYDEN

Dolores Hayden's work is well known. An architectural historian, Hayden has distinguished herself as a scholar and author. Her work on the material feminists (Hayden 1981) and the development of the American single-family suburb (Hayden 1984) and their meaning for contemporary planning is internationally recognized. Hayden clearly links the social meaning of reproduction to traditional planning and architectural built environment thought and action. Using history as her point of departure, she shows that the implicit assumptions of traditional thought and practice are based on the assumption that women and children have either no "urban experiences" or they have the same experiences as men (Hayden 1984). She challenges conventional thought about the opportunities presented to women in the Progressive Era to seize power in the public domain and points out that the already established separate spheres for women and men enabled (and continue to enable) men to exclude women's contributions to public life.

Hayden's contributions to our understanding of women's historic place are not contained only within the covers of her excellent books and articles. She has been energetically involved in saving women's urban heritage (along with that of ethnic and labor groups) since 1982, when she founded a small, nonprofit corporation, the Power of Place, in Los Angeles. She describes it:

> We are committed to identifying landmarks of ethnic, women's and labor history not yet seen as cultural resources, and creating more balanced interpretations of existing landmarks to emphasize the ethnic diversity of the city. We publish walking tours and scholarly research about historic sites and buildings, sponsor community history workshops, make proposals for historic preservation and sponsor public art (Hayden 1990, p. 12).

Through the Power of Place, Hayden is breaking new ground in emphasizing the importance of gender, class, and ethnicity in understanding the meaning of the built environment. She is helping change the premises on which historic preservation activities are planned and conducted and is reshaping urban historical scholarship. However, the Power of Place is more than a scholarly endeavor. It reaches out directly to the community through a series of walking tours, maps, and public art projects. It is a growing rather than a static project with endless possibilities for enriching both the scholarly knowledge about feminist, ethnic, and labor history and the documentation and preservation of sites of historical importance. It also presents exciting possibilities for replication in other places, making Hayden's work staggering in its potential impact nationwide and worldwide. She links her work directly to a changed urban environment that

> can create a stronger urban sense of place and a more egalitarian approach to the urban landscape, where attention is given to every urban neighborhood, not just those where commercial real estate ventures are profitable. This is the kind of city The Power of Place would like to help create (Hayden 1990, p. 17).

JACQUELINE LEAVITT

A founding member of the Planning and Women Division of the APA, a longtime member of the steering committee of the Planner's Network, and more, the word advocate only begins to describe Jacqueline Leavitt's tireless efforts to improve the lives of the disenfranchised. Best known as an expert on socially responsible housing policy and design, Leavitt has been a tireless advocate for the improvement of women's place in the profession of planning. She was the author (Leavitt 1980) of the first dissertation to be devoted to the subject of women in planning and the impacts of planning on women. She has developed and written extensively about feminist advocacy as a theory of planning.

Leavitt strives to create linkages between the worlds of architecture and planning. The historical retreat of planning from its physical roots and from housing policy is a consistent source of concern that frames much of her scholarly and practical work. Not only does she address the needs for a more collaborative framework in theory but she has extensively participated in actual design projects in which she has teamed up with an architect to design housing more sensitive to the needs of women and their changing families. In 1984, two of these collaborative efforts, with architect Troy West, won first place in national competitions.

Leavitt's contributions to an understanding of low-income women's housing problems and solutions are holistic and innovative. Her most recent book, *From Abandonment to Hope* (with Susan Saegert, 1990), examines the experiences of tenants who lived through the experience of landlord abandonment of their homes in Harlem. It shows how women in this community cope with adversity by creating an interlinked world of household and community. The authors draw on their respondents' interviews and the existing literature on women's behavior to create a "community-household model," which has as its root "the valuing of housework itself as the most basic level of organization" (Leavitt and Saegert 1990, p. 241).

A believer in practical education, Leavitt consistently involves her students with low-income housing tenants in Los Angeles, where she is a board member of two community housing corporations. She is also a member of the board of directors of the National Low Income Housing Coalition and an adviser to numerous housing agencies throughout the country.

Her current research includes an examination of the meaning of "exclusion and containment" in the context of American communities and a feminist conceptualization of issues of safety and security in low-income neighborhoods. Again linking theory and practice, her goal is to use this research to help develop more "woman-friendly" security and safety policies for Los Angeles public housing.

BETH MOORE MILROY

In her own words, Beth Moore Milroy has "an abiding passion for theories, especially social, feminist and planning theories" (Moore Milroy 1990). Her scholarly work focuses on feminist and Postmodern interpretations of community life. She recently edited and contributed a paper to a special symposium issue on Postmodern thought for the *Journal of Planning Education* (Moore Milroy 1991a) and moderated the first panel ever devoted to feminist epistemology at a national planning conference in the United States.

Moore Milroy's work reveals an ability to segue effectively from the sometimes heavy-handed jargon of contemporary theorists to the practicalities of women's daily community life. The effect of space and time and the impact of the temporal and functional separations of home and work on women's lives are explored in her work. She emphasizes the need for theory and research to develop together and writes of feminist research: "Its premise is that knowledge and action are inter-related, the one affecting the nature of the other but neither necessarily taking precedence" (Andrew and Moore Milroy 1988, p. 180).

Moore Milroy's current work is a funded three-year research project on the influence of community and domestic and paid labor on women's lives in the twentieth century, which includes a case study of their contributions to the civic maintenance of one Canadian city.

She is actively involved in a variety of community housing projects, is a board member of a forty-six unit, low-income housing project for women and their children sponsored through the Kitchner-Waterloo YWCA, and is a member of the local Community Housing Coalition. In addition, she is involved with a research issue that focuses on empower-ment issues especially as they relate to the lives of the institutionalized and deinstitutionalized mentally ill.

Moore Milroy's teaching, research and community agendas are intertwined. She writes:

> It seems to me that I understand teaching, research and community work as all of a piece. I have the sense that I and others are making small, piecemeal gains as we share our bits of experience and knowl-edge in cooperative ways, gradually moving projects forward that, were I faced with them alone, would seem formidable. I like this feeling of a circle. And this is why I do what I do (Moore Milroy 1991b, p. 1).

GERDA WEKERLE

Starting as a sociologist with an interest in the built environment, Gerda Wekerle has been identified with teaching, research, and commu-nity work related to women and the urban environment for more than sixteen years. She was the cofounder and editor for the initial eight years of its existence of the first journal in the field, *Women and Environ-*

ments. She was an editor (Wekerle et al. 1980), as mentioned earlier, of one of the first two collections of research on women and the built environment (see also Wekerle 1981) and the author of the first article synthesizing the diverse body of literature in the field. She is currently at work on a book that "will make linkages between urban change and restructuring over the past two decades and changes in women's lives in the same period. It will focus on women as urban activists who have created new spaces and new urban services through community and local struggles" (Wekerle 1990, p. 1).

Wekerle began her practical work in the community in 1980 when she was elected to the executive board of the National Action Committee on the Status of Women (the Canadian equivalent of the National Organization of Women in the United States) and began to raise issues of housing and environmental policies and their impact on women. She has been involved with the Toronto Metro Task Force on Violence Against Women and Children and has worked extensively on issues related to women's use of public transit, including, but not limited to, issues of safety and security. Her work has substantially changed the Toronto transit system, making it more user-friendly to women. With Carolyn Whitzman, she has worked to facilitate training workshops for the planning and development staff of the city of Toronto on planning safer cities for women.

Housing research is another aspect of Wekerle's contributions. Her study of eight women's housing projects was the first to document housing developed especially for women residents. It included the women residents' first person evaluations of life in these projects.

Wekerle speaks of the braiding together of her scholarly and community activities:

> All of these efforts at community activism have built on my scholarly work and feedback to enrich it. I have been able to share my work with community groups and politicians concerned with creating social change; my own involvement has given me access to new perspectives on my research and to new data sources. As a result of these activities, I have become much more interested in research on the policy process, how social change is implemented, and how grass roots groups affect change in urban environments. This is the direction in which my research is currently moving (Wekerle 1990, p. 1).

MARSHA RITZDORF

It is a hallmark of much feminist work that personal stories frame the content and context. In this tradition, I offer a few words about my own work. Since 1985, I have published a series of articles addressing the relationship between land use and zoning issues and the changing lives of women. Specifically, I addressed the power of municipal zoning ordinances to spatially direct our lives, the location of our support systems, and the very composition of our intimate household arrangements (through the enforcement of outdated definitions of family).

Lynda Schneekloth writes of my work: "Because of her theoretical work which uses critical theory analysis to reevaluate existing technical regulations, Ritzdorf is able to expose the hidden agenda of land use controls to those responsible for the regulation and enforcement of these codes" (Schneekloth 1987, p. 319).

My theoretical work is grounded in empirical research, including a 1984 nationwide survey of municipal zoning practices, which I am replicating in 1994 to create a longitudinal analysis. In addition, my explorations of the use of land to enforce traditional social values and gender roles led me to question the historical role of middle-class women in helping promote and enforce these agendas, and I am currently writing a book exploring the historical relationships between gender roles and municipal land use planning.

I am interested in the transformation of zoning regulation into a proactive tool for social change, but, being a realist, I focus my community work on hopefully achievable and, alas, incremental changes that respond to the changing demographics of family life. I teach workshops all over the country for zoning and planning administrators and community activists. I recommend zoning ordinance changes that respond to the changing needs of women and their families (child care–friendly ordinances, for example) and teach planners and advocates how to lobby for such revisions in ways that will be politically acceptable to their communities.

I also focus my work and service on improving the status of women in planning education and practice. This work included completing a national survey and research report for the Association of Collegiate Schools of Planning on the issues of recruitment and retention of women and persons of color in planning education.

Conclusion

Women are still outsiders in the world of planning academia in general (only 18 percent of all tenured and tenure-track American planning professors are women).[2] Even a smaller number identify themselves as feminists and/or theorists, as indicated by their conference participation and the nature of their published work.

Unfortunately, many women planners are unwilling to rock the boat or to jeopardize their "appeal" to their male colleagues. Therefore, they accept the prevailing notion that planning theory and planning practice are gender blind. "The paradigms on which planning and theorizing have been based are informed by characteristics traditionally associated with the masculine in our society" (Sandercock and Forsyth 1990, p. 36).

While there are male planning theorists who may self-identify themselves as "feminists," they are few. In addition, it is fair to say that there is probably no male theorist who would be so identified by all, or even the majority, of the women working in the field.

The common assumptions that bind the work of feminists can contribute to more egalitarian planning theory. Joan Scott sums them up elegantly:

> We need theory that can analyze the workings of patriarchy in all its manifestations—ideological, institutional, organizational, subjective— accounting not only for continuities but also for change over time. We need theory that will let us think in terms of pluralities and diversities rather than of unities and universals. We need theory that will break the conceptual hold, at least, of those long traditions of (Western) philosophy that have systematically and repeatedly construed the world hierarchically in terms of masculine universals and feminine specificities. We need theory that will enable us to articulate alternative ways of thinking about (and thus acting upon) gender without either simply reversing the old hierarchies or confirming them. And we need theory that will be useful and relevant for political practice (Scott 1988, p. 33).

The good news is that planning theorists are beginning to explore the potential contribution of feminist thought, including feminist ethics, to the field and that feminists are choosing to address the issues of planning theory. The bad news is that a long and arduous road lies ahead before planning theory, education, and practice genuinely reflect the fact that men and women's lives, needs, and thoughts are of equal importance.

Notes

I wish to thank John Forester (1990) and Ann Forsyth (1990), who gave generously of their time to discuss feminist theory and planning theory with me during the 1990 fall term I spent at Cornell University. Thanks also to William Simonsen at the University of Oregon for his excellent editorial suggestions.

1. For example, as of August 1991, I personally knew that at least the following academics were working on manuscripts containing or completely based on narrative research with planners (John Forester, Charles Hoch, and Norman Krumholz), female planning students (Marsha Ritzdorf), and citizens (Linda Keyes and Kenneth Reardon).

2. No absolutely accurate accounting of planning faculty exists. These figures are from the 1989 study done for the Association of Collegiate Schools of Planning (ACSP) entitled "The Recruitment and Retention of Women and People of Color in Planning Education" published in the *ACSP UpDate* (University of Wisconsin at Madison, August 1990, 1–27).

Bibliography

Acker, J., Barry, K., and Essveld, J. 1983. Objectivity and truth: problems in doing feminist research. *Women's Studies International Forum* 6, 423–435.

Ahrentzen, S. B. 1990. Rejuvenating a field that is either coming of age or aging in place: feminist research contributions to environmental design research. *EDRA 21*. Environmental Design Research Association Conference Proceedings, Washington, D.C., 11–18.

Andrew, C. and Moore Milroy, B., eds. 1988. *Life spaces: gender, household, employment*. Vancouver: University of British Columbia Press.

Association of Collegiate Schools of Planning. 1990. *ACSP UpDate*. Madison, WI: Association of Collegiate Schools of Planning. August.

Beauregard, R. 1990. Raising the questions: the meeting of feminist theory and planning theory. Unpublished manuscript.

Collins, P. H. 1989. The social construction of black feminist thought. *Signs* 14, 745–773.

Cook, J. and Fonow, M. 1986. Knowledge and women's interests: issues of epistemology and methodology in feminist sociological research. *Sociological Inquiry* 56, 2–29.

Fonow, M. and Cook, J., eds. 1991. *Beyond methodology*. Bloomington: Indiana University Press.

Forester, J. 1990. Personal correspondence and conversations with the author.

Forsyth, A. 1990. Personal correspondence and conversations with the author.

Gilligan, C. 1982. *In a different voice: psychological theory and women's development*. Cambridge: Harvard University Press.

Hayden, D. 1981. *The grand domestic revolution*. Cambridge: MIT Press.

———. 1984. *Redesigning the American dream*. New York: Norton.

———. 1990. Using ethnic history to understand urban landscapes. *Places* 7, 11–17.

Hess, B. B. and Ferree, M. M. 1987. *Analyzing gender: a handbook of social science research*. Newbury Park, CA: Sage Publications.

Jayaratne, T. and Stewart, A. 1991. Quantitative and qualitative methods in the social sciences: current feminist issues and practical strategies. In Fonow, M. and Cook, J., eds. *Beyond methodology.* Bloomington: Indiana University Press, 85–106.

Jones, K. B. 1988. Citizenship in a woman-friendly polity. *Signs* 15, 781–812.

Leavitt, J. 1980. *Planning and women, women in planning.* Ph.D. dissertation, Columbia University, New York.

————. 1986. Feminist advocacy planning in the 1980's. In Checkoway, B., ed. *Strategic perspectives in planning practice.* Lexington, MA: Lexington Books, 181–194.

Leavitt, J. and Saegert, S. 1990. *From abandonment to hope: community-households in Harlem.* New York: Columbia University Press.

Moore Milroy, B. 1990. Personal correspondence with the author.

————. 1991a. Into postmodern weightlessness. *Journal of Planning Education and Research* 10, 3: 181–87.

————. 1991b. Planning, space and gender: taking stock. *Journal of Planning Literature* 16: 3–15.

Okin, S. M. 1979. *Women in Western political thought.* Princeton, NJ: Princeton University Press. In Nelson, B. J. Women and knowledge in political science: texts, histories and epistemologies. *Women and Politics* 9, 1–25.

Ritzdorf, M. 1990. Unpublished survey of University of Oregon Faculty Women, Committee on the Status of Women, University of Oregon, Eugene.

————. 1993. The fairy's tale: teaching planning and public policy in a different voice. *Journal of Planning Education and Research* 12, 99–106.

Sandercock, L. and Forsyth, A. 1990. Gender: a new agenda for planning theory. Berkeley: Institute of Urban and Regional Development, Working Paper No. 521.

Schneekloth, L. 1987. Advances in practice in environment, behavior and design. In Zube, E. H. and Moore, G. T., eds. *Advances in environment, behavior and design.* Vol. 1. New York: Plenum Press, 307–331.

Scott, J. 1988. Deconstructing equality versus difference: or the uses of post-structuralist theory for feminism. *Feminist Studies* 14, 33–50.

Tannen, D. 1990. *You just don't understand: women and men in conversation.* New York: William Morrow.

Wekerle, G. 1981. Women in the urban environment. In Stimpson, C., ed. *Women in the American city.* Chicago: University of Chicago Press, 185–211.

————. 1990. Personal correspondence with the author.

Wekerle, G., Peterson, R., and Morley, D., eds. 1980. *New spaces for women.* Boulder, CO: Westview.

PART II

Ethical Theory
and
Planning Practice

ELIZABETH HOWE

Introduction

The five chapters in this part are concerned with the relationship between ethical theory and planning practice. Ethical theory can be enlightening in itself. As the first part of this book has demonstrated, it is not by any means a monolithic body of thought (Harper and Stein 1992). Utilitarian ideas of ethics have vied with deontological ones for ascendancy over Western thought since the eighteenth century. In recent years, neo-Marxist ethics as interpreted in the critical theory of Jürgen Habermas (Benhabib and Dallmayr 1990; McCarthy 1978) has been receiving considerable attention in planning (Forester 1980, 1985; Innes 1990). Communitarian ethics has just begun to have an impact in planning but has its intellectual roots in ancient Greece (MacIntyre 1985). Having some understanding of these various ethical theories and controversies can provide insight into the nature of ethical dilemmas in planning and can help each person to clarify his or her own particular approach to ethics.

However, understanding one's approach to ethics still begs the central question. Ethical theory does not exist simply because of its philosophical elegance. Ethics are supposed to regulate behavior in the so-called "real" world. Professional ethics, in particular, are intended to shape not only thought but action as well. This part is concerned with the normative question of how planners should behave in practice and to a lesser extent, what kind of ethical theories they do or do not use.

In fact, the questions in this set of readings are cast more narrowly. All the chapters in this part focus on social justice in planning. These analyses are basically liberal, as opposed to Marxist, and, because of their concern with justice, are largely deontological as well. Even James A. Throgmorton, whose analysis of energy planning draws on the Postmodern image of planning as a rhetorical activity and who seems to share much with critical theorists, still relies in chapter 10 on a liberal view of ethics suggested by this author (Howe 1990) and discussed by several authors in part I. Given the general similarity of theme and approach among these articles, I focus here primarily on why social justice should be an ethical principle in planning, to what degree it should be a binding one, and how closely this corresponds to actual practice among planners.

SOCIAL JUSTICE IN PLANNING

The central issue raised by all five chapters in this part is how planners can work in practice to achieve social justice. This is not the only, or even the most common, ethical issue faced by planners in practice. Issues concerning basic honesty, truthfulness in analysis, keeping of confidences, fairness to colleagues or to members of the public, or accountability to superiors are often more common in day-to-day practice (Howe 1994).

Why, then, should justice be the particular focus of attention here? Historically, planning has been a profession more strongly committed to large-scale visions of the "good" or the "right" than its sister public professions of public administration and policy analysis (Alterman and MacRae 1983). A utopian thread has always drawn people committed to making cities and other forms of human development more aesthetically pleasing, more socially just, or less environmentally damaging, as well as more economically efficient. Professional ethics in planning might be thought of in part as balancing daily issues such as fairness to development applicants or loyalty to departmental superiors, and these larger social purposes. While, as we will see, the former may be more apparent to practicing planners, the latter are particularly evident to academics and theoreticians.

Since the housing reformers of the Progressive period, there have always been planners concerned with improving living conditions of the poor. This commitment has even older roots in the moral crusades of the nineteenth century (Boyer 1983) and continues today, even in a more secular society, to have a strongly moral flavor. So its strong representation in a reader on ethics should hardly be surprising.

Finally, justice poses dilemmas for planning that touch on many other ethical responsibilities as well. Fairness, for example, is one aspect of justice itself. Serving justice may produce especially difficult conflicts with agency policy and responsiblity or loyalty to appointed and elected superiors.

While social justice can be a powerful principle for guiding public policy, it presents planners and others who would choose to use it with two significant practical issues or problems. One is how to define it. This sounds like an academic quibble, but how one defines justice or equity significantly shapes the kind of policy interventions required to achieve it.

The second issue is what kind of obligation a commitment to social justice requires. Is it a strict obligation owed to all other people in all circumstances or is it something looser? If it is a less binding obligation, how much of a duty is it? Again, while this general formulation may seem rather theoretical, this is a central practical problem because in many cases the claims for social justice are politically weak and the duty to try to achieve it is a difficult one.

The practical nature of these issues can be explored using the information available about the ways that planners deal with the issue of social justice in practice. However, first it may be useful to clarify what the issues and choices are.

DEFINING JUSTICE

Justice can mean any of a number of things. This can create problems since different ideas can be a source of policy disagreements, even among people who think they are trying to accomplish the same thing. Conversely the diversity may be useful, as different ideas of equity may be needed singly or in combination for different policy contexts or problems.

This diversity of definitions can be seen in the articles here and is developed by others as well (Beatley 1984, 1988a,b,c; Lucy 1981; Reamer 1982). One common idea of equality of shares or benefits requires equality of inputs. It is often invoked for the distribution of resources for public services, such as street improvements. Equal risk or sacrifice is the other side of equal benefits. It is used by Reg Lang in chapter 9 in considering fairness in the location of LULUs (locally unwanted land uses) such as waste management facilities, and by Randal Marlin in chapter 7 in relation to impacts of traffic.

Equal opportunity may be the most common image of equity in North American culture. Again, this idea of equity primarily focuses attention on equal inputs or equal life chances. Equal opportunities in housing and education were the basis of the New York Yonkers decision, as discussed by Marcia Marker Feld in chapter 11. Three of Harvey M. Jacobs's equity criteria in chapter 8 also draw on the idea of equal opportunity. Intergenerational equity preserves opportunities in the future while tenure equity for prospective homeowners and for new farmers preserves opportunities for present people.

However, disillusionment with the effectiveness of approaches based on equal opportunity has led some people to focus instead on equal outcomes or results. Perhaps the most widely discussed version of this approach is John Rawls's theory of justice (1971), which is advocated here by Marlin. Rawls (1971, p. 12) argues that if a group of people were developing a social contract for a society and as "behind a veil of ignorance," the members had no knowledge of what social or economic positions they would hold in that society, they would choose to organize institutions that would maximize benefits to the least advantaged people since any of them might end up in that position. This standard would allow absolute inequalities to exist but only if they served to maximize benefits to the least advantaged. Moreover, such inequalities would be constrained by the "principle of fair equality of opportunity" (Rawls 1971, p. 75), which would require access for all to basic primary goods such as education, jobs, health care, and a minimum income. While Lang and Throgmorton do not cite or draw on Rawls, their concern for improving the lot of the least advantaged draws on the same idea of more equal results.

The difference between equality of inputs or of opportunity and equality of outcomes is very significant. There is an obvious uneasiness that justice is not really just if great inequalities exist among individuals and social groups. Alternatively, many people are made uneasy by the idea that equality of results would deprive people of significant freedom and would result in a stultifying uniformity. As Rawls (1971) indicates, this is not an either/or proposition—all freedom or all equality—but because of the tension, policy arguments do often take place over definitions of justice.

These are all substantive ideas of the meaning of equity, but several of these authors—Lang, Throgmorton, and Jacobs—are also careful to include the idea of equity as fair process. Two quote David Harvey (1973, p. 98) concerning "a just distribution justly arrived at." Promoting a just distribution of resources through means that are dehumanizing or unethical would undermine the ultimate purpose of a humane society in which people can have authentic relationships. This idea of procedural justice is another variation on equality of opportunity, of access to decision-making processes. Marlin raises a particularly interesting issue that primarily relates to procedural justice: "Is it enough that the planners be satisfied that the worst-off are likely to fare better under the scheme, or is it essential that the worst-off themselves should make this judgment?" Ultimately, he suggests that it is important to take seriously the perceptions—indeed, often the fears and uncertainties—of those affected but to accept them using a test of whether they are reasonable to an uninvolved observer.

What is also notable about these five chapters is how many of the authors use multiple ideas of equity. Jacobs has five, related to process, substance, and the needs of different groups who can own agricultural land. Marlin contrasts the idea of those most disadvantaged by traffic impacts with those most disadvantaged in economic terms. In other contexts, Timothy Beatley (1984, p. 463) adds to the Rawlsian standard a variety of "second order . . . constraints on the maximization of benefits within any particular socio-economic group." These include holding people culpable for harm done, rewarding contributions or effort, and allowing for the benefit principle of contribution in fair proportion to benefit received.

As a practical matter, however, achieving equal results would be far more difficult than achieving equal opportunity. This distinction in approach highlights the second dilemma planners face in trying to achieve social justice: deciding how strict an obligation it is.

While serving social justice may have a strong moral claim, politically and practically its claims are weak. This difficulty is clearly recognized in a number of these chapters. Feld's discussion of the Yonkers case particularly explores the role of planners who supported elected officials in politically expedient discrimination against minorities in housing policy. Lang begins the discussion of his proposed equity-based approach to waste facility siting with the assertion that it

> is unlikely to be eagerly embraced by decision makers. Politicians know that such an approach, besides reducing the pool of available sites, would require tough decisions sure to displease one or another interest group. Crisis decisions are easier to justify. It is also less controversial to go along with staff proposals that appear to be logical, scientific, unbiased, and inevitable (see the section "An Equity-Based Approach" in Lang's chapter 9).

Marlin describes how the largely unarticulated claims of less affluent residents of Pretoria Avenue in the Glebe, a community in Ottawa, Canada, were disregarded because they would probably have jeopardized the mayor's support for the Glebe traffic planning effort.

Why, then, should planners try to struggle with the problem of justice? If they should struggle with it, how much of an obligation should it be? The first answer—that it is required by the American Institute of Certified Planners (AICP) *Code of Ethics and Professional Conduct* (1981)—only begs the question, especially since the code says nothing about how binding the obligation is. Curiously, a number of these chapters, and much of the broader normative literature on social equity in planning (Davidoff 1965; Davidoff et al. 1970; Forester 1980; Friedmann 1987; Krumholz and Forester 1990; Krumholz et al. 1975), do not really make much of a case for why planners should take on such a politically risky issue or how much they should press for it. Many simply assume that it is self-evident that achieving social justice is a moral obligation that everyone must recognize and work toward. The obvious difficulty is that we would not need these exhortations if planners and others in policy-making roles were actually doing it.

What are the arguments for the morally binding nature of justice? The exact nature of the obligation depends in part on what kind of ethical theory is being used and what kind of obligation it is thought of as imposing. In a consequential ethical theory such as utilitarianism, justice is one of many good principles that are subsumed under the duty to achieve the greatest good for the greatest number. The English philosopher John Stuart Mill (1985 [1863]) argued that it is a special principle, but even so, if the greater good could, in some instances, be achieved by imposing costs on a minority, this would be an acceptable moral action.

The central test is the aggregate good or bad consequences of action. Consequentialist arguments on moral issues have a very practical quality. Equality must be useful; it has no intrinsic worth of its own. Publicly subsidized revitalization projects, which destroy or convert run-down housing, are justified as benefiting the city as a whole, even if they seem unfair to the low-income minority whose housing is taken. A consequentialist argument about the long-term costs and benefits of poverty would focus on such arguments as the trade-off between having a substantial potential pool of low-wage workers versus the problems created for the larger society by the growth of an increasingly isolated underclass.

This consequentialist idea of justice has always bothered many people because they are not convinced by the general logic of consequentialist ethics. Rawls (1971), for one, takes a critique of utilitarianism as the point of departure for his argument for social justice. A deontological ethical framework defines some actions as intrinsically right or wrong, regardless of their consequences, and seeks to protect some aspects of life as rights or duties, exempt from trade-offs and the calculation of social costs and benefits.

Rights require acceptance of the idea of reciprocity—of identification of one person with another. Immanuel Kant (1964), in one formulation of his famous Categorical Imperative, focuses on the idea that people should be treated as ends in themselves, not as means to the ends of others. To be an effective principle, this requires an ability to universalize, to put oneself in the shoes of the other person, to accept the idea that if you feel dehumanized by being used by others, they, in turn, would feel the same way. The Golden Rule—"Do unto others as you would have them do unto you"—captures this reciprocity. A sharper version, in the face of misfortune or injustice, is the formulation "There but for the grace of God, go I." This is the essential insight in Rawls's idea of the veil of ignorance. Rights are concerned with basic things that make us human and allow us to have authentic interactions with other people, things that we want to protect. A right, in turn, creates a duty. If I expect or want others to treat me fairly—if I want to assert that I have a right to be treated fairly—then I have an obligation to do the same to others.

Marlin's discussion of his use of Rawls's difference principle in the Glebe traffic planning process highlights the difference of perspective between utilitarian and deontological approaches to policy issues. In the dispute over Carling and First avenues, the majority of residents at the meeting actually voted for a plan that would have forced increased traffic on the residents of these already heavily trafficked streets because this would have served the best interests of the neighborhood as a whole. However, the residents of Carling and First and a number of others as well argued that a close majority vote did not give the decision sufficient legitimacy for implementation because of the injustice involved. The majority, in this case, accepted this logic and ultimately a modified plan was adopted.

Some deontological duties, according to Kant (1964), are "perfect duties," owed all the time to all other individuals, regardless of inclination. These have, in some contexts, been called "duties of justice" (Baron 1984; Howe 1994). Truthfulness, fairness, promise-keeping, and not doing harm are all examples. Other duties, though, can be thought of as looser, "imperfect" duties or "duties of benevolence" that are by their nature desirable but that create an impractical burden if they are always owed to everyone you come into contact with. Helping others struggling with hardships is the example given by Kant (1964). One has a duty to help but there is some leeway in deciding who and when to help. We are not obligated to help everyone all the time.

Is justice a duty of justice, as its name suggests, or only a duty of benevolence? Fairness seems to have the quality of a duty of justice. Justice is an enlargement of the idea of fairness from the level of the individual to the level of the social group. Is justice, then, the same as fairness? Surely fairness and justice overlap but are not the same thing. Fairness is not only more individual but it is more procedural. A planner's obligation to be procedurally fair could just as easily be owed to a powerful developer as to a powerless homeless person; but would a planning system concerned primarily with procedural fairness necessarily produce results that most people would think of as socially just?

It might. This is the faith of procedurally oriented planners who are concerned about citizen participation and open access. This is the procedural version of equal opportunity—the opportunity to affect policy outcomes. Access is not necessarily related to power or to political skill, though, and it is not unreasonable to think that people with more resources of all kinds will have disproportionate influence over the outcome of the policy-making process. So equal results would hardly be automatic, even if truly equal access could be guaranteed. Marlin's examples of planning in Ottawa appear to support this idea.

The difference here is that it is possible to expect planners to be procedurally fair to everyone—that is part of their duty as public servants. They may also have an obligation, though probably a less certain one, to see that diverse groups have a chance to be involved in the planning process. Conversely, the duty to achieve social justice is not only more difficult to visualize in person-to-person terms, it would be an enormous, perhaps impossible, task, for any individual. This suggests that justice is discretionary, a duty of benevolence, and not a binding duty of justice.

LAWS AND MORAL DUTIES

Rights are especially important for protecting the weak against the strong. They may be either legal or moral rights. Kant, for example, was concerned with the latter. Such moral rights are enforced simply by custom and an implicit ability to put oneself in the shoes of another. Because of this, they may be particularly effective between approximately equal individuals.

Legal rights, though, seem to arise out of unequal relationships where at some point the weaker minority is able to appeal to the majority on moral (and sometimes on practical, perhaps even consequentialist) grounds for protection against harmful or unequal treatment. Such legally created rights may not necessarily be fully accepted by the broad public or by certain groups within it, but once they exist in law, members of the protected group have some recourse in the courts against violation of these rights.

As a purely moral duty, justice is weak. It seems at most to be a duty of benevolence. Few people feel that they or anyone else has an obligation to strive in all circumstances to right the injustices of racism or social class, for example. Indeed, it is easy with a duty of benevolence to think that while it may be important in principle, it might just as easily be carried out by other people in other circumstances. Acting for justice involves incurring individual costs while the benefits are largely collective in nature.

Perhaps equally troubling is the possibility that working for justice may involve a kind of paternalism or noblesse oblige. Those with more advantages try to help those with fewer, and this may not be entirely welcome to the recipients.

Given these problems with the purely moral obligation to work for justice, minority groups have often sought instead to gain legal rights, for instance, to equal access to jobs or housing. Characteristically, these rights guarantee equal access, not necessarily equal results. Legal acceptance of rights to minimum levels of basic goods such as food, shelter, health care, or income has been much less common in the United States. Comparison with Canada in the area of health care, for example, is instructive.

Thus, as a practical matter, we seem to rely on legal rights more heavily than on moral rights in the realm of justice. In these chapters, this is most clear in the Yonkers case where a U.S. District Court ruled that Yonkers had violated the legal rights of black residents by intentionally maintaining and strengthening patterns of housing and school segregation. However, despite the hope that political decision making could be encouraged to be more attuned to issues of social justice, the pressure for this in actual decisions related, for example, to the siting of noxious facilities, often seems to come from the legal system in which more and less powerful groups use the rights created by law to jockey for position in the political process.

Clearly, all planners are bound by law and must respect rights created by it; but beyond adherence to the law, do planners have a residual moral obligation to try to right social injustices? We will see below some planners' answers to this question. The writers of these five chapters and those of the AICP *Code of Ethics* (1981) certainly do think that such an obligation exists. These are calls for the members of the profession to interpret this duty of benevolence more individually and more actively.

As a discretionary duty, how is one to know how much of an obligation one owes to social justice? This may depend on one's idea of social justice. Certainly, all of the authors here would insist on the idea of procedural fairness. Lang and Feld both argue that just outcomes should result from an open and fair process while Throgmorton and Jacobs, in rather different ways, focus on aspects of the decision-making process that could promote more equitable outcomes. Jacobs, for example, lays out a framework for analysis of impacts on different groups affected by agricultural land preservation decisions that could contribute not only to considering their interests in decision making but perhaps also to encouraging their active participation in that decision-making process. Marlin, though, argues, largely on the grounds of political practicality, that a planner did not have a binding obligation to encourage the active participation of the apathetic Pretoria Avenue residents.

The idea of justice as equal outcome goes considerably further. It would seem to require such evaluation of more decisions—both public and private—but evaluation would, in this case, have to be linked to a commitment to equality or to improving the lot of those with the fewest advantages. The Rawlsian idea of justice used by Marlin and by Beatley (1984, 1988a,b,c) and the somewhat similar ideas used by Jacobs and Lang would place the criterion of social justice at the center of any decision making concerned with noxious public facilities, with energy policy, with growth management, or with the funding of infrastructure. However difficult it may be in practice to open up the planning process to a wider range of groups or to ensure equal opportunity in housing and schools, these are surely lighter duties than trying to ensure that the outcomes that might result, for example, from education or from housing policy, would benefit the least advantaged.

Marlin points out that Rawls himself states that his principles of justice "primarily" apply to "the basic structure of society," not to individual allocative decisions. It may sometimes be difficult, though, to disentangle basic structures and smaller decisions. Institutions such as zoning, for instance, are in part the accretion of many individual decisions.

This leads Marlin and others (Krumholz et al. 1975) to use Rawls's difference principle as a guide for individual decisions. As a standard, it can be useful, though Marlin argues that it is not always obvious in its application. What this perspective misses, however, is that planners like Marlin or Krumholz who chose to use the difference principle did so in a society whose basic structures were and are not shaped by a Rawlsian idea of justice. In this situation, the planner operates at the margins, constrained by considerable political limitations that Marlin, himself, discusses quite explicitly.

Thus, beyond legal obligations, the discretionary moral duty to work for justice can be interpreted in stronger or weaker, easier or more difficult ways. The question of how binding an obligation it is has no obvious answer. How, then, do actual planners answer it in practice?

JUSTICE IN PRACTICE

Since the Progressive movement, a concern with social justice has been one thread in the values of planners. It waxes and wanes in salience but seems always to exist as an undercurrent in professional values. It is one of the definitions of the public interest in the AICP *Code of Ethics and Professional Conduct* (1981).

A study based on interviews with ninety-six planners in California, Texas, Tennessee, Maryland, and New York[1] (Howe 1994) found that justice did not play a very central role in planning ethics. Many of the practicing planners in this study did not see justice as an important issue directly applicable to their everyday practice. Only a few had institutionalized roles concerned with achieving equity or a personal commitment strong enough to impel them to raise this issue. For most, raising issues of justice in their jobs challenged the values of elected officials and of many citizens in their communities. It challenged deep injustices built into the social and political institutions of our society. Yonkers stands as a dramatic example of this, but one that is not atypical. Raising the issue of equity could create significant conflict and place planners at risk of a loss of effectiveness in other areas of their work— and possibly at risk of a loss of their jobs as well.

What encouraged planners to be at all concerned about justice? Procedural fairness was accepted as an important ethical obligation by most of the planners in this sample. One aspect of any bureaucratic role is the application of universalizable rather than particularistic values— being consistent and treating like cases alike. Many planners talked particularly about fairness to developers. There was also a group of about 11 percent of these planners whose central professional commitment seemed to be to promote an open planning process. These planners extended the idea of procedural fairness to less active, less powerful groups.

The ideas of open access and democracy are powerful symbols, if ones whose full implications are not always accepted. The greater commitment of the planning profession since the 1960s to the idea of citizen participation has been real, even if somewhat uneven in practice. Planners certainly grant to citizens the right and ability to define the problems faced by their communities, but they still worry about a loss of professional control if participation were to become pervasive in the planning process (Howe and Kaufman 1981). Even given these caveats, this evocation of the basic value of democracy provides support for justice as fair procedure.

In older central cities, the idea of representative democracy, joined to the dominance of poor and minority residents, could by itself give legitimacy to an advocacy role such as that played by Cleveland planning director Norman Krumholz in the late 1960s and 1970s (Krumholz and Forester 1990; Krumholz et al. 1975). This was a majority that obviously should be represented, and planners could play a role in this representation. Neighborhood planning, still supported by the Community Development Block Grant program in the United States, helps to keep this advocacy role alive in many cities. Among the ninety-six planners were four who formally worked as neighborhood planners or as low-income housing advocates in such cities.

Finally, there were some who did not work in older central cities but who still went beyond a purely procedural interpretation of the idea of justice. They wanted planning to be an active force for justice in society. Altogether, about 10 percent of the planners talked about having a strong professional concern about social justice. By and large, they had brought it into the profession with them. They came from families with strong religious or with liberal-to-radical, secular values that inculcated this concern. A few had seen injustice as teenagers, which gave them the ability to imagine being in the other person's shoes. A number had also gone to college or graduate school in the 1960s and had been influenced by movements for peace and justice there.

What they did with these values as professionals took two radically different forms. Half were active optimists. They carefully created political legitimacy in their jobs that would allow them to raise issues of justice. They were very much concerned with seeing results from their work and were proactive in trying to achieve them. They primarily worked on housing—either neighborhood revitalization or the construction of high-density, affordable housing in suburban areas. They believed that an open participatory process of planning was the only way to deal usefully with issues that were politically volatile. This was a process in which they were active organizers of information and procedure but in which they expected other actors with very different values to play an active role as well. They did not shy away from conflict. However, they did accept the right of their elected officials to make the final decisions about the "public interest," though they wanted to have an active role in shaping those decisions so that social justice would be considered. They did not spend all or, in most cases, probably even the majority of their time on these issues. They saw this as a discretionary duty but still as a real, personal obligation in their particular communities.

While a sense of personal obligation was clearly a strong motivating force for these planners, they did not act alone, without support. They seem to have worked in liberal communities, mostly in California, where the state government at the time had a policy of encouraging "affordable" housing. They did seem willing to play a leadership role but with the support of colleagues and other like-minded people in their communities.

The other half of the planners who were strongly concerned about justice seemed overwhelmed by the difficulty of acting on such a controversial issue. They were not active optimists like their colleagues. Personally, they did not like conflict and sought out jobs in internal administration or research, for example, which removed them from the possibility of having to deal with it. As a result, they had no network of support for raising controversial issues. While this was their own choice, though, it was also a source of feelings of frustration and guilt. They thought planning ought to be an active force for social justice, but they knew that they were not fulfilling this role.

The contrast here is, of course, dramatic. It suggests the possibility for action on equity issues but also some of the pitfalls. Even more clearly, the discussion of this sample shows that almost 90 percent of the planners did not take justice to be a serious moral obligation at all. A few others did talk about it, but for every planner who worried about not being able to convince his or her council that apartments would not be harmful to a suburban community, there was another like the planner who talked proudly about his role in the Yonkers Redevelopment Authority during the heyday of urban renewal. For most of the planners, justice seemed to be an abstraction that had little connection to their daily professional lives. It may be that both their own values and the political structures in which they worked served to keep issues of social justice off the planning agenda.

SOCIAL EQUITY AND THE ENVIRONMENT

An interesting additional subtheme appears in a number of the chapters in this part. The issue of achieving social justice is posed in the context of specific areas of planning, such as agricultural land preservation, energy conservation, or solid waste management, where there is also a sometimes only implicit ethical commitment to preserving the environment. The authors are all posing the possibility, at least, that environment values may be served at the expense of justice—landfills may be located in poor communities that cannot effectively fight them and "efficiency"-oriented energy planning may result in high utility rates that fall most heavily on the poor. Even when these trade-offs are not made explicit, they lie behind the concern that in these various substantive areas planning should be both environmentally sound and socially just.

The image that environmental values might often conflict with those concerned with social justice is one that is commonly held. Interestingly, however, several members of my sample of planners made a particular point of arguing that this conflict was overplayed, in part by people who used it to undermine the legitimacy of environmental concerns about specific projects. These active planners saw no conflict in their own practice of working to serve both sets of values. Still, while equity-oriented planners often held active environmental values as well, environmental planners seemed less concerned about justice.

CONCLUSION

The lack of attention paid by practicing planners to issues of justice brings us back to the larger question of why should we, as a profession, care about justice. The Rawlsian argument about the veil of ignorance highlights the need for a sense of moral reciprocity discussed earlier. With a few notable exceptions, these planners did not put themselves in the shoes of those unable to afford to live in their communities. Faced with urban ghettos, they did not think "There but for the grace of God, go I." In any case, most were not actively faced by the reality of slums due to urban patterns created and sustained at least in part by planning itself.

However, there is another argument for the importance of a commitment to social justice or, for that matter, to an environmental ethic. Robert Bellah and his colleagues, in a study of the values of middle-class Americans, focus on the question of how to "preserve or create a morally coherent life" (1985, p. vi; see also chapter 4). They explore the evolution and impact of the idea of individualism in American life. They argue that in a highly complex, urban/industrialized society in which people have little sense of understanding or control, many retreat to the private spheres of family, work, life-style, and therapeutic self-actualization to find meaning in their lives. Individual happiness becomes the only guide and standard. Objective criteria of right and wrong or of what a good society should be like are lost because people believe that all values are purely individual or relative and that it is impossible to have a rational discussion over conflicting values or ends. Substantive values that are central to a liberal democracy become lost. Justice is one such value:

> In the absence of any objectifiable criteria of right and wrong, good or evil, the self and its feelings become our only moral guide. What kind of world is inhabited by this self, perpetually in progress, yet without any fixed moral end? There each individual is entitled to his or her own "bit of space" and is utterly free within its boundaries. In theory, at least, this civil and psychic right is extended to everyone . . . [but] only those who have enough money can, in fact, afford to purchase the private property required to do their own thing (Bellah et al. 1985, p. 76).

> The litmus test that both the biblical and republican traditions give us for assaying the health of a society is how it deals with the problem of wealth and poverty. . . . The American dream is often a very private dream of being the star . . . the one who stands out from the crowd of ordinary folk. . . . And since we have believed in that dream for a long time and worked very hard to make it come true, it is hard for us to give it up, even though it contradicts another dream that we have—that of living in a [just] society that would really be worth living in (Bellah et al. 1985, p. 285).

These authors call for a revitalization of the public realm based on cultural communities that, through common history and traditions, link individuals with institutions that have the legitimacy to develop substantive ideas of the common good, not just out of the clash of competing pluralist claims but out of rational discussion. Such ideas of the common good could provide a firmer foundation for the kind of legal and moral rights discussed earlier that now are often only partly accepted.

This argument about the importance of a revitalized public sphere speaks directly to public planners. It suggests that an effort to build political consensus on the base of technical expertise is flawed, as is an approach that focuses only on access to the planning process and procedural fairness. Both are compatible with our current individualistic ideas of the role of public professionals since they accept the logic that no useful discussion of ends is really possible. However, they may both lead ultimately to ineffectiveness and to frustration with "politics" for planners and for the public they serve (Baum 1983). Both Lang and Throgmorton, in rather different ways, focus on the inadequacies of a scientific/technical approach for developing any true, authentic consensus on a plan.

Bellah and his associates (1985) give a number of examples of people they interviewed who were engaged more actively in the difficult process of trying to build a new concept of the public good around social justice or an environmental ethic. Their exemplars sound a great deal like the small group of active, optimistic planners committed to social justice in my study of planners (Howe 1994).

In the articles included here, Throgmorton is probably the most explicit in trying to imagine a role for planning that builds communities bound together by common goals. He sees planners as "active mediators" between the clashing "rhetorics" of participants in the planning process. In this role, the planner would be committed to specific values, such as justice, but would also play an active role in translating these incompatible rhetorics. While this image of planning is still largely procedural, it holds the promise of building "new interpretive communities" out of a "fusion of horizons" among conflicting participants.

Throgmorton portrays this role as furthering social justice. Would it always? There is nothing in this discussion that indicates that it would. Throgmorton, like the other authors here, including myself, does not really come to grips with the inequalities of power and the racist values that keep social justice from being accepted as a strict duty of justice. The problem is perhaps clearest here in Feld's discussion of the problems of the imposed solution to the Yonkers housing case. No "fusion of horizons" produced a "new interpretive community" there. Lines of social and racial division were hardened. She argues for a more locally based, participatory planning process for achieving a socially just policy that would be accepted by the various sides in the conflict. But is this just a pleasant dream?

In a liberal ethical framework, which is what most practicing planners use, this kind of participatory process may be the only real leverage for building new interpretive communities capable of changing social inequalities. It depends on getting people to see that "There but for the grace of God, go I" and out of that insight to build a more just society one decision at a time. However, as long as this is the primary leverage held by planners, it should not be surprising to find that only a few optimistic, committed, and active planners take on this challenge.

Note

1. This study consisted of face-to-face interviews with a sample of ninety-six public planners in each of these states. Generalization from the results must be limited. The sample is not especially random. With an equal number of respondents from each state, it was not proportional to the numbers of public planners in each. It was also strongly biased to senior-level planners because members were chosen from the APA membership roster. Finally, the states themselves were quite diverse in their cultures of planning; there is no way to know what other states would be like. In the interviews, the planners were primarily asked what kind of issues they had encountered in their practice that had posed ethical issues and how they had dealt with those issues.

Bibliography

Alterman, R. and MacRae, D., Jr 1983. Planning and policy analysis: converging or diverging trends. *Journal of the American Planning Association* 4, 200–215.

American Institute of Certified Planners. 1981. *Code of ethics and professional conduct.* Washington, DC: American Institute of Certified Planners.

Baron, M. 1984. *The moral status of loyalty.* Dubuque, IA: Kendall/Hunt.

Baum, H. 1983. *Planners and public expectations.* Cambridge: Schenkman Publishing.

Beatley, T. 1984. Applying moral principles to growth management. *Journal of the American Planning Association* 50, 459–469.

———. 1988a. Ethical issues in the use of impact fees to finance community growth. In Nelson, A., ed. *Development impact fees: policy rationale, practice, theory, and issues.* Chicago: Planners Press (American Planning Association), 339–361.

———. 1988b. Development exactions and social justice. In Alterman, R., ed. *Private supply of public services.* New York: New York University Press, 83–95.

———. 1988c. Equity and distributional issues in infrastructure planning: a theoretical perspective. In Stein, J., ed. *Public infrastructure planning and management.* Urban Affairs Annual Reviews, Vol. 33. Newbury Park, CA: Sage Publications, 208–226.

Bellah, R., Madsen, R., Sullivan, W., Swidler, A., Tipton S., 1985. *Habits of the heart: individualism and commitment in American life.* Berkeley: University of California Press.

Benhabib, S. and Dallmayr, F. 1990. *The communicative ethics controversy.* Cambridge: MIT Press.

Boyer, C. 1983. *Dreaming the rational city.* Cambridge: MIT Press.

Davidoff, P. 1965. Advocacy and pluralism in planning. *Journal of the American Institute of Planning* 31, 331–339.

Davidoff, P., Davidoff, L., and Gold, N. 1970. Suburban action: advocate planning for an open society. *Journal of the Amreican Institute of Planners* 36, 12–21.

Forester, J. 1980. Critical theory and planning practice. *Journal of the American Planning Assocation* 46, 275–286.

———, ed. 1985. *Critical theory and public life.* Cambridge: MIT Press.

Friedmann, J. 1987. *Planning in the public domain: from knowledge to action.* Princeton, NJ: Princeton University Press.

Harper, T. and Stein, S. 1992. The centrality of normative ethical theory to contemporary planning theory. *Journal of Planning Education and Research* 11, 105–116.

Harvey, D. 1973. *Social justice and the city.* London: Edward Arnold.

Howe, E. 1990. Normative ethics in planning. *Journal of Planning Literature* 5, 123–150.

———. 1994. *Acting on ethics in city planning.* New Brunswick, NJ: Center for Urban Policy Research, Rutgers—The State University of New Jersey.

Howe, E. and Kaufman, J. 1981. The values of contemporary American planners. *Journal of the American Planning Association* 47, 266–278.

Innes, J. E. 1990. *Knowledge and public policy: the search for meaningful indicators.* 2nd ed. New Brunswick, NJ: Transaction Publishers.

Kant, I. 1964. *Groundwork of the metaphysic of morals.* Translated by H. J. Paton as *The moral law.* New York: Harper Torchbooks.

Krumholz, N. and Forester, J. 1990. *Making equity planning work: leadership in the private sector.* Philadelphia: Temple University Press.

Krumholz, N., Cogger, J., and Linner, J. 1975. The Cleveland Policy Planning Report. *Journal of the American Institute of Planners* 41, 298–304.

Lucy, W. 1981. Equity and planning for local services. *Journal of the American Planning Association* 47, 447–457.

McCarthy, T. 1978. *The critical theory of Jurgen Habermas.* Cambridge: MIT Press.

MacIntyre, A. 1985. *After virtue.* 2d ed. London: Duckworth.

Mill, J. S. 1985. *Utilitarianism.* New York: MacMillan. Originally published in 1863.

Rawls, J. 1971. *A theory of justice.* Cambridge: Harvard University Press.

Reamer, F. 1982. *Ethical dilemmas in social service.* New York: Columbia University.

RANDAL MARLIN

7   *Rawlsian Justice and Community Planning*

Are the insights of John Rawls's *A Theory of Justice* (1971) applicable only to the most basic structures and practices of a society or are they also relevant to low-level planning? I approach this question from two different points of interest. The first is from that of extensive involvement in a planning process, trying to control traffic through a neighborhood in a core area of a large city. This process took place some twenty years ago, and I have now had ample opportunity to see the long-term effects of decisions taken at that time. The second point of interest is theoretical. Do high-flown abstract principles ever give genuine guidance to practical problems?

An early critic of Rawls, Benjamin Barber, has reiterated his negative answer to this second question in his comparatively recent book, *The Conquest of Politics* (Barber 1988). He there attacks Rawls, along with a number of other theorists, for his foundationalist approach to political actuality. The device of the original contractors fails, Barber thinks, to give the results Rawls derives from it. The Difference Principle, with the

Reprinted from *The International Journal of Applied Philosophy* 4, 4 (1989), 36–44 with permission of the publisher. This article has been slightly revised for publication in the present volume.

141

"maximin" strategy of choosing policies that will make things best for the worst off, seems, for example, to emerge from Rawls's hypothetical contractors only if we import a psychological aversion to risk-taking into their mentalities. Why, though, do we have to suppose such psychological conservatism? Barber thinks the political process is not helped by applying abstract, blind, ahistorical standards to an existing political situation. The goal should not be "cognition" (Barber 1988, p. 203) but rather "citizenship" (Barber 1988, pp. 199–200), meaning the desire to "act rightly, not to know for certain . . . to cooperate with others, not to achieve moral oneness" (Barber 1988, p. 209). The goal should be political judgment, meaning "the forging of common actuality in the absence of abstract, independent standards" (Barber 1988, p. 209).

Rawls himself states that his two principles of justice—the equal liberty principle and the Difference Principle (with equal opportunity)—"primarily" apply to "the basic structure of society" (Rawls 1971, p. 61). This leaves it open as to whether his principles can be applied to less basic relations in society. On the face of things, there would seem to be no good reason why an insight into justice, if it is a good one, should be allowed to function only at the most basic level of social arrangements. It may be that at a less basic level other considerations will intrude and the clarity of the original directives will become obscured; but surely they will have some bearing on the justice of various aspects of community planning.

In what follows, I will sketch the details of a real, complex political problem—that of getting the agreement of a whole community (population: about 15,000; location: the Glebe, Ottawa, Canada; time: 1972–74) to a whole set of traffic proposals on a then unprecedented scale. This concrete example does reveal difficulties in applying Rawls's principles to real-life circumstances. At the same time, I can vouch for the fact that in this case, at least, they were not irrelevant because I did take account of the Difference Principle—or my own interpretation of it—while working out the scheme that was finally adopted.

My experience has led me to confirm wholeheartedly Barber's important observation, made in a criticism of Robert Nozick, that "Political argument begins with concrete givens. If abstract alternatives prove indefensible, we do not return to point zero; we are left rather with the givens—with a logic in process that will have consequences even if no choices are made" (Barber 1988, p. 114). Yet I do not think that the application of Rawls's views is harmful to the political process or involves a "conquest of politics"; on the contrary, as I hope to show.

The Glebe community traffic planning experience reveals, I think, the following. (1) It is difficult to interpret how one is to understand the "most disadvantaged person" when considering planning for the community. (2) When one has what seems like a reasonable interpretation of the Difference Principle, an absolutely unyielding application of it, impervious to political realities, does not seem right. (3) Nevertheless, a Difference Principle that is able to accommodate modification in the light of political exigencies does seem to yield right results. (4) In the calculation of whether the worst off will gain under a scheme, there will be uncertainties. Is it enough that the planners be satisfied that the worst off are likely to fare better under the scheme or is it essential that the worst off themselves should make this judgment? The evidence I have points to the latter, but not as an exceptionless matter having no regard to political realities.

The events began with the presentation to the community of an elaborate scheme for controlling traffic and improving the community by an imaginative Ottawa architect, John Leaning, whose work had been supported by the National Capital Commission. At this time, the community had undergone a continuous state of decline and was threatened, as so many inner-city communities were, with redevelopment in favor of high-rise buildings and fast arterial traffic. The aim of the new scheme was to revitalize the neighborhood, which had excellent existing housing stock for raising families. The key to revitalization lay in controlling traffic. Increases in commuter traffic volume on residential streets were threatening to split up the community into isolated fragments. Child safety and pedestrian peace of mind had to be secured if the community was to be restored as a viable place to raise families.

The problem was with selling this plan both to the politicians and the bureaucrats of the city of Ottawa, to the Regional Municipality of Ottawa-Carleton, and to the community residents themselves. People from each of these groups were sometimes apathetic and downright hostile to the idea of erecting barriers to the free flow of traffic, despite the fact that the plan would be in the community's overall best interest.

It will be necessary first to spell out, with the help of the accompanying map (Map 7-1), some of the details connected with the plan. The community, known as the Glebe, is divided by heavily trafficked north-south arterial roads known as Bank Street and Bronson Avenue. Downtown Ottawa lies to the north. Heavy traffic along east-west lines followed Carling Avenue and First Avenue. Commuter traffic tended to spill over heavily into Percy, Lyon, and particularly O'Connor streets. Key features of the plan that was finally accepted included erecting barriers at points B and C to encourage traffic to use arterial roads and the Queen Elizabeth Driveway to pass through and around the Glebe. An original plan went further and involved, for example, complete closures of First,

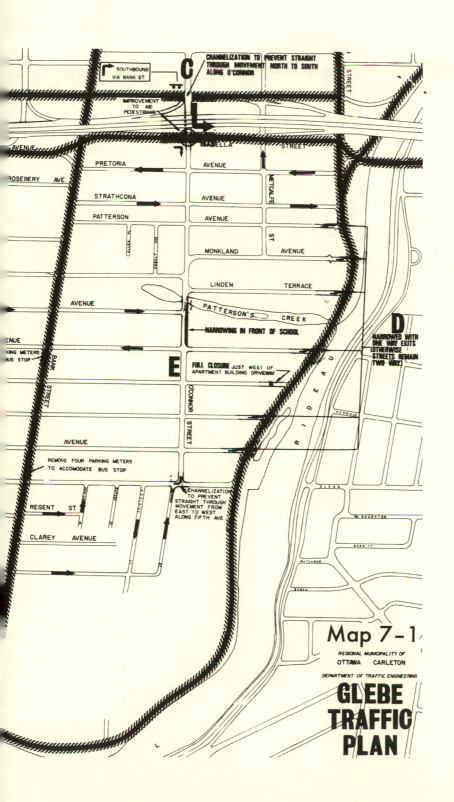

SOUTHBOUND VIA BANK ST.

CHANNELIZATION TO PREVENT STRAIGHT THROUGH MOVEMENT NORTH TO SOUTH ALONG O'CONNOR

C

IMPROVEMENT TO AID PEDESTRIANS

ISABELLA STREET

PRETORIA AVENUE

ROSEBERY AVE.

METCALFE

STRATHCONA AVENUE

PATTERSON AVENUE

ST.

MONKLAND AVENUE

LINDEN TERRACE

AVENUE

PATTERSON'S CREEK

NARROWING IN FRONT OF SCHOOL

D

NARROWED WITH ONE WAY EXITS (OTHERWISE STREETS REMAIN (TWO WAY)

ENUE

KING METERS US STOP

BANK STREET

E

FULL CLOSURE JUST WEST OF APARTMENT BUILDING DRIVEWAY

O'CONNOR STREET

HERRIDGE

RIDEAU

AVENUE

REMOVE FOUR PARKING METERS TO ACCOMODATE BUS STOP

CLEGG

CHANNELIZATION TO PREVENT STRAIGHT THROUGH MOVEMENT FROM EAST TO WEST ALONG FIFTH AVE.

McNAUGHTON

REGENT ST.

MERRITT

CLAREY AVENUE

HUTCHMOR

BOWEN

Map 7-1

REGIONAL MUNICIPALITY OF
OTTAWA CARLETON

DEPARTMENT OF TRAFFIC ENGINEERING

GLEBE
TRAFFIC
PLAN

Second, and Third avenues at Bronson Avenue. This would have turned those wide avenues into recreational space at the Bronson end, but it would also have meant increased traffic on Carling (renamed Glebe Avenue, east of Bronson, as part of the scheme) and First avenues. All things considered, I do not think the plan imposed a great burden on commuters. In the case of southbound O'Connor traffic, cars were already causing a bottleneck as they reached the traffic light at Fifth and Bank. The time savings with the shortcut were becoming increasingly less and would likely have vanished in time.

The main problem with the original plan, from the point of view of gaining acceptance within the Glebe community, was the increased traffic on Carling and First avenues that would result from the full closures. Those two streets were among the worst sufferers from existing commuter traffic. Some channelization at point A on the map was meant to encourage the west-east traffic to follow Bronson, Chamberlain, and Isabella, and bumps in Carling Avenue between Bronson and Park were meant to further discourage traffic there. However, residents there were understandably reluctant to approve a plan that would give them the certainty of increased traffic with the uncertain prospect of reduced citywide through traffic. In my own mind, it was a fair trade-off, but I could see that it was not unreasonable for those residents to suppose otherwise. A First Avenue resident put it forcefully to me as we traveled to work: "Why do you support a scheme which is going to make the worst-off streets in the community still worse off than they are now?" When it came to a vote after a very bitter meeting with vigorous protests from Carling and First avenue residents, the plan passed with a very slight majority. As past president of the Community Association and as the Traffic Committee chairman, I had some influence on what was to happen next, and I argued (along with others) that the plan not be implemented with such opposition. The fact that the community as a whole stood to benefit ought not to be decisive as to the rights of a segment of the community who might be worse off under the scheme (though that was a matter of which judgments differed). If one interpreted "worst off" in traffic terms alone rather than in socioeconomic terms (it was one of the better-off streets in the latter reckoning), the residents of those streets might well be right to complain of unjust treatment based on an interpretation of Rawls's Difference Principle. The fact that the residents mounted such a well-organized campaign of opposition to the plan made me think of a real-life counterpart to Rawls's principle. When people are intelligent and aware of what a scheme involves, when they are put (as they see it) to disadvantage in order to improve the situation for the already better off, they get very angry. They organize and fight, goaded not only by their particular interests but also by a sense of impending injustice.

The plan was recast in such a way as to avoid increased traffic on Carling and First avenues. This was done by replacing the closures at Bronson with narrowings, thus obviating the necessity of cars from First, Second, Third, and Fourth avenues having access to Bronson by Carling, First, or Fifth avenues. In this way, the latter worst-off streets had only to gain from the scheme. There remained a question of justice regarding Pretoria Avenue, from which no significant protest had been heard. This residential street in the northeast quadrant stood to get increased traffic as a result of restricting access to the avenues from the Queen Elizabeth Driveway. Here there were not closures (except at point E, and that closure was eventually removed) but only one-way signs permitting cars to exit onto the driveway but not enter from there. This meant that Pretoria Avenue would have to accept more traffic. At that time, it was a street threatened with redevelopment. It did not have heavy traffic, but it was one of the least well off streets in socioeconomic terms. Once again, the question arose: Will this plan benefit the people on this street as well as elsewhere in the Glebe? And once again, in my own mind, the answer seemed quite possibly affirmative—but the people on that street might well have a different opinion. In my judgment, the street was threatened in any case because its zoning included commercial uses. With revitalization of the whole community, one could expect this area to share to some extent in the overall benefit and perhaps have some of the residential properties renovated instead of torn down (something that, in fact, was to happen). However, the residents themselves might have decided differently in view of the immediate and certain impact of increased traffic. Should the Glebe Community Association have made special consciousness-raising efforts to ensure that the views of Pretoria residents were based on adequate information and properly heard?

Any attempt, though, to stir up potential opposition from that street would have had very serious political implications. The planning staff of the regional government had devoted many months of work to this scheme, which was dragging into a second year. It was made clear by the mayor at that time—Pierre Benoit—that support for this planning would not continue indefinitely. The likely result of smoking out opposition from Pretoria residents would have been jettisoning the whole plan, which would have produced far worse results for the community as a whole and probably even for the residents of Pretoria themselves (something one can say with more confidence now as the street has shown visible signs of improvement in the intervening years) than adoption of the plan, even with its possible injustice.

Let us be clear about what was at issue. It was not that the plan would clearly have made Pretoria residents worse off. That was a questionable matter. It was, rather, that the people of Pretoria might well have seen the plan as inimical to their interests, just as residents of Carling and First—or a significant number of them—had done. The latter protested effectively; the former did not, the reason being, as I thought at the time, that Pretoria residents were less aware, less concerned, or less articulate (though there was also the possibility that they were simply more public-spirited). Now justice is justice, and it ought not to depend on whether a group is articulate or not. Consistency would seem to have dictated an elaborate canvassing of the opinion of Pretoria residents to make sure that their judgment, and not the judgment of the planners (both the technical and community kinds), should apply so far as assessment of their own interests were concerned. For the practical political reasons already mentioned, this demand for consistency was not met, but it does raise important questions for the treatment of similar or analogous situations that might arise in the future regarding community planning.

Out of curiosity, I did some investigating years later as to why opposition from Pretoria had not been heard. What I found out was not conclusive; many of the residents at the time were transients and had moved. In at least one instance, though, a resident-owner was fully cognizant of the plan and its possible unfavorable outcome for Pretoria but was simply public-spirited and not interested in standing in the way of an overall good thing.

It would seem likely that there would arise many cases where a plan might benefit a whole community to the detriment of one section of the community. Should those who perceive themselves worse off under some such scheme be allowed, in the name of Rawlsian justice, to block it? Among several objections to such a conclusion is the following: What if their judgment is clearly, in the minds of planners and any objectively minded person, unreasonable? Perhaps at some point we must say that Rawlsian justice (if we can call it that, when thus applied) can extend only so far as to accommodate *reasonable* perceptions by the worst off that a scheme will further worsen their situation. Not any irrational assessment by the affected party should be allowed to block a scheme. Conversely, it is not unreasonable to require that planners' assessment of costs and benefits should be compared to the assessments of the people affected by the plans and possibly be made to yield to the latter. In the extreme cases, where there is a very probable disutility to a group, from a plan that will greatly benefit the rest of the community, there should be a provision for some kind of compensation. This might take the form of a much lower assessment of a property for tax purposes or some improvement that does to that particular segment of the community a kind of compensation, such as a neighborhood park, fancy streetlighting, or whatever might appeal to those residents as a desirable quid pro quo. Informal trade-offs of this kind are common occurrences in municipal politics. What Rawlsian justice suggests to me is that compensation should be considered, not only in cases where powerful opposition demands it but also where the unaware, inarticulate, or politically powerless are involved. The nature of the mechanisms to provide appropriate compensation may not be easy to discover, but the impetus to discovering them should be there. In the case of Pretoria, it turned out that the street did get a net benefit; but the situation might have been otherwise, and residents might reasonably have predicted otherwise.

The plan as outlined on Map 7-1 was accepted by a two-thirds majority, with the support of Carling and First avenue residents. The benefits were as anticipated. Traffic on residential streets became greatly curtailed and people developed a new confidence in the community's future prospects. The Glebe as a result has become one of the most desirable places to live in Ottawa. The immediate effect was a reduction of traffic accidents with injuries by 24 percent. The long-term effect has been reconversion of many divided houses into single-family dwellings. The area has become a very stable one and has provided benefits to the Ottawa-Carleton region by accommodating various kinds of halfway houses, thus contributing to the solution of social problems in the region.

The traffic plan also inspired similar developments elsewhere, usually with comparable benefits to other communities. The result has been so successful, in fact, that a quite different problem has arisen. Instead of deterioration, there has come "yuppication," that is, extensive renovation with upscale living styles by new residents. Subsequent large-scale increases in tax assessments have forced many of the community's less wealthy residents to sell their houses and move out. Students have found their stock of rooms in the former declining neighborhood reduced. Stores that used to sell basics have been replaced with expensive boutiques. Perhaps a farsighted scheme would have included devices to protect what until then had been a desirable mix of income levels in the neighborhood. The long-term experience suggests that when we take into account the "worst off" we should be thinking on more levels than immediate traffic effects alone. The idea would be not to nullify things like the traffic plan but to anticipate the undesirable side effects and try to forestall them.

For simplicity's sake, I have not considered the Glebe traffic plan in relation to its impact on the surrounding community. I believe that with one possible exception only, the plan simply shifted traffic onto arterial roads with no great cost in time or inconvenience, compared to the likely travel times that would have developed anyway in the absence of the plan. Some other Ottawa residents might disagree, and the matter would have to be argued. One of the points in discussion at the time was that since core-area residents had funded, through their taxes, the development of roads and sewers to the newer outlying areas, it was only fair that they should get some protection from the harmful effects of traffic coming from those areas. As against that, it might be argued that since some of the poorest families had come to be living in subsidized housing on the outskirts of the city (by foolish planning—but that is another story), these worst-off people would not have to be made worse off by increases in commuting time. This argument can become very complex and might be persuasive in connection with some proposals. I don't think it applied forcefully to the Glebe plan, though, for reasons pertaining to the wider traffic layout of the city and region. Without a much bigger map, pursuit of this question would be pointless, so I shall not consider it further here.

I have also not treated the right to drive a car on any route one wishes as a basic liberty right. If one were to do so, Rawls's first principle, that "each person is to have an equal right to the most extensive basic liberty compatible with a similar liberty for others" (Rawls 1971, p. 60), might arguably take precedence over traffic-restricting plans. Clearly, though, this liberty is not as fundamental as the right to profess one's religious beliefs or the right to vote. One good reason for not treating it as a basic liberty right is that it interferes with pedestrian movement and something more basic—namely, security of life and limb, particularly regarding children and the elderly.

Was the kind of application of Rawls's principle, as I interpreted it, beneficial in the case I have described? I believe so, but my reasons are open to dispute. It is open to anyone, including the original architect, John Leaning, to argue that the original plan with its closures would have been better off for the community than the plan that was adopted. Perhaps the Carling and First avenue residents would have been worse off under the first proposal than under the plan that was adopted; but in retrospect, it seems they would still have been better off than they would have been with no plan at all. So, arguably, letting those residents have the final determination as to what would make their area better off or worse off was not a wise move. In reply, I would say that when the plan was first implemented, there was considerable opposition from people outside the Glebe. Without the internal cohesion that came with the modified plan, it might well have been doomed. So politically, I would say, the introduction of the Rawlsian dimension to the thinking was indeed beneficial.

Given the subsequent acceptance of the traffic plan, I suspect that its replacement with the original plan would produce something better overall for the community, but there would now be the problem that residents of the present Glebe Avenue (formerly Carling) and First Avenue would be asked to approve a plan that would clearly be worse for their streets than what they have now. Judged in terms of the situation quo ante the whole 1973 plan, they would be better off, but judged in terms of the present situation, they would be clearly worse off.

These reflections bring out aspects that seem likely to be duplicated with any practical applications of Rawls's principles—namely, considerations of a historical nature. Those with a historical sense might well recognize the justice of implementing the full scheme with all its closures; but new people will have moved into the area, and these people will not have any sense of history of the traffic on the streets or a sense that some street has debts to pay to other streets in the matter of accommodations made to fears that, in retrospect, seem to have been exaggerated. I have here in mind the fear that the original plan would have left those streets worse off than before. The channelizations and four-way stop signs introduced later to replace the bumps have been very successful at cutting down on through traffic. Additional traffic from closures at Second, Third, and Fourth would not have added sufficiently to create a net disutility. So we have here a very short-term example of a phenomenon with many possible long-term counterparts: namely, that we get different perceptions of justice or injustice depending on the time frame within which a political determination is viewed and the overall context within which it is located.

If I am right, there is a way in which at least the spirit of Rawls's Difference Principle does find application to low-level planning, but there is nothing cut-and-dried about how it should be interpreted nor must it be conceived as an unyielding principle, such that political realities should never be allowed to override a perceived injustice of this kind. Still, it does provide an impetus to a desirable kind of fairness that may easily be forgotten in the usual political bargaining process. Taking account of this sort of justice in advance is likely to make political planning in a well-informed democracy ultimately easier rather than more difficult. As I interpret the principle, it should lead planners to take account of the needs of the worst-off in society to ensure that schemes do not further diminish their lives but also to listen to the judgments of those people themselves as to what is likely to enhance or adversely affect their interests. There is reason to suppose that the ordinary political process does not pay enough attention to those needs.

It may be that Rawls himself would prefer to retain the Difference Principle at a high level of abstraction where it might operate free from all the compromises and uncertainties of political life. If so, his views would be more vulnerable to Barber's critical assessment about philosophical principles, that they are irrelevant or have a dangerous tendency to undermine necessary give-and-take in a democratic political process. By contrast, if the Difference Principle, or some variant thereof, does find application in the way I have indicated, the upshot would be that Barber's assessment would at least be in need of some qualification. My feeling is that the democratic political process is greatly improved if bargainers can transcend their immediate perceived interests in favor of some form of principled accommodation rather than relying on raw power. In a cynical, Postmodern time, the prospects for acceptance of philosophical principle do not seem very encouraging. I hope that this particular case study may contribute in some way to improving those prospects.[1,2]

Notes

1. This is slightly revised and reprinted from the 1989 *International Journal of Applied Philosophy* 4, pp. 36–44, by permission of the publisher. It takes into account helpful comments by Benjamin Barber, whom I wish to thank.

2. I would like to thank my Carleton colleague, Professor Tony Ward, and the Planning Commissioner of the Regional Municipality of Ottawa-Carleton, Nick Tunnacliffe, for helpful comments on an earlier draft. I would also like to thank the Regional Municipality of Ottawa-Carleton for permission to reproduce its map.

A great many individuals at the community, city, regional, and federal levels gave much assistance to this plan. It may be worth putting some of those names on the record here: John Leaning, Bruce McNabb, Michael Pine, Michael and Diana Cooper, Pat Kealey, Jack Commerford, Gwen McKinnell, Gerry La Forest, Ross Cleary, and Sylvia Holden from the community; Toivo Rukholm and Keith McLean from regional traffic; Mayor (as he then was) Pierre Benoit, former Mayor Lorry Greenberg, and Alderman Don Lockhart from the city; Douglas Fullerton and Roderick Clack from the National Capital Commission; and Gérard Pelltier, from the federal government, for a Local Initiatives Program that provided funds for door-to-door explaining of the plan and for gathering a communitywide petition.

I would like to thank the Maison Française at Oxford for sponsoring a conference devoted to Rawls's theory of justice in January 1988. It was in the course of a discussion there that the idea came to me of recording the planning experience I have described.

Bibliography

Barber, B. 1988. *The conquest of politics: liberal philosophy in democratic times.* Princeton, NJ: Princeton University Press.

Rawls, J. 1971. *A theory of justice.* Cambridge: Harvard University Press.

HARVEY M. JACOBS

8 Ethics in Environmental Planning Practice: The Case of Agricultural Land Protection

Introduction

Agricultural land protection has been a prominent landscape planning issue for American policymakers, citizens, and planners for more than a decade. Two foci have dominated the examination of agricultural land protection. One is an assessment of the actual amount and rate of acre-equivalent land loss per year, with estimates ranging from less than one million to nearly nine million acre-equivalents per year, and the resulting criticalness of this loss for the agricultural production system (Baden 1984; Fisher 1982; Gustafson and Bills 1984; *Journal of Soil and Water Conservation* 1981; National Agricultural Lands Study 1981; Raup 1982). The second, more common, focus is on the policy alternatives available to implement agricultural land protection programs. The experience and literature in this area are wide ranging, with experimentation occurring in all aspects of taxation, regulation, direct action, and public-

This chapter is a slightly revised version of Harvey M. Jacobs, "Social equity in agricultural land protection," *Landscape and Urban Planning* 17 (1989), 21–33. It is included in this volume with permission of Elsevier Science Publishers B.V.

private collaboration policy (Brenneman and Bates 1984; Conklin 1980; Coughlin and Keene 1981; Fisher 1982; Furuseth and Pierce 1982; Steiner and Theilacker 1984). While no consensus emerges from the work to date as to which technique should be used to protect agricultural land, if such land is even in need of protecting, there is a largely unwritten consensus about the use of an efficiency criterion to evaluate public policy alternatives. This criterion (Duncan 1984) is stated or implied to be: How well does a policy alternative work to prevent/retard the conversion of agricultural land to competing uses?

An issue left largely unaddressed has to do with social equity of alternative agricultural land protection policies. While research continues to be necessary into the efficiency of policy alternatives, answers to queries over how well alternatives will work to protect land need to be supplemented with research into how equitable these efficient solutions are likely to be.

The lack of literature on the subject of social equity in agricultural land protection is not surprising. It is a direct reflection of the general lack of literature on the social equity of land planning policy in the United States (Jacobs 1985). With the exception of housing discrimination in suburban land use controls, the subject is largely unexplored. Why it should be surprising, however, is because of the clear recognition of the unique social nature of land and land policy in work in the developing world. Major international conferences, such as the U.N. (United Nations) Habitat meeting in 1976, and reports on international organizations, such as the U.N. and the World Bank, stress this point (Darin-Drabkin 1977; United Nations 1976). Concerns along these lines have begun to appear in discussions on U.S. land planning policy in general (Brooks 1976; Geisler and Popper 1984; Kaufman 1980; Popper 1979) and very recently with regard to agricultural land policy in particular (Ebenreck 1983; Sampson 1979; Shrader-Frechette 1984; Wunderlich 1984).

This chapter seeks to contribute to this discussion in several ways. Even among those who wish to examine and discuss the equity of land planning policy, there is confusion over the bounds of the discussion. Toward this end, the first part of this chapter outlines an approach to understanding the concept of social equity, specifying its place within a discussion of environmental ethics and clarifying its meaning for the purpose of this discussion. Then the general concept of social equity is modified in two ways, first to reflect the special geophysical and social nature of land, land ownership, and land policy and, second, within the particular circumstance of agricultural land planning policy in urban-rural fringe areas of the United States. In the third part of this chapter, alternative policies for agricultural land protection are outlined and assessed. The chapter ends with thoughts on the utility of social equity analysis to land planning policy for agricultural land and other land resources along with suggestions for further research.

Defining "Social Equity"

Social equity is an issue of long-standing debate throughout human history. Religions and political systems have been founded and fought for because of specific conceptions of equity. John Rawls (1971) tried to formulate an approach to understanding justice that could be applied to policy analysis, but even this formulation is subject to direct attack (Nozick 1974) and alternative formulations continue to be developed (Bookchin 1982; see part I).

Futher, a relationship of social equity to environmental ethics may not be at all obvious. As "classically" understood (that is, as classic as a relatively new and evolving field can be), environmental ethics addresses the relationship of people to the natural environment, the nonhuman world—wild places, animals, natural resources, and so on. In this way, though, environmental ethics ends up addressing a set of long-standing moral questions about duties, obligations, and responsibilities. However, to the extent that contemporary science and philosophy together argue the position that the human species is itself only one part of the natural world, then one portion of environmental ethics must address human-to-human relationship duties, obligations, and relationships, both for themselves and how they impact upon the nonhuman, natural world. Thus, issues of social justice and social equity are a legitimate and necessary part of an environmental ethics framework (Beatley 1989).

In the area of land policy, Dean Misczynski (1978, p. 143) has noted that "equity . . . is a slippery concept." The reason, according to another researcher, is that "inequity is a subjective concept, related to ethics and values and undefinable in exact terms" (Meadows 1977, p. 136). There is, though, general agreement about the nature and dimensions of the concept of social equity.

Equity has two primary dimensions—the *substance* or outcome of the act, in this case the application of public policy, and the *process* by which the act, that is, public policy, is formulated and implemented (Ervin et al. 1977). In common terminology, these two foci are denoted as just-ness (justice) and fairness. The dimension of just-ness focuses on outcomes or ends, the allocative results, of policy decisions. The dimension of fairness focuses on procedures, for example, the impartiality of access to decision processes, whereby individuals and groups can get ideas and concerns expressed.

The concept of *social* equity further specifies a discussion of allocative and procedural equity as an examination of impacts of policy decisions on groups or classes of people rather than on individuals (Ervin et al. 1977). The principal dimensions of social, that is, group or class, equity are identified as horizontal or vertical equity. Horizontal or vertical equity distinguishes between whether a public policy affects people within a group or class (horizontal equity) or among groups or classes (vertical equity).

An example of horizontal and vertical equity in the area of housing policy has to do with property tax relief proposals. Proposals to relieve the burden of local property taxes can take the form of a horizontal equity proposal, through a relief measure aimed at the class of existing homeowners, or a vertical equity proposal, through relief proposals that include provisions for renter participation, another group of sheltered persons affected by rises in property taxes.

These two major components of social equity, the type of equity and its class impact, can be combined to form a four-part description of the ways in which social equity can be discussed (Table 8-1). Some of the confusion about social equity is perhaps clarified through this table. It shows that it is possible to use the phrase social equity and yet be concerned with very different issues.

TABLE 8-1

Social Equity Analysis Framework

| | *Type of Equity* | |
| | Allocative | Procedural |
Class Impact		
Vertical	Allocative/ vertical[1]	Procedural/ vertical[2]
Horizontal	Allocative/ horizontal[3]	Procedural/ horizontal[4]

Notes:
1. Redistribution of resources among separate classes.
2. An open, democratic policy process.
3. Distribution of resources to a particular class.
4. Restricted access to representation and administration.

For the purposes of this discussion, social equity is defined as "a just distribution, justly arrived at" (Harvey 1973, p. 98). This means that social equity will be a combination of states number 1 and number 2 in Table 8-1. A social equity assessment of agricultural land protection policies will thus seek to determine if policy alternatives are fair, open to participation and influence by a range of interest groups and classes, and just. However, the just-ness of policy needs to reflect the particular nature of land as a resource and commodity in urban-rural fringe areas.

Specifying Social Equity Assessment Criteria

Land economists, soil scientists, conservationists, and others have long asserted the unique nature of land, as both a resource and as a commodity. These unique features of land can be summarized into six points (Harvey 1973; Kelso 1972; Lichfield 1980; Misczynski 1978; Ratcliffe 1976):

1. Land is nonuniform. Parcels of land can be vastly different from one another in resource capability. This difference is important because it is difficult and expensive to create or re-create certain resource characteristics, such as productivity.
2. Land is a limited resource that, in the usual sense of the word, cannot be produced. It is a resource that, though durable if properly cared for, is susceptible to depletion.
3. Land cannot be moved. It has a fixed location to which use in it is tied.
4. Land uses have ripple effects. A given use of land can set into motion dynamic forces that over time establish new land use relationships.
5. Land is an absolute social necessity. A person cannot exist without occupying and using physical space for living, working, and all the other aspects of individual and social life.
6. Land is owned in two important ways. In the present time, the ownership of land is distributed among society's members by some set of social–political–economic rules. This ownership results in certain legal and social–political–economic rights and privileges (Popper 1979). At the same time, all members of the present generation own land to the exclusion of future generations. For both private and public land, those in the present decide the intensity for use and therefore the range of

land use options that will be available to future users (Doeleman 1980; Page 1977).

One specification of the just-ness basis of social equity in agricultural land protection policy comes from combining the concern with the future in point number six with the first and second points outlined above. A concern with the limited, nonuniform basis of land combined with a perceived ethical obligation to deliver to future generations a sufficiently broad set of land use choices leads to the articulation of an intergenerational equity criterion. Specifically, it can be stated as—land policy should preserve long-run options for resource use.

Balanced against the intergenerational criterion for social equity are concerns for social justice implications of current patterns of land ownership and use. These are commonly denoted as tenure concerns. Three classes of persons would seem to be most directly affected by agricultural land protection policy in the urban-rural fringe: (1) the owners of the land; (2) prospective homeowners; and (3) prospective agricultural users of the land, that is, new farmers. This list of groups affected by proposed agricultural land policy is not exclusive. Instead, it represents, in this author's opinion, the groups with the most pressing equity concerns.

For existing owners of agricultural land, the concern is with the impact of proposed policy on the market value of the land. For many owners of agricultural land, particularly those characterized as family farmers, the economic value of the land represents their major item of personal investment and wealth (Ervin et al. 1977; Lapping 1979). An equity criterion for existing owners should seek a fair return on the value of the land or, conversely, policy should not wipe out the land's value to the individual landowner. While there is considerable disagreement as to what constitutes "fair" or "just" compensation under the taking clause of the Fifth Amendment to the U.S. Constitution (for example, given that agricultural land protection policies single out owners of agricultural land for differential treatment from other classes of landowners in an area and since these owners may be among those least able to bear the individual and class burden of providing a public good), the equity criterion for this group suggests that the owners receive some reasonable, though not necessarily full market equivalent, return for the value of their land.

The second group identified above is prospective homeowners. In the urban-rural fringe, agricultural land is under particular pressure from competing land uses, especially residential uses, because (1) many of the characteristics of land that facilitate agricultural use also facilitate residential development—the land is generally flat and well drained—and (2) in a regional housing market, the input variable with the most elasticity is likely to be the cost of land, so that land acquired and used for housing at the urban-rural fringe can significantly lower the average price of housing. In this situation, public policy that restricts the availability of agricultural land at the urban-rural fringe could possibly lead to higher prices for housing for new prospective homeowners. An equity criterion would thus be: any policy action should not adversely affect the opportunity for prospective homeowners to acquire new housing at prices comparable to those absent the program.

The third and final group is new farmers. One of the purposes of any agricultural land protection program is to retain land in agricultural use. For agricultural land to be in agricultural use requires a number of things, including, importantly, farmers (Lapping 1979). The age profile of American farmers is growing older. They are generally over fifty years of age, and the number of young people entering farming is small, in large part because of the capital costs of starting new farm operations, a significant part of which is attributable to land costs. An agricultural land protection program whose aim is to ensure the long-term utilization of the land must be concerned with the ability of new producers to get access to that land and thus the impact of any policy program on this factor. An equity criterion with regard to this consideration would therefore be: policy action should moderate land purchase costs, below fair market value, at the time new producers seek to acquire such land.

In summary, it is argued that a social equity basis for assessing agricultural land protection policy has five equity criteria, drawing from the general nature of social equity as a concept and from the particular nature of land, and especially agricultural land, as a resource. These criteria are:

- *Intergenerational equity*—policy should preserve long-run options for resource use;
- *Tenure equity for existing landowners*—policy should provide the opportunity for a fair return on land value;
- *Tenure equity for prospective homeowners*—policy should not adversely affect housing prices by unduly restricting land for residential development;
- *Tenure equity for new farmers*—policy should moderate the price and availability of land such that farmers can acquire land to use in agriculture; and
- *Process equity*—policy should be open for participation by a wide

range of groups and interests, in both policy formation and administration.

It is important to recognize, though, that a social equity assessment of alternative agricultural land protection policies will reflect the particular orientation of the commentator or policy advocate. Environmentalists and conservationists have traditionally afforded more weight to the intergenerational aspects of land protection policies for agricultural and other land resources. Legislators and policy administrators have afforded more weight to process equity issues, asserting that a fair process for making decisions will result in fair decisions. Tenure equity concerns have been brought forth by those adversely affected by a policy approach, most often existing landowners arguing against strict regulatory policy.

Policy Alternatives for Agricultural Land Protection

As noted, there is wide-ranging experimentation in agricultural land protection policy. Various forms of policy have been tried or proposed for all levels of government. This includes taxation, regulation, direct action, and collaborative public-private policy by local, state, and national government (Conklin 1980; Coughlin and Keene 1981; Duncan 1984; Grillo and Seid 1987; Hiemstra and Bushwick 1986; National Agricultural Lands Study 1981; Rozenbaum and Reganold 1986; Steiner and Theilacker 1984). For the purposes of this chapter, a single, prominent example of each type of policy is assessed against the five social equity criteria. These policies are (1) differential property taxation, (2) large-lot agricultural zoning, (3) purchase of development rights programs, and (4) private land trusts. This section briefly explains each alternative. (The description of these four programs is drawn principally from the literature noted immediately above. Each characterization is thus not an accurate description of any particular state or local approach to agricultural land protection but is instead a generalized description that captures the most common features of the four programs. These features will, in turn, be modified as a program is actually implemented by a state or local government.)

Differential property taxation is a common policy approach in the United States, with programs in forty-nine states. Under constitutional amendment and enabling legislation, real property law is modified to allow for the taxation of agricultural land on a basis different from other types of land. Voluntary incentive programs are established that offer agricultural landowners, sometimes only farmer agricultural land-owners, some method to reduce the burden of real property taxes. Programs between and among states differ on which method is offered to landowners, for example, a fixed amount per year or a fixed percent of the floating, actual amount and whether and how, if at all, the state seeks to guarantee commitment from a landowner in return for a tax abatement, that is, a recapture provision for all or a portion of abatements granted if a contract is broken, or a resource management plan. States also differ on whether the program is administered solely by the state or only enabled by the state and implemented through a local program.

Large-lot agricultural zoning is an application of the government's police power—the power to regulate on the basis of the public health, safety, morals, and general welfare—to the issue of agricultural land being converted into other, competing uses. Zones are established in which agricultural use of land is the primary permitted use. The minimum lot size assigned to this preferred use is not uncommonly forty acres or more. Other agricultural uses of land are permitted, including the building of barns and other outbuildings, as well as dwelling units to house agricultural employees. Most nonagricultural uses of the land are treated as conditional uses. Alternative land use proposals are reviewed individually on the basis of how strongly they will negatively affect the use of land for agriculture. A report by William Toner (1984) shows a pervasive use of some form of large-lot agricultural zoning by different levels of substate, local government. Under large-lot agricultural zoning, pressures to convert agricultural land to competing residential and commercial development uses are not removed but are instead held in check and discouraged through the use of the regulatory authority. Modifications of the rules are possible, with the frequency and extent varying from community to community.

Purchase of development rights (PDR) programs are dramatic examples of direct-action policy on the part of the government. Instead of, or in addition to, responding to a perceived problem in the land market by offering incentives, through taxation, or setting rules for behavior, through zoning, the government participates directly in the land market. The goal is to remove market pressures and assure long-term agricultural use of the land. The vehicle used to achieve the goal is voluntary purchase by the government, from the individual agricultural landowner, of the property right that represents the authority to execute land use change, such as to a nonagricultural land use. With the purchase of that right, the property legally loses the ability to be used in nonagricultural uses while remaining in private ownership. The land is still held by a private owner, who can exercise all the other rights in the land, including private party transfer of the land. Prominent examples of this approach to agricultural land protection are conducted by the commonwealth of Massachusetts; King County in the state of Washington; and Suffolk County, New York. In all cases, the program is expected to require tens of millions of dollars to implement.

Private land trusts are to land policy what nonprofit housing corporations are to housing policy or community development corporations are to local economic development policy. Land trusts are an attempt to use the financial advantages offered private, nonprofit corporations to achieve public-interest land use goals. They exist as a supplement to other forms of public land policy and have the potential to exercise a wide variety of management tools with regard to land policy objectives. Land trusts can acquire development rights, hold land, develop land, or manage land or rights in land for themselves or on behalf of other parties. There have been some interesting developments in land trust activity for agricultural land protection at the national, state, and local level, most commonly through the managed donation of development rights from the landowner to a land trust. In the United States, the activities of the Vermont (State) Land Trust, the Marin County Land Trust in California, and the American Farmlands Trust nationally are the most prominent examples of this approach to agricultural land protection.

A Social Equity Assessment of Alternative Policies

A social equity assessment of alternative agricultural land protection policies is necessarily a slippery exercise. It involves a set of subjective judgments that can, at best, be made as explicit as possible for examination for reassessment by others. Table 8-2 is a summary of this assessment. The four policy alternatives outlined above and the five social equity criteria are arranged in a matrix. This allows for (1) an examination of each single policy against the five criteria, by going down a column; (2) a rough, summary social assessment of each policy alternative, "summing" values associated with each cell in a column; and (3) a comparison among policies, on the basis of an individual equity criterion, by comparing policies across rows and by comparing their "total" assessments.

Alphabetic values in the cells are notations for a simple three-point scale: "E" denotes an excellent fit between the structure of the policy program and the equity criterion; "G" denotes a good fit; and "P"

TABLE 8-2

Summary of a Social Equity Assessment
of Agricultural Land Protection Policies

	Policy Programs			
	Taxation (differential assessment)	Regulation (large-lot zoning)	Direct Action (purchase of development rights)	Public/ Private (private land trusts)
Equity Standards				
Intergenerational	P	P	E	E
Tenure				
Landowners	E	G	E	E
Prospective Buyers	P	G	P/G	P/G
New Farmers	P	P	E	G/E
Process	E	E	E	G
"Total" equity[1]	G−	G−	E−	G+

"P" denotes a poor fit between the program and the equity standard; "G" a good fit; and "E" denotes an excellent fit.

1. A simple sum average that assumes equal weight among the five criteria in the column.

denotes a poor fit. These values are, however, more accurately probability statements about the likely fit between an individual program, as developed by a state or local government, and the equity criteria. "E" suggests that it is more than likely that the policy program will satisfy the equity criterion, "G" suggests likely, and "P" suggests less than likely, though for each cell value there are numerous exceptions because of the many variables that impact upon the formulation and administration of public policy programs. This section presents the rationale for the values assigned to the cells of Table 8-2, with the discussion structured around the four policy programs. The data for assigning values to cells in Table 8-2 are drawn from the following principal sources: Conklin (1980); Coughlin and Keene (1981); and Steiner and Theilacker (1984) and, with regard to private land trusts in particular, Brenneman and Bates (1984) and the Institute for Community Economics (1982).

DIFFERENTIAL PROPERTY TAXATION

Differential property taxation is the most common state policy program in the United States. The reason is most likely that it does not require a direct expenditure of funds. Instead, it allows for a sometimes relatively small, and almost always hard to identify, shift in property tax burden away from agricultural land uses to other uses of land. This program is also popular from the users' point of view. Policy programs offer some method for direct reduction in property tax burden, with anywhere from zero to ten or more years of commitment as to agricultural use. Almost all contractual arrangements can be broken by the agricultural landowner at any time during the contract period, and even when tax recapture provisions exist, they rarely outweigh the financial gain that can be accrued through selling out to a competing, nonagricultural use. Even for those who choose to fulfill a contract period, there is evidence to suggest that unless programs require twenty and more years of commitment from the landowner, abatements may be granted to landowners for whom such an incentive will not prevent eventual land conversion (Brown et al. 1981).

In Table 8-2, intergenerational equity is rated as poor. The short- to medium-term contractual nature of the program and the ease with which most programs can be voided by a participant remove any guarantee that land will remain in agricultural use. Studies have shown little direct relationship between differential property taxation and a reduction in the rate of agricultural land conversion. Among the three tenure equity criteria, the landowner's equity is rated as excellent while that of home buyers and new farmers is poor. For the landowner, from the perspective of the defined equity criterion, differential taxation is a windfall. For the period the land is in agricultural use, it is eligible for reduced property taxes—and yet at almost any time the property can be sold on the market, for fair market value, with little or no additional burden other than repayment of abated tax amounts for a specified period. For the home buyer, the program has poor equity implications because if there is widespread participation in a region, the supply of land for housing may be restricted and land that is available will be selling toward the top end of a market range. For the new farmer, the equity implications are also poor for many of the same reasons given in assessing intergenerational equity. Nothing about the program guarantees the availability of land to new farmers, at any price, and especially not at a less than full market value price. In the area of process equity, differential property taxation is given an excellent rating, not so much from the experience of how these programs have been set up and run but because there is nothing about the structure of the program that prevents an open, democratic process of policy formation and administration.

LARGE-LOT AGRICULTURAL ZONING

Large-lot agricultural zoning programs have the advantages and disadvantages of zoning policy applied to other types of land resource management issues. As regulatory policy, such action is a relatively direct yet inexpensive method for public sector action with regard to a perceived problem. However, as regulation, it cannot compel proper behavior on the part of individual landowners but rather can establish rules that define the realm of improper and unacceptable behavior. In this way, large-lot agricultural zoning is an example of negative, reactive policy rather than positive, initiative policy.

Large-lot agricultural zoning is given a poor rating for intergenerational equity. The reason for this has to do with the administrative history of zoning in the United States. Since its formulation in the early part of this century, zoning has been used as a land management device that is expected to change with changing land market and socioeconomic characteristics in a locale. It is not designed, and is ill suited, to guarantee the long-term use of land in a particular use class. This is the reason for the extensive use of legislative and administrative procedures to amend and vary the requirements of regulations. Therefore, if large-lot agricultural zoning is like other uses of zoning, it will be unable to withstand pressures to use land in competing uses, where a market for such uses exists. Transference of the land to future generations is in no way guaranteed.

For the tenure criteria, Table 8-2 shows two good ratings and one poor rating. Following from the discussion immediately above on intergenerational equity, landowners' equity, in terms of receiving a fair price for land value, is unlikely, in the long term, to be harmed by the existence of a zoning program. While the opportunity to sell for maximum market value will be impeded for certain landowners at certain points in time, many other landowners are likely to be able to receive some variation on the requirements of a program where it would cause undue personal harm for the land to remain solely in agricultural use. This may involve the permission to receive nonagricultural prices for a portion or all of the land. For prospective home buyers, the rating is also good for many of the same reasons. Where sufficient pressures to use agricultural land in nonagricultural uses exist, buyers are unlikely to see zoning withstand pressures for the availability of reasonably priced land. However, demands for land will be balanced against the goal of keeping land in agricultural use, and as such, there is likely to be some restriction on land availability. From the perspective of new farmers, this approach to agricultural land protection gets a poor rating. Zoning actions are largely directed at current owners of property. There is nothing about the program that ensures that land will be made available at below-market costs so as to allow new farmers to facilitate the start of agricultural enterprises. In terms of procedural equity, large-lot agricultural zoning receives an excellent rating because, like differential property taxation, there is nothing about the structure of the program that prohibits an open process of participation. In fact, zoning, among the four alternatives discussed here, may have the best potential in this regard because many state enabling laws require extensive public hearing and review procedures for the formulation, adoption, and administration of a zoning law.

PURCHASE OF DEVELOPMENT RIGHTS PROGRAMS

PDR programs are significant departures from the preceding two approaches to agricultural land protection because they involve substantial direct financial outlay and commitment on the part of the governmental unit. As noted in Table 8-2, this approach to agricultural land protection suggests equity impacts substantially different from either taxation or regulatory policies.

The intergenerational equity of PDR is excellent. With the development right to property purchased away, and the fundamental legal status of the land changed, it is all but assured that the land will not be put into an incompatible, competing land use. (PDR programs do not assure, though, that the converse will be true—that the land will remain in productive, agricultural use.) Among the tenure criteria, two are excellent and the other poor to good. Landowners' equity is rated as excellent because under PDR a qualifying and interested landowner is paid market or near market value for the development right. As the program is voluntary, no landowner is required to accept the separation of the development right from the property rights bundle or the particular price offered for a right. Prospective homeowners' equity is rated as poor to good. It will likely be poor if there is an extensive amount of agricultural land in the area covered by a program. If there is widespread participation, the equity impact of prospective homeowners will be moderated. For new farmers, the tenure equity of

PDR programs should be excellent. Experience and theoretical analysis have shown that development rights cost from 50 to 95 percent of total land value, depending on the nature of the land market (Coughlin and Keene 1981; Coughlin and Plaut 1978). In theory, new farmers should be able to purchase land for agricultural use at a cost that directly reflects the development right purchase. Most of the current programs are as yet too new to have any evidence in this regard. In terms of process equity, PDR programs are rated as excellent. Largely because they do require substantial outlay of funds, PDR programs have been subject to intensive public screening and input. They are initiated as a result of public interest in more direct action for agricultural land protection, and they are administered in such a way as to make the identification of purchase sites and areas a matter of public record and discussion.

PRIVATE LAND TRUSTS

Private land trusts that are established as tax exempt, nonprofit corporations under federal and state tax codes exist to implement public interest land use goals. They do not have the authority to compel participation in their activities. Trusts rely on the powers of persuasion, relating to both the economic self-interest and land ethic principles of agricultural landowners. As private corporations, they can be extremely flexible in applying a range of land management powers in such a way as to meet the very specific and particular needs of an individual landowner.

The intergenerational equity consequences of private land trust activity in agricultural land protection should be excellent. Land or development rights acquired by the trust will change the legal status of the land, so that it will be nearly impossible for agricultural land to be put into incompatible, competing uses. The equity for landowners is also excellent. The trust allows a landowner to receive payment (sometimes indirectly through tax savings) for changes in property rights status. As a voluntary transaction, the value of the payment will be of a satisfactory nature, even if it does not always represent full, fair market value. For prospective home buyers, the activities of land trusts will have poor to good equity impact, depending on the activeness and success of the trust. An active and successful trust may have significant impact on land availability in an area and result in higher prices for remaining land for housing. If, and more likely, a trust will be active but will be unable to have a signficant effect on land holdings or prices, then prospective home buyers would not find prices inflated and the equity standard could be rated as at least good and perhaps excellent. The equity assessment for new farmers is good to excellent, with the difference being how sensitive the trust is to the goal of land acquisition for new farmers. If a trust is very sensitive and conditions its participation on access for new farmers, the equity results should be excellent; even if it does not, the results should be at least good if landowners who participate in the activities of the trust sell land for its agricultural use value. Finally, the process equity impacts should be good but could be poor. Many trusts are membership organizations that seek to involve people in a community and regional area concerned with agricultural land protection. However, the limitations on process equity have to do with the actual accessibility of the organization to a range of persons (that is, membership fees, meeting times, and so on) and the power afforded members to form and direct the organization's policy (that is, whether members elect members of the board of directors, how priorities are formalized, and so on).

PATTERNS OF SOCIAL EQUITY

As is clear from the final row of Table 8-2, as well as the pattern of individual cell values, different policies for agricultural land protection appear to have different social equity impacts. The final row of Table 8-2 is constructed by assigning each of the cell designations a numerical value of one, two, or three, corresponding to poor, good, and excellent, and then simply summing and averaging the values from the preceding five cells in the column. The values that result thus assume that each of the individual criteria should be afforded equal weight. What results is a differentiation between two sets of policies: differential taxation and large-lot zoning are designated as "good-minus," whereas purchase of development rights and private land trusts are designated as "excellent-minus" and "good-plus," respectively.

Perhaps the most striking pattern in Table 8-2 is the difference for intergenerational equity between the two sets of policies. The taxation and regulatory options for agricultural land protection are rated as offering poor chances for intergenerational equity while the direct-action and public-private options offer excellent chances to protect land for future generations. The equity impacts for new farmers show a similar sharply contrasting pattern. All of the policy alternatives examined here appear to have roughly equal equity impacts for existing agricultural landowners, with only large-lot zoning possibly interfering with the ability of owners to obtain a fair and reasonable price for property rights. Because it is the program most likely to be developed within a context of a comprehensive land use plan, large-lot zoning appears to have the best equity implications for prospective home buyers, though none of the programs are rated as excellent on this criterion. Finally, in terms of how programs appear to facilitate public participation in program formulation and implementation, all three of the public programs have the potential to be excellent in this regard, with the capability of private land trusts moderated because of their private nature.

Social Equity Analysis of Land Policy

This chapter presents one attempt to articulate what fairness in land policy means and to apply that specification to an assessment of the equity implications of alternative agricultural land protection policies. It is necessarily exploratory in nature. It is intended to be valuable in two ways: (1) by making clear the basis for discussing social equity in land policy and showing how persons concerned with it can legitimately differ over the framework for policy assessment, and (2) by offering an assessment framework to which others can bring different arguments and conclusions, based on, for example, assigning unequal weights among equity criteria.

The conclusions that follow from this analysis are different from those that focus solely on issues of efficiency, effectiveness, or political feasibility. This additional insight into the impacts of land policy action is valuable because it helps to respond to some of the bases of public interest in land policy action in the first place and identifies early on, in a clear way, some of the trade-offs that occur with the choice of one policy alternative over another. Ultimately, the application of this type of approach to assessment of agricultural and other land resource policy options should allow for policy that is better at achieving stated goals because of the recognition of the broad range of constraints and impacts flowing from alternative actions.

Clearly, though, this attempt at social equity analysis is preliminary in nature. The data for the assessment are secondary information on the actual or expected performance of a limited range of policy alternatives. If social equity analysis is to be more fully developed so that it can be of continuing help to the policy analyst and planning practitioner, at least three things need to be done with the analysis: (1) the assessment should be expanded to include other policy alternatives for agricultural land protection; (2) the data for determination of cell values in Table 8-2 need to be supplemented by case studies of actual equity outcomes of applications of alternative policies; and (3) the conceptual work that underlies an equity analysis needs to be refined and expanded. For example, are the five stated social equity criteria the only and best criteria to use in assessing land policy alternatives?

Land use policy in general and agricultural land protection policy in particular have significant social impacts. Certain interests, classes, and groups in society will gain as the result of certain types of policy action while others will lose. Throughout history and in other parts of the world, land policy is recognized as being at the crux of social, economic, and political relations and power. Social equity assessment of alternative policies can help planners and land resource managers to better understand the emotion generated by proposed policy actions and to propose more specific land policy solutions that best combine concerns for efficiency and equity.

Bibliography

Baden, J., ed. 1984. *The vanishing farmland crisis: critical views of the movement to preserve agricultural land.* Lawrence: University Press of Kansas.

Beatley, T. 1989. Environmental ethics and planning theory. *Journal of Planning Literature* 4, 1–32.

Bookchin, M. 1982. *The ecology of freedom.* Palo Alto, CA: Cheshire Books.

Brenneman, R. L. and Bates, S. M., eds. 1984. *Land saving action.* Covelo, CA: Island Press.

Brooks, M. E. 1976. *Housing equity and environmental protection: the needless conflict.* Washington, DC: American Institute of Planners.

Brown, J. H., Philips, R. S., and Roberts, N. A. 1981. Land markets at the urban fringe. *Journal of the American Planning Association* 47, 131–144.

Conklin, H. E., ed. 1980. *Preserving agriculture in an urban region.* New York's Food and Life Sciences Bulletin 86. Ithaca, NY: Cornell University.

Coughlin, R. E. and Keene, J. C. 1981. *The protection of farmland: a reference guidebook for state and local governments.* Washington, DC: U.S. Government Printing Office.

Coughlin, R. E. and Plaut, T. 1978. Less-than-fee acquisition for the preservation of open space: does it work? *Journal of the American Institute of Planners* 44, 452–462.

Darin-Drabkin, H. 1977. *Land for human settlements: some legal and economic issues.* New York: United Nations.

Doeleman, J. A. 1980. On the social rate of discount: the case for macroenvironmental policy. *Environmental Ethics* 2, 45–58.

Duncan, M. L. 1984. Toward a theory of broad-based planning for the preservation of agricultural land. *Natural Resources Journal* 24, 61–135.

Ebenreck, S. 1983. A partnership farmland ethic. *Environmental Ethics* 5, 33–45.

Ervin, D. E.; Fitch, J. B.; Godwin, R. K.; Shepard, W. B.; and Stoevener, H. H. 1977. *Land use control: evaluating economic and political effects*. Cambridge: Ballinger.

Fisher, P., ed. 1982. Special issue on regional development and the preservation of agricultural land. *International Regional Science Review* 7, 249–302.

Furuseth, O. J. and Pierce, J. T., eds. 1982. Special issue on farmland preservation in North America. *GeoJournal* 6, 498–560.

Geisler, C. C. and Popper, F. J., eds. 1984. *Land reform, American style*. Totowa, NJ: Rowman and Allanheld.

Grillo, K. A. and Seid, D. A. 1987. *State laws relating to preferential assessment of farmland*. Staff Report No. AGES870326. Washington, DC: Economic Research Service, U.S. Department of Agriculture.

Gustafson, G. C. and Bills, N. L. 1984. *U.S. cropland, urbanization and landownership patterns*. Agricultural Economic Report No. 520. Washington, DC: Economic Research Service, U.S. Department of Agriculture.

Harvey, D. 1973. *Social justice and the city*. London: Edward Arnold.

Hiemstra, H. and Bushwick, N. 1986. How states are saving farmland. *American Land Forum* 6, 60–65.

Institute for Community Economics. 1982. *The community land trust handbook*. Emmaus, PA: Rodale Press.

Jacobs, H. 1985. Progressive land-use planning. *Planners Network* 55, 3–4.

Journal of Soil and Water Conservation. 1981. The national agricultural lands study—an interview with Robert Gray. *Journal of Soil and Water Conservation* 36, 62–68.

Kaufman, J. L. 1980. Land planning in an ethical perspective. *Journal of Soil and Water Conservation* 35, 255–258.

Kelso, M. M. 1972. Resolving land use conflicts. In Thompson, D. L., ed. *Politics, policy and natural resources*. New York: The Free Press, 145–178.

Lapping, M. B. 1979. Agricultural land retention strategies: some underpinnings. *Journal of Soil and Water Conservation* 34, 124–126.

Lichfield, N. 1980. *Settlement planning and development: a strategy for land policy*. Vancouver: University of British Columbia Press.

Meadows, D. 1977. Equity, the free market and the sustainable state. In Meadows, D. L., ed. *Alternatives to growth I*. Cambridge: Ballinger, 135–153.

Misczynski, D. 1978. Efficiency and equity. In Hagman, D. and Misczynski, D., eds. *Windfalls for wipeouts*. Chicago: American Society of Planning Officials, 141–160.

National Agricultural Lands Study. 1981. *Final report*. Washington, DC: U.S. Department of Agriculture.

Nozick, R. 1974. *Anarchy, state and utopia*. New York: Basic Books.

Page, T. 1977. Equitable use of the resource base. *Environment and Planning* 9, 15–22.

Popper, F. J. 1979. Ownership: the hidden factor in land use regulation. In Andrews, R. N. L., ed. *Land in America: commodity or resource.* Lexington, MA: Lexington, 129–135.

Ratcliffe, J. 1976. *Land policy: an exploration of the nature of land in society.* London: Hutchinson.

Raup, P. M. 1982. An agricultural critique of the national agricultural lands study. *Land Economics* 58, 260–274.

Rawls, J. 1971. A theory of justice. Cambridge: Harvard University Press.

Rozenbaum, S. J. and Reganold, J. P. 1986. State farmland preservation programs with the Upper Mississippi River Basin: a comparison. *Landscape Planning* 12, 315–336.

Sampson, R. N. 1979. The ethical dimension of farmland protection. In Schnepf, M., ed. *Farmland, food and the future.* Ankeny, IA: Soil Conservation Society of America, 89–98.

Shrader-Frechette, K. 1984. Agriculture, property and procedural justice. *Agriculture and Human Values* 1, 15–28.

Steiner, F. R. and Theilacker, J. E., eds. 1984. *Protecting farmlands.* Westport, CT: Avi Publishing.

Toner, W. 1984. Ag zoning gets serious. *Planning* 50, 19–24.

United Nations. 1976. *Report of Habitat: United Nations conference on human settlements.* New York: United Nations.

Wunderlich, G. 1984. Fairness in landownership. *American Journal of Agricultural Economics* 66, 802–806.

9 An Equity-Based Approach to Waste Management Facility Siting

The siting of solid waste management facilities—sanitary landfills, incinerators, transfer stations, energy from waste plants, and the like—presents municipalities and their planners with an urgent and confounding problem: everyone benefits from these facilities but no one seems to want them nearby. The problem is often characterized as NIMBY, narrow self-interest. Yet "Not in my backyard" can also be heard as "Why us? Why here?"—a cry for fair treatment (Simmons 1985). Accepting this interpretation offers promise for finding waste management sites that are not only technically feasible but also politi-

This chapter is a slightly revised version of Reg Lang, "Equity in siting solid waste management facilities," *Plan Canada* 30, 2 (1990), 5–13. It is included here with permission of the editor of *Plan Canada*. An earlier version of the paper was published as "Fair Siting in Waste Management" in *Proceedings. An International Symposium on Hazardous Materials/ Wastes: Social Aspects of Facility Planning and Management,* Institute for Social Impact Assessment, Winnipeg, Manitoba, Canada (1990), 237–242.

While the author's thinking on waste management facility siting has evolved considerably since publication of the article on which this chapter is based, equity principles similar to those discussed here remain central to development of a viable waste management strategy.

cally and publicly acceptable and more equitable for those directly affected.

This chapter begins by exploring the concept of equity and the nature of the waste management "crisis." Drawing mainly on the Ontario, Canada, context and the author's experience as an expert witness at a 1988 environmental assessment hearing on a major landfill project, evidence is presented of inequity in the siting of solid waste management facilities.[1] An alternative framework is proposed for siting facilities based on principles of equity. Since such an approach would be a significant departure from current practice, there is a discussion of the implications of introducing equity up front, when policies and siting guidelines are being established, rather than leaving it to be determined at environmental assessment hearings when it may be too late.

Equity

Equity here refers to the fairness of siting a facility at a particular location and the fairness of the process for reaching that decision—"a just distribution, justly arrived at," in the words of David Harvey (1973). Equity, therefore, is a matter of distributive justice and of procedural fairness. It calls for equal treatment of equals and, conversely, for unequals to be treated unequally.

How can we decide what is equitable, fair, just? William Lucy (1981) suggests that five concepts of equity be considered: equality (everyone should receive the same service, within reason); need (those requiring a service should get more of it); demand (those showing an active interest in a service should be rewarded); preference (to include those whose interest in a service is not revealed through its use); and willingness to pay (only people who use a service should pay for it). This typology usefully exposes not only the various dimensions of equity but also how complex it can be. The five conceptions of equity are often in conflict: some have thresholds, others are difficult to measure, and all are subject to varying interpretations.

In practice, it is seldom possible to distribute society's goods and bads equally, to the satisfaction of all. Likewise, it is often difficult to sort out competing claims between efficiency and equity, that is, maximizing total benefit to the community versus distributing benefits fairly among its members. Small wonder that practitioners are inclined to consign confusing equity issues to the larger mess called "politics." As I argue later, though, that stance is neither ethical nor effective in addressing equity, especially in an atmosphere of crisis.

The Waste Crisis

That much overworked word, "crisis," certainly applies to waste. At least half of the landfills in the more than eighty-eight thousand municipalities in the United States will be closed during the 1990s.[2] A comparable figure for Canada is not available but in Ontario landfill sites serving half of the population will run out of capacity in the next ten years (Martin 1989) and some one hundred and sixty landfills have less than two years of remaining capacity (Ontario Ministry of the Environment 1990). To make matters worse, garbage production rates are on the increase. Each year, Canadians generate more than a ton of residential and commercial waste per capita, half again as much as twenty-five years ago and more than any other country in the world (L. Howard 1990). In Metro Toronto, the Works Department has registered an annual increase in waste volume of more than 15 percent; other large urban centers report a similar trend.[3] Metro councillor Richard Gilbert (1988a, p. 29) sums up:

> We've achieved excellence in many areas of municipal government but in our management of waste, we are just one of a large majority of North American urban areas that face imminent crises in their ability to dispose of the wastes they produce.

If new waste disposal facilities were being sited and constructed at an appropriate rate, there would not be a crisis—but they are not; far from it. The Greater Toronto area is a case in point. It relies heavily on three landfills for disposal of the four to five million tons of solid waste generated each year. Two of these facilities are practically full now and the third was to have reached its capacity in 1993. Siting new facilities, including environmental assessment, takes a lot longer than two years; hence, the crisis. Garbage in this urban area of nearly four million people could soon be piling up in the streets, with profound consequences. "Development will stop, businesses will close, municipal budgets will explode, and disease will spread," warns Gilbert (1988a, p. 29). Other parts of the province of Ontario face a similarly grim prospect.

This is the crisis, then: an increasing volume of waste alongside a rapidly decreasing capacity in existing waste management facilities; new facilities not coming on stream fast enough; and formidable barriers to speeding up the process. How can this critical situation have come to be? The answer lies in its root causes, which run deep, and are as follows.

1. *Our "throwaway" culture.* Waste is something we no longer want, need, or have a use for. It is culturally determined and its

definition in our culture has changed over time. From the mid-1940s onward, Canadians began consuming more resources per capita and substituting goods, such as plastics for wood, detergents for soap, synthetic for natural fibers, and so on. These trends combined with population growth to create rapid increases in the amount of waste, new kinds of waste far more difficult to dispose of, and wasteful attitudes and behaviors that endure today. For example, fully half of all garbage by volume consists of packaging, which consumers have come to expect (McInnes 1989).

Awareness of a fundamental contradiction in our society is finally finding its way into the popular consciousness: economic growth, at least in its current North American form, exceeds the capacity of the natural/human environment to assimilate the waste such growth generates. Environment ministries and departments created to manage this contradiction can no longer contain it. Waste has become essential to "progress," not merely an unfortunate by-product of it. The economy's health depends on many kinds of goods being disposable, on consumers wasting rather than conserving, and on somehow getting rid of what is left over.

Consequently, waste management processes have tended to emphasize quick pickup and efficient removal of whatever is put out on the curb rather than reducing the amount of waste requiring disposal. These attitudes are changing, but only slowly. A 1989 series in Canada's "national newspaper"—the *Globe and Mail*—found business to be increasingly interested in stemming the tide of waste by turning used materials into salable products (Lush 1989). Attracted by potential profits, stimulated by government initiatives such as Ontario's Municipal Industrial Strategy for Abatement, pushed by environmentally aware customers and sky-rocketing costs of waste disposal, and threatened by tougher laws including stiff fines and even jail terms, firms across the country are responding to this newfound "opportunity." Yet these advances are dwarfed by the mountains of waste being generated and by opposing trends, such as the rapid growth in the private sector's waste stream (cardboard and plastics are prime culprits), the supply of recycled material running way ahead of the demand for it, the continued insistence that recycling be market-driven, and the huge profits to be made in the illegal disposal of hazardous chemical wastes. The overwhelming reality continues to be a society that is extremely wasteful and that is just beginning to face the consequences. In that sense, a crisis is both inevitable and necessary.

2. *A technical approach to waste management.* Technical rationality dominates waste planning and management. This mind-set stresses scientific method as an objective means of providing information to decision makers, relies on facts separated from values as the basis for knowledge, emphasizes analysis over interaction, and searches for the "best" solution to problems (Lang 1988a). While the technical approach has valuable applications, especially in science, it also has significant limitations (Armour 1988). It is unsuited to complex situations, such as waste management, in which key conflicts are about values and where a multiplicity of perspectives must be respected. Then, a technical/analytic approach needs to be combined with one that is interactive and political (Lang 1988b).

Unfortunately, this happens all too rarely.[4] Typically, engineers, planners, and others do their studies, prepare their reports, and tack public participation onto this process. Affected interests are informed, perhaps consulted, but the dominant reality for decision makers and their advisers remains grounded in technical rationality. For example, environmental assessments routinely treat noise solely as an objective measure of sound determined by arbitrary standards without acknowledging something obvious to the ordinary person, that it is the meaning we attach to sound that makes it pleasant and desired or stressful and "noisy." This technical bias carries over into environmental hearings. When these occur in quasi-judicial, adversarial settings monopolized by lawyers, "hard" data and "objective" testimony by experts receive the most attention.

Exacerbating the problem is government environmental assessment legislation that, in Ontario, at least, "presently perpetuates and further entrenches the model of technical rationality and the 'technical approach' to solid waste management planning" (McMillan 1989, p. 127). For instance, Ontario's Environmental Assessment Act requires a comprehensive examination of all alternatives, narrowed down through evaluation to one. Consideration of alternatives is laudable, but when conducted in the minute detail required to sustain legal challenges at hearings, the inevitable result is a massive technical exercise that is lengthy and costly without assurance of a positive outcome. In the case of Halton Region, Ontario, the siting process took more than fifteen years, cost taxpayers upward of $30 million (including $80,000 a month to export waste to New York State), and as of 1990 was still bogged down in appeals.

3. *A clash of "moral universes."* A related root cause of the waste crisis is both moral and philosophical. The essential problem, according to Peter Timmerman (1992, p. 244), is that "the system asks people involuntarily to take on unknown personal health risks on behalf of the larger social good." A means-oriented managerial approach based on bureaucratic rationality clashes with an ends-oriented "mutualistic community" perspective. The latter, he says, "is predicated on the refusal to treat people as means to ends, no matter how worthy; nor will it countenance the slightest addition to the burden of risk on members of that group. . . . To accept knowingly a possible future risk is to commit moral outrage" (Timmerman 1984, p. 11). When these two universes collide—for example, when a local government proposes that residents of a smaller community bear the brunt of the cost, inconvenience, and risk associated with a waste management facility in order that the larger community of which they are part may benefit—trouble is sure to follow. Because it is fundamentally about competing moral perspectives, the ensuing controversy is especially difficult to handle and particularly dangerous to the legitimacy of "the system." Perhaps that is why governments are loath to impose such facilities, no matter how strong the objective arguments, and why they prefer to keep waste management issues in the technical realm.

These kinds of root causes are seldom addressed quickly or easily. Equity is one promising point of entry because it is embedded in each of the three causes outlined above. In the throwaway culture, some generate much more waste than others and some benefit a lot more from the economic growth that produces this waste; yet these individuals and groups do not bear a proportionate share of the costs represented by waste. A technical approach to waste planning and management distorts this distributional injustice (Kemp 1982). It also favors certain kinds of information inputs to decision makers while discriminating against other kinds, often to the disadvantage of those adversely affected by the proposed facilities. Finally, the clash of moral universes and the renegotiation of the social contract that it implies call for choices that are fundamentally about equity.

Inequity in Waste Management

Specific evidence of inequity in waste management is not hard to find. Moreover, attempts to deal with the waste management crisis as often as not aggravate inequity.

This problem is occurring at all levels. At the global scale, developing countries attempt to unload their worst wastes on less-developed countries, "often offering development-for-dumping deals that are attractive to nations worried about paying off their growing debts."[5] Closer to home for Canadians was the Québec government's attempts to send PCB-contaminated waste to a plant in Wales. When British dock authorities refused to allow the freighter to unload, the waste was rerouted to storage in Baie-Comeau, Québec, where vigorous local opposition was quelled only by the riot squad.

In Ontario, as regional municipalities scramble for solutions to their waste crises, equity appears to be low on the list of concerns. Consider the case of Metro Toronto. Its strategies for responding to the crisis have included creating an "interim landfill" in the Rouge River Valley, an environmentally significant area designated for a provincial park; paying a neighboring municipality to accept Metro's waste (a deal embraced by the recipient, which would have enjoyed revenue in excess of $250 million); expanding an already huge existing dump in another adjoining municipality; and transporting waste far away to the northern Ontario towns of Kapuskasing and Kirkland Lake, where it would be input to recycling and energy from waste plants. These proposals have been and continue to be strenuously opposed by local groups on environmental and equity grounds.

How could politicians and their planners have let things go so far without taking preventive action? The warning signs of an impending crisis were readily apparent years ago. It is difficult not to suspect that the situation has been allowed to become a crisis in order that (1) the provincial government will jump in to rescue the municipalities, effectively removing from them the responsibility to dispose of the waste their growth generates, and (2) environmental and equity considerations can be "trumped" by urgency and local interests can be subordinated to "the larger good."[6] Moral objections, such as those of Toronto alderman Robert Hollander, who says "to dump our garbage in someone else's backyard is just not right," have been overshadowed by the bottom-line position expressed by Metro Toronto chairman Alan Tonks: "We can't let the existing economic system seize up" (Lalonde 1989; Moon 1989).

Equity issues will not go away, though. It is becoming more difficult to hide the inequity in waste management or to get residents to accept it. Landfills alone seldom yield benefits to people who live beside them. Instead, such facilities are likely to result in increased hazards and reduced environmental quality (such as pollution, heavy truck traffic, noise, odor, and other nuisance effects), along with the stigma of being labeled a garbage dump, having to live with an eyesore, fear of reduced property values, stress, and an assortment of other ills, both "real" and "perceived." Whichever community is unlucky enough to be the recipient of a landfill will experience some or all of these impacts and may well feel unfairly treated. A far more inequitable situation exists if the community has already been living with a landfill for a long time. Its residents can justifiably claim that they have done their share for the larger good and now it is someone else's turn.

However, this argument seems not to impress those responsible for facility siting; quite the contrary. Data obtained from the Ontario Ministry of the Environment in 1987 indicated that the selection of a site next to an existing landfill, rather than being a regrettable last choice, is actually preferred by most municipalities:

> Of the twenty-two waste management planning exercises that had reached the stage of selecting landfill sites under The Environmental Assessment Act at that time, twelve included as one of the candidates a site that was an expansion of or adjacent to an existing landfill. Six of the remaining ten did not have this option, for various reasons. Therefore, three of every four municipalities who had the opportunity to make use of a site adjacent to an existing landfill actively pursued this option. Only three of the sixteen did not do so and only one municipality decided, as a matter of policy based on equity, to locate its landfill elsewhere.
>
> Of the twelve municipalities who selected a candidate site next to an existing landfill, nine went on to designate, as their preferred site, one that was an expansion of or adjacent to an existing landfill. In addition, eight of the municipalities conducting environmental assessments expanded or were seeking to expand their existing landfill operations in order to buy time to find longer-term solutions.[7]

These data show that a clear majority of Ontario municipalities engaged in waste management planning favored the "proximity option"— locating new facilities next to existing ones. More recent research indicates that add-on sites are still preferred, especially for "interim" and "temporary" facilities (which have the unfortunate tendency to become permanent).[8]

What explains this apparent predisposition toward such sites? The reasons, seldom articulated officially, include the following:[9]

- The existing site was proved to be reasonably satisfactory and therefore we can expect another one beside it to be equally so. Besides, a landfill next to another landfill is a compatible land use.

- We already have a monitoring system in place at the existing landfill. This will save us having to install another.
- The environment at the existing landfill (for instance, the groundwater) is already degraded. Why spoil another part of the municipality?
- The people who live near the existing landfill and along the haul routes have gotten used to it.
- It is much easier to get government approval for an expansion than for a new facility.

Ontario's then Minister of the Environment, Ruth Grier, seemed to support the proximity option, at least in times of crisis: "It is better to contemplate, in an emergency, going to an existing site rather than opening up a new site," she stated (Gorrie and James 1990).

Arguments such as these convey a disturbing impression: elected representatives and their advisers figure that it will be easier to locate new facilities alongside existing ones. Facing urgent requirements to get these facilities sited (often because they waited so long to begin planning or misjudged the amount of time it would take), and afraid that ruling out an adjoining site on equity grounds could deprive them of a suitable location for the facility, they feel justified in exercising the proximity option.

Residents who have lived with a landfill or other such facility for many years are understandably infuriated by these arguments, not just because they are unfair but also because they are seriously flawed. Combined monitoring of an existing and a new landfill makes it difficult if not impossible to determine the source of leachate migration; as a result, accountability suffers. Also, degraded environments call for remedial action, not more degradation. In addition, residents are most offended by the suggestion that they have somehow become acclimatized to landfilling nearby. This is not borne out either by their experience or by the literature on individual and community stress.[10] For three reasons, people who have lived near landfilling and suffered its adverse impacts are likely to be more rather than less vulnerable to the stressful effects of another landfill in their midst. First, their perceptions of a landfill's effects will be negatively conditioned by their experience (unlike residents of a community that has never known a landfill).[11] Second, damaging stress can be cumulative in its effects; as it adds up, the individual may be increasingly prone to significant illness. Finally, stress experienced by people is worse if they believe they have little control over a particularly stressful event—a feeling that certainly would exist if they were to get another landfill despite their opposition and one that would be heightened if problems with the present landfill had continued in past years despite their opposition (Baum et al. 1983).

Whether is is fair to locate a new landfill beside one that has been there for a long time is a question that is both procedural and substantive. Procedurally, it *may* be fair to consider a site adjoining an existing landfill if affected communities and residents are fully included in the study. Substantively, however, it is manifestly unfair to require that the environmental and social impacts of garbage disposal be borne over a long period of time by a single community or part thereof. The political principle of equality provides that people have a right to equal treatment, that is, to the same distribution of goods or opportunities as anyone else has or is given (Beehler 1983). While there cannot be a totally fair distribution, to deliberately place the burden of waste disposal on one segment of the community, generation after generation, is undeniably unfair. "Deliberately" is a key word because random inequity can be much more bearable than inequity that is or appears to be intentional.

How to be fairer to those living in close proximity to a waste management facility is therefore a complex and difficult problem. A shift in attitude is part of the solution—for example, from the typical facility planner's attitude, that "local opposition frequently threatens the feasibility of siting these facilities," to one that is more respectful of the threat these facilities pose for the receiving environment (E. Howard 1990, p. 11). Beyond attitude change, though, there is a deeper need to make equity considerations explicit in the policy guidance given to appointed officials and consultants when they begin looking for sites.

An Equity-Based Approach

A facility-siting approach based on equity is unlikely to be eagerly embraced by decision makers. Politicians know that such an approach, besides reducing the pool of available sites, would require tough decisions sure to displease one or another interest group. Crisis decisions are easier to justify. It is also less controversial to go along with staff proposals that appear to be logical, scientific, unbiased, and inevitable. In any case, if the technical approach produces a politically undesirable recommendation, politicians feel they can always overrule it. They may also hope that when a site is finally designated, the support of the many who benefit (relieved that the garbage problem is being taken care of and not in their backyards) will greatly outweigh the complaints from the directly impacted few.

The problem with this approach is that it often does not work either in producing acceptable sites or in avoiding controversy. Furthermore, claims of unfair treatment persist far beyond the fatal siting decision, as does broader public uneasiness about trampling on individual rights.

Clearly, equity *is* a matter of politics, for politics is about the allocation of resources, that is, who gets what. Equity thus deserves up-front consideration in waste management decisions. Leaving equity to be dealt with at the end of the siting process is tantamount to giving it no consideration at all. By the time that a long and costly selection process has designated a site, it may be quite difficult for elected decision makers to rule it out on equity grounds. To do so would invite the counter agument, "If you now reject the site because you believe that to locate a landfill there would be inequitable, why did you consider that site in the first place?"

Accepting political responsibility for equity means debating equity principles openly, at the outset, and then providing guidelines for site selection. Ten such principles are proposed below.[12] As this list is an interrelated set, it is best used as a whole rather than in part.

1. All elements of society share responsibility for the generation of waste and its disposal.
2. Each region has a responsibility to take care of its own waste. One region should not export its waste problem to another without previously agreed-on reciprocal arrangements that were democratically arrived at.
3. Adverse impacts should not be imposed on people and their environments, or on future generations, if these impacts can be avoided. Every effort should be made, prior to facility siting, to reduce the amount of waste that requires disposal.
4. Waste creates social and environmental costs that are not borne equally. Within the region, all efforts must be made to distribute waste management facilities equitably, in space and in time. Each community within the region must bear its share of the responsibility in proportion to its share of the region's waste stream.
5. Integrated regional and interregional strategies are necessary to provide the long-range context for equitable siting of waste management facilities. This should include multiple siting—identifying all facilities required in the future rather than siting one facility at a time—based on consideration of each region's ultimate future size and scale, integration of its

waste production with its land development, and establishment of a pattern of facilities that is as equitable as can be.

6. Inevitably, some individuals, groups, and communities will have to assume a disproportionate amount of the impacts and risks associated with waste disposal. Every effort must be made to render the imposition of such facilities as voluntary as possible, minimize adverse impacts, share unavoidable risks, mitigate the impacts that remain, and compensate fully those who bear the burden of these residual impacts.

7. Individuals and interest groups affected by a proposed facility can reasonably expect that an analytically sound and politically fair process will be followed in site selection.

8. A community, or part thereof, that is selected for a waste management facility can expect, and should receive firm assurance, that it will not be selected for further waste management facilities in the future.

9. After the facility is in place, there should be ongoing opportunities for those directly affected to be kept informed about and involved in its operation. Their involvement should include a measure of control (for example, a shutdown of the facility when it exceeds operating guidelines) to ensure conformance, and the appearance of same, to requirements and promises of performance set out when the facility was assessed and approved.

10. Imposing unwanted risks and impacts upon the few for the benefit of the many is fundamentally an ethical problem. It therefore deserves open explicit consideration at the beginning of a facility siting process. That process, and the planning that precedes it, must have sufficient lead time so that site selection will not occur in an atmosphere of crisis that may override other equity principles, such as provision for full environmental assessment.

Front-end guidance on equity would still need to be complemented by back-end assessment of a designated proposal's equity impacts, as part of the environmental and social impact assessment. Equity impact assessment could take this form:

- Establishment of criteria for considering equity, making these explicit rather than leaving them hidden, as impact assessments tend to do. This requires interaction with the various "stake-

holders," the effecting and affected interests who have or perceive they have a direct stake in the siting decision.

- In-depth examination of the history of solid waste disposal in
the region served by the proposed facility, including to what
extent, over time, each area had assumed responsibility for its
own waste and that of other areas.
- Identification and analysis of the equity concerns of residents
at each site, recognizing that equity has both objective and
subjective dimensions.
- Retrospective assessments of environmental/social and cumulative impacts of existing and recent waste management facilities.
- A summary and comparison of the equity-related social impacts at each site, as the basis for further discussions with
stakeholders.

The foregoing principles are not cast in stone but are intended to
be adapted, through public discussion, to each locality. A useful by-
product of such discussion could be the surfacing of deeper issues that
tend to be disguised by, among other things, a technical approach that
narrowly defines all this as no more than a siting problem. It is fast
becoming a lot more than that; Michael Heiman (1990, p. 359) makes
this clear in his account of a growing grass-roots movement that claims
all facilities should be opposed—"Not in anybody's backyard" is its
rallying cry—until government and industry commit themselves to levels
of source reduction of waste "well beyond the process, recycling and
waste stream modifications" now being implemented. While extreme,
this view dramatizes the main message of the waste crisis, namely, the
nonsustainability of present economic and population growth.

Implications

Applying the foregoing equity principles would have certain implications.

Principle 1 establishes the importance of not separating acts from
their consequences. Principle 2, for example, questions the export of
waste, irrespective of how willing the "host community" may appear to
be. There are likely to be some objectors in any community, which raises
the issue of whether the municipal council, often dominated by business
interests, can or should speak for the community on such matters.[13] At
a deeper level, Principle 2 challenges the dubious moral justification of
one area taking care of another's waste. Because "bartered consent" is

becoming increasingly popular, such questions are urgently in need of public debate (Kasperson 1986). The Alberta government took a negotiated approach when it sited its hazardous waste treatment center at Swan Hills (Armour 1988; Fagan 1989). Similarly, Greater Vancouver negotiated a contract to take 20 percent of its garbage to a wood-chip plant at Cache Creek in British Columbia's interior (Donville 1989). A voluntary "invitational" approach is also being implemented by the Canadian federal Task Force on Low-Level Radioactive Waste (Armour 1988). While the voluntary and compensatory aspects of these activities may be consistent with other principles, there remains the danger that willing-host communities will be ones "where the inclination or ability to resist is minimal . . . communities that are rural and small, where unemployment is high, and where the residents are more likely to trade safety and environmental quality for material gain" (Kasperson 1986, p. 133).

Principle 2 may appear to be inapplicable to developed urban areas that have no space left for landfills. A solution then could be in the interpretation of "reciprocal arrangements"; for instance, municipalities near Metro Toronto have argued that it should share its substantial business and industrial tax revenue in exchange for asking them to share in the waste burden. Alternatively, it may be necessary to revise municipal boundaries so that every municipality has space for managing its waste.

Principle 3 calls for full adoption of the four Rs—reduction, recycling, reuse, and recovery of waste—and in the appropriate sequence. It is unfair to impose a landfill or incinerator on a local community before all possible efforts have been made by the larger community to reduce the waste load.

Principle 4 relates closely to Principles 2 and 8. Equitable distribution of waste management facilities will not be easy to determine. Equity applies both to whole municipalities and to smaller communities within them.

Principle 5 significantly affects present practice. Simultaneous siting of facilities (Morell 1984)—preferably all at once but at least two sites at a time so that there is always one in reserve—sounds like and is a common sense planning principle. Taking a holistic, long-range perspective, however, opens up two thorny issues: the optimum size of an urban area and the possibility that the ability to dispose of its waste may limit its growth. Also, if this principle resulted in the building of more numerous, smaller facilities, new trade-offs between equity and efficiency would be required.

Principle 6 introduces compensation, being experimented with in various jurisdictions (O'Hare et al. 1983). It is to be applied, though, only after the impacts of the facility in question have been avoided or mitigated to the maximum possible extent.

Principle 7 speaks to the deeper issue of public distrust of institutions, a major part of the siting problem. Siting processes must be perceived as legitimate. No waste management program can succeed unless people have confidence in industry and government proponents: first, to give health, safety, and environmental concerns top priority (not to sacrifice them for political popularity or profit) and, second, to treat all parties with respect and scrupulous fairness. In the absence of such trust, governments have recourse only to imposition—overriding local interests to site needed facilities. For nonhazardous solid waste management, the justification for that approach is questionable and the political price can be high.

Principle 8 requires that equity considerations take precedence over technical ones. That position will not go unchallenged.

Principle 9 addresses the ongoing management of waste facilities and the need to relinquish some control to the local community. Acceptance of this principle could reduce local opposition during the siting process. Provisions for representativeness and accountability would be necessary.

Principle 10 makes equity an integral part of waste management planning from the outset. Sufficient lead time is essential if a crisis is to be averted: Waste + Haste = Inequity.

An equity-based approach has a further implication for land use planners. Roger Kasperson (1986, p. 138) makes it clear that the problem involves a great deal more than finding sites for waste management facilities:

> It is crucial to understand that *this is a systems-level, not a facility-level task* (original emphasis). Waste management must be undertaken with an understanding of the relationship between disposal strategies and opportunities for reducing the generation of waste. It is also clear that what is at stake is not the deployment of a facility but a network of waste generation, waste processing, waste movement, and storage or disposal, a system that needs to be integrated with land-use planning.

Integration is a trendy term, capable of disguising needed action of a more controversial nature (Lang 1988b). In this case, it is not merely a matter of coordinating planning for waste management with planning for economic and physical development. What happens when a municipality or region can no longer handle the waste generated by its growth? Until now, solid waste has not been one of the "growth shapers." The main infrastructure investments influencing the amount, type, and timing of urban growth have been sewage capacity, water supply (sometimes), and transportation facilities. The assumption has been that somewhere, either in the municipality or in its hinterland, solid waste will be disposed of. Equity principles and environmental considerations bring this assumption sharply into question. They raise the specter of having to limit a municipality's growth to a level consistent with its ability and willingness to dispose of the waste it generates.

If taking account of an ability to deal with outputs (waste) when admitting inputs (new growth) seems to be a radical idea, that says something about how superficially the ecological paradigm has penetrated the mind-sets of our political decision makers and their advisers. The same principle underlies "sustainable development," another fashionable concept whose full implications are as yet unrecognized. Unless humankind shoots its garbage into space (which would be morally suspect, to say the least), limits to growth must be confronted eventually. The longer we ignore this reality, the more difficult it will be to face and the more unfair it will be to generations to come.

Waste as a "limit to growth" need not mean a halt to development. Countries such as Japan have demonstrated the vast scope for the four Rs; there are forms of development that are less waste-intensive than others, and the waste crisis itself opens up opportunities. Taking waste as a growth limit seriously, however, constitutes a major challenge for planners, especially in areas where growth pressures are strong and development interests are well entrenched in the political system—the very areas that produce the most waste and therefore are in greatest need of this limit.

A postscript on Metro Toronto illustrates this point. Without having overcome the waste crisis and without consulting the public, Metro's politicians decided to increase their area's population by 300,000. Metro council was pushed in this direction by the previous provincial government that, despite its "war on waste," favored growth through increased density in Metro Toronto because it would cost less than growth in outlying communities that would require new sewers, roads, and other services. Decisions on urban growth and decisions on what to do with the waste it generates are still made in isolation; and growth continues to be pursued avidly, on the assumption that somehow and somewhere the waste will be disposed of.[14]

In all this, there are further ethical implications. Equity and ethics are intertwined; most of us agree that it is wrong to treat people unfairly—and doubly wrong to do so intentionally—but how do planners sort out what should be considered unfair? How do we deal with the uncomfortable reality that waste management decisions are likely to create hardship no matter what is done—hardship for those living near a facility and along haul routes versus hardship for everyone if no site can be found? Such questions and others beg for our attention. It is an evasion of professional responsibility to sweep them under the political rug or to hide behind an instrumental role definition. For instance, is it ethical to make or contribute to decisions that will result in a clearly inequitable distribution of costs and benefits without at least first assessing the equity impacts and making every effort to minimize them? Is it ethical to distort communication so that inequity is disguised? Is it ethical to promote and facilitate growth that may not be sustainable and to turn a blind eye to impending crises?

Ethics is inherently about conflicting obligations. That is what planners and decision makers face, especially when waste management is approached from an equity perspective. It is essential, therefore, that the ethics of waste management be addressed directly and openly.

Conclusions

The set of equity-based principles outlined herein could provide the foundation for such an approach. The principles are grounded in a systems perspective that reframes the waste problem from a siting of facilities to formulation of regional strategies that address both the disposal and the generation of waste—the inputs and the outputs together. Integration of planning for waste management with planning for economic and physical development is part of the capacity of the people and organizations in a region collectively to handle the waste they generate individually. The challenge this presents to planners and decision makers is to find new forms of development that are sustainable and fair and to take a stand against development that is not; to admit equity directly into their deliberations; and to address the ethical implications that inevitably accompany it.

Equity is now part of the waste management problem. Somehow, it will have to be made part of the solution, if there is to be one.

Notes

1. I appeared before the Joint Board (which combined the Ontario Environmental Assessment Board and the Ontario Municipal Board) for three

days in August 1988 on behalf of the Canadian Environmental Law Association and the West Burlington Citizens Group (WBCG), who were opposing a proposal by the Regional Municipality of Halton to site a landfill in their community alongside an existing landfill. My testimony was based on a report I had presented for the WBCG on the facility's social impacts (Lang 1988a).

The emphasis in this chapter is on solid waste management. Reference is made, however, to relevant literature on siting hazardous and radioactive waste facilities.

2. See "Governments face solid waste crisis," *PA Times*, March 31, 1989.

3. Niall McMillan (1989) notes that much of the increase is in waste generated and handled by the private sector, which in Metro Toronto recently exceeded a growth rate of more than 33 percent per year.

4. An exception is the social impact assessment for the Region of Peel, located immediately west of Metro Toronto, by Armour and Associates and the Institute of Environmental Research (1987).

5. "Garbage Imperialism," in *The Futurist*, November–December 1988, p. 5, cited the city of Philadelphia, which offered Panama 250,000 tons of toxic dioxin-laden fly ash as part of a development project to build a road through untouched wetlands in that country. The project would have endangered precious wildlife habitat and seriously affected the region's already degraded coral reef, according to the Earth Island Institute.

6. The provincial government that took office in the fall of 1990 seemed willing to fulfill the first condition. The then Minister of the Environment, Ruth Grier, assured Greater Toronto area politicians that garbage would not be allowed to pile up in the streets. She canceled the previous government's decision that would have allowed two interim landfills to be created without environmental assessment, announced strong waste reduction measures to postpone the crisis (but retained the power to expand existing landfills if this did not work), and was to establish a provincial-municipal authority to find a permanent solution. Municipal leaders in the Greater Toronto area reacted to these announcements with relief mixed with concern about possible landfill expansions. The chairman of Metro Toronto was quoted as saying, "I'm happy because the province is assuming the major risk" (James 1990, p. A6).

7. These data were collected as part of the preparation of my report (Lang 1988a). As of October 1987, more than ninety waste management planning exercises were under way in Ontario but only twenty-one of these had reached the stage of selecting candidate sites.

8. This research was assisted by Janice Cumberbatch; I'm grateful for her help. We were unable to get data directly comparable to those gathered in 1987, but the information we obtained does suggest a continuing trend toward the proximity option.

9. The first four reasons were advanced by officials of Tiny Township (one of those preferring the proximity option) to graduate students who used it as a case study in one of my courses. The last reason was offered by an official of Halton Region (DiGregorio 1987).

10. Stress is commonly defined as either a stimulus or the body's response to it. Lazarus and Folkman (1984, p. 19) define psychological stress as "a particular relationship between the person and the environment that is appraised by the person as taxing or exceeding his/her resources and endangering his/her well-being." Community (or endemic) stress refers to a problem that (1) affects a large number of people in an area and (2) cannot be resolved by the individual alone and therefore requires collective action (Bachrach and Zautra 1985). Fried (1982) defines community stress as a condition of continuing and manifold changes, persisting or increasing scarcity, perduring conditions of loss or deprivation, and ongoing experiences of inadequate resources or role opportunities.

11. A key to the definition of stress advanced by Lazarus and Folkman (1984) is the judgment, or "cognitive appraisal," that a particular person-environment relationship, such as living near a landfill, is stressful. The authors argue that it is the way we interpret events, not the events themselves, that produce the physical and psychological effects called stress (or, more accurately, distress) and that affect our adaptive or coping response.

12. This list is derived from Lang (1988a). Ethical bases for facility siting can also be found in Easterling and Kunreuther (1990), Kasperson (1983, 1986), and Morell (1984).

13. For example, the Temiskaming Anti-Garbage Coalition disputes Kirkland Lake's town council presenting itself as a willing-host community. The coalition carried out a local survey that claims to have found 60 percent of respondents opposed and only 20 percent in favor (Allen 1990).

14. An article in the *Ontario Planning Journal* (Miller 1990) noted that the Greater Toronto area is now expected to grow to six million by 2021. An underlying assumption is that "sufficient infrastructure would be provided to achieve a similar level of service to that experienced in 1986." Transit, roads, open space, and storm water quality were mentioned as "significant infrastructure elements." Solid waste was not referred to in the article, either as significant or as a growth constraint.

Bibliography

Allen, G. 1990. Make metro keep trash, Pollution Probe urges. *Globe and Mail* December 19.

Armour, A. 1988. Facility siting: a no-win situation? Part 2. *Canadian Environmental Mediation Newsletter* 3, 1–6.

Armour and Associates and the Institute of Environmental Research. 1987. *Investigation for landfill sites in Areas I, II, and VI in the city of Brampton: social impact assessment.* Brampton, Ontario: Regional Municipality of Peel.

Bachrach, K. M. and Zautra, A. J. 1985. Coping with a community stressor: the threat of a hazardous waste facility. *Journal of Health and Social Behavior* 26, 127–141.

Baum, A., Fleming, R., and Singer, J. E. 1983. Coping with victimization by technological disaster. *Journal of Social Issues* 39, 117–138.

Beehler, R. 1983. The concept of fairness. In Case, E. S. et al., eds. *Fairness in environmental and social assessment.* Calgary, Alberta: Faculty of Law, University of Calgary.

DiGregorio, R. 1987. Region's dump plans "dirty pool": Little. *Globe and Mail* June 12.

Donville, C. 1989. Cache Creek finds its rejuvenation in garbage. *Globe and Mail* June 12.

Easterling, D. and Kunreuther, H. 1990. Siting strategies to instill trust and legitimacy: the case of radioactive waste depositories. Paper delivered at the International Symposium on Hazardous Materials/Wastes: Social Aspects of Facility Siting and Planning, October, Toronto.

Fagan, D. 1989. Swan Hills' welcome for waste plant a sharp contrast to NIMBY syndrome. *Globe and Mail* March 15.

Fried, M. 1982. Endemic stress: the psychology of resignation and the politics of scarcity. *Journal of Orthopsychiatry* 52, 4–19.

Gilbert, R. 1988a. Toronto region's looming waste management crisis. *City Planning* 1, 29–33.

———. 1988b. *The solid waste crisis and some solutions.* Toronto: Municipality of Metropolitan Toronto.

Gorrie, P. and James, R. 1990. NDP scraps 2 proposed dump sites. *Toronto Star* November 22.

Harvey, D. 1973. *Social justice and the city.* London: Edward Arnold.

Heiman, M. 1990. From "not in my backyard!" to "not in anybody's backyard!" grassroots challenge to hazardous waste facility siting. *Journal of the American Planning Association* 56, 359–362.

Howard, E. 1990. Other people's waste is everybody's business. *Ontario Planning Journal* July/August, 11–12.

Howard, L. 1990. Canadians called largest garbage producers. *Globe and Mail* March 29.

James, R. 1990. Province assuming major trash "risk." *Globe and Mail* November 22.

Kasperson, R. E. 1986. *Hazardous waste facility siting: community, firm and governmental perspectives.* Worcester, MA: Center for Technology, Environment and Development, Clark University.

———, ed. 1983. *Equity issues in radioactive waste management.* Cambridge: Oelgeschlager, Gunn and Hain.

Kemp, R. 1982. Critical planning theory—review and critique. In Healey, P., McDougal, G., and Thomas, M., eds. *Planning theory: prospects for the 1980s.* Oxford: Pergamon Press, 59–67.

Lalonde, M. 1989. Kapuskasing willing to house incinerator for Toronto's waste. *Globe and Mail* September 11.

Lang, R. 1988a. *Potential social impacts of Halton's landfill proposal on communities at Site F in Burlington.* Toronto: Canadian Environmental Law Association; available from the author.

———. 1988b. Planning for integrated development. In Dykeman, F. W., ed. *Integrated rural planning and development.* Sackville, New Brunswick: Department of Geography, Mount Allison University.

———. 1992. Fair siting in waste management. *Proceedings.* International Symposium on Hazardous Materials/Wastes: Social Aspects of Facility Siting and Planning. Institute for Social Impact Assessment, Toronto, 237–242.

Lazarus, R. and Folkman, S. 1984. *Stress, appraisal and coping.* New York: Springer.

Lucy, W. 1981. Equity and planning for local services. *Journal of the American Planning Association* 47, 447–457.

Lush, P. 1989. Goodness from the garbage pile. *Globe and Mail, report on business.* February.

McInnes, C. 1989. Bad news comes in all sizes. *Globe and Mail.* October.

McMillan, N. 1989. Ontario's "crisis" in solid waste management: an alternative perspective. Master of Environmental Studies major paper, Faculty of Environmental Studies, York University, Toronto.

Martin, T. 1989. Up to our ears. *Globe and Mail.* August.

Miller, G. 1990. Province tackles GTA problems, searches for solutions. *Ontario Planning Journal* 6 (July–August), 3–6.

Moon, P. 1989. Huge dump in Rouge suggested for garbage. *Globe and Mail.* November.

Morell, D. 1984. Siting and the politics of equity. *Hazardous Waste* 1, 555–571.

O'Hare, M., Bacow, L., and Sanderson, D. 1983. *Facility siting and public opposition.* New York: Van Nostrand Reinhold.

Ontario Ministry of the Environment. 1990. Towards a sustainable waste management system: a discussion paper. Toronto: The Ministry.

Simmons, J. 1985. Rights and wrongs in hazardous waste disposal. In *Not-in-my-backyard.* Charlottesville: Institute for Environmental Negotiation, University of Virginia, 11–19.

Timmerman, P. 1984. *Ethics and hazardous waste facility siting.* Solid and Hazardous Waste Management Series, Department of Civil Engineering and the Institute for Environmental Studies. Toronto: University of Toronto.

———. 1992. The ethical sphere. *Proceedings.* International Symposium on Hazardous Materials/Wastes: Social Aspects of Facility Siting and Planning. Institute for Social Impact Assessment, Toronto, 243–248.

JAMES A. THROGMORTON

10 *Ethics, Passion, Reason, and Power: The Rhetorics of Electric Power Planning in Chicago*

Rhetoric is, both theoretically and practically, an extremely important part of planning.[1] Simply by making such a claim, this chapter turns away from the dominant scientific or Modernist conception of planning (see part 1) and begins to propose an alternative view. According to the Modernist view, planners can use scientifically verified facts and laws to guide social process (Friedmann 1987). Persuasion and audiences are, in the Modernist view, at best irrelevant and at worst positively dangerous. The contrary view expressed here is that persuasion and audiences are at the very core of planning. Planners are embedded in a complex rhetorical situation created by the interaction of three broad audiences—lay advocates, scientists, and politicians—and three core impulses—passion, reason, and power.[2] Rather than conceiv-

This chapter is a revised version of James A. Throgmorton, "Passion, reason and power: the rhetorics of electric power planning in Chicago," *Journal of Architectural and Planning Research* 7, 4 (1990), 330–350. It is included here with the permission of Locke Science Publishing Co., Inc.

ing of planning rhetoric as "mere words" or manipulation, I argue that it can and should also be thought of as a hermeneutic dialogue in which planners who occupy specific roles (to be defined later in this chapter) attempt to understand, persuade, and be persuaded by their three primary audiences. Through this process, planners and their audiences fuse into new interpretive communities, and the demarcation between planners and their audiences gradually disappears in all but name only. In this Postmodern conception, planners do not guide action or simply try to influence decision makers nor do they try to perfectly represent each of their core audiences. Rather, planners actively mediate between fundamentally different audiences and thereby help to create and sustain a broadly inclusive community of advocates, politicians, and scientists.

In the following pages, I describe and justify the proposed conceptual framework in greater detail. Once having done so, I illustrate the framework with a concrete example drawn from a recent effort to restructure the electric power industry in the Chicago area. The example serves primarily to reveal the complexity of the rhetorical situation in which practicing planners find themselves, but it also shows how planners in Chicago's Department of Planning attempted to deal with that complexity. I end this chapter by discussing what the conceptual framework implies for planning practice and by assessing the relationship between the framework and various theories of planning ethics.[3]

The Rhetorics of Planning: A Conceptual Framework

According to the traditional view, rhetoric is the use of style to manipulate or seduce others into behaving or thinking in some desired way (McGee and Lyne 1987). In this sense, rhetoric threatens to reduce all judgments to immediate persuasive effect rather than sound intellectual argument. This traditional view has recently been challenged, however. According to new rhetoricians, such as John Nelson, Allan Megill, and Donald McCloskey (1987), it is persuasive discourse within a community; it is "the quality of speaking and writing, the interplay of media and messages, the judgment of evidence and arguments" (Nelson et al. 1987, p. ix). Accordingly, one who investigates rhetoric within a discipline would analyze actual arguments among scholars (see, for example, Bazerman 1988; McCloskey 1985; and Nelson and Megill 1986). Students of rhetoric would begin with texts and consider the roles of various audiences for inquiry; they would explore how backings are shared, the extent to which warrants are accepted, and why. They would be concerned with figures of speech, arguments, and other devices of language authors use to persuade audiences in particular disciplines.

Building on the prior work of these new rhetoricians, as well as on recent studies of planning practice and ethics (Baum 1983; Dalton 1988; Forester 1989; Howe 1980), I have been developing a conceptual model of the rhetorics of planning (Throgmorton 1989, 1990a,b, 1993). The model initially assumes that individual planners occupy one of three pure roles: scientist, politician, or advocate (Figure 10-1). It further assumes that these planners have three parallel audiences for their work—scientists, public officials, and lay advocates—and that planners have to persuade each applicable audience to cite, use, or trust their work. Ultimately, though, the model argues that the pressing needs of practical action force practicing planners to actively mediate among those audiences.

FIGURE 10-1

Conceptual Model of the Rhetorics of Planning

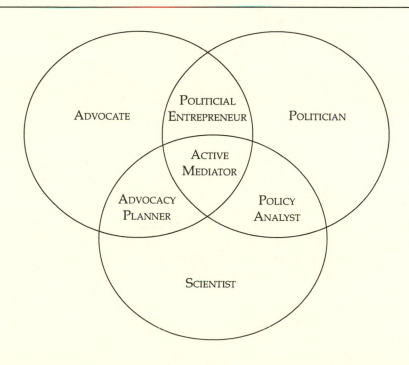

Three Core Rhetorics of Planning

Planners address three core audiences. To be persuasive, they have to use rhetorics appropriate for (and expected by) each of those audiences. That is not an easy task, for those rhetorics vary dramatically.

Scientists seek to increase the cumulative stock of knowledge in a particular discipline. Guided by a theoretical framework provided by their home discipline, they seek to describe, explain, and predict phenomena in a theoretically coherent way. They tend to address technical peers (primarily through technical journals and reports), and their rhetoric is dispassionate. As John Ziman (1984, p. 62) puts it, scientists write a paper

> as if it were addressed to a hypothetical, very skeptical reader, who is already very well informed on the subject, and might therefore form the spearhead of critical opposition. It is couched in formal technical language, thus indicating the professional competence of the author. Other research bearing on the subject is religiously cited, both to authenticate the basic premises of the investigation and to indicate that the author is thoroughly familiar with all the background material. The theoretical arguments and experimental results are expressed impersonally, in the passive voice, as if to emphasize the objectivity . . . and disinterestedness . . . with which the research was undertaken, and the conclusions are given quasi-logical weight, suggesting the rational necessity . . . of this particular outcome.

Politicians define public problems as part of the "game" of politics. For them, the challenge is to "get things done" (produce desired consequences) in a legislative and regulatory world that is characterized by incremental change, fragmented authority, legal constraints, and self-interested competition for electoral position, power, and survival (Matthews 1988). Seeking to gain and hold power, they try to show that they are qualified for elected office, are like their constituents, and empathize with their constituents' problems (Fenno 1978). They speak of friends, enemies, alliances, favors, deals, loyalty, reputation, spin (that is, managing expectations and reactions to performance), and positioning (such as presenting a desired self-image to others). Seeking to be elected or reelected, politicians tend to emphasize good trends and ignore bad ones, claim credit for what is good and shift blame for what is bad, and criticize others for past decisions and for unpopular trends and events, regardless of the extent to which the others actually caused them.

Advocates define problems in the moral language of right and wrong. Whether they are promoting the rights of women, gays, African-

Americans, consumers, the unborn, future generations, or the natural environment, advocates speak of right, justice, and, in many cases, freedom from oppression. Through words and deeds, they try to transform perceptions, express demands, and mobilize action. They tend to write and speak in the vernacular, and they communicate with the public through community meetings, slogans, songs, pamphlets, paperbacks sold in bookstores, and routine face-to-face interaction. When necessary, they use emotional appeals and symbolic actions, such as demonstrations and marches, to create a groundswell of public support for favored policies and programs (Stewart et al. 1984). They believe that important public decisions should not be made without their informed participation and that pluralist politics helps maintain a system of oppression. They tend to reject compromise as capitulation.

As this brief review indicates, the contrast among the rhetorics of "explaining phenomena in a theoretically coherent way," "putting the right spin on things," and "demanding rights" is stark. The conversations within these disparate audiences can be thought of as "normal discourses" (Rorty 1979) within "interpretive communities" (Fish 1979). Each of these communities has "an agreed-upon set of conventions about what counts as a relevant contribution, what counts as answering a question, what counts as having a good argument for that answer or a good criticism of it" (Rorty 1979, p. 320). When disagreements arise within these communities, members try to persuade one another with rhetoric authorized by their "agreed-upon conventions." However, when communication between interpretive communities is required—that is, "when someone joins in the discourse who is ignorant of these [normal] conventions or who sets them aside" (Rorty 1979, p. 320)—members of these interacting communities have to engage in "abnormal discourse." At this point, the criteria for persuasion become much more ambiguous. Hermeneutics becomes necessary.

Hermeneutics can be thought of as the study of an abnormal discourse from the point of view of some normal discourse (Rorty 1979). As Alasdair MacIntyre (1988, p. 350) puts it, "[T]here is no standing ground, no place for enquiry, no way to engage in the practices of advancing, evaluating, accepting, and rejecting reasoned argument apart from that which is provided by some particular tradition or other." Thus, scientists who seek to understand the political community would approach that community from the traditional perspective of the scientist. They would provisionally concede authority to the political, seeking to understand it better. At this point, dialogue between the two communities would become crucial; scientists would have to be prepared to accept their own fallibility and to discover the real strength of the political perspective. Successful dialogue would produce a shared understanding, or "fusion of horizons" (Bernstein 1983), that reflects a transformation of the initial positions of both communities. They would construct a new common language.

The experiences of engaging in "abnormal discourse" and trying to "fuse horizons" are common ones for planners. As they become more experienced, move from one role setting to another, or delve more deeply into planning problems, planners must engage a wider range of planning audiences. In doing so, planners tend to act hermeneutically and thereby become more like the audiences they try to persuade. Over time, new forms of normal discourse develop between some members of each of these communities. The three initially "pure" impulses tend to shade into one another and thus create new, and more realistic, roles for planners.

Fused Horizons: Three Blended Rhetorics of Planning

As some scientists, politicians, and advocates interact, the incoherence of "abnormal discourse" becomes less confusing. Interacting members gradually "fuse horizons" and construct new interpretive communities: policy analysts, advocacy planners, and political entrepreneurs (see Figure 10-1). To persuade within these new communities, planners have to use rhetorics appropriate for (and expected by) each of those communities. As we see below, however, each of these new rhetorics contains conceptual ambiguities and ethical tensions.

One role might be termed *client advocate* (Jenkins-Smith 1982), *strategic planner* (McClendon and Quay 1987), or *policy analyst* (Wildavsky 1979). Blending science and politics, these planners try to persuade elected and appointed officials to use the planner's advice (Majone 1989). How they proceed depends in part on whether the planner initially sees himself or herself as a political or scientific planner. Scientifically oriented analysts (Stokey and Zeckhauser 1978) emphasize the importance of methodological rigor, but they also stress the importance of brevity, clarity, and timeliness. Politically oriented analysts (Meltsner 1976, Wildavsky 1979) stress the importance of addressing problems that the client has the authority to solve, using language and concepts the client can understand. From this point of view, analysts must be willing to delete material from reports and do whatever else—within vague limits—is necessary to help gain acceptance of their advice and their client's policies (Meltsner 1976).

A second new role might be termed *partisan analyst* (Lindblom

1980), *advocacy planner* (Davidoff 1965), or *issue advocate* (Jenkins-Smith 1982). Disclaiming value-neutrality, these planners use rigorous scientific techniques in support of a chosen set of values or interests. As Paul Davidoff (1965, p. 279) puts it, "the planner should do more than explicate the values underlying his prescriptions for courses of action; he should affirm them; he should be an advocate for what he deems proper." According to this view, advocate planners help clarify and express their client's ideas, help inform the public about the range of available alternatives, point out biases in other plans, and ground the evaluation of plans in a clearly articulated (and passionately held) set of values.

The third new role might be termed *mobilizer* (Rabinovitz 1969) or *political entrepreneur* (Mollenkopf 1983). Blending advocacy and politics, and relying heavily on "ordinary knowledge" (Lindblom and Cohen 1979), these nontechnical planners bring diverse constituencies (or advocacy groups) into new coalitions, which, in turn, push for the expansion of programs and provide organizational and political support for the political entrepreneurs who established them. According to John Mollenkopf (1983, p. 6) the " 'political entrepreneur' . . . does not simply play by the rules of the game, but attempts to win the game by changing them. Using government to create new beneficiary groups, political entrepreneurs create supportive new constituencies."

The emergence of the policy analyst, advocacy planner, and political entrepreneur roles demonstrates that rhetoric can help bind interpretive communities together, but each of these rhetorics incorporates conceptual ambiguities and moral tensions. By acting as policy analysts, planners can increase their ability to influence decision making, but they do so at the risk of losing legitimacy in the eyes of particular rights-oriented communities (Levine 1982). Scientists will accuse analysts of being "too applied" or contaminated by politics, and lay advocates will accuse analysts of being untrustworthy mercenaries who systematically perpetuate wrongs, for example, racial segregation (Feld 1989). Occupying the role of advocacy planner earns the planner greater credibility and legitimacy with particular communities, but it does so at the risk of losing credibility in the eyes of elected officials. Advocacy planners are also open to the scientist's charge that values contaminate their work and to the analyst's charge that such planners are substituting their own political values for those of the broader public (as represented by elected officials; Hill 1989). Planners who assume the role of political entrepreneur are more likely to get things done in a way that satisfies both elected officials and particular communities, but they do so at the risk of being accused by scientists of producing decisions that are technically incompetent, ineffective, and guided by emotion.

Active Mediation: Practical Action in a Context of Rhetorical Complexity

It is in the mixing of roles and audiences, in the effort to make practical sense out of being caught among three audiences and three rhetorics, in the effort to "fuse horizons" and thereby "do good, be right, and get things done," that the complex rhetorics of practicing planners emerge. This effort has led to the development of the three blended rhetorics of policy analysis, advocacy planning, and policy entrepreneurship. However, as we have seen, each of these blended rhetorics expresses difficult conceptual ambiguities and moral tensions. Can those ambiguities and tensions be elminated in practice? I have suggested elsewhere that they can be eliminated by "planning teams" that "synthesize" politics, rationality, and advocacy (Throgmorton 1989). In this view, successful planning organizations and coalitions would have practitioners who specialize in each of the roles but who also cross-fertilize and compensate for each other's limitations.

I am no longer persuaded by this notion of "synthesis." It now strikes me as nothing more than the old Modernist conception of planning in new garb; it seeks to eliminate the differences between rhetorical communities by creating a new rhetoric. Rather than eliminating difference, I want to suggest that planners need to actively mediate between and among those different rhetorics. They need to be able to argue persuasively at specific times, in specific places, on specific issues, and before specific audiences, and that implies an ability to understand diverse rhetorics and to translate one rhetoric into another. To determine what this notion of "active mediation"—or "active mediator (see Figure 10-1)—actually entails, though, and to assess its viability, we need to conduct detailed studies of planners in action. It is for that purpose that I now turn to a discussion of electric power planning in Chicago.

Electric Power Planning in Chicago[4]

THE CONTEXT: SCIENTISTS, ADVOCATES AND POLITICIANS

Electric power planning in the Chicago area reflects both nation-wide tendencies and a unique local context. Nationally, the electric power industry has undergone fundamental structural change (Hyman 1988; Joskow and Schmalensee 1983; Kahn 1988; Rudolph and Ridley 1986). As a result, there have been numerous "scientific" studies of the industry and how it is likely to change. Locally, the Commonwealth Edison Company (Com Ed) has been trying to complete an expensive nuclear plant construction program, but its effort has been opposed by a vocal coalition of local advocacy groups. Perhaps more importantly, Com Ed now finds that the city of Chicago's elected officials are seriously considering the possibility of removing the city from Com Ed's system. Thus, planners concerned with electric power in the Chicago area have three core audiences: scientists, advocates, and politicians.

There have been several scientific studies of the electric power industry and how it is likely to change, including those by Paul Joskow and Richard Schmalensee (1983) and Edward Kahn (1988), and numerous articles in journals, such as the *Bell Journal of Economics, American Economic Review,* and *Energy.* None of these studies directly addresses the Chicago area, but collectively they provide (and reproduce) a common language that dominates the discourse about electric power planning. This rhetoric conceptualizes the industry in terms of public utility economics and is laced with technical concepts, such as "natural monopoly," "economies of scale," "rate base," "rate of return," "revenue requirements," "used and useful," and "marginal and average costs." To the specialized community, this rhetoric is necessary and useful, but to nonexperts, it is "a fog of specialized verbiage" (Hyman 1988, p. 3). Planners and others who share this framework agree the goal of electric power planning is to maximize economic efficiency.

Com Ed has not been immune from the pressure for structural change. Even though it is the nation's third largest electric utility, Com Ed has been facing major difficulties. Projecting (and counting on) a steady increase in the demand for electric power, Com Ed in the early 1970s initiated the nation's largest nuclear power plant construction program. To the utility's surprise, though, the expected increase failed to materialize, and Com Ed was left with substantial amounts of excess generating capacity. In order to recoup the capital costs of building those plants, Com Ed had to petition the Illinois Commerce Commission (ICC) to approve a series of large rate increases. The earliest requests generated little opposition, but the ones that sought to recoup the $7.1 billion capital cost of Com Ed's last three nuclear plants stimulated intense opposition.[5]

The coalition that has opposed Com Ed's requests for rate increases is diverse in membership and interests. At the coalition's core is a set of community, consumer, antinuclear, environmental, and labor groups, including the Citizens Utility Board (CUB), which represents residential ratepayers in utility regulation issues; Business and Professional People for the Public Interest (BPI), a public interest law firm that represents low-income consumers and environmental concerns; the Center for Neighborhood Technology (CNT), a technical assistance group that aids community organizations; Citizens for a Better Environment; and numerous "Alinsky-style" community organizations that seek both to mobilize and empower low-income communities. These groups generally agree that Com Ed has—in a shortsighted pursuit of profit—drastically overbuilt its power generating capacity, made northern Illinois one of the highest-cost electric power regions in the country, driven businesses and jobs away from the region, and greatly increased the risk of nuclear accidents in northern Illinois.

With approximately $2 billion in sales annually within the city of Chicago (roughly one-third of the utility's total revenues), Com Ed is also a large and important part of the local economy (Commonwealth Edison [Com Ed] 1988a). As a result, the utility has also received critical attention from the city's elected officials. Disturbed both by Com Ed's rate increase requests and by the ICC's willingness to approve rate increases larger than the city thought were justifiable, the city began—subsequent to the election of Harold Washington as mayor in 1983--to explore options to remaining on Com Ed's system.

The city's effort to explore options has taken place in a complex and highly volatile political context: "Chicago politics"—the very words conjure up images of smoke-filled rooms and under-the-table deals. It seems no exaggeration to say that many, if not most, Chicago residents believe that the city's elected officials are hopelessly corrupt, racially biased, and care little for the public's welfare (Squires et al. 1987). To many of those residents, however, things seemed to have changed substantially in 1983 with the election of Washington. To them, Washington's victory initiated a progressive effort to distribute the city's resources more fairly, to emphasize neighborhood economic development, to challenge politically powerful businesses, and to establish a more open, participatory decision-making process (Moberg 1988).

EXPLORING THE CITY'S OPTIONS TO REMAINING ON COM ED'S SYSTEM

The city of Chicago and its residents currently obtain their electric power from Com Ed pursuant to a franchise agreement that was adopted forty years ago and that was scheduled to expire in December 1990. Disturbed by Com Ed's rate increases, knowing that the franchise had to be either renegotiated or terminated, and encouraged by his energy advisers in the Planning Department, Mayor Washington announced on October 10, 1985, that the city would not renew Com Ed's franchise without first critically exploring other options (Richards 1987a; Williams 1990; Ziemba 1986). Perhaps by somehow bypassing Com Ed, the city could avoid the full brunt of the utility's rate increases and their adverse effects on the city's economy. The mayor instructed the city's Planning Department to conduct a one- to two-year study of electric power supply options.

The idea of conducting such a study was strongly supported by CNT, CUB, the Illinois Public Action Council (IPAC), the Chicago 1992 Committee, the Organization of the Northeast (ONE), the Logan Square Neighborhood Association, the Nuclear Energy Information Service (NEIS), and other members of the informal coalition referred to previously. It was strongly opposed by Com Ed: Com Ed Vice President Donald Petkus said that the utility would move its corporate headquarters (and $140 million in annual tax revenues) out of Chicago if the city went through with its threat (Biddle 1985). Undaunted, the city's planners hired R. W. Beck and Associates, a nationally recognized consulting engineering firm, to conduct the study.

Beck and Associates (1987) submitted their report to the city in November 1987. The report was clearly not a scientific study, for it did not burden the reader with theory, disciplinary jargon, references, quotations, methodological detail, or other trappings of scientific analysis, but it did rely heavily on the conceptual language provided by public utility economics: "bulk power purchases," "interconnection and coordination services," "discounted present values," "levelized costs of electric service," "reliability" of supplies, "excess capacity," and "disallowances of costs" for nuclear power plants that had been built but not yet been put in the "rate base." It also adopted the antirhetorical stance (that is, the passive voice and a generally somber appearance) favored by scientific planners: "This study was undertaken," the report said, "to explore various options with respect to the furnishing of electricity to the City and the citizens of Chicago," and its purpose "is to summarize the results of the studies undertaken by the Consulting Engineer and to provide information as may be helpful to the policy makers in Chicago" (Beck and Associates 1987, p. I–1). Also, without providing any details, the report stated that "The costs of electric service were estimated by using the PWRCOST and APCAP series of computer programs developed by Beck and Associates" (1987, p. I–14).

The report was also clearly not a political analysis, for it did not focus on the political consequences of pursuing alternative courses of action. Deftly avoiding the ticklish question of whether any new public power system might be corrupted by the "Chicago Pols," the report simply said that "in the event the City would decide to pursue any form of the options studied, prompt attention would need to be paid to the development of an appropriate structure for governance, management, and operation of the municipal utility" (Beck and Associates 1987, p. I–13).

Neither political nor scientific, the Beck Report was an example of planning as policy analysis: it relied heavily on the language and tools of public utility economics but limited its attention to the city's concerns. Thus, the report adopted the city's definition of the problem, compared a few economic consequences of four specific alternatives, and presented a series of contingent recommendations. In the end, Beck and Associates (1987, p. I–14) concluded that "the potential exists for the City to reduce the aggregate costs of electric services to consumers within the City during the next twenty years" by $1.1 billion to $18 billion, depending on the option chosen.

Mayor Washington publicly accepted and commented on the report at a press conference on November 4, 1987. Calling Com Ed's rate increases "a tidal wave threatening to wash this city's economic foundation out to sea" and claiming that the city had a "once-in-a-lifetime opportunity to do something about this threat," the mayor stressed that "we would be remiss . . . if we did not further explore these potential savings," that "we've made no final choices," and that "we challenge Edison to focus on our mutual threat" (Anonymous 1987). By speaking this way, the mayor retained considerable maneuvering room. Com Ed wanted its existing franchise renewed, advocacy groups wanted the city to municipalize the operation, and the mayor needed the threat of municipalization as leverage to negotiate a more favorable franchise agreement.

Accompanying the mayor's press conference was an overview of the Beck Report prepared by the Chicago Department of Planning (1987). The cover page both symbolically appealed to the anti–Com Ed coalition for support and selectively portrayed the department's view of the city's relationship to Com Ed: low on the horizon lay a small representation of Chicago's skyline and looming above that skyline were electric transmission lines that stretched between two immense transmission towers. Com Ed has power over Chicago, the cover implied, but Chicago is free to explore the options to remaining dependent on Com Ed.

The remainder of the overview reinforced the symbolism expressed on the cover page. The department argued that Com Ed mismanagement had caused electric power rates to soar, that those soaring rates had caused enterprises to avoid investing in Chicago, that Com Ed's "traditional monopoly supply arrangements" had "stifled" competition, and that the city had the responsibility to explore options to remaining on Com Ed's system. However, the overview also portrayed the department as a publicly accountable, politically responsive organization that sought technical advice from experts, solicited advice from a broad range of interests in Chicago, was sensitive to political needs of the mayor and the aldermen, and sought to keep the public informed.

On the same day that Mayor Washington accepted the Beck Report, Com Ed's Communication Services Department responded with a press release (Com Ed 1987). This was just the start of a barrage of advertising that soon spewed forth from the utility. For at least the next eighteen months—on radio and television, in newspapers, and through a series of neighborhood meetings—Com Ed advertised its case against the city's effort to "take over" Com Ed's facilities.

In these advertisements, Com Ed consistently portrayed itself as a model citizen of a world-class metropolis whose growth and progress vitally depended on a steady supply of safe, clean, reliable, and reasonably priced electric power. It further portrayed itself as an experienced, skillfully managed corporation that was trying to protect and advance the interests of its consumers and shareholders and of the Chicago region as a whole. Conversely, Com Ed tried to delegitimize any challenges to its expertise. Regardless of the fact that the Chicago City Council had the legal authority and responsibility to reconsider the franchise with Com Ed in the very near future, and regardless of the evident right of the city's citizens to voice their opinions about what the council should do, Com Ed pointedly warned that a few red-tinged "bureaucrats and activists" were propagating the idea that the city should "take over your [the consumers'] electric power system" (Com Ed 1988b). Relying heavily on a few striking symbols and typically writing in simple, lay language, it charged that such a "take over" was a "seriously flawed bad idea" that would result in an inefficient, politicized electric power system that would dole out favors "at the whim of the City Council" (Com Ed 1988b).[6]

Let me present two striking examples of the symbolism and language used in Com Ed's advertising. Here is the "Taxi" radio spot that Com Ed ran in late 1987 and in 1988:

> [*Guy* voice-over]:
> Ya know, I can't rightly explain it, but nobody seems to
> know more about sports than your average cabdriver. So

I wasn't surprised the other day when mine turns to me
and asks what I thought about all this talk over changing
managers. I said, well, to tell you the truth, I thought
pitching was the biggest problem. Oh, no, he tells me.
He meant how people have been talking about the city
managing its own electric company. I said, I thought
Commonwealth Edison already did that. Oh, they do,
he said. Been doing it for over a hundred years, in fact.
Why this summer alone they set seven all-time peak load
records and they did it without those power shortages
like the East Coast had. I said, well, then, why do some
folks think the city can do a better job? . . . He said, oh
most folks don't. In fact, in one survey, two out of three
said they were against it. I said, well, I'm no expert, but
seein' as how the people have already spoken, maybe the
problem is that some folks just aren't listenin.

[*ACR* (Com Ed representative) voice-over]:
Commonwealth Edison. We're there when you need us.

Com Ed also ran a very interesting "Windmill/New" television spot
that sought to persuade the public that the city's "take over" campaign
would cause Chicago to abandon an era of progress and prosperity
(fueled by Com Ed's power) and to enter an era of risk, decay, and
declining expectations (all because the city was going to force people to
use untrustworthy technologies). The ad contained twelve separate
scenes. The first seven displayed the beauty of downtown Chicago at
night, illuminated by electric lights. With music in the background, an
offscreen narrator said, "Every hour of every day . . . Commonwealth
Edison works to keep down . . . the cost of the electricity we produce.
. . . We'll even go outside Illinois for energy. . . . If we can get it for you
at a better price." Then the scene suddenly shifted to the upper three
stories of an older apartment building. On the roof was a rather old-
looking windmill. The lights in the three rooms directly below the
windmill were off in the first scene, then on, then off, then on, then off.
Again offscreen, the narrator said, "The fact is, more reliable . . . more
economical . . . electricity . . . would be hard to come by . . . even if you
made it yourself." Superimposed over the windmill in the last scene were
the words "Commonwealth Edison We're There When You Need Us."

It is ironic that Com Ed chose to use the image of decaying inner-
city apartments to convey what would happen *if* the city took over the
power system. That decay was not something that would happen. It had
already happened . . . during the time that Com Ed had been managing

the electric power system! Equally ironic is the contrast between Com Ed's effort to define itself as the local expert in electric power and its choice not to back up its specific claims with credible, publicly available technical analysis. Given Com Ed's self-portrait, one would have expected it to release technical studies to counter, indeed, overwhelm, the city-sponsored Beck Report. To the best of my knowledge, however, Com Ed did not publicly reveal any such report.[7]

Though it did not make its own technical studies available for public critique, Com Ed did—through its advocacy advertising—identify several potentially important objections to the city's review of options. It claimed that (1) Chicago consumers would be *required* to invest in conservation and reduce their consumption of electric power; (2) the city did not know where it would obtain long-term replacement power; (3) there was not enough existing transmission capacity to carry the needed replacement power; (4) the company's "rate freeze alternative" (see note 5) would be cheaper than the city's buyout options; and (5) the city's options would generally lead to higher taxes, higher rates, less reliability, delivery bottlenecks, and so on. By not placing its studies in the public record, though, Com Ed opened itself up to the charge that its objections lacked any firm basis and were nothing more than an effort to limit the planning agenda to those few alternatives that were acceptable to the utility.

Com Ed's advertisements passionately attacked the "few activists and bureaucrats" and "extremists" who were promoting a "take over of your electric system." Whether "extremists" or not, several local organizations denounced Com Ed and pressed the city to continue its exploration. In a variety of newsletters, public reports, and public demonstrations, these groups consistently portrayed themselves as nonprofit, nonpartisan, citizen-based organizations that wanted to "educate" the public about Com Ed's mismanagement and about the need to achieve fundamental changes in how electric power and other services are produced and delivered in the Chicago area (Chicago Electric Options Campaign [CEOC] 1989; Fremon 1988; Hellwig 1989; Nuclear Energy Information Service [NEIS] 1988).

Initially, these groups acted separately, and they still do to some extent. In late 1987, however, twelve organizations (including CUB, IPAC, ONE, CNT, and NEIS) created a coalition called the Chicago Electric Options Campaign (CEOC). One of the campaign's first actions was to sponsor referenda concerning the city's exploration. "We chose this tactic," said organizer Josh Hoyt, "because politicians only understand two things. . . . Dollars and votes. . . . When you go door to door, you talk their language" (Burleigh 1989, p. 3). After collecting five thousand signatures in support, the following nonbinding referendum was placed on the March 1988 ballot in the Forty-Seventh Ward: "Should the City of Chicago actively pursue all options which would give residents and business cheaper electric rates, including the possibility of ending the Commonwealth Edison monopoly?" The vote showed 8,050 in favor and 1,884 against. Eight months later, CEOC members placed similar questions on ballots in fifteen more wards. More than 111,000 voters supported the pursuit of options; only about 18,000 opposed it (Hellwig 1989).

The CEOC and other members of the coalition claimed that Com Ed was disseminating erroneous and misleading information. In one of its newsletters, for example, NEIS (1988, p. 2) claimed that Com Ed's aggressive $630,000 advertising campaign (at the ratepayer's expense) constituted "deliberate deceptions designed to mislead the public." In a report to consumers, David Fremon (1988, p. 2) of the Chicago 1992 Committee charged that Com Ed was a "utility octopus whose main concern is providing its stockholders maximum profits" and that "Com Ed scaremongers" and "peddlers of panic" were trying to maintain Com Ed's "stranglehold" and "smokescreen the other options available to the city short of complete takeover." Most importantly, Fremon implied that U.S. Congressman Dan Rostenkowski, chairman of the House Ways and Means Committee, was in Com Ed's hip pocket. "How else," wrote Fremon (1988, pp. 18, 25), "can one explain his sponsorship of a bill [which prohibits the use of tax-exempt municipal bonds to buy out existing utilities] whose sole effect was to cripple the city in its negotiations with Commonwealth Edison?" At a workshop for potential speakers that it held in April 1989, the CEOC (1989) urged the speakers to remind their audiences that Chicago's citizens had "a DEMOCRATIC RIGHT to explore all the options" and a "once in a lifetime opptny [sic] to change from [the] monopoly squeezing us."

These advocacy organizations believed (or assumed) that the large recent increases in Com Ed's electric power rates were due to Com Ed mismanagement, particularly its rapid shift to nuclear power and its noticeable lack of enthusiasm for energy conservation and alternative sources of electric power. Com Ed's rates were indeed high, but to the best of my knowledge, none of the neighborhood groups carefully documented the extent to which those rates differed from the national average or from rates charged by similar utilities in similar areas. Conversely, some of these organizations (especially CNT) had significant technical expertise and intimate knowledge of Chicago's neighborhoods and residents, and they wanted to see that knowledge and expertise used. They acted as "political entrepreneurs": by prodding and supporting the city's exploration of options, they created the possibility that the city would turn to them for assistance when implementing a new electric power structure.

Throughout 1989 and 1990, the community coalition continued to pressure the city of Chicago to fully explore its options and to involve the public in that exploration. Whether their effort will prove successful is not yet clear. In November 1987, Mayor Washington passed away unexpectedly, thus placing his reform agenda in considerable jeopardy. At first, the new mayor, Eugene Sawyer, continued to follow the broad outlines of Washington's agenda. By late 1988, though, it was no longer clear that the Washington agenda would survive his death (Moberg 1988). After considerable political jockeying for position, Richard M. Daley became mayor in the spring of 1989. The new mayor said little about the franchise, kept a much tighter rein on city-sponsored research, and shifted responsibility for the city's exploration of options away from the department's energy planners. To the pleasure of the CEOC and other community groups, Mayor Daley and the city council in late December 1989 quietly notified Com Ed of the city's intent to terminate the franchise. However, he seemed to be far less interested in "exploring options" than he was in renegotiating the franchise. His administration spent the first eight months of 1990 negotiating with the utility over the specifications of a new franchise then, in August 1990, agreed to a one-year extension. Though the situation might still change, Com Ed continues to supply power to the city of Chicago and its residents.

Discussion and Conclusion

I began this chapter by arguing that rhetoric is an important part of planning but that it should not be construed exclusively to mean the use of style to manipulate others. I suggested that Modernist planners are "antirhetoricians" who seek to guide development on the basis of the best available scientific facts, theories, and models and who explicitly deny any need to persuade others. I then presented an alternative framework, one that recognizes that planners are embedded in a complex rhetorical situation involving three primary audiences—scientists, politicians, and lay advocates—each of which can be thought of as an "interpretive community" engaged in a "normal discourse." Interaction with those diverse audiences causes planners to engage in a hermeneutic dialogue that leads to new forms of normal discourse: policy analysis, advocacy planning, and political entrepreneurship. Claiming that each of these blended rhetorics expressed conceptual ambiguities and ethical tensions, I proposed that planners should seek to "actively mediate" the discourse among the rhetorics of passion, reason, and power. To assess the practical viability and implications of active mediation, I investigated the rhetorics of electric power planning in Chicago.

The story is not yet closed on this particular project, so the results discussed in this concluding section should be considered tentative. Notwithstanding this caveat, some important conclusions can be presented. First, the Chicago electric power planning case amply supports the claim that rhetoric is an extremely important part of planning. Modernist planning—in the "antirhetorical" sense of trying to plan the city's electric power future purely on the basis of the best available scientific facts, theories, and models—simply disappeared. In its place, we find a deeply rhetorical version of planning. Throughout the Chicago case, we see actors using diverse planning rhetorics to persuade others to adopt their definition of the problem and their view of the range of possible solutions and to mobilize potential supporters of preferred alternatives. Let me explain.

Chicago's exploration of options began in the context of the "agreed-upon conventions" of public utility economics. Of course, much of that discourse took place within scientific journals and was not directly or immediately relevant to electric power planning in the Chicago area. However, much of that discourse also occurred in Illinois Commerce Commission—the ICC—hearings. There, policy analytic planners attempted to persuade ICC commissioners in terms of the agreed-upon conventions of public utility planning and regulation. Though the city's planners continued to participate in relevant ICC hearings, Mayor Washington set aside those agreed-upon conventions when he decided to investigate alternatives to remaining on Com Ed's system. By doing so he moved electric power planning in the Chicago area into an "abnormal discourse."

The Beck Report initiated that "abnormal disclosure." By adopting a somber and passive style, and by relying heavily on the rhetoric of public utility economics, Beck and Associates conveyed the impression of having conducted an objective, scientific study. This "antirhetorical" stance enabled Beck and Associates to persuade the city that it had conducted a technically sound study. It also supported the city's effort to persuade elected officials and the public at large that establishment of a new electric power structure would be in the best interests of the city and its residents. The Beck Report's claim to be "scientific" or "objective" (in the sense of being value neutral) was, of course, quickly challenged.

Setting aside the policy analytic rhetoric and conventions of the Beck Report, Com Ed responded with the rhetorical conventions provided by the normal discourse of advocacy. Denigrating its opponents as "bureaucrats and activists" who wanted to "take over your electric power system" and throw the Chicago region into an era of economic decay, and relying heavily on provocative symbolism (such as the windmill on the dilapidated apartment), Com Ed sought to manipulate the opinions of vast numbers of voters and consumers through an expensive barrage of advertising.

Com Ed's advertising blitz led its opponents to respond, partly as advocates and partly as political entrepreneurs. They tried to sway the hearts of those same voters and consumers with claims that Com Ed was a "utility octopus" whose "scaremongers" and "peddlers of panic" were keeping the people of Chicago in the utility's "stranglehold." They also acted as political entrepreneurs, trying through the CEOC's referendum and related efforts to mobilize political support for the city's exploration of options.

This disappearance of Modernist, "scientific" planning, and its replacement by an interaction of the rhetorics of passion, reason, and power, could be interpreted as just another retelling of the old story about how "planning" always loses out to "politics." According to this view, technical analysis on the basis of public utility economics in "real planning" and the advertisements, press releases, demonstrations, referenda, and so on, are "downstream," part of the politics of adoption and implementation. Such a Modernist interpretation would be precisely the wrong one to make. Planning in the "scientific" sense disappeared from the Chicago story precisely because it is only one part of a rhetorically complex concept and activity. Planning is not simply good technique. It is also passionate argument over rights and political efficacy. Accordingly, I want to argue that the Chicago story shows that planning is inherently an "abnormal discourse," a discourse that is always scientific, political, and normative. "Scientific" planning did not "disappear," it was part of the abnormal discourse that is planning.

So, let us now take as a given the claim that planning is a deeply rhetorical activity. What does such a claim imply for planners and for what planners should do, that is, for planning ethics? The first thing to note about this question is that "plans" (in the sense of professionals who occupy jobs labeled "planner") seemed to fall out of (or disappear from) the Chicago story as much as Modernist, scientific planners did. The exploration of options (planning) was deeply affected by diverse actors, none of whom (with one notable exception) were educated as planners or occupied jobs formally labeled "planner."

The one exception, about whom I have said very little up to this point, deserves special attention. Recall that Mayor Washington asked the city's Planning Department to conduct a one to two-year study of the city's electric power options. That task was assigned to a small group of energy planners in the department. Those planners did not try to prepare a "scientific" analysis of the city's options—they sponsored the Beck analysis—nor did those planners try to identify some broad set of goals and objectives that all Chicagoans could agree to. They allied themselves with the energy efficiency and economic justice objectives favored by the community and consumer groups. Nor did they act as sterilized laboratory technicians who wanted to avoid contamination by the dirty world of politics. They identified themselves with Mayor Washington's political agenda and sought to both influence it and help bring it to fruition. The city's planners, in other words, drew upon Beck's policy analytic research (which in turn was based in part on the "scientific" electric power planning literature), promoted the values and interests of energy conservation and neighborhood development groups, and were part of Mayor Washington's pragmatic reform agenda.

I want to suggest that the department's planners did not act as scientists, advocates, or politicians; nor did they act as policy analysts, advocacy planners, or political entrepreneurs. Rather, they sought to link Mayor Washington, the community coalition, and energy scientists by "mediating" (that is, understanding and then translating) their diverse rhetorics. However, they did not mediate in a neutral fashion, as if they did not care what the city did with regard to the Com Ed franchise. They "actively" mediated the discourses: they personally identified with the mayor's pragmatic but progressive reform agenda; they agreed with the community coalition's desire to encourage energy conservation and local empowerment; and they knew enough about the technical literature on electric power planning to stick within the realm of the possible.[8] The department's energy planners did not, therefore, try to achieve some grand synthesis. They acknowledged that the claims each actor made were legitimate and worthy of consideration, but in order to ensure that each claim was fairly considered, they had to place Com Ed's interests on the periphery and to support the advocacy coalition that Com Ed sought to delegitimize.

The city's planners "actively mediated" the discourse among the diverse planning rhetorics at play in the city's exploration of electric power options. How might their actions be characterized in terms of planning ethics? To answer this question, I draw heavily on Elizabeth Howe's (1990) article about normative ethics in planning. She creates a fourfold typology of normative theories concerning planning ethics: act-deontological, rule-deontological, act-teleological, and rule-teleological, and then she observes that the presence of these four theories produces "ethical pluralism" in planning. "Each group thinks its own perspective is obvious," she says, "and that of the others is basically flawed. Each can justify its position, but neither can convince the other" (Howe 1990, p. 128).

Using Howe's terminology, we could characterize the rhetoric of the scientist and the politician as being teleological, that is, concerned with the goodness (or utility) of an act's consequences. Scientists (public utility economists, for example) seek to predict or explain likely consequences. Similarly, we could characterize the rhetoric of the advocate as being deontological, that is, concerned not with consequences of action but with the rightness of the acts themselves. Com Ed, for instance, stressed the rights associated with ownership: it characterized the Beck study as part of the city's effort to "take over" its electric power system. Conversely, the community coalition stressed the democratic right to have a say in what the city did. So, drawing on Howe's article, we can conclude that when planners speak the rhetorics of science or politics, they are also speaking in terms of teleological or consequentialist ethics; when they speak the rhetoric of advocacy, they are also speaking in terms of deontological ethics.

What then of the department's planners who tried to "actively mediate" among the diverse rhetorics? What ethical theory were they articulating? My sense is that such a planner could be characterized, again in Howe's terms, as "a moral agent balancing a number of ethical principles" (Howe 1990, p. 147) in specific places (Chicago) at specific times (1985–88) on specific issues (an exploration of electric power options) in a context of rhetorical and ethical pluralism. The planner who actively mediates is concerned with trying to "do good," "be right," and "get things done" and rejects the notion that a planner can objectively determine what is right and wrong or objectively calculate the good and bad consequences of alternative courses of action. Conversely, such a planner would also reject the notion that "right" and "good" are purely relative concepts. The notion of "active mediation" in a context of rhetorical and ethical pluralism rests not on objectivity and relativism but between them. It does so by requiring planners to discursively redeem their acts, at least in principle, before relevant audiences or, as Sissela Bok puts it, through "public arguments capable of convincing reasonable people" (Howe 1990, p. 145).

We find, therefore, that the city of Chicago's exploration of options proceeded in a context of rhetorical and ethical pluralism and that a small number of the city's energy planners tried to actively mediate the discourses between and among the diverse rhetorical communities involved in that exploration. This finding strongly reinforces the claim that rhetoric (in the deep sense of persuasive discourse within and between interpretive communities) is an extremely important part of planning; indeed, that rhetoric should be thought of as a defining characteristic of planning practice. The Chicago case also lends support to the claim that for planning to be meaningfully effective, someone has to "actively mediate" among the diverse discourses of passion, reason, and power and that such active mediation involves—from an ethical point of view—acting as a moral agent who balances a number of ethical principles in a local context of rhetorical and ethical pluralism. How and whether such a heavy burden can be sustained over a long period of time are questions that need attention.[9]

Notes

1. Not all planning is performed by professional planners (Dalton 1988). Accordingly, I distinguish between "planners" (any person who is engaged in a conscious social effort to guide change) and "professional planners" (any person who is formally trained or employed as a planner).

2. Michael P. Brooks (1988, p. 241) reminds us of the first when he appeals for "a return to the utopian, visionary, reformist spirit that previously fueled the profession" and claims that we bear "critical responsibilities . . . for the well-being of all who reside in the communities we purport to serve" (Brooks 1988, p. 246). Charles Hoch (1984) reminds us of the importance of both passion and reason when he writes that planning involves "doing good" and "being right." Bruce McClendon and Ray Quay (1987) and William Lucy (1988) remind us that to "master change" (get things done) we have to be "close to power."

3. This chapter should not be interpreted as an empiricist effort to verify or falsify a scientific model of electric power planning. Rather, it can best be thought of as an effort to develop a more sophisticated, and perhaps more helpful, understanding of the complexity of planning practice and of how rhetoric fits into (and helps shape) that practice.

4. This discussion focuses primarily on the period from mid-1985 through early 1988.

5. Seeking the desired rate increase, Com Ed proposed in December 1986 an "innovative rate freeze plan" that would raise rates 13 percent in 1987 and then freeze the rates for the next five years. Though supported by Governor James B. Thompson, Attorney General Neil F. Hartigan, and Cook County State's Attorney Richard M. Daley, this proposal was rejected by the ICC in September 1987. Com Ed subsequently asked the ICC to approve a 27 percent rate increase. That case has not yet been resolved (see Throgmorton 1990b).

6. John Hogan (1986), director of Com Ed's Communication Services Department, implies that Com Ed executives expect politicians to bluster in public (in order to obtain public support) but wheel and deal in private, all the time trying to enhance their personal wealth and power.

7. Com Ed did hire a Chicago-based consulting firm, Planmetrics, to analyze the Beck Report. Howard Axelrod, vice president of the firm, reportedly said that "My advice to the city of Chicago . . . would be to put the Beck study on the shelf and cut your losses" (Richards 1987b). However, Com Ed has not yet made Planmetrics's work available for public inspection.

8. The department's energy planners continued to play this role until the Daley administration came into office. In late 1989, the new mayor put a new planner in charge who was expected to help the city "renegotiate the franchise" as a policy analyst, rather than help the city "explore options" as an active mediator. The energy planners formally in charge of the exploration were assigned technical tasks pertaining to energy conservation (Williams 1990).

9. I wish to thank the people who reviewed and critiqued the earlier version of this chapter that was published in the *Journal of Architectural and Planning Research*. Of special note are John Forester of Cornell University, Charles Hoch of the University of Illinois at Chicago, members of the University of Iowa's project on the Rhetoric of Inquiry, and three anonymous reviewers. Work on the paper was supported in part by the National Science Foundation's Ethics and Values Studies branch, and I am grateful for its support. I also wish to acknowledge the support services provided by University House, the center for advanced study at the University of Iowa. This project was not undertaken by or on behalf of the foundation or any other agency of the U.S. government.

Bibliography

Anonymous. 1987. Talking points for Mayor Harold Washington on electric power options study. November 4.

Baum, H. S. 1983. *Planners and public expectations*. Cambridge: Schenkman Publishing.

Bazerman, C. 1988. *Shaping written knowledge: the genre and activity of the experimental article in science*. Madison: University of Wisconsin Press.

Beck, R. W. and Associates. 1987. *Electric supply options study*. Prepared for the City of Chicago, Department of Planning. Indianapolis: R. W. Beck and Associates.

Bernstein, R. 1983. *Beyond objectivism and relativism: science, hermeneutics, and praxis*. Philadelphia: University of Pennsylvania Press.

Biddle, F. M. 1985. Edison may leave if city pulls plug. *Chicago Tribune* October 14. Section 4, p. 3.

Brooks, M. P. 1988. Four critical junctures in the history of the urban planning profession: an exercise in hindsight. *Journal of the American Planning Association* 54, 241–248.

Burleigh, N. 1989. Power plays: the public relations battle between community organizers and Commonwealth Edison. *Neighborhood News* January 13. p. 3.

Chicago Department of Planning. 1987. *Electric power options for Chicago: an overview*. Chicago: Department of Planning.

Chicago Electric Options Campaign. 1989. Notes for neighborhood presentations. April 14.

Commonwealth Edison. 1987. *City buyout of Edison would be costly, unreliable, analysis shows*. Chicago: Commonwealth Edison.

————. 1988a. *1987 Annual Report*. Chicago: Commonwealth Edison.

————. 1988b. *Candle, candle, burning bright, could be Chicago every night*. Chicago: Commonwealth Edison.

Dalton, L. C. 1988. Emerging knowledge about planning practice. Paper delivered at the thirtieth annual conference of the Association of Collegiate Schools of Planning, October 27–30, Buffalo, New York.

Davidoff, P. 1965. Advocacy and pluralism in planning. *Journal of the American Institute of Planning* 31, 331–337.

Feld, M. M. 1989. The Yonkers case and its implications for the teaching and practice of planning. *Journal of Planning Education and Research* 8, 169–175.

Fenno, R., Jr., 1978. *Home style: house members in their districts*. Boston: Little, Brown.

Fish, S. 1979. *Is there a text in this class? The authority of interpretive communities*. Cambridge: Harvard University Press.

Forester, J. 1989. *Planning in the face of power*. Berkeley: University of California Press.

Fremon, D. 1988. *Commonwealth Edison: a consumer's report*. Chicago: Chicago 1992 Committee.

Friedmann, J. 1987. *Planning in the public domain: from knowledge to action*. Princeton, NJ: Princeton University Press.

Hellwig, M. 1989. Consumer advocate urges: "Look at all options." *ONE CITY* January/February: 5.

Hill, E. W. 1989. Yonkers' planners acted ethically: its citizens and politicians acted illegally. *Journal of Planning Education and Research* 8, 183–187.

Hoch, C. 1984. Doing good and being right: the pragmatic connection in planning theory. *Journal of the American Planning Association* 50, 335–345.

Hogan, J. 1986. *A spirit capable: the story of Commonwealth Edison*. Chicago: Mobium Press.

Howe, E. 1980. Role choices of urban planners. *Journal of the American Planning Association* 46, 398–409.

————. 1990. Normative ethics in planning. *Journal of Planning Literature* 5, 123–150.

Hyman, L. S. 1988. *America's electric utilities: past, present and future*. 3d ed. Arlington, VA: Public Utilities Reports.

Jenkins-Smith, H. C. 1982. Professional roles for policy analysts. *Journal of Policy Analysis and Management* 2, 86–99.

Joskow, P. L. and Schmalensee, R. 1983. *Markets for power: an analysis of electric utility deregulation*. Cambridge: MIT Press.

Kahn, E. 1988. *Electric utility planning and regulation.* Washington, DC: American Council for an Energy-Efficient Economy.

Levine, A. 1982. *Love Canal: science, politics, and people.* Toronto: D.C. Heath.

Lindblom, C. 1980. *The policy-making process.* Englewood Cliffs, NJ: Prentice Hall.

Lindblom, C. and Cohen, D. 1979. *Usable knowledge.* New Haven, CT: Yale University Press.

Lucy, W. 1988. *Close to power: setting priorities with elected officials.* Washington, DC: American Planning Association.

McClendon, B. W. and Quay, R. 1987. *Mastering change: winning strategies for effective city planning.* Chicago: American Planning Association, Planners Press.

McCloskey, D. N. 1985. *The rhetoric of economics.* Madison: University of Wisconsin Press.

McGee, M. C. and Lyne, J. R. 1987. What are nice folks like you doing in a place like this? Some entailments of treating knowledge claims rhetorically. In Nelson, J. S., Megill, A. and McCloskey, D. N., eds. *The rhetoric of the human sciences: language and argument in scholarship and public affairs.* Madison: University of Wisconsin Press, 381–406.

MacIntyre, A. 1988. *Whose justice? Which rationality?* Notre Dame, IN: University of Notre Dame Press.

Majone, G. 1989. *Evidence, argument, and persuasion in the policy process.* New Haven, CT: Yale University Press.

Matthews, C. 1988. *Hardball: how politics is played, told by one who knows the game.* New York: Harper and Row.

Meltsner, A. 1976. *Policy analysts in the bureaucracy.* Berkeley: University of California Press.

Moberg, D. 1988. One year without Washington: What did he accomplish? How long will it last? *The Reader* 18 p. 1.

Mollenkopf, J. H. 1983. *The contested city.* Princeton, NJ: Princeton University Press.

Nelson, J. S. and Megill, A. 1986. Rhetoric of inquiry: projects and prospects. *Quarterly Journal of Speech* 72, 20–37.

Nelson, J., Megill, A., and McCloskey, D. 1987. *The rhetoric of the human sciences.* Madison: University of Wisconsin Press.

Nuclear Energy Information Service. 1988. Com Ed ads—an exercise in deception? *NEIS News* January. p. 1.

Rabinovitz, F. 1969. *City politics and planning.* New York: Atherton Press.

Richards, B. 1987a. High electric rates are hindering Chicago's rebound. *Wall Street Journal* September 21. p. 6.

———. 1987b. Chicago mulls plan to cut electric rates by buying or bypassing utility's plants. *Wall Street Journal* November 5. p. 45.

Rorty, R. 1979. *Philosophy and the mirror of nature.* Princeton, NJ: Princeton University Press.

Rudolph, R. and Ridley, S. 1986. *Power struggle: the hundred year war over electricity.* New York: Harper and Row.

Squires, G. D., Bennet, L., McCourt, K., and Nyden, P. 1987. *Chicago: race, class, and the response to urban decline*. Philadelphia: Temple University Press.

Stewart, C., Smith, C., and Denton, R., Jr. 1984. *Persuasion and social movements*. Prospect Heights, IL: Waveland Press.

Stokey, E. and Zeckhauser, R. 1978. *A primer for policy analysis*. New York: W. W. Norton.

Throgmorton, J. A. 1989. Synthesizing politics, rationality, and advocacy: energy policy analysis for minority groups. *Policy Studies Review* 8, 300–321.

———. 1990a. The rhetorics of policy analysis. *Policy Sciences* 24, 153–180.

———. 1990b. Revealing deals: electric power ratemaking in the Chicago area, 1985–1990. Draft manuscript submitted to the *Journal of Policy Analysis and Management*.

———. 1993. Planning as a rhetorical activity: survey research as a trope in arguments about electric power. *Journal of the American Planning Association* 59, 334–346.

Wildavsky, A. 1979. *Speaking truth to power: the art and craft of policy analysis*. New Brunswick, NJ: Transaction Books.

Williams, C. W. 1990. Personal interview with author in Chicago, April 19 and 20.

Ziemba, S. 1986. Edison rates may cut jobs. *Chicago Tribune*, Section 1, page 1.

Ziman, J. 1984. *An introduction to science studies: the philosophical and social aspects of science and technology*. Cambridge: Cambridge University Press.

MARCIA MARKER FELD

11 Education Planning: Ethical Dilemmas Arising in Public Policy Decision Making

Introduction

AN ETHICAL FRAMEWORK

For more than two decades, during the 1960s and 1970s, the most important battle against racism in the United States concerned school desegregation. It is still a source of national tension. Planners have remained out of this battle, partly because it was outside of the scope of their work. Comprehensive planning, as usually practiced in the United States, has simply ignored decisions that have affected schools, their

This chapter represents an expanded version of Marcia Marker Feld, "Preface," "The Yonkers case and its implications for the teaching and practice of planning," and "Reprise," *Journal of Planning Education and Research* 8, 3 (1989), 167–168, 169–175, 195–196. This material is included here with permission of the *Journal of Planning Education and Research.*
    Some content is also taken from Marcia Marker Feld and John D. Hohman, Jr., "Planning leadership: a tale of two cities," *Journal of the American Planning Association* 55, 4 (1989), 479–481, and Marcia Marker Feld, "Planners guilty on two counts: the city of Yonkers case," *Journal of the American Planning Association* 52, 4 (1986), 387–388. This material is reprinted with permission of the *Journal of the American Planning Association.*

construction and location, and their place in the mix of government services. These complex dynamics of communities helped create school segregation in the first place; the planning profession, however, has lost sight of that fact, taking the attitude that school planning is not the business of city planners. Instead, planners seem to have adhered to the notion that the effect of neighborhood segregation on schools is an unintended outcome of unrelated circumstances. The political separation of school districts from the city government—where planners traditionally are located—has reinforced that ideology, but even in dealing with issues where planning has usually been involved, the housing field, planners have promoted or acceded to housing and transportation plans that resulted in segregated patterns of housing (Feld 1986).

A few planners have spoken out on the implications of housing location decisions for de facto segregation of schools. Paul Davidoff, writing in the late 1960s, described how government-supported construction of segregated housing was widening the gulf between white and black residents (Davidoff et al. 1970). A decade later, Gary Orfield examined the connection between housing policy decisions and the racial isolation of students in the public schools (Orfield 1981, 1983). Nonetheless, the effects of public housing, land use, and transportation policy on school segregation have been largely ignored by city planning practitioners and academics alike. School administrators and city planners generally have paid little attention to each other—to the detriment of American cities and suburbs and their inhabitants. Despite the often-stated commitment to comprehensive planning of professional planners and academics, and the call to social justice and equal access that is articulated in the American Institute of Certified Planners (AICP) *Code of Ethics,* the planners and the public decision process that they influence fail, often deliberately, to meet these ethical commitments (American Institute of Certified Planners [AICP] 1991; American Planning Association [APA] 1987).

This documented practice of unethical decision making by the planners in Yonkers, New York, suggests a need for planners to focus on issues of professional ethical decision making in potentially hostile practice environments. The purpose of this chapter is to discuss the Yonkers case and shed light on ethical questions regarding the planner's role in promoting social equity.

THE CITY OF YONKERS AND ITS PLANNERS: A CRITIQUE

In 1985, a court decision was handed down that highlighted this situation and demanded corrective action. Judge Leonard B. Sands of the U.S. District Court for the Southern District of New York (SDNY), in *United States v. City of Yonkers et al.* (Southern District of New York [SDNY] 1985), found a causal relationship between the segregation of housing and the segregation of schools in the city of Yonkers, New York. Judge Sands found that segregation in both housing and schools was brought about by the policy decisions of federal, state, local, and school system agencies, sometimes separately and sometimes in collusion.

Since the enactment of the National Housing Act of 1949, as Judge Sands's massive 665-page opinion meticulously documents, actions by federal and local agencies[1] have deliberately located public housing in one area of Yonkers: the heavily minority-occupied downtown neighborhood of southwest Yonkers. Of the twenty-seven family housing projects approved by the political and planning processes in Yonkers, all but one were located in the southwest neighborhood. Through minutes of meetings, official memoranda, correspondence, and public hearing transcripts, the court established racial bias intent. The criterion used by Yonkers and, particularly, the Yonkers Planning Department for determining public housing sites—"political feasibility"—helped to create and maintain a pattern of segregated housing that, in turn, supported the local school board in intentionally creating and maintaining racial segregation in the public schools.

In this situation, as in many—albeit undocumented—others, planners were confronted with explicit calls for community-based comprehensive planning in their role as professional planners. The problem in Yonkers was not that planning failed in the attempt to prevent or remedy racial discrimination but that planning methods were applied in order to achieve discriminatory results. The relationship between housing patterns and school segregation is evident and policy driven (Dimond 1984). Even though municipal elected and staff officials, officials of the U.S. Department of Housing and Urban Development (HUD), and officials of the New York State Urban Development Corporation (UDC) knew of the widely acknowledged negative economic and social effects of concentrating subsidized housing in one area, these location decisions prevailed. Racial discrimination had a chronic and pervasive influence on the decision process. If it had not been for the configuration of public housing that resulted, Judge Sands concluded, the racial mix of students in public schools would have been distinctly different.

The planners in Yonkers were guilty on two counts, as shown in the forty-year history of planning in their city. First, the planning process was not truly comprehensive since it did not include schools, thereby omitting a critical element of community life. Second, Yonkers planners ignored both the notion of redistributive justice and social equity demanded in the Brown decision in 1954[2] and the planning profession's commitment to equal opportunity espoused in the AICP *Code of Ethics*. The ethical principles prescribed in the *Code of Ethics*— including serving the public interest; supporting citizen participation in the planning process; recognizing the comprehensive and long-range nature of planning decisions; and expanding choice and opportunity for all persons—were either ignored or subverted by the planners and elected officials.

The History of the Yonkers Case

BACKGROUND

In 1980, the Yonkers branch of the National Association for the Advancement of Colored People (NAACP) filed a complaint with the U.S. Department of Justice stating that there was deliberate segregation of public housing projects and therefore segregation of the public school system. Responding to this complaint, the U.S. Department of Justice filed a suit against the city of Yonkers, the Yonkers Board of Education, and the Yonkers Community Development Agency, charging the city with deliberately segregating its public housing and schools. In November 1985, a decision by Judge Sands of the U.S. District Court for the SDNY found the city of Yonkers guilty of intentionally segregating its public housing and schools and of enacting policies that maintained racial segregation within the borders of the city. An appeal of this decision was denied by the U.S. Court of Appeals for the Second Circuit on December 28, 1987. On June 14, 1988, the U.S. Supreme Court, without recorded dissent, refused to hear an appeal of the 1985 ruling. The political decision-making bodies of Yonkers were found guilty and were mandated to remedy the situation by desegregating the public schools and by locating new public housing in other neighborhoods of the city. The discussion that follows charts the decisions taken by the officials concerning the location of public housing.[3]

THE DEMOGRAPHICS OF YONKERS

Yonkers consists of three distinct geographical areas. East Yonkers has been a middle- and upper-class residential area. Northwest Yonkers has served as a middle ground between low- and middle-income people. Southwest Yonkers contains the original central business district (CBD) and the city's least expensive housing. As a result, it serves a large number of low-income and minority people.

Yonkers, on the northern border of New York City, covers some twenty square miles (5,180 hectares) and borders on the Hudson River. The 1980 population was 195,331, which reflects a 4 percent decrease over the previous decade.

The city's population has changed significantly since World War II, particularly between 1960 and 1980. The minority population increased by almost 325 percent and has been concentrated in the southwestern section of the city. The white population has resided in the eastern and northwestern parts of the city. Spatial segregation is pronounced, as illustrated by the 1980 census data showing southwest Yonkers with 37.5 percent of the city's total population but more than 80 percent of the city's total minority population.

Several residential and economic factors have led to this distribution of racial groups. Both the northwestern and eastern sections of the city are middle- and upper-income suburban neighborhoods with spacious, well-maintained single-family homes. These neighborhoods are served by shopping centers and are interspersed with apartment complexes. By contrast, the southwestern section of Yonkers is characterized by poorly maintained housing. There are old and poorly kept pre–World War II walk-ups and stark, crime-ridden high-rise apartment buildings. Southwestern Yonkers also contains Getty Square, the city's CBD, which fell victim to the successful suburban malls in eastern Yonkers and surrounding communities. Economic conditions in southwestern Yonkers have deteriorated since 1950, and, despite urban renewal efforts, the area continues to succumb to the pressures of suburban retail centers, as well as internal problems such as crime, unemployment, and economic stagnation. These conditions have changed the employment patterns of Yonkers residents. For instance, only 31 percent of the working population works in Yonkers.

As the minority population citywide grew from 2.9 percent in 1940 to 18.8 percent in 1980, the concentration of minorities in southwest Yonkers also increased (Table 11-1).

The location of low-income subsidized housing corresponds to the concentrations of minority residents. By 1982, the city had 6,800 units of subsidized housing; of these, 6,566 units (96.6 percent) were located in southwest Yonkers. Only two subsidized housing projects were not in a southwest Yonkers neighborhood, one a family project located in a black enclave, Runyon Heights, and the other a mostly white senior citizen project in east Yonkers.

TABLE 11-1

Increasing Minority Population in Southwest Yonkers

Year	Percent Minority	Percent Minority in Southwest	Percent Minority Outside Southwest
1940	2.9	3.5	2.0
1950	3.2	4.5	1.6
1960	4.5	6.7	2.8
1970	10.2	19.8	3.9
1980	18.8	40.4	5.8

KEY ACTORS

Many persons and organizations participated in the decision-making processes for the development and location of public and subsidized housing in Yonkers between 1949 and 1982 (Table 11-2). Yonkers's governing body was its city council, consisting of the mayor, elected in a citywide election, and twelve councillors, each elected from one of the city's twelve wards. Mayors Alfred D. Del Bello and Angelo Martinelli played key roles in establishing policies that maintained the siting of low-income housing in southwest Yonkers. They served successive terms during the late 1960s and 1970s, a period during which much of the illegal siting took place.

The Department of Development (DOD) was established in 1971 with jurisdiction over three offices: the Planning Bureau (called the Planning Department until 1971), the Community Development Agency (CDA), and the Bureau of Housing and Buildings. The administrator of DOD was charged with coordinating and administering community development activities within Yonkers. The DOD was the first contact point for individuals and firms with proposals for development. Morton Yulish became director in 1971 and served until 1974. He was succeeded by Alphons Yost, who served until 1980.

The Planning Bureau served as the technical support to the Planning Board. Philip Pistone served as the director of the Planning Bureau for thirty years.

Other key organizations included the Planning Board, consisting of seven unpaid citizens appointed by the mayor, and the Municipal Housing Authority (MHA), a public corporation organized in the 1930s pursuant to the New York State Public Housing Law. The MHA was the entity authorized to propose, construct, and operate public housing.

The Yonkers Urban Renewal Agency (YURA) operated from 1964 to 1971. It was authorized to coordinate and implement various federal and state-assisted urban renewal projects. It had a five-member board consisting of the city manager, the mayor, the corporation counsel, the city comptroller, and the planning director. The Community Development Agency (CDA) replaced YURA in 1971. When this change took place, the board was expanded to include two community members appointed by the mayor and approved by the city council. CDA was named, along with the city of Yonkers and HUD, as a codefendant in the housing portion of the case.

The plaintiffs contended that the housing practices of the city were designed in part to achieve and preserve segregation in area schools. They sought to show that the city had helped to maintain such segregation through mayoral appointments to the CDA of people known to advocate preservation of the segregated neighborhoods and neighborhood schools.

The evidence showed that several of the key actors acted in concert to encourage and maintain racial segregation. The city council frequently voted against MHA proposals for public housing in certain council members' wards, particularly those in eastern and northwestern Yonkers, due to public outcry from residents of white majority neighborhoods. Under state law, federal funding could not be requested for a site proposed by MHA until the site was either (1) approved by a majority vote of both the planning board and the council or (2) approved by at least three-quarters of the council if less than a majority of the planning board approved. According to the testimony of one member of the council, the opposition by any councillor to a project proposed for his or her own ward was routinely honored by the other council members. This suggests that the desires of the constituents of the council members played a great role in influencing the decision of the city council and that the members of the city council did not adhere to their oaths to maintain equality and justice throughout the city but rather attempted to maintain their livelihoods and popularity with their neighborhood constituents.

THE COURT CASE

In 1980, responding to a complaint filed by the Yonkers branch of the NAACP, the U.S. Department of Justice filed a suit against the city of Yonkers and the Yonkers Board of Education. This court decision, handed down in 1985 (*United States v. City of Yonkers et al.* [SDNY 1985]),

TABLE 11-2
Key Players

Players	Appointed by/ Elected	Responsibilities	Tenure
City Council	Twelve members, elected by ward members plus mayor	All legislative powers, including budget, public programs, and improvements/ use of public land.	
		Approves MHA (Municipal Housing Authority) projects; can override planning board with three-quarters vote	
Mayor	Elected citywide	Appoints agency board members	1960s, 1970s (during much of illegal siting): Alfred D. Del Bello, and Angelo Martinelli
City Manager	Appointed by city council	Administers city government and appoints agency department heads	
Department of Development (DOD)		Oversees Planning Bureau (Planning Department before 1971), Community Development Agency (CDA),	

		and Bureau of Housing and Buildings
		Coordinates and administers community development activities in Yonkers
New York State Urban Development Corporation (UDC)	Formed by state legislature	Catalyst to development; could override local zoning laws and condemn land	1971 to present: Directors: Morton Yulish, 1971–74; Alphons Yost, 1974–80
U.S. Department of Housing and Urban Development (HUD)		Administers federal programs	1968 to present
		Encouraged placement of some but not all relocation housing near urban renewal activities	
		Encouraged (but did not enforce) scattered site housing after 1970	
Local and national interest groups		White majority interest groups vocally opposed location of subsidized housing in their neighborhoods; others (NAACP, League of Women Voters, Urban League) criticized discriminatory decisions	Involved in Yonkers since mid-1960s with application for funds for major project in southwest

TABLE 11-2 (continued)

Key Players

Players	Appointed by/ Elected	Responsibilities	Tenure
Private developers		Targeted southwestern Yonkers for subsidized housing projects due to relative ease of approval	
Planning board	Seven unpaid citizens appointed by mayor	Reviews zoning amendments, capital budget, parking lot locations, exception usages, subdivision plans, urban renewal plans, public housing sites, subsidized housing projects, and MHA projects	
Planning Bureau		Provides technical support to planning board	Director: Philip Pistone
Municipal Housing Authority (MHA)	Appointed by city manager	Proposes, constructs, and operates public housing	1935 to present

Yonkers Urban Renewal Agency (YURA)	1964–1971	Five-member board consisting of city manager, mayor, corporation counsel, city comptroller, and planning director; staff reports to city manager	Coordinates and implements federal- and state-assisted urban renewal projects.
Community Development Agency (CDA)	1971 to present: Director: Alphons Yost	Same as YURA with addition of two citizens appointed by mayor and approved by mayor and city council	Replaced YURA in 1971
Consultants			Surveyed vacant land sites, which were ranked by suitability for subsidized housing; list was abandoned after mayoral election due to public opposition to sites outside southwestern Yonkers
			Subsequent study by different firms recommended redevelopment and location of subsidized housing in southwestern Yonkers

has changed the legal perception of the relationship between school segregation and the location of public housing. In a thoroughly documented opinion, the intimate public policy link between the deliberately segregated site location decisions for public housing by all parties and the deliberately sanctioned segregation of the public schools by a school board has been articulated by Judge Sands, who found a causal relationship between the segregated conditions of the city's housing and its schools. This segregation was brought about by a juxtaposition of policy decisions of federal, state, local, and school agencies, sometimes separately and sometimes in concert. Since the passage of the National Housing Act of 1949, as the opinion discloses, the actions of the federal government, the Yonkers MHA, the city planning board (and its consultants), the Yonkers City Council, the mayor, and the city manager deliberately located badly needed public housing in one area of Yonkers, the heavily minority-occupied downtown neighborhood of southwest Yonkers. Of the twenty-seven housing projects for families approved by the political planning process in Yonkers, all but one were located in the southwest neighborhood. The court established racial intent through the minutes of planning board meetings and city council meetings; memoranda from the planners to HUD, from city officials, and from the mayor; correspondence of citizens groups; and transcripts of public hearings. Yonkers's criterion of "political feasibility" for site location helped to create and maintain a pattern of segregated housing that, in turn, supported the school board's intentionally creating and maintaining racial segregation in the public schools.

Judge Sands held the city of Yonkers housing authority and public school district jointly responsible for the segregation of public schools in Yonkers. Earlier, a third defendant, HUD, separately settled the housing portion of the suit after admitting a "failure to insist" on equitable placement of public housing. The judge found that the city and school officials in Yonkers had "illegally and intentionally" segregated the city's public schools and housing since 1949. Judge Sands ruled that for forty years, Yonkers housing officials located all low-income housing in a mile-and-a-half square (388.5 hectares), mainly nonwhite section of southwestern Yonkers. They, along with the school officials, who gerrymandered attendance zones and school locations, perpetuated discriminatory conditions in their arguments. The defendants contended that "any relationship between the public housing and school segregation was coincidental" (SDNY 1985). School officials argued that they were unable to desegregate the schools in light of the housing pattern imposed on the city.

Conversely, the plaintiffs contended that the city's actions played a significant role in determining the segregated housing pattern and in preserving the eastern and northwestern sections of Yonkers as overwhelmingly white communities. The city's twenty-seven subsidized housing projects stigmatized the southwest as a minority area, thus shaping and maintaining demographic configurations. In deciding for the plaintiff, the court quotes the weight of expert testimony on this point, particularly that of the late Paul Davidoff, planner and lawyer. Identified in the opinion as an expert witness on urban planning, Davidoff testified on behalf of the United States that the location decisions did stigmatize the southwest as a minority area. The court reports that it found his statements persuasive.

The city, in response to the housing component of the case, contended that it did not select sites for public housing on the basis of race and that "any segregative effect which the site selections may have had was entirely unintended" (SDNY 1985).

The court ruled that the city had, in fact, illegally and intentionally created or maintained racial segregation in its public housing and schools. The decision was hailed as a landmark ruling since a federal court accepted the argument that housing and school segregation were causally linked, the first being, in part, responsible for the second. The court found that the actions of responsible city, state, and federal authorities and of the Yonkers school district had created and maintained a segregated school system. The housing policy decisions often caused (and certainly exacerbated) racial segregation in Yonkers. Judge Sands determined that city officials, in response to extreme opposition by communities outside the southwest, effectively transformed a legislative requirement to provide adequate housing and relocation into a mandate to construct as much public housing as possible in the southwest.

EVIDENCE AGAINST THE CITY

In formulating his ruling, Judge Sands cited several recurring patterns that arose from the city's efforts to select sites and construct public housing:

1. The emergence of strong community opposition to proposed subsidized family housing when sites were located in predominantly white eastern Yonkers;
2. The political structure likely to make community opposition unusually effective; and

3. The consistency with which the sites in eastern Yonkers and other heavily white areas that promoted opposition were subsequently rejected, abandoned, or otherwise opposed by city officials.

The court found that planning objectives stated in the local plans and state and federal programs were disregarded or compromised, that the degree to which a proposed site was supported or rejected depended on whether it was in the eastern or western part of the city, and that planning criteria were applied inconsistently. A variety of evidence supports the ruling that the city encouraged the segregation of schools. First, the city was well aware of the relationship between segregated neighborhoods and segregated schools. White residents opposing the construction of minority housing in their predominantly white neighborhoods mentioned the schools as one of their concerns. Nearly all the councillors from eastern Yonkers stated explicitly that their constituents opposed minority housing in their neighborhoods in part because they sought to keep minority children out of their schools.

Second, on several occasions, city officials sought to have white neighborhoods allocated to school attendance zones that already had a predominance of white students. The effect, had the school board not rejected these requests, would have been to increase the degree of school segregation. The city had offered no justification for the requests. The court thus inferred from these attempts at further segregation that the city desired white students to attend schools that had as large a proportion of white students as could be arranged. The mayor's forthright packing of the school board with persons he believed would adhere to the neighborhood school policy provided clear support for the finding that the city deliberately sought to preserve segregation in the schools as well as in the neighborhoods.

THE DISTRICT COURT FINDINGS

The city was ordered to take steps to remedy the segregation for which it had been found liable. The district court held that the city, through its practice of confining subsidized housing to the southwestern section of Yonkers, had intentionally increased racial segregation in housing in violation of Title VIII of the Civil Rights Act of 1964 and the Equal Protection Clause of the Fourteenth Amendment to the U.S. Constitution. The court found that the school board's selective adherence to a neighborhood school policy in light of the city's segregative housing practices, combined with its failure to implement measures to alleviate school segregation, constituted intentional racial segregation of the Yonkers public schools in violation of Titles IV and VI of the Civil Rights Act of 1964 and the Equal Protection Clause. The court held that the city had contributed to the segregation of the Yonkers public schools by means of its segregative housing practices and that its segregative intent was revealed by the clear evidence of the foreseeable effects of its housing practices, its direct involvement with certain schools, and the mayor's appointing people to the board who were firmly committed to maintaining the segregated state of the schools.

The court emphasized that its findings of the city's discriminatory intent rested not on a failure to act but on a forty-year practice of consistently rejecting the integrative alternative in favor of the segregative, a practice that had the unsurprising effect of preserving and significantly exacerbating existing patterns of racial segregation in Yonkers. The remedy was to mandate a school desegregation plan and a plan for locating public housing in a desegregated pattern.

THE SEQUEL

In *United States v. City of Yonkers et al.* (SDNY 1985), in which the U.S. Department of Justice filed suit against the city on behalf of the NAACP, Judge Sands found against the city; his remedy required that the school board and superintendent develop a school desegregation plan and the planners and city council develop a public housing desegregation plan. In September 1986, the school system was successfully desegregated. However, for years, the city council balked at creating and implementing the housing desegregation plan. In September 1988, Judge Sands imposed severe fines on the city of Yonkers to spur action on the housing desegregation plan. In June 1989, when no housing remedy plan had been approved by the Yonkers City Council, the court appointed a "master," a well-known city planner, to design one. While the Yonkers planners' complicity in the events leading up to the litigation has been detailed and is well known, their role in the events subsequent to the court order to develop an appropriate housing plan is no less counter to the professional ethics adhered to by the planning field. The Yonkers planners and political decision makers have refused to participate in the planning process to create the remedy mandated by Judge Sands in his decision. Despite the fines levied against the city and the threatened wholesale layoff of city employees, the Yonkers City Council refuses to vote for selection or acquisition of public housing sites. This intransigence prevented any genuinely participatory settlement of the housing situation in a comprehensive framework and, indeed, seems to have foreclosed a role in the remedy planning process for the Yonkers Planning Department, with its concurrence.

The hope that the court-ordered housing settlement could accomplish some genuine comprehensive, community-based planning was frustrated. Thus, planning of a kind that takes into account the needs of all the citizens, as set forth in the AICP *Code of Ethics* (AICP 1991), has yet to be achieved in Yonkers, even with the impetus of a court-ordered housing remedy.

Moreover, the court-ordered remedy failed equally to recognize the public interest embodied in a truly locally based comprehensive framework. Despite the efforts of the court-appointed "master" to reach the community directly, a number of factors—the absence of a comprehensive framework; the barriers against community participation in the political process presented by the Yonkers Planning Department and the mayor and city council; and the "master's" inability to structure a remedy through a community-based process—resulted in a "sock-it-to-them" plan. This type of redistributive plan, familiar to those who have been involved with other school desegregation fights, is often formulated by outside experts who narrowly construe their assignments.

A more just solution could have evolved if the court-ordered remedy had followed the ethical principles endorsed by AICP. Had the court-appointed "master" developed the housing plan in conjunction with the successful school remedy plan, in place for three years and implemented by a courageous superintendent, school board, and parents, the proposed housing plan might have been more balanced and more responsive to all the citizens of Yonkers.

What role did the local planners and the community have in developing the court-ordered housing remedy? It seems none—and it certainly reflects none. They chose to stand aside and not support the court "master's" efforts to develop a community-based comprehensive housing remedy. Missing in this dilemma is a leadership role for the local planners buttressed by a commitment to the ethical principles of the profession. In the face of political opposition, the local planners would not lead—even with the court's support. The planners did not take their opportunity to make amends for past inaction. As a result, the housing plan is narrow and lacks a sense of equal access. Ironically, the unethical actions of the Yonkers planners in the last fifty years are still plaguing the city, even after their wrongs have been judged and a solution mandated (Feld and Hohman 1989).

THE CODA

Ten years after the U.S. Department of Justice sued the city of Yonkers for discriminating against minorities in its housing and schools, and nine years after Judge Sands prescribed a remedy mandating the desegregation of the public schools and the construction of low-income housing units in mainly white neighborhoods, the demographic pattern of the city of Yonkers has not altered. The 1990 U.S. Census of Population shows that this city of 188,082 seems to be integrated, with 31,476 Hispanic residents, 24,534 blacks, and 5,420 Asians—but, in fact, the 1990 census shows the same residential pattern of segregation of the previous decade. The northeast section bordering on Bronxville, Tuckahoe, Eastchester, and Greenburgh was 95 percent white in 1980 and is 92 percent white today. The southeast, north of Woodlawn and Van Cortlandt Park sections of the Bronx and next to Mount Vernon, was 98 percent white in 1980 and is 95 percent white today.

At the end of August 1993, seven years after Judge Sands ordered the city of Yonkers to create a program to desegregate its school system, he found that the effort has so far proved incomplete and that "vestiges of segregation" remained throughout the city's schools (*New York Times,* August 31, 1993). Unlike the city's response to desegregating public housing, the judge found that the school board has made a sincere effort to desegregate the schools but "although minority students in Yonkers attend school in the same buildings as majority students, they are undergoing different educational experiences." The school system stated that without additional funding from the state of New York, the desegregation plan would not be completed.

That same order, judicially linking housing and school segregation for the first time in an American court, also mandated that subsidized housing be built in white residential areas. This housing—of a small scale and low-density on scattered sites with three-fourths consisting of town houses of no more than forty-eight units per site—should improve the possibility of the projects blending into the neighborhoods (Galster and Keeney 1993).

The 1986 housing remedy order and a 1988 consent decree required the city to build two hundred public housing units and eight hundred "affordable" housing units outside of the southwest sector. Today, about 75 percent of the public housing units are under contract and about six of the affordable units have been built. In 1984, when HUD agreed to fund two hundred units of public housing on the east side, the city refused to select sites for the housing. In 1987, Oscar Newman was employed as an adviser to the court and presented twenty sites for the housing. The city council approved seven of these. Several rounds of RFP's have produced very few bids; financing for them has been effectively stifled by Yonkers residents picketing the local branches of the bank that proposed to fund the projects. The city thus continues to fight against the housing desegregation component of the court decision (Stern 1991).

THE ROLE OF THE PLANNER: A REPRISE

The professional planner's role in Yonkers during the last fifty years has been viewed by the planners as one of technician and adviser to the elected officials. According to the planners' testimony, their role was to see that the spatial and human environments were harmonious and that the physical and social relationships within the city fit together. Nevertheless, the records of the planning board meetings and other meetings since 1949 do not seem to corroborate this claimed role. The planners, in some instances, made recommendations that they knew would meet the approval of the appointed and politically elected officials—recommendations that did not conform to their professionally based knowledge of the consequences of these proposed actions on the community.

In other instances, the planners recommended courses of action that were in concert with their professional expertise and code of ethics. When these alternatives were rejected by the officials, however, the planners carried out the decisions of the planning board and council, seemingly without objection. The outcome was a series of site location decisions that reflected the pressure exerted by the white majority population opposed to public housing in their neighborhoods.

In behaving this way, the professional planners who worked in Yonkers between 1949 and 1980 carried out the will of the city council and the planning board that opposed public housing in white majority neighborhoods. The first ethical failure of the planners was to ignore the relationship between the concentrated location of public low-income housing and resultant geographic and school segregation. The second failure of the planners was not using their professional expertise to influence site selection. They declined to utilize their technical skills and potential influence to recommend sites that were both physically acceptable and socially just.

Contextually, the planners who were involved in the Yonkers housing situation, either through direct employment with the city or through employment with consulting firms or New York State UDC, worked during a period of paradigm change in the theory and practice of planning emphasizing a shift in the role of the planner and a new understanding of the implications of an ethical dimension in the field. In 1949, the classic comprehensive planning paradigm drove professional planning activities through a technical assessment of information. As this new approach to assessing information was presented to the planning board, they began to view the planners' behavior as apolitical. Planners were viewed as technicians and therefore apart from the political process. This, in turn, influenced the planning board in discouraging a leadership role for the practicing planner. Nor did they consider the ethical dimension, in part because the public interest was still defined as a unitary one of the public good, which needed no elaboration. In any case, the planner's job, as they saw it, ended with their report to the planning board. As planning education and practice broadened and shifted during the more than three decades of the school and housing discrimination in Yonkers, the nationally accepted planning paradigm changed its emphasis toward more activist stances, including advocacy of differing needs and stressing a multiplicity of possible public interests. The planner often became a more sensitive political adviser (and quick-response artist) to the political chief of the community. The Yonkers planners, however, remained unchanging in their professional behavior. The boundaries of comprehensive planning in Yonkers did not expand to include social and economic concerns, as they did in many other communities.

Thus, the planners were unresponsive to the contemporary notions of planning ethics that grew out of a history of abuse in professional practice and the respondent articulation of the norms of the field. Yonkers planners did not play a leadership role because activist, client-oriented behavior did not mesh with their preception of what a planner working for a city should do. In addition, the Yonkers planners had no larger professional community to which they could turn for peer support in modifying the technician planner mold. Ultimately, the self-perceived role and place of the planners in the decision process structured their behavior.

ETHICAL QUESTIONS IN RESPONSE TO THE YONKERS CASE
AND THEIR BROADER CONSIDERATIONS

Questions have been raised in assessing the critical ethical concerns for planning practitioners and academics that emerged from this case:

- What are the responsibilities of planners in applying their knowledge of the complex dynamics of communities and their schools to a situation involving political conflict?
- What are the roles and responsibilities of the professional planner in a politically troubled situation? Does a planner who "gets along by going along" bear a moral responsibility for the political outcome?
- What guidelines are being taught to prepare planners for making the ethical and moral choices that are inherent in these situations? What is being taught to provide the will and skills necessary to implement such decisions?
- How can the isolating effect of practice be resolved to meet the need for peer support and review? Is the AICP *Code of Ethics* (1991) a useful guide for American planners in their decision-making process? Do contextual issues prevent an autonomous role for planners?

Responses to these questions are generally centered around the ethical concerns of the planner. There is a moral imperative to validly apply professionally shaped knowledge and values when employed by a community whose majority political consensus is contrary to that of the profession's commitment to the equitable city. Several themes are raised in addressing these questions, particularly about the nature of ethical action and the definition of a professional in practice. In one theme, in the reality of practice, planners were powerless against the authority of the political process of the community. To what extent, then, should planners be blamed for not promoting a more just society? It can be argued that this action, instead, would be unethical. Nonetheless, planners are strategically situated in government and can play key roles in influencing public policy; it is their professional responsibility to do so.

A second theme assumes that planners have some power. However, planners, as employees of the political officials who are themselves the representatives of the community, should eschew independent thought and action. In this view, planners ought to embrace the role of technician and adviser as the only rightful stance. From this perspective, it can be proposed that the most appropriate role is to educate the public about the consequences of its collective action—but even this is seen by others as a wrongfully activist model. It is clear, though, that this position ignores a major stream of planning theory and history during the last quarter of a century that emphasizes active roles for planners driven by norms of equity and redistributive justice.

A third theme relates to how planners use their professional education, particularly that of the comprehensive assessment of the consequences of a particular course of action. Has professional planning education provided the will and the skills necessary to address equity and redistributive issues in practice? Most planners view housing as a singularly physical element of a community, one related to property values and real estate. Others suggest that housing is a complex, socially dynamic force with a normative dimension that impacts many aspects of the lives of the residents. From this latter perspective, planners need the support of each other as members of a professional community if they are to apply their expertise to questions involving activist behaviors and political conflict.

Responses to these questions lead to further inquiry. What are the norms of professional behavior? Is there a legitimacy by which planners may transcend their immediate boundaries? Do planners have a responsibility to utilize their expertise independently to bring about a more just society? On the contrary, are planners accountable only to their employers, the elected or appointed officials designated by the community as the arbiter of its will? Is there an ethical community to which professional planners belong, in which accountability and responsibility to broader norms reside? Is there a role for a professional code of ethics, and, if so, how is it enforced? Finally, the underlying questions raised by Paul Davidoff: Who is the client for the professional planner? For whose goals are we planning and how is this determination made? While other chapters in this book address some of these queries, the debate has clearly only just begun. Cases such as that of Yonkers presented in this chapter provide valuable starting points for such discussions. Detailed investigations of planners' decisions, behaviors, values, and environments are needed in order to more fully understand and appreciate why planners do what they do and how their actions fit into their own, and their profession's, ethical constructs.[4]

Notes

1. Actions include those by the federal government (what is now the U.S. Department of Housing and Urban Development), the Yonkers Municipal Housing Authority, the city planning board and its consultants, the Yonkers City Council, the mayor, and the city manager.

2. This case (*Brown v. Board of Education of Topeka*) constituted the central victory of the civil rights movement in the United States in the 1950s with its call for desegregation of the public schools. The Brown case, brought by the NAACP against the board of education of the city of Topeka, Kansas, argued that separate school facilities for white and Negro students were inherently unequal

and therefore unconstitutional. This suit overturned the previous precedent, *Plessy v. Ferguson* (1896), which first enunciated the "separate but equal" services doctrine for different races. Brown said racially separate facilities were at all times unequal and that separate segregated schools placed Negro students at a disadvantage in society. This case was innovative in introducing, on behalf of the plaintiffs, social science information supporting their contentions. As the notion of adequate schooling had become a part of the American dream after World War II, the Brown decision marked, for the first time, a formal governmental commitment to include blacks in the promise of access to the American economic growth both through access to economic development and as an ethical concern in and of itself. The Yonkers case represented the first time that the relationship between segregated schooling and segregated housing was acknowledged by a federal court.

3. The facts of this case are based upon the city of Yonkers opinion by Judge Leonard B. Sands and by Cathy Holden (1987) and this author (Feld et al. 1989).

4. The author would like to thank the participants of the Paul Davidoff Memorial Symposium, "Equity, Empowerment and Planning: Lessons from the Yonkers Case," for their insights: Howell S. Baum, Barry Checkoway, Edward W. Hill, Jerome L. Kaufman, and Seymour J. Mandelbaum. Thanks for their assistance are extended to Cathy Holden and John D. Hohman, former research assistants in the graduate program in community planning at the University of Rhode Island in Kingston. Also, a thank you to Professor Alan L. Feld for his editorial comments.

Bibliography

American Institute of Certified Planners (AICP). 1991. *Code of ethics and professional conduct.* Washington, DC: American Institute of Certified Planners.

American Planning Association (APA). 1987. *Statement of ethical principles for planning.* Washington, DC: American Planning Association.

Brown v. Board of Education, 74 S Ct 686, 347 US 483.

Davidoff, P., Davidoff, L., and Gold, N. 1970. Suburban action: advocate planning for an open society. *Journal of the American Institute of Planners* 36, 12–21.

Dimond, P. 1984. *Beyond busing: inside the challenge to the urban segregation.* Ann Arbor: University of Michigan Press.

Feld, M. M. 1986. Planners guilty on two counts: the city of Yonkers case. *Journal of the American Planning Association* 52, 387–388.

Feld, M. M. and Hohman, J. D., Jr. 1989. Planning leadership: a tale of two cities. *Journal of the American Planning Association* 55, 479–481.

Feld, M. M.; Baum, H. S.; Checkoway, B.; Hill, E. W.; Kaufman, J. L.; and Mandelbaum, S. J. 1989. Paul Davidoff Memorial Symposium. Equity, empowerment and planning: lessons from the Yonkers case. *Journal of Planning Education and Research* 8, 167–196.

Galster, G. and Keeney, H. 1993. Subsidizing housing and racial change in Yonkers, New York. *Journal of the American Planning Association* 59, 172–181.

Holden, C. 1987. Public housing in Yonkers: the impact of planners on site selection in a segregated community. Unpublished master's research project, University of Rhode Island Graduate Curriculum in Community Planning and Area Development, Kingston.

Orfield, G. 1981. *Towards a strategy for urban integration: lessons in school and housing policy from twelve cases.* New York: Ford Foundation.

———. 1983. *State housing policy and urban school segregation.* Denver, CO: Education Commission of the States.

Plessy v. Ferguson, 16 S Ct 1133, 163 US 437.

Southern District of New York (SDNY). 1985. *United States v. City of Yonkers, et al.* Civil Action #80 CIV 6761 LBS, November 20.

Stern, J. 1991. Yonkers gives in. *Planning* 57, 8–11.

PART III

Ethical Theory
and
Planning Education

RICHARD E. KLOSTERMAN

Introduction

The following four chapters on ethical theory and planning education provide an appropriate conclusion to this collection of essays examining the role of ethics in urban and regional planning. Ending the
discussion with issues of pedagogy is important because only education
can ensure that future professionals are aware of the ethical issues that
pervade their practice and are provided with the concepts, tools, and
perspectives needed to deal with these issues intelligently.

These chapters provide insightful and informative reports on four
pioneering attempts to introduce professional planning students to the
extensive body of literature comprising traditional and contemporary
ethics. Although differing in detail, the essays represent the latest stage
in planners' rejection of the perception of planning as a "value-neutral"
applied science for a richer appreciation of planning as an inherently
social, communicative, and ethical undertaking.

Thus, for example, Jonathan E. D. Richmond demonstrates in
chapter 14 that fundamental issues of distributive justice pervade transportation planning—ostensibly the most "technical" form of planning.
Transportation planning has been traditionally regarded largely as an
engineering activity of providing roads wherever they were needed to
allow cars to flow quickly and efficiently. However, Richmond asks,
"What use are freeways—which provide *vehicles* with 'free' access—to
people who don't own cars?" Thus, he makes clear, questions of differen-

tial access associated with larger issues of education, race, and class are fundamental to what superficially appears to be a simple problem of physical movement.

The chapters also reflect Timothy Beatley's view in chapter 15 that, for most students, graduate planning school is their last opportunity to engage in informed moral reflection and to clarify and critically assess their personal values before entering the world of professional practice, political compromise, and economic expedience. As a result, exposure to the literature on ethics is particularly useful in helping students develop their own personal ethical frameworks, sharpening their sense of professional purpose.

This introductory essay does four things. First, it traces the increased emphasis that ethics has received in planning education over the last twenty years. It then briefly reviews the different approaches that these four authors have taken in pursuit of their common objective of introducing planning students to ethical issues and concepts. Next, it draws on the authors' experiences to suggest general guidelines for instructors who may wish to follow in their footsteps. Finally, it speculates on the future role of ethics in planning education.

THE INCREASED APPRECIATION FOR PLANNING ETHICS

Jerome L. Kaufman is undoubtedly correct in chapter 12 in suggesting that the first semester-long course on planning ethics offered at a graduate city planning program was offered in 1979 by him and Elizabeth Howe. At that time, the field of planning ethics lacked depth and definition and planning educators and practitioners gave the topic little attention. Today he identifies six courses in planning ethics currently being offered at North American planning schools and the publication of roughly fifty articles and book chapters on the topic during the decade of the 1980s.

Three approximately decennial surveys of planning theory courses provide useful snapshots of the increased concern with ethics in planning education. The first survey was conducted by Henry Hightower in the late 1960s. The informal summary of the survey findings (Hightower 1969) mentions only one "planning ethics" reading, Melvin Webber's "Comprehensive Planning and Social Responsibility" (Webber 1963). However, it also identifies several extremely influential articles and books that introduced the profession to the "politics of planning" (Altshuler 1965; Davidoff and Reiner 1962) and to explicitly normative approaches such as advocacy planning (Davidoff 1965). The importance that these writings had in helping planners recognize the value-laden nature of their professional practice, thereby setting the stage for an appreciation of issues of planning ethics, became clear a decade later, as is shown below.

The general neglect of planning ethics in the 1960s reflected the tremendous changes in the planning profession's self-image that were taking place during the preceding decade. Until then, planning had generally been assumed to be a form of "architecture writ large" in which the perspectives and procedures of architects and landscape architects were applied to the city and its hinterlands. Ethical issues of what should be done were assumed to be resolved by relying on professional expertise and the principles of "good practice" in pursuit of the objectives of "the client"—generally assumed to be some poorly articulated conception of the "public interest."

This conception of "planning as architecture" had been replaced in the 1960s by a new image of "planning as an applied science." The core ideals of professional practice shifted from professional expertise and intuitive design to "objective" science and quantitative technique. In professional education this conception of planning-as-science was reflected by an abandonment of the once ubiquitous design studio for an increased emphasis on statistics, quantitative methods, and the substantive theories of economics, regional science, and the other positive social sciences. Underlying this new emphasis on applied science was a view of the planner as a "value-free means technician" who collects and analyzes "factual" data concerning alternative means for achieving public policy ends but avoids entirely the "value" questions of defining these objectives. From this perspective, there was little need for planning professionals or educators to be concerned with apparently "subjective" and "unscientific" issues of ethics.

A second, more extensively reported course survey conducted in 1979 (Klosterman 1981) found that things had changed remarkably in a decade's time. The survey found "ethical issues of planning practice" listed as a topic for 39 percent of the fifty-seven master's-level course outlines in the survey. It also identified five articles on "professionalism and ethics" that were required reading for 10 percent or more of the fifty courses in the sample: John Friedmann (1973)—14 percent, Elizabeth Howe and Jerome Kaufman (1979)—12 percent, Richard E. Klosterman (1978)—16 percent, Peter Marcuse (1976)—26 percent, and Melvin Webber (1963)—18 percent. Marcuse's "Professional Ethics and Beyond" is the only reading in the entire list that had been published in the later half of the 1970s and was required for more than one-quarter of the courses in the sample.

A more extensive listing of all readings that were required in three or more of the fifty graduate courses in the sample (Klosterman 1980) lists a total of ten articles dealing with planning ethics. These articles are indicated in the appendix at the end of this introduction by the number 1979 (denoting the 1979 survey), the number of times the reading was required, and the percentage of the fifty courses in the sample that required the readings. Thus, for example, the second reading on the list, the American Institute of Planners (AIP) *Code of Professional Responsibility* (1962), was required in four courses or 8 percent of the reading lists in the 1979 sample: [1979; 4; 8%]. The list of readings in the appendix is examined in some detail below.

The survey results indicate that planning ethics was receiving much more attention among planning educators than it had only ten years previously, largely as a result of the fundamental transformation of planners' view of their practice that had taken place during the 1970s. The results also revealed that students were no longer being taught that planning was an apolitical technical activity, based firmly on an abstract model of perfect procedural "rationality." Instead, they were being taught that planning was an inherently political undertaking and were being introduced to a wide range of topics, including alternative procedural models, public participation, and the radical critiques of planning. The increased interest in planning ethics was a natural outgrowth of this new concern with the "politics of planning."

The final point of reference is provided by a third survey of planning theory courses conducted in 1989 (Klosterman 1992). The survey found professional ethics to be on 59 percent of the master's courses in the sample—the third most popular of the twenty specific topics identified in the survey—up from 39 percent in the 1979 survey. The topic also appeared in one-third of the undergraduate courses in the sample. Ten articles on professional ethics were required readings for 10 percent or more of the master's reading lists in the sample. Two articles, Howe and Kaufman's "The Ethics of Contemporary American Planners" (1979) and Marcuse's "Professional Ethics and Beyond" (1976), were among the ten articles required on more than a quarter of the reading lists.

The twenty-four readings that were required on three or more reading lists in the sample are identified in the appendix by the number 1989 (referring to the 1989 survey), the number of times the reading was required, and the percentage of the courses in the sample that required it. Thus, for example, the first reading in the list, the American Institute of Certified Planners (AICP) *Code of Ethics and Professional*

Conduct (1981), was a required reading for thirteen courses or 19 percent of the courses in the 1989 survey: [1989; 13; 19%].

The list in the appendix is suggestive in several ways. First, it identifies five articles that are at least candidates for "classic" articles on planning ethics, having been required on 10 percent or more of the reading lists in both the 1979 and 1989 surveys. In alphabetical order by authors, these articles are: John Friedmann's "The Public Interest and Community Participation" (1973); Elizabeth Howe and Jerome Kaufman's "The Ethics of Contemporary American Planners" (1979); Richard E. Klosterman's "Foundations for Normative Planning" (1978); Peter Marcuse's "Professional Ethics and Beyond" (1976); and Melvin Webber's "Comprehensive Planning and Social Responsibility" (1963).

Second, like the larger sample of planning theory readings of which it is a part (Klosterman 1992), the survey results clearly indicate the importance of an edited text on professional education. Eleven of the twenty-three most widely required readings for 1989—and three of the five "classics" identified above—are included in Martin Wachs's (1985) edited collection on ethics in planning. It is, of course, impossible to tell whether (1) these readings are popular because they are readily available in an edited collection or whether (2) the collection includes articles that would have become popular in any case. Either way, Wachs's collection has clearly had a major impact on the teaching of ethics in contemporary planning education.

As Kaufman points out, the increased academic interest in planning ethics during the 1980s was paralleled by similar developments among planning practitioners. The AICP adopted a revised code of ethics in 1981 (AICP 1981) and published a two hundred–page *A Guide to Ethical Awareness in Planning* for planners in 1986 (Barrett 1986). The American Planning Association (APA) published its own code of ethics in 1987 (American Planning Association [APA] 1987). Sessions on planning ethics have also become a regular feature of national, state, and regional conferences and the annual meetings of the Association of Collegiate Schools of Planning (ACSP).

The increased concern with planning ethics during the 1980s reflected more general trends in the fields of philosophy, society, and other professions. Academic philosophy underwent a radical transformation during the mid-twentieth century as the overly simplistic views of the "logical positivists" were rejected for an appreciation that substantive ethical issues of right and wrong, good and bad, could be rationally analyzed and debated. These views were introduced to a more general public in the 1970s with the publication of John Rawls's landmark *A Theory of Justice* (1971) and Robert Nozick's *Anarchy, State and Utopia*

(1974) and the introduction of the journal *Philosophy and Public Affairs*. These developments provided the intellectual foundations for a new concern with ethical issues in the field of philosophy, in new fields such as environmental ethics, and in public policy issues from medicine to law.

In society, the tremendous optimism and general faith in the efficacy of science, technology, and professional expertise of the 1950s and 1960s were replaced by a widespread belief that the professions were, indeed, "a conspiracy against the public." These developments and widely publicized scandals involving professionals sparked a concern with ethical issues in fields such as business and in professions such as medicine, law, and planning. As a result, questions of ethics assumed a new importance in all realms of professional education, including our particular concern here, urban and regional planning (The Hastings Center 1980).

ALTERNATIVE APPROACHES

The following chapters describe four pioneering efforts to introduce these general concerns into the planning curriculum. In chapter 12, Jerry Kaufman describes five attempts over a twelve-year period to teach three different versions of a planning ethics class. The current version divides the semester-long course into four sections. The first part introduces students to the literature on ethics in order to provide them with a new language for dealing with ethical issues and concerns. This part of the course relies heavily on the work of what Kaufman calls the "planning interpreters" of moral philosophy (including many of the contributors to this volume) who have linked the general concepts of moral philosophy directly to planning issues and concerns. He has found this literature to be particularly helpful in capturing the attention of students and helping them appreciate better the significance of normative ethics for planning. Other strategies he uses to keep students' interest include listening to taped interviews of planners talking about ethical issues in their professional lives, conducting in-class discussions of ethical issues drawn from contemporary events, and even playing an ethics game.

The second part of the course examines the ethical views and attitudes of contemporary planners, relying heavily on the landmark study he conducted with Elizabeth Howe (1979) and similar studies. Several mechanisms are used to encourage students to explore their own ethical views, thereby enriching their understanding of planners' ethics: answering the Howe and Kaufman questionnaire, debating a few bellwether scenarios from that survey, and responding to a series of ethically problematic actions that a planner might take.

The third part of the course introduces students to several approaches for ethical analysis that they can use to think more systematically about the ethical issues they will face in their careers as planners. The discussion here starts by examining interviews with practicing planners to see how they made ethical choices and then progresses to consider more structured approaches, such as Rawls's (1971) Wide Reflective Equilibrium. The final part of the course examines the ethical codes that have been developed during the 1980s (AICP 1981) that provide ethical directives for planners to follow.

In chapter 13, Charles Hoch describes the two courses that he teaches dealing with planning theory and ethics. Both courses reflect his general belief that useful planning theory ideas must remain closely tied to practical affairs. In his provocative metaphor, he does not view planning theory as a sun illuminating a world of dark and shadowy uncertainties. Instead, he sees it as a narrowly focused and relatively short-range flashlight that is no better than the purposes and competence of the person using it.

The first course attempts to combine traditional planning theory topics and ethical concerns by focusing on the arguments that planners use to justify their plans and policies. Hoch begins by soliciting examples of advice-giving based on the students' experiences and then raises questions about their arguments, nudging them to offer justifications for their actions. These concrete examples drawn from students' experiences are then used to introduce a historical survey of the different moral perspectives (such as beauty, efficiency, and the like) that planners have used to analyze problems and attempt to solve them.

The remainder of the course uses two central concerns to frame different moral orientations toward planning. The first issue, the problem of rationality, is used to consider the rational planning model and alternative approaches within a larger context of different moral conceptions of what counts as good reasons. The second issue, the problem of the public good, is used to examine different conceptions of the nature and scope of social collectives and alternative procedures for dealing with issues of justice.

Hoch's second course, "The Professional Development Seminar," raises ethical issues in a field studies seminar that frames contrasting moral orientations in the context of professional experience. Hoch devotes a great deal of time and effort to encouraging students to relate their individual experiences and explore common or especially difficult problems professionals encounter in their practice. In the process, Hoch tries to direct the class's attention to ethical issues that emerge as students tell their experiences, purposely avoiding the more formal and distinctly philosophical approaches employed in most planning theory courses.

Hoch attempts to promote three kinds of learning activities as the class listens to the students' stories. The first activity, storytelling, suggests that professional communications are forms of stories and correspond only occasionally to the norms of the rational planning model. The second activity, critical interpretation, tries to demonstrate ways in which students can interpret the same narrative in many different ways. For the final activity, creative design, the class is broken into small groups and engages in different conflict resolution situations. Students are then required to write a story about the planning that occurred in these situations in an attempt to help future participants improve their effectiveness and better serve the public good.

Chapter 14 describes Jonathan Richmond's innovative attempt to incorporate philosophical concepts into a course dealing with a substantive area of planning—urban transportation planning. The major objective of the course is helping students to recognize, criticize, and move beyond the assumptions that lie at the hidden core of many planning problems. The course begins by reviewing the evolution of the urban transportation system and examining the impacts that this history has had on current transportation policies and institutions. The remainder of the course introduces students to major philosophical approaches, such as utilitarianism, and demonstrates their application to real-world transportation issues.

Three major class assignments are employed to encourage students to use the theories introduced in class to uncover and criticize the assumptions underlying traditional transportation planning practice. The first exercise requires students to critically evaluate the justifications for two very different transportation systems and the transcript of an actual debate on transportation policy. For the second, students must write an essay that applies one of the theories discussed in class to practical examples. In the final assignment, class presentations prepared by groups of students are used to unearth and criticize the assumptions underlying actual transportation planning examples.

Chapter 15 describes Timothy Beatley's efforts over the course of several years to teach a course in environmental ethics within a broader specialization in environmental planning. The course has three primary objectives: (1) sensitizing students to the pervasive ethical dimensions of environmental policy and planning issues; (2) introducing them to the variety of ethical propositions, theories, principles, and points of view that can help guide environmental decision making; and (3), most importantly for Beatley, helping students develop and clarify their own particular environmental ethic or ethics.

The initial classes are devoted to preliminary issues, such as basic terminology and understanding what environmental ethics is and how it might be helpful in environmental planning and policy-making. The remainder of the course considers a number of specific perspectives, defined along two primary ethical dimensions: (1) the extent to which a perspective is teleological (ends-based) or deontological (duty-based or nonconsequentialist); and (2) the extent to which it is anthropocentric (human-centered) or nonanthropocentric (life-centered or ecosystem-centered).

The course begins with a relatively narrow conception of one's ethical obligations to the environment and gradually expands this view over the course of the semester. The discussion takes an applied-philosophical approach in which half of each class session is devoted to a discussion of ethical theories, concepts, and principles. The second half of each class applies these general topics to specific environmental policy issues or conflicts illustrated by hypothetical scenarios prepared by the instructor or by recent newspaper articles.

The final paper requires all students to develop their own environmental ethic or set of ethics. Each student is assigned an anonymous paper that she or he must present and critique. The author has a chance to rebut the critique and the class then discusses the paper. For Beatley, this exercise is an important element of the course pedagogy because it forces students to sharpen and clarify their ethical views in order to make them understandable to others.

LESSONS LEARNED

These four chapters provide a wealth of practical experience derived from four innovative attempts to introduce planning students to ethics issues, concepts, and concerns. There are significant differences in course content and pedagogical style, as one would expect. Thus, for example, Kaufman is alone in introducing students to the profession's ethical norms while Richmond's course is uniquely structured around an attempt to uncover the assumptions that underlie planning practice or what he calls "bursting bubbles." Nevertheless, the authors provide a remarkable consensus on their general objectives and strategies that provides a useful set of guidelines for anyone who wishes to follow in their footsteps.

First, all of the authors agree that ethics should be an integral part of the professional education of students not only in specialized sub-fields, such as environmental and transportation planning, but in all areas of planning. They also agree that it is important for instructors to, as Kaufman puts it, charge students' moral batteries by exposing them to the fundamental moral ethical issues that they will inevitably face in their professional work.

The authors suggest several different mechanisms for exciting students' moral imaginations. Kaufman relies heavily on the surveys and interviews of practicing planners that he has conducted with Elizabeth Howe. Beatley uses newspaper clippings and hypothetical scenarios that he has developed. Hoch extracts moral issues and concerns from the stories students relate of their personal experiences. Richmond utilizes transcripts of actual policy debates and texts representing different perspectives on important policy issues. All of these approaches are extremely useful in making students concretely aware of the inherently ethical nature of planning and public policy-making.

The authors also agree that instructors cannot merely increase students' ethical awareness; they must also help students develop their analytical skills for making ethical judgments and introduce them to some of the most important principles and techniques for dealing with these issues. Here again, they agree that students' interest cannot be maintained by introducing moral concepts and principles in the abstract. Instead, they must be applied directly to the concrete concerns of practicing planners. For example, Kaufman does this by relying on the work of "planning interpreters" who have linked the concerns and insights of moral philosophy directly to planning. Beatley does it by introducing ethical principles and perspectives and their application to public policy in the same class period, helping students see how abstract theories and concepts can (and cannot) help guide planning and policy-making.

The authors also emphasize the importance of using a final paper that requires students to apply the ethical concepts they have learned in class to a real—or at least simulated—planning issue. This exercise is particularly important in forcing students to develop their ethical views and apply them to real public policy issues, a practice that will continue throughout their professional careers.

Perhaps most importantly of all, the authors agree that it is essential that courses in planning ethics be conducted in an atmosphere of free and open dialogue in which all points of view are treated as equally legitimate and worthy of respect. It is especially important that instructors avoid "imposing" their own ethical views upon students, intentionally or unintentionally. In Beatley's words, the instructor should be primarily an ethical facilitator, not a lecturer.

FUTURE ROLE OF ETHICS IN PLANNING EDUCATION

It seems appropriate to end this introduction by considering an issue that Kaufman raises in his essay—the future role of ethics in planning education. As he points out, several fundamental factors suggest that few new courses on planning ethics will be offered in an era of declining—and aging—faculty resources at most planning schools. Few incentives exist for younger planning scholars to do their doctoral research or teach in this area. There is also little reason for more senior faculty members to undertake the difficult task of learning this new and somewhat complex topic. In addition, as the following chapters illustrate well, teaching an ethics course requires more preparation and better skills at directing—but not controlling—classroom discussions than more traditional courses dealing with better defined and less controversial topics.

As Kaufman points out, there are countervailing tendencies, however. Most importantly, the current Planning Accreditation Board guidelines for accrediting planning programs in the United States require accredited planning programs to "provide students with a basis for becoming ethical practitioners, who are aware of, and responsible for, the way their activities affect and promote important values" (Planning Accreditation Board 1992, p. 21). In addition, the wealth of articles and edited books (including this one) relating ethical concerns to planning (Howe 1990) makes it much easier to incorporate ethics into courses than it was when these authors began doing so.

The most likely result of these conflicting trends will be the incorporation of ethics into required planning "core" courses and, on rare occasions, into methods and specialty courses. The 1989 planning theory survey described above suggests that this is already happening to a large degree. While this is clearly less exposure than ethics deserves in the professional education that planners receive, this is equally true of most topics that crowd planning curricula. The obvious danger is that ethical issues introduced in planning theory courses will be ignored in the rest of the curriculum. The good news is that planning students— and educators—*are* much more aware of planning ethics than they have ever been and are somewhat better prepared to deal with these issues. One can only hope that planning practice will be improved by this realization.

Bibliography

Altshuler, A. A. 1965. *The city planning process.* Ithaca, NY: Cornell University Press.
American Institute of Certified Planners. 1981. *Code of ethics and professional conduct.* Washington, DC: American Institute of Certified Planners.
American Institute of Planners. 1962. *Code of professional responsibility and rules of procedure.* Washington, DC: American Institute of Planners.
American Planning Association. 1987. *Statement of ethical principles for planning.* Washington, DC: American Planning Association.
Barrett, C. 1986. *A guide to ethical awareness in planning.* Washington, DC: American Institute of Certified Planners.
Davidoff, P. 1965. Advocacy and pluralism in planning. *Journal of the American Institute of Planners* 31, 331–338.
Davidoff, P. and Reiner, T. A. 1962. A choice theory of planning. *Journal of the American Institute of Planners* 28, 103–115.
Friedmann, J. 1973. The public interest and community participation. *Journal of the American Institute of Planners* 39, 2–12.
The Hastings Center. 1980. *The teaching of ethics in higher education.* Hastings-on-Hudson, NY: The Hastings Center.
Hightower, H. C. 1969. Planning theory in contemporary planning education. *Journal of the American Institute of Planners* 35, 326–329.
Howe, E. 1990. Normative ethics in planning. *Journal of Planning Literature* 5, 123–150.
Howe, E. and Kaufman, J. 1979. The ethics of contemporary American planners. *Journal of the American Planning Association* 45, 243–257.
Klosterman, R. E. 1978. Foundations for normative planning. *Journal of the American Institute of Planners* 44, 37–46.
———. 1980. *Readings in planning theory: results of a course survey.* CPL Bibliography No. 34. Chicago: Council of Planning Librarians Bibliographies.
———. 1981. Contemporary planning theory education: results of a course survey. *Journal of Planning Education and Research* 1, 1–11.
———. 1992. Planning theory education in the 1980s: results of a second course survey. *Journal of Planning Education and Research* 11, 130–140.
Marcuse, P. 1976. Professional ethics and beyond: values in planning. *Journal of the American Institute of Planners* 42, 264–275.
Nozick, R. 1974. *Anarchy, state and utopia.* New York: Basic Books.
Planning Accreditation Board. 1992. *The accreditation document: criteria and procedures of the planning accreditation program.* Ames, IA: Planning Accreditation Board.
Rawls, J. 1971. *A theory of justice.* Cambridge: Harvard University Press.
Wachs, M., ed. 1985. *Ethics in planning.* New Brunswick, NJ: Center for Urban Policy Research, Rutgers—The State University of New Jersey.
Webber, M. M. 1963. Comprehensive planning and social responsibility: toward an AIP consensus on the profession's roles and purposes. *Journal of the American Institute of Planners* 24, 232–241.

American Institute of Certified Planners. 1981. *Code of ethics and professional conduct.* Washington, DC: American Institute of Certified Planners. Reprinted in Wachs, M., ed. 1985. *Ethics in Planning.* New Brunswick, NJ: Center for Urban Policy Research, Rutgers—The State University of New Jersey. [1989 (date of survey); 13 (number of times reading was required); 19% (percentage of the courses in the sample that required the readings)]

American Institute of Planners. 1962. *Code of professional responsibility and rules of procedures.* Washington, DC: American Institute of Planners. [1979; 4; 8%]

———. 1973. *The social responsibility of the planner.* Washington, DC: American Institute of Planners. Reprinted in Wachs, M., ed. 1985. *Ethics in planning.* New Brunswick, NJ: Center for Urban Policy Research, Rutgers—The State University of New Jersey. [1989; 4; 6%; 1979; 4; 8%]

American Planning Association. 1987. Statement of ethical principles for planning. *Planning* 53, 35–38. [1989; 7; 10%]

Bolan, R. S. 1983. The structure of ethical choice in planning practice. *Journal of Planning Education and Research* 3, 23–34. Reprinted in Wachs, M., ed. 1985. *Ethics in planning.* New Brunswick, NJ: Center for Urban Policy Research, Rutgers—The State University of New Jersey. [1989; 7; 10%]

Fainstein, S. and Fainstein, N. 1971. City planning and political values. *Urban Affairs Quarterly* 6, 341–362. [1979; 3; 6%]

Friedmann, J. 1973. The public interest and community participation. *Journal of the American Institute of Planners* 39, 2–12. [1989; 7; 10%; 1979; 7; 14%]

Gardiner, J. A. 1985. Corruption and reform in land-use and building regulation: incentives and disincentives. In Wachs, M., ed. 1985. *Ethics in planning.* New Brunswick, NJ: Center for Urban Policy Research, Rutgers—The State University of New Jersey. [1989; 3; 4%]

Hoch, C. 1984. Doing good and being right: the pragmatic connection in planning theory. *Journal of the American Planning Association* 50, 335–343. [1989; 7; 10%]

———. 1984. Pragmatism, planning, and power. *Journal of Planning Education and Research* 4, 86–95. [1989; 3; 4%]

Howe, E. and Kaufman, J. 1979. The ethics of contemporary American planners. *Journal of the American Planning Association* 45, 243–255. Reprinted in Wachs, M., ed. 1985. *Ethics in planning.* New Brunswick, NJ: Center for Urban Policy Research, Rutgers—The State University of New Jersey. [1989; 21; 31%; 1979; 6; 12%]

———. 1981. The values of contemporary American planners. *Journal of the American Planning Association* 47, 266–278. [1989; 9; 13%]

Kelman, S. 1982. *Cost benefit analysis and environmental, safety, health regulation: ethical and philosophical considerations.* In Kelman, S. *Cost benefit analysis and environmental regulations: politics, ethics and methods.* Washington, DC: Conservation Foundation. Reprinted in Wachs, M., ed. 1985. *Ethics in planning.* New Brunswick, NJ: Center for Urban Policy Research, Rutgers—The State University of New Jersey. [1989; 4; 6%]

Klosterman, R. E. 1983. Fact and value in planning. *Journal of the American Planning Association* 49, 216–225. [1989; 4; 6%]

———. 1978. Foundations for normative planning. *Journal of the American Institute of Planners* 44, 37–46. Reprinted in Wachs, M., ed. 1985. *Ethics in planning.* New Brunswick, NJ: Center for Urban Policy Research, Rutgers—The State University of New Jersey. [1989; 9; 13%; 1979; 8; 16%]

———. 1980. A public interest criterion. *Journal of the American Planning Association* 46, 323–333. [1989; 9; 13%]

Lucy, W. H. 1988. APA's ethical principles include simplistic planning theories. *Journal of the American Planning Association* 54, 147–149. [1989; 4; 6%]

MacIntyre, A. 1977. Utilitarianism and the presuppositions of cost-benefit analysis: an essay on the relevance of moral philosophy to the theory of bureaucracy. In Sayre, K., ed. *Values in the electric power industry.* Notre Dame, IN: University of Notre Dame Press. Reprinted in Wachs, M., ed. 1985. *Ethics in planning.* New Brunswick, NJ: Center for Urban Policy Research, Rutgers—The State University of New Jersey. [1989; 4; 6%]

Marcuse, P. 1976. Professional ethics and beyond: values in planning. *Journal of the American Institute of Planners* 42, 264–274. Reprinted in Wachs, M., ed. 1985. *Ethics in planning.* New Brunswick, NJ: Center for Urban Policy Research, Rutgers—The State University of New Jersey. [1989; 21; 31%; 1979; 13; 26%]

Moffit, L. C. 1975. Value implications for public planning: some thoughts and questions. *Journal of the American Institute of Planners* 41, 397–405. [1979; 3; 6%]

Patton, C. V. 1983. Citizen input and professional responsibility. *Journal of Planning Education and Research* 3, 46–50. [1989; 3; 4%]

Stollman, I. 1988. The values of the city planner. In So, F. S., and Getzels, J., eds. *The practice of local government planning.* 2d ed. Washington, DC: International City Management Association. [1989; 6; 9%]

Taylor, N. 1980. Planning theory and the philosophy of planning. *Urban Studies* 17, 159–172. [1989; 3; 4%]

Wachs, M. 1982. Ethical dilemmas in forecasting for public policy. *Public Administration Review* 42, 562–567. Reprinted in Wachs, M., ed. 1985. *Ethics in planning.* New Brunswick, NJ: Center for Urban Policy Research, Rutgers—The State University of New Jersey. [1989; 8; 12%]

Wachs, M. ed. 1985. *Ethics in planning.* New Brunswick, NJ: Center for Urban Policy Research, Rutgers—The State University of New Jersey. [1989; 5; 7%]

Webber, M. 1963. Comprehensive planning and social responsibility: toward an AIP consensus on the profession's roles and purposes. *Journal of the American Institute of Planners* 29, 232–241. Reprinted in Faludi, A., ed. 1973. *A reader in planning theory.* New York: Pergamon Press. [1989; 9; 13%; 1979; 9; 18%]

Wheaton, W. L. C. and Wheaton, M. F. 1970. Identifying the public interest: values and goals. In Erber, E., ed. *Urban planning in transition.* New York: Grossman. [1989; 4; 6%; 1979; 4; 8%]

JEROME L. KAUFMAN

12 *Reflections on Teaching Three Versions of a Planning Ethics Course*

Over the past twelve years, I have taught three different versions of a planning ethics class at five different times. During this period, my thoughts about how to teach such an uncommon class continued to evolve, change, and be refined. In this chapter, I reflect on these experiences by describing, assessing, and occasionally critiquing what I did in the classroom, devoting most attention to the most recent version of the course. After discussing the several courses, I present some of the key lessons I learned from my teaching experiences that may be of interest to others contemplating offering such a course. I conclude by speculating about the likelihood that more planning ethics teaching will occur in the future in planning schools.

The first class on planning ethics that I taught was in the fall of 1979 and was a collaborative effort with my colleague, Elizabeth Howe. Fresh from completing a research project on the ethics of American planners (Howe and Kaufman 1979), we plunged into the murky waters

From Jerome Kaufman, "Reflections on teaching three versions of a planning ethics course," *Journal of Planning Education and Research* 12, 2 (Winter 1993), 107–115. © 1993 Association of Collegiate Schools of Planning. Reprinted with permission.

of planning ethics to teach a semester-long course—to our knowledge, the first one ever given on this subject in a graduate planning program.

At that time, the literature on planning ethics was meager.[1] Not only did the field of planning ethics lack definition and depth but the great majority of planning educators gave it scant attention. When ethics was treated in planning curricula, it was clearly as an "add-on" to a regular planning course.[2] Among planning practitioners at the end of the 1970s, interest in planning ethics was also quite limited. The American Institute of Certified Planners (AICP; 1981) inherited the code of ethics of the American Institute of Planners (AIP; 1962), the organization it succeeded in the mid-1970s, but few planners were familiar with the contents of that code and rarely was an ethics charge ever filed against a planner for allegedly violating that code's provisions.

I waited until the spring semester of 1982, two and a half years later, before trying to teach another planning ethics course, this time by myself. Although I planned initially to offer a semester-long sequel to the one Howe and I gave in 1979, modifying somewhat the structure and content of that course, I ended up pursuing a less ambitious agenda by offering an eight-week noncredit colloquium on ethics and planning.

Between my first and second teaching ethics forays, only three new articles on planning ethics had been published in journals (Howe 1980; Howe and Kaufman 1981; Wachs 1982), two of them growing out of the Howe/Kaufman research study on the ethics of American planners. The interest of planners in planning ethics picked up slightly in the United States, due mostly to widespread circulation of the newly adopted AICP *Code of Ethics and Professional Conduct* (AICP 1981).

After finishing my noncredit colloquium, I took a long break from teaching a planning ethics course. In a sense, I was like a homesteader who, finding it somewhat difficult living out on the frontier, decided to return to the relatively familiar and more comfortable environs of the bigger city. Seven years later, in 1989, I returned again to the frontier to teach another planning ethics class.

I benefited from the break because during the 1980s increased scholarly attention, accompanied by other developments on the planning ethics front, occurred. Consequently, anyone who now decides to teach a planning ethics class could draw on a much richer array of writings than in the early 1980s.

From 1981, when the AICP code was adopted, to the end of the 1980s, at least twenty-five articles on planning ethics were published in planning journals.[3] A book of ethics readings was published under the title *Ethics in Planning* (Wachs 1985). The American Planning Association (APA; 1987), following the path of AICP, adopted its own code of ethics. Sessions on planning ethics are now commonplace at national, state, and regional planning conferences. A two hundred–page *A Guide to Ethical Awareness in Planning* was prepared for the AICP (Barrett 1986). Intended for use in training practitioners, the *Guide* contains more than forty scenarios depicting ethical dilemmas faced by planners, techniques of ethical analysis, and an annotated bibliography of more than 20 readings on planning ethics.

An indicator of the increased status of ethics in planning education is reflected by the action taken in 1989 by the Planning Accreditation Board (PAB; 1990), which sets criteria and procedures for accrediting master's degree planning programs in the United States, to elevate ethics to a more prominent place in the curricula of planning programs. A graduate planning program must now assure the PAB that its graduates will have had substantial exposure to basic subject areas under three components: knowledge, skills, and the new area of values. The values section begins with the following sentence: "The planning program shall provide students with a basis for becoming ethical practitioners, who are aware of, and responsible for, the way their activities affect and promote important value" (PAB 1990, p. 18). Although the PAB does not expect graduate programs to offer a course in values or ethics, they are specifically advised to discuss such issues as "the ethics of professional practice and behavior" within existing courses and in other noncourse contexts.

Nowadays, several planning educators are teaching planning ethics courses in North American universities.[4] However, unlike other new areas of planning interest, such as alternative dispute resolution, geographic information systems, and real estate/development—where courses on these subjects are beginning to proliferate in planning schools—planning ethics courses are still few and far between.

The First Version: 1979

The research on the ethics of American planners that Howe and I did (Howe and Kaufman 1979) whetted our appetites for developing a course on ethics (Kaufman 1981). We approached the task with some trepidation since neither of us had any training in philosophy nor were we particularly conversant in moral or normative ethical theories. We asked ourselves whether we had enough material for a full-semester course. Metaphorically speaking, could we prepare enough of a main course to eat? If we could, would there be anyone interested in coming to dinner?

In initially preparing for the course, we relied heavily on what we knew best—the planning context of ethical issues drawing mainly on scenarios from our ethics questionnaire that described planners behaving in certain ways that had ethical implications. Our first cut was to design the course around cases in planning, but we began to have doubts about that format, reasoning that a case study approach would take us only so far.

It became increasingly clear to us that we needed to gain a better understanding of the broader context in which to reflect on issues of planning ethics. So we changed direction and took our own crash course in moral philosophy to learn more about those illuminating theories and arguments that had been devised to deal with recurrent ethical dilemmas, not just with professional ethical dilemmas. We read selectively from the works of past masters such as Plato, Immanuel Kant, William David Ross, Jeremy Bentham, and John Stuart Mill, as well as from the works of more contemporary philosophers like John Rawls, William Frankena, John Dewey, and Sissela Bok. This allowed us to become better informed about central concepts in moral philosophy, such as deontology and teleology; act and rule forms of utilitarianism, intuitionism; communitarianism; distinctions between metaethics, normative ethics, and descriptive ethics; and so on. We were thus preparing ourselves to better convey this "broader" moral philosophical context to our students.

In addition to introducing students to moral theories and concepts, we also wanted them to know something about methods of ethical reasoning to help them make ethical judgments. Here, too, we devised our own crash course by reading about various approaches to the analysis of ethical issues, including writings of Baum (1975), Bok (1978), Frankena (1973), and Rawls (1971).

The class as we conducted it in 1979, although structured in design, was fluid in the way we carried it out. A couple of early sessions were devoted to ethical theories and concepts drawn from moral philosophy literature. We followed the initial sessions by giving the students a heavy dose of material on specific ethical issues in planning, drawing mainly on the results of our recent empirical study of planners' ethics. We paid particular attention to the impacts of values and of the social setting of professions on ethics. We also took a look at what codes of ethics were like, particularly the old AIP *Code of Ethics* (AIP 1962), which we felt left much to be desired. Our intention was to apply pertinent theories and concepts of moral philosophy to better understand the roots of ethical issues in planning. Exposing students to several methods of ethical analysis was also done. A few of these methods were used experimentally to try to resolve specific ethical dilemmas faced by planners drawn from our case materials.

Ultimately, what we attempted to do in the course was to balance our knowledge of how ethical issues were woven into planning as it took place in the real world with a better knowledge of ethical theory and techniques of ethical analysis drawn from moral philosophy. Were we successful? On reflection, only somewhat.

We never seemed to be able to get over the hump. For several sessions of the class, we were literally only a day or two ahead of the students, scampering to soak up as much of the new material from our readings in moral philosophy as possible. The problem is that by having to learn so quickly about normative ethics to broaden the course beyond the planning contexts we knew best, we never got sufficiently on top of this material to use it comfortably in the course. Then, too, we experimented with some topics that in retrospect added little to the class, for example, a session on what constitutes a profession. We were also disappointed in the small number of students who signed up. Only five enrolled, good students to be sure but far fewer than we anticipated or would have liked to have had.[5]

Yet the course did work in some respects. It helped stimulate the moral imaginations of the students. They became more aware of the moral dimensions of the planning and public policy fields. In addition, the class allowed them to learn about some analytical tools to arrive at more informed and carefully thought out moral judgments.

In retrospect, however, the class was probably a lot more valuable to us than it was to the handful of students who took it. It forced us to become more conversant with key moral theories and concepts, thus giving us a better appreciation of the roots of the ethical dimensions of the planning field. It also enabled us to sharpen our thinking about what we needed to do in the way of research to deepen our understanding of the ethics of American planners. The dialogue we had with the students and between ourselves convinced us that we had to go beyond what we learned about the ethics of American planners from using just the findings from a lengthy questionnaire. To acquire a deeper and fuller understanding of the ethics of American planners, we needed to engage in more two-way communications with planners by interviewing them "in the flesh" about their ethical views.[6]

The Second Version: 1982

I intended to offer a planning ethics course by myself in the spring semester of 1982, making some modest adjustments to the one that

Howe and I taught. By then, I was more comfortable with the moral philosophical theories, concepts, and methods than I was in 1979, but I was still concerned about the "market" for the course. My preliminary soundings to gauge the level of student interest in taking an ethics course were not reassuring. Consequently, I got cold feet and decided to scale down the course. Instead of teaching a semester-long planning ethics class for credit that semester, I offered one for no credit that ran for only half a semester.

Fifteen students chose to be the guinea pigs. They were asked to read an article a week and sometimes to do an "ethics" exercise in class. Discussion questions about each assigned article were given to them in advance of the class session.

The eclectic nature of this course can be seen in the assignments. These included reading and discussing two articles written by planning educators about planning ethics, for example, Klosterman (1978) and Marcuse (1976); reading and discussing parts of Bok (1978) using the technique of moral negotiation developed by Rosen to resolve an ethical disagreement in planning; answering some questions from a questionnaire on ethics developed for the magazine *Psychology Today* (Hassett 1981) to probe into one's own personal ethics; and discussing the differences between the 1962 and 1981 (AICP 1981) professional planning codes of ethics.

The class worked reasonably well. Since no papers were required, few readings assigned, no attendance taken, and no grades given, the work load was, to say the least, manageable. Participation remained steady from beginning to end of the eight-week period. Discussions were invariably lively. What also was useful were the discussion questions students were given in advance pertaining to the weekly readings. However, a course for no credit that lasted only eight weeks hardly allowed for enough wide-ranging and in-depth discussion to do justice to the complexities of planning ethics.

The Third Version: From 1989 to 1991

I took a seven-year break from teaching planning ethics after 1982. The main reason was that I was not convinced I was having much impact on the students. Those who took the earlier versions of the course were at most titillated with planning ethics but hardly satiated. Nevertheless, my interest in teaching planning ethics was sustained during the 1980s. I continued to plug a session or two on planning ethics into two other courses I regularly taught—a required introductory course on planning thought and practice and an elective course on strategies for increasing planning effectiveness. In addition, I continued to write articles on different aspects of planning ethics throughout the eighties (Howe and Kaufman 1983; Kaufman 1985, 1987a,b, 1989), give numerous talks on the subject at planning conferences and at other universities,[7] and serve on the AICP Ethics Committee through 1986.

In 1989, I returned to the frontier to teach yet another planning ethics course. This class was for credit but ran for only six weeks. In design, it differed little from the one I had offered seven years before. Students were asked to respond to questions about the assigned readings handed out in advance of the class session, albeit this time there were more readings to choose from, reflecting the modest surge in publications on the topic.

In 1990, I expanded the class to nine weeks, introducing more new material into the course. By 1991, I was ready to offer a full-semester version of the planning ethics course.

In the current version, I divide the semester into four main parts, with a few tributaries running off the main streams. I begin with discussing the application of normative theory to planning, move on to treat planners and their views on ethics and the ethical dilemmas they face in their work, then turn to consider approaches to ethical inquiry to help decide what to do when faced with ethical issues. I conclude by examining principles of ethical behavior for planners.

Throughout the semester, I hand out discussion questions keyed to issues raised in the weekly assigned readings so that everyone comes to class prepared to discuss the readings.[8] I rarely cover all the questions in class, though. My intent is to use the discussion questions merely as wedges to get into the topics for that class session rather than slavishly cover all of them.

In the beginning of the course, I concentrate on introducing the students to key elements of normative ethical thought drawn directly from the rich veins of moral philosophy. My aim is to provide them with the rudiments of a new language they can use in considering the kinds of moral issues and problems professional planners encounter, as well as ones the students themselves might encounter when they work eventually as planners.

We spend time in this part of the course learning the differences between deontological and teleological or consequential approaches and about various offshoots of these two central strands of moral philosophy. Although I use some "original" source material to lay this groundwork— for example, a section of Plato's *Crito* pertaining to Socrates's moral dilemma about whether or not he should escape from prison illustrates distinctions between act and rule forms of both deontological and consequential thinking (Frankena 1973)[9]—much of what I use in this early part of the course comes from the writings of "planning interpreters" of moral philosophy. This new breed of planning scholars, few in number, have begun to publish more interpretive pieces that link moral philosophy to the arena of planning (Beatley 1984, 1987, 1988, 1989; Harper and Stein 1992; Howe 1990, 1994). Howe (1990) and Beatley (1984, 1989) are particularly useful examples.

For pedagogical reasons, I find the writings of these "interpreters" of moral philosophy better to use than having students—few of them having any background in moral philosophy—read directly from the original works of moral philosophers. The writings of these interpreters help more in capturing the attention of graduate planning students. Not only are ideas of moral philosophers such as Rawls or Nozick, for instance, put into planning contexts for the students but the students seem to appreciate more the significance of normative ethics for planning because this small body of planning literature affords it instant credibility.

Although I provide a strong dose of normative ethics at the beginning of the course, at the same time, I find it useful to leaven the dosage by bringing in some practical, down-to-earth material to make contemporary ethical issues come more alive for the students. I employ several teaching strategies.

In the first class session, for example, not only do we discuss the logic of Socrates's reasoning whether or not to escape from prison, as a way of introducing normative ethical schools of thought, but we also listen to snatches of taped interviews of contemporary planners talking about ethics as it is woven into their professional lives. This smorgasbord is intended to show students right from the beginning that some planners do indeed recognize and reflect on ethical dimensions of their work. It is another way of giving planning ethics more credibility as a topic.

I use an ethics game called *Where Do You Draw the Line?* (Simile II 1977) in the second class session.[10] My purpose is to begin very early in the course stimulating the students' moral imaginations by asking each of them to decide for themselves whether people who behave in certain ways in everyday life are acting ethically or unethically.[11] Invariably, this exercise leads them to realize that their judgments about what is right or wrong for people to do in everyday life are not necessarily shared by everyone. The tendency for some to decide what is right and wrong along more situational ethics lines and others to rely more upon general moral principles is clearly revealed in this game. Because the exercise easily elicits opinions from students about what is right and wrong, it sets a good tone for the course, that is, having them participate in class discussions without feeling intimidated.

In addition, during the first phase of the course, and throughout the semester, I will occasionally bring to the students' attention issues with ethical dimensions drawn from current events, as well as encourage them to bring such issues to class. As their normative ethical "language" improves, they begin to see more readily the ethical content embodied in many contemporary issues that on the surface are not cast in ethical terms. This also helps activate their moral compasses and stimulates their moral imaginations.[12]

The second part of the course focuses on planners and their views of ethics. What are the ethical values and attitudes of contemporary planners? What are important ethical issues and dilemmas planners face in their work? How do planners deal with such issues and dilemmas? I rely heavily on the findings of studies of the ethics of planners that Howe and I did in 1978 (Howe and Kaufman 1979) and 1982 (in an unpublished study) in answering these questions. In addition, Elizabeth Howe's book, *Acting on Ethics in City Planning* (Howe 1994), which probes even more deeply into the ethics of planners by drawing on the 1982 interviews we conducted of planners, provides very useful information for this part of the course.

Other empirical studies I use are ones done of planners in other countries. Sue Hendler (1991) studied Canadian practicing planners and planning students and compared their views of ethics. Two Swedish researchers used our ethics questionnaire in a study of Swedish planners (Khakee and Dahlgren 1990), comparing their views on ethics to those of the American planners we studied. I also use material from the cross-cultural study I did on the ethics of Israeli planners and American planners (Kaufman 1985).[13]

I also find it helpful in this part of the course to supplement the empirical findings with portions of taped interviews of planners from our 1982 study of one hundred planners. Hearing planners talk about ethical dilemmas encountered on the job, how they dealt with these, and whether they thought they acted ethically or unethically in such instances provides a sense of reality that the students find believable, sometimes absorbing. Particularly revealing are taped accounts of planners who discuss candidly how data were manipulated to justify a predetermined policy outcome, how pressure was exerted on them to change their professional judgments, and how fairness was or was not adhered to in specific situations. In addition to the tapes, I also invite at least one planning practitioner to class to discuss job-related ethical issues. The opportunity this provides for students to question and probe into the planner's ethical views adds another important reality dimension to the course. Readings on the Yonkers, New York, housing segregation case (Baum 1989; Checkoway 1989; Feld 1989a,b; Hill 1989; Kaufman 1989; Mandelbaum 1989) are also used to show how several planning academicians come to different conclusions about the ethical dimensions of this intriguing case (see chapter 11).

An excellent way to deepen the students' understanding of the ethics of planners is to engage them directly in exploring their own ethical views. I do this in three ways—by having them answer the Howe/ Kaufman questionnaire on ethics that was part of our 1978 study (Howe and Kaufman 1979), discuss and debate a few bellwether ethics scenarios from that questionnaire, and respond to a series of ethically problematic actions a planner might take.

At the beginning of the course, I give each student the same fourteen-page questionnaire on ethics and values that we sent in 1978 to a random sample of 1,178 members of AIP, approximately 10 percent of its membership. I then, in this part of the course, have them compare their responses to those of planning practitioners in both the 1978 and 1982 samples to gauge the fit.[14]

Secondly, I have students discuss their answers to a couple of the scenarios from this questionnaire in class. One in particular has proven to be an excellent way to show why planners hold different opinions about what is ethical or unethical to do. The scenario deals with a regional planner who, without authorization, gives a draft of the findings of a wetlands preservation study to an environmental group because the planner believes the agency's director purposely left out these findings from the draft report. In discussing this scenario, differences of opinion among the students invariably arise about whether the planner behaved ethically or unethically. Some judge the planner's behavior to be ethical, others unethical, and still others say they are not sure. At least five ethical principles embodied in this simple scenario emerge during the course of the discussion to explain the students' judgment. Two reasons are usually given by those who view the planner's behavior as unethical: disloyalty to the agency and deceitfulness in leaking information. Three reasons are usually given by those who view the planner's behavior as ethical: the public has a right to know, professional integrity, and the "good" inherent in preserving an environmental resource such as wetlands. Some students cite reasons on both sides of the fence but weight these reasons differently. For example, a student who says the planner acted unethically may still recognize that the public has a right to know but in this instance gives more weight to the planner being loyal to the agency.[15]

The third way I try to deepen students' appreciation for planners' ethics is to have them respond to a series of thirteen behaviors to determine whether they would never, rarely, or occasionally do each of them. These range from accepting a bribe and falsifying data (the least acceptable behaviors) to withholding certain information from someone who is on the opposite side of an issue from you and is looking for data to prove that a predetermined policy choice is best (the most acceptable behaviors). The exercise shows which students tend to think more deontologically and which more consequentially. It gives students insight into their own "ethical compasses" and the balance point between their deontological and consequential sides.

In the third part of the course, I shift focus to introduce students to several approaches to ethical analysis. My rationale stems from the belief that because they will inevitably face ethical dilemmas in their careers as planners, students should know more about how to think more systematically about resolving such dilemmas. As a starting point, I focus on how planners themselves make decisions when confronted with an ethical choice. Here I draw on material from our 1982 interviews of planners.

Some planners decide in a convoluted way by trying to avoid situations that have a potential for unethical action. As one said, "I'm a lover, not a fighter. So I try to skate around the problem areas I can't solve. . . . I don't go looking for brick walls to penetrate." Others follow a mixed deontological-consequential approach—"When faced with a decision about whether to do something or not, I'd try to finesse the conflict . . . not do violence to honesty, but also try to hype my substantive value preferences." Still other planners seem to base their decisions on a version of Kant's categorical imperative. One said succinctly, "In what I do on a day-to-day basis as a planner, I'd want to act in a way that I'd want others to act toward me." Most often, though, planners would say that they would try to test their prospective decision against some set of moral standards before deciding what to do.

The last response leads to a discussion of methods of ethical inquiry put forth in various writings by contemporary philosophers and others. One article I use shows, in an imaginatively constructed dialogue between a planning consultant and a consultant specializing in ethics, how careful ethical reasoning can be helpful in illuminating the ethical dimensions inherent in as mundane an issue as drafting a contract between a planning consultant and a client (Hendler and Kinley 1990).

More structured techniques of ethical inquiry are also presented.

Bok (1978), for example, discusses a three-step method of ethical analysis that, although keyed to the question of whether "to lie or not to lie," has wider applicability for deciding whether other contemplated ethically questionable actions are justifiable. She calls her scheme "practical moral reasoning." First, a person should consider alternative forms of action that could resolve the difficulty without using a lie; second, the person should consider what might be the moral reasons brought forth to excuse the lie and what reasons can be raised as counterarguments; and, third, as a test of these two steps, the person should ask what a public of reasonable persons might say about such lies.

Other methods of ethical analysis are also introduced. Among them are the moral negotiation technique of Rosen and Rawls's Wide Reflective Equilibrium (see chapter 3 of this book). Both are used to try to reach consensus among different parties to an ethical dispute. I have the students do an exercise in which they apply Rosen's moral negotiation technique to a planning situation. The technique involves a careful description of the moral issue in question by describing the planning situation in terms that reflect rather than hide the disagreement. Then everyone is asked to present reasons—pro, con, undecided—for each side and to list the reasons in the form of if/then conditional statements. Ultimately, the discussion should revolve around factual disagreements about the items in the "if" statements (the antecedents) that underlie the moral disagreement. Rosen contends that this process can lead to more rational discussion of the ethical issue, possibly even to resolving the ethical dispute.

In the final part of the course, I zero in on that body of ethical principles that has emerged in the 1980s constituting directives for ethical planners to follow. Before 1980, what normative prescriptions existed that were aimed at planners were slim indeed. For American planners, the AIP Code of Professional Responsibility and Rules of Procedure (AIP 1962) provided the only set of ethical norms for planners, and few took that code seriously—but now not only are there two completely revised codes of ethics for American planners—the AICP (1981) and APA (1987) codes—but a number of planning educators are speaking out about what is right or wrong for planners to do. These include ethical prescriptions put forth by Wachs (1989) on guidelines for the planner/forecaster to use, Beatley (1991) on ethical principles to guide land use policy, and Howe (1994) on encouraging ethical action.

The well of ethical prescriptions for planners is filling up. Although there are legitimate criticisms that can be raised about certain provisions in the revised codes of ethics, in terms of appropriateness and content (Hendler 1990; Kaufman 1990; Lucy 1988), the codes still constitute the planning profession's best statement to date of what ethical standards it holds its members to. Consequently, every planning student, not only the ones who take a planning ethics course, should be exposed to their provisions. The normative positions being taken by some planning scholars, whose writings are well known in the ethics area, are an indication that there will be even more advice given in the future about what constitutes ethical behavior for planners. The neophyte planners who take classwork in ethics need to be informed about what in the codes of ethics and in the writings of various planning scholars constitutes ethical behavior for planners. This alerts them to the prevailing ethical norms in the profession they choose to enter. I do this now in my class; but in the late 1970s, when I first started to teach planning ethics, I did this in a much more limited way because the normative well was fairly dry.

Lessons Learned

In reflecting on my experiences in teaching planning ethics over the past dozen years, I've distilled the following points that might be useful for planning educators contemplating teaching such a course to consider.

Early in the course, students need to gain an understanding of important moral, philosophical theories, and concepts that underpin the ethical issues planners face. Rather than have them acquire that understanding by assigning them too many readings from moral philosophers themselves, I find it more useful to convey such knowledge using the works of the new breed of "planning interpreters" who link moral philosophy directly to the arena of planning.

The moral imagination of students needs to be stimulated. My assumption is that all of us have ethical compasses that provide us with directions about what is right and wrong, but these ethical compasses tend to be dormant. They need to be activated in the course. Helpful in this regard is to have students answer self-administered ethics questionnaires and discuss the results, to have them play games that require them to make ethical choices and justify their choices, and to get them accustomed to looking for signs of ethical issues embodied in current events.

Planning students need to have an understanding of the kinds of ethical issues and dilemmas that planners actually face in their work—ranging from being pressured to change their professional judgments to being tempted to manipulate information for "good" ends to reconciling conflicts between loyalty to one's employer and loyalty to the public interest. Reporting the results of studies of the ethical views of planners, playing portions of taped interviews of planners, and inviting selected planners to speak in class about their ethical dilemmas and how they resolved them are useful ways of bringing this "reality" dimension into the classroom.

Planning students should be helped to develop analytical skills to arrive at ethical judgments. A casual "quick and dirty" approach to arriving at ethical judgments is a start, but only that. More helpful is to give them an understanding of principles and techniques of ethical analysis and some opportunity to sharpen their developing ethical analysis skills on the marrow of real planning issues.

Planning students need to be appraised of the ethical norms of the profession they are choosing to enter. This means exposing them to the provisions of the codes of planning ethics and to the views of reflective educators and practitioners about what is right and wrong for planners to do. At the same time, there needs to be balance to avoid teaching ethics in a way that is too strongly normative—for example, this is the right thing to do or this is the wrong thing to do. Above all, it is important to make sure that students do not end up feeling that the course was a vehicle for transmitting the private prejudices of the instructor.

Finally, it is important to conduct rigorous class discussions to elicit a fuller consideration of issues. To do this, the instructor needs to have a clear plan of the central points to make in the class session and steer the discussion back on track when it is going off course. In a class such as planning ethics, where students sometimes differ sharply with each other because of the different weights they attach to ethical principles, it is essential that the instructor be adept at keeping discussions from degenerating into windy exchanges of student opinions.

Will Planning Ethics Be Taught More in Planning Schools?

In the 1970s, the teaching of ethics in higher education began to pick up a head of steam. The Hastings Center's (1980) Institute of Society, Ethics, and the Life Sciences documented the increased activity in teaching ethics in a number of professional schools, including law, journalism, business, engineering, and public administration. Interest in teaching ethics in planning schools came later, but now several such courses are being offered by planning educators to supplement the more widespread "add-on" approach to dealing with ethics in planning school curricula.

I was initially drawn to teaching such a class not just because of the study of planners' ethics that Howe and I did in the late 1970s but because I believed then, and still do, that much of the behavior of planners both reflects ethical choices and carries with it ethical consequences. Ethical judgments are involved, sometimes explicitly but more often implicitly, in many planning activities, including collecting and analyzing data, forecasting, cost-benefit analysis, dealing with the public, administering and managing programs, drafting plans and policies, and implementing plans. Part of the challenge to those of us teaching ethics in planning schools is to help charge up the ethical batteries of students so that they see more clearly the pervasive ethical dimensions involved in planning work.

If ethics is as ubiquitous in planning as I believe it to be, are we likely to see more planning ethics courses offered in planning programs in the 1990s? I suspect we will see a modest increase. On the constraint side, the incentives for younger planning faculty to teach planning ethics are limited. Few aspiring planning educators will likely choose to do their doctoral dissertations on planning ethics topics. For one, funds to support doctoral dissertation research on issues centrally related to planning ethics are meager. In addition, although much more published material on planning ethics exists today than ten years ago, it is doubtful that many young planning educators will be lured away from teaching opportunities in core areas of planning, such as land use, economic development, environmental planning, planning methods, and planning theory, to teach a planning ethics course. Few incentives exist to make the option of teaching a course on planning ethics attractive to all but a small minority of younger planning faculty. The greater likelihood is that the quality of the ethics add-ons plugged into the "standard" planning courses that younger planning educators will offer should be improved given the greater range and depth of the planning ethics literature that can be drawn upon.

With respect to more senior planning faculty, some might become interested enough to try their hand at offering a planning ethics course. Those who already add on an ethics session to their theory, methods, and substantive area courses—that is, who already have an appreciation for the ethical issues inherent in the courses they offer—are probably the most likely to leap into the uncharted waters of a planning ethics course. However, the steep learning curve for those who have little knowledge of moral philosophy, as I discovered more than ten years ago when I first decided to offer a planning ethics course, may deter some of the potential leapers.

Despite these drawbacks, there are signs that ethics will be given more attention in American planning schools in the 1990s. The most important reason can be traced to the decision of the PAB (1990) in May 1989 to elevate the ethics and values component of the curricula to the same level as the knowledge and skills components. This "stamp of approval" should lead to giving ethics greater visibility and legitimacy as a subject in planning curricula. It should also lead to a more concerted effort on the part of graduate planning programs to beef up the ethics and values components of their course offerings. The sheer expansion of scholarly work on the topic of planning ethics is another reason why ethics may become more prominent in planning education. It is even possible, ironically, that the practitioner community might exert some pressure on planning schools to devote more attention to ethics. Why? Because more and more planning practitioners are becoming more sensitive to the ethical dimension of their work. It remains to be seen, though, whether planning schools and planning educators will respond to this challenge.

Notes

1. Apart from Peter Marcuse's (1976) excellent article in which he identified several sources of sometimes conflicting ethical prescriptions affecting planners on the job, less than a handful of articles relating directly to planning ethics had been published. These included David Allor (1970–71), Robert C. Hoover (1961), and Richard E. Klosterman (1978).

2. In a survey of graduate planning theory courses in 1980, Klosterman (1981) found that readings dealing with ethical issues of planning practice appeared in 39 percent of the course outlines he investigated, indicating that some attention was being given in the core theory courses to the ethical dimensions of planning.

3. These twenty-five articles were published in the four leading North American planning journals, *Journal of the American Planning Association,* the *Journal of Planning Education and Research, Plan Canada,* and the *Journal of Planning Literature.* In contrast, during the 1970s only three articles were published in these journals. It should also be noted that since 1981 at least as many planning ethics articles were published in planning journals as were published in nonplanning journals and as chapters in books.

4. Among them are Timothy Beatley, University of Virginia; Marcia Campbell and Kenneth Pearlman, Ohio State University; Thomas Harper and Stanley Stein, University of Calgary; Susan Hendler, Queen's University; Charles

Hoch, University of Illinois–Chicago; and Martin Wachs, University of California, Los Angeles.

5. For many years, I believed that the relatively small number of students who took the course was due to the average student's perception that a course in planning ethics would not help him or her in getting an entry-level job in planning. My reasoning was that ethics had little "market" value, so unless it was a required course or some other incentives were used, few planning students would choose ethics as an elective course. Other elective courses I taught, which dealt with more basic skill and knowledge areas of planning, had relatively high enrollments.

6. In the summer of 1982, we moved into a second phase of our research when we interviewed a randomly selected group of one hundred planners in five states to acquire that deeper and fuller understanding. The class gave us a clear insight that the questionnaire was only the first step in our research.

7. From 1982 to 1989, I gave fifteen talks to different groups on the subject of planning ethics.

8. In 1989 and 1990, I asked two or three students to serve as discussion leaders for an assigned reading. Unfortunately, a few students, unless specifically assigned the role of discussion leader, were not keeping up with the readings. Now, by asking everyone to be prepared to answer the discussion questions in class, students are kept more on their toes. I find this approach works better.

9. William Frankena, a widely respected professor of ethics, begins his well-known book on ethics (1973) with Socrates' dilemma from Plato's *Crito*.

10. The class is divided into five groups for the ethics game. Each group is given brief but different scenarios about the same four people who behave in ethically problematic ways. While the issue for each person is the same, the circumstances surrounding the issues differ. One issue deals with someone who has "stolen" $10 worth of cash or goods for different purposes. The other issues deal with the proper use of influence, income avoidance or evasion, and breaking a law that makes no practical difference to anyone. Each class group is asked whether the behavior described is acceptable or not.

11. I used this exercise when I taught the course in 1989 and 1990, but not until the end of the course. Now that I use it at the beginning of the course, I find it to have more value. Because we do not usually consciously think in philosophical ethical terms, the earlier the ethical palates of the students can be stimulated the better. Although students find the exercise interesting to do early or late in the course, it has more "nutritional" value if done earlier. Other exercises can be used for this purpose. One is to have the students answer questions from the June 1981 issue of *Psychology Today* (Hassett 1981), which also probe for reactions to the rightness or wrongness of behaviors drawn from everyday life.

12. Particularly good examples of current events that reflected a number of ethical issues covered in the course—including loyalty, fairness, harm to an individual, deception, rights of privacy, adherence to a code of professional

ethics, and consequential thinking—surfaced at the time I gave the course in the fall 1991 semester. These included the U.S. Senate hearings concerning the nominations of Clarence Thomas for the Supreme Court and William Gates for director of the Central Intelligence Agency and the "right to die" controversy that surfaced around the actions of Dr. Jack Kevorkian, who assisted some of his terminally ill patients to die. The ethical dimensions of these cases were discussed in class to heighten the students' appreciation for the ubiquitousness of ethics in contemporary society.

13. Shulamith S. Gertel (1990) replicated my research on Israeli planners for her master's thesis by doing a study of a much larger sample of Israeli planners five years later.

14. I also compare the ethics students' responses to those of other groups of students who filled out the same questionnaire in other years. Elizabeth Howe and I have been giving out our ethics questionnaire to students at the beginning of their first semester in the master's program for the past ten years.

15. During the past ten years, I've spoken on planning ethics in many forums and have used this particular scenario as a way of getting planners to surface their ethical values. The opinions have ranged widely about the planner in the wetlands scenario—from a high of 75 percent for one group who viewed the planner's behavior as ethical to a low of 7 percent for another group. Thirty-one percent of the planners in our original 1978 sample viewed the planner's behavior in the wetlands scenario as ethical. The point is that different planners obviously weigh ethical principles differently.

Bibliography

Allor, D. 1970–71. Normative ethics in community planning. *Maxwell Review* 7, 113–137.

American Institute of Certified Planners. 1981. *Code of ethics and professional conduct.* Washington, DC: American Institute of Certified Planners.

American Institute of Planners. 1962. *Code of professional responsibility and rules of procedure.* Washington, DC: American Institute of Planners.

American Planning Association. 1987. *Statement of ethical principles for planning.* Washington, DC: American Planning Association.

Barrett, C. 1986. *A guide to ethical awareness in planning.* Washington, DC: American Institute of Certified Planners.

Baum, H. S. 1989. Yonkers: the case for community planning. *Journal of Planning Education and Research* 8, 177–179.

Baum, R. 1975. *Ethical arguments for analysis.* New York: Holt, Rinehart and Winston.

Beatley, T. 1984. Applying moral principles to growth management. *Journal of the American Planning Association* 50, 459–469.

———. 1987. Planners and political philosophy. *Journal of the American Planning Association* 53, 235–236.

————. 1988. Ethical dilemmas in hazard management. *Natural Hazards Observer* 12, 5:1–3.

————. 1989. Environmental ethics and planning theory. *Journal of Planning Literature* 4, 1–32.

————. 1991. A set of ethical principles to guide land use policy. *Land Use Policy* 3, 3–9.

Bok, S. 1978. *Lying: moral choice in public and private life*. New York: Pantheon Books.

Checkoway, B. 1989. Equity in education: is planning enough? *Journal of Planning Education and Research* 8, 181–182.

Feld, M. M. 1989a. Preface. *Journal of Planning Education and Research* 8, 167–168.

————. 1989b. The Yonkers case and its implications for the teaching and practice of planning. *Journal of Planning Education and Research* 8, 169–175.

Frankena, W. 1973. *Ethics*. 2d ed. Englewood Cliffs, NJ: Prentice Hall.

Gertel, S. 1990. *Ethics for planners amidst political conflict*. Master's research thesis, the Technion-Israel Institute of Technology, Haifa, Israel.

Harper, T. and Stein, S. 1992. The centrality of normative ethical theory to contemporary planning theory. *Journal of Planning Education and Research* 11, 105–116.

Hassett, J. 1981. Is it right? An inquiry into everyday ethics. *Psychology Today* June, 49–56.

The Hastings Center. 1980. *The teaching of ethics in higher education*. Hastings-on-Hudson, NY: The Hastings Center.

Hendler, S. 1990. Professional codes as bridges between planning and ethics: a case study. *Plan Canada* 30, 22–29.

————. 1991. Ethics in planning: the views of students and practitioners. *Journal of Planning Education and Research* 10, 99–105.

Hendler, S. and Kinley, J. 1990. Ethics and the planning consultant: a play in one act. *Plan Canada* 30, 29–32.

Hill, E. W. 1989. Yonkers' planners acted ethically: its citizens and politicians acted illegally. *Journal of Planning Education and Research* 8, 183–187.

Hoover, R. 1961. A view of ethics and planning. *Journal of the American Institute of Planners* 27, 293–304.

Howe, E. 1980. Role choices of urban planners. *Journal of the American Planning Association* 46, 398–409.

————. 1990. Normative ethics in planning. *Journal of Planning Literature* 5, 123–150.

————. 1994. *Acting on ethics in city planning*. New Brunswick, NJ: Center for Urban Policy Research, Rutgers—The State University of New Jersey.

Howe, E. and Kaufman, J. 1979. The ethics of contemporary American planners. *Journal of the American Planning Association* 45, 243–255.

————. 1981. The values of contemporary American planners. *Journal of the American Planning Association* 47, 266–278.

————. 1983. Ethics and professional practice. In Dunn, W., ed. *Values, ethics, and the practice of policy analysis*. Lexington, MA: Lexington Books, 9–31.

Kaufman, J. 1981. Teaching planning ethics. *Journal of Planning Education and Research* 1, 29–35.

———. 1985. American and Israeli planners: a cross-cultural comparison. *Journal of the American Planning Association* 51, 352–364.

———. 1987a. Hamlethics in planning: to do or not to do. *Business and Professional Ethics Journal* 6, 67–77.

———. 1987b. Teaching planning students about strategizing, boundary spanning and ethics. *Journal of Planning Education and Research* 6, 108–116.

———. 1989. U.S. vs. Yonkers: a tale of three planners. *Journal of Planning Education and Research* 8, 189–192.

———. 1990. American codes of planning ethics: content, development and after-effects. *Plan Canada* 30, 29–34.

Khakee, A. and Dahlgren, L. 1990. Ethics and values of Swedish planners: a replication and comparison with an American study. *Scandinavian Housing and Planning Research* 7, 65–81.

Klosterman, R. E. 1978. Foundations for normative planning. *Journal of the American Institute of Planners* 44, 37–46.

———. 1981. Contemporary planning theory education: results of a course survey. *Journal of Planning Education and Research* 1, 1–11.

Lucy, W. 1988. APA's ethical principles include simplistic planning theories. *Journal of the American Planning Association* 54, 147–149.

Mandelbaum, S. J. 1989. Claiming rights warily. *Journal of Planning Education and Research* 8, 193–194.

Marcuse, P. 1976. Professional ethics and beyond: values in planning. *Journal of the American Institute of Planners* 42, 264–274.

Planning Accreditation Board. 1990. *The accreditation document: criteria and procedures of the planning accreditation program.* Ames, IA: Planning Accreditation Board.

Rawls, J. 1971. *A theory of justice.* Cambridge: Harvard University Press.

Simile II. 1977. *Where do you draw the line? An ethics game.* Del Mar, CA: Simile II.

Wachs, M. 1982. Ethical dilemmas in forecasting for public policy. *Public Administration Review* 42, 562–567.

———. ed. 1985. *Ethics in planning.* New Brunswick, NJ: Center for Urban Policy Research, Rutgers—The State University of New Jersey.

———. 1989. When planners lie with numbers. *Journal of the American Planning Association* 55, 476–479.

CHARLES HOCH

13 *Teaching Ethics and Planning Theory*

Introduction

I have long been convinced that useful planning theory ideas remain closely tied to practical affairs. People who do planning use ideas to justify and guide their actions. The kinds of reasons and arguments they use I call planning theory. This belief is by no means universally held. Many students of planning theory spend considerable time and effort arguing for the primacy of a theory that stands on its own, over and above practice. They want a theory that like the sun illuminates the shadows cast by the uncertainties we face in charting our collective destiny (Branch 1983, 1990, 1992; Faludi 1973, 1987; Friedmann 1987). These analysts hope the comprehensive and even transcendent qualities of a coherent rational planning model will provide a reassuring and secure frame of reference for charting the diverse destinations of practice.

In contrast, my expectations are more modest. Planning theory works, I think, more like a flashlight than the sun. In a world composed of dark and shadowy uncertainties shaped by many irrational and complex conditions, the beam cast by planning ideas is narrow and of a relatively short range (Rittel and Webber 1973). Furthermore, a flashlight does not enjoy a lofty and secure home in the heavens above

(Mandelbaum 1979). The quality of the light cast by a flashlight is no better than the purposes and competence of the person gripping it.

Efforts to turn a flashlight into the sun usually do little more than produce a huge spotlight. While the spotlight can illuminate objects at a great distance, only people equipped with binoculars or telescopes can see the objects. Most onlookers see only the bright beam. Instead of seeking a single source of illumination, it would be better to pursue a wider variety of sources. Sticking with the metaphor, we can imagine all sorts of innovations that have emerged to put narrow beams of light to practical use, whether headlights on automobiles or laser beams on weather satellites.

This brings up the topic of ethics. Planning ideas are inspired by the intention to do good with and for others. When we undertake a journey, our destination is set not only to meet our own expectations but the purposes of other people as well. The social conventions and lessons we have learned chart both where we hope to go and the proper way to conduct the journey. Ethics refers to those ideas each of us uses to judge the merit of our purposes and the quality of our conduct, especially when we have doubts about our own actions or when conflicts emerge with the actions and expectations of others.

I teach planning theory as part of two courses in the curriculum: one entitled "History and Theory" and the other "The Professional Development Seminar." The former introduces students to the major theoretical arguments about rational planning; the latter takes up the problems of practice. I teach both classes to improve how students understand and apply moral distinctions in understanding and coping with moral problems common to planners. The first course offers a survey, the second an immersion in my own version of applied theory.

Teaching History and Theory of Planning

In order to teach planning theory in a way that focuses on ethical concerns, I begin with practical planning problems. First, I solicit examples of advice-giving based on the experiences of students and ask them to tell the arguments they made at the time. Then I raise questions about their arguments, nudging them to offer justifications for their rationale. Was it good advice? How do you know? Why should I believe your argument? (Krieger 1981).

We use theory to answer such questions, I point out. When we experience doubts about our rational beliefs, we use theory to construct a reasonable answer. Furthermore, these beliefs matter to us in practical moral and emotional ways, not just intellectually. I offer a working definition with three elements. Planning refers to those reasonable actions we take to identify, anticipate, and prepare for collective uncertainty and promote the common good (Christensen 1985; Marris 1982, 1987). In other words, planners offer advice about what to do to resolve future collective (versus individual or corporate) uncertainty. Planning theories provide diverse rational justifications for the different ways in which people can, do, and should give advice.

History

Planning theories emerged over time in response to different conditions and traditions of planning. While the formal planning profession has existed for less than a century, the history of planning ideas is complex, filled with contesting interpretations justifying, analyzing, and criticizing what planners do. In the context of one class, I make no effort to teach a thick historical account of planning in the twentieth century. Rather, I construct historical periods using moral themes to frame the orientation of planning in each period. The distinctions are organized to focus on one moral problem central to each period and how planners analyzed the problem and tried to solve it. I use readings that offer contrasting and frequently competing interpretations of planning and planning thought for each period. For instance, I contrast the historical assessments of planning in the United States by Christine Boyer (1983), Peter Hall (1988), and Donald Krueckeberg (1983):

1. *Beauty 1890–1910:* Here I provide cursory review of the late nineteenth century urbanization in the United States and the associated problems. How should we characterize the City Beautiful Movement as a response to these? (Fogelsong 1986; McKelvey 1982; Manieri-Elia 1979; Weber 1967).
2. *Efficiency 1910–30:* I discuss the emergence of professional planning in the context of the progressive reform movement. I lay out some of the tensions here between social reformers and the more analytically oriented engineers and architects and consider the development of the master plan, zoning, and especially the plan for the New York region (Friedmann and Weaver 1980; Hays 1959; Lubove 1967; Nolen 1929; Scott 1969; Sussman 1976).
3. *Security 1930–60:* I discuss the U.S. federal government response to the Great Depression and the expanded role of

national and regional planning as part of the welfare state. Planning takes root here as a government function (Conkin 1975; Gellen 1984; Merriam 1944; Selznick 1953; Tugwell [1939] 1975).

4. *Equity 1960–80:* I emphasize the institutionalization of urban planning through federal government subsidy and support: urban renewal, public housing, transportation, water and sewer provision, and the U.S. Section 701 comprehensive planning grants. I explore how these changes are paralleled by the rapid expansion of university-based education and the adoption of social science methods. Finally, I take up the conflicts that emerged in the 1960s as social movement activists and advocates questioned the efficacy of rational planning, the bureaucratization of planning, and the inequality of state-sponsored planning programs. Radical calls for reform accompany modest efforts to implement redistributive community planning efforts (Gerckens 1988; Heskin 1980; Hoch 1985; Needlman and Needlman 1974; Perloff 1957; Scott 1969).

Theory

After completing the historical sketch, the remainder of the course focuses on the rational planning model and its competitors. I organize such a large and complex subject by focusing on two central moral problems for planning and planners that change with shifts in theoretical orientation: rationality and public good. I discuss these problems for each kind of planning theory:

1. *The problem of rationality.* How do we recognize what counts as reasonable or well-argued advice? When we say, "That sounds reasonable and persuasive," what do we mean? I focus on the issue of truthfulness and what it means in applied settings. How do we use arguments to bridge the gap between being sure and making do? Different conceptions of what counts as reasonable lead to conflicting forms of interpretation about not only what should be done but how best to go about doing it. How do we reconcile multiple truths?

2. *The problem of public good.* How do we go about deciding the nature and scope of the collective—the "we," the "public," the "group" that does or is likely to bear the burden of uncertainty we expect our plans to reduce? What criteria do we use to include and exclude actors, players, recipients, constituents, and so on? How do we

identify the commons in relation to individual desires and rights? Who do our plans address? Who is likely to listen and be willing and able to act usefully on the advice offered? I focus on the problem of justice. Competing conceptions of planning lead to conflicting interpretations about what counts as collective goods. How do we compare different conceptions of justice among the diverse theories of planning?

3. *Theories of planning.*
   A. The rational planning model and the formal criteria for good reasoning (Meyerson and Banfield 1955). The use of scientific reasoning as a model for the conduct of planning thought. The virtue of righteous implementation of the canons of scientific method marked by abstract, detached assessment. Case example from Alan A. Altshuler's (1965) book on city planning in St. Paul, Minnesota.
   B. The common sense planning model and the tacit conventions for persuasive argument (Lindblom 1959; Simon 1957). The use of applied reasoning as a model for the conduct of planning thought. The virtue of wise implementation that respects the customs of everyday life based on concrete, engaged judgment. Selection from Aaron Wildavsky and Jeffrey L. Pressman's book (1973) telling of implementation of a federal program in Oakland, California.
   C. Revising the rational model and integrating the analytic and practical:
      a. Social learning theories focus on the quality of participation and kinds of social relations among planners and clients. The central importance of trust and communication as the basis for rational deliberation with useful practical consequences that respect democracy (Friedmann 1973, 1987; Michael 1973; Schön 1983). Case example of local zoning administrator from Donald Schön (1983).
      b. Contingency and strategic choice. This approach acknowledges the contextual quality of planning within complex organizations and attempts to put an adaptive rationality to use using Machiavellian political craft (Benveniste 1989) or conceptions of leadership and entrepreneurial innovation (Bryson 1988; Bryson and Crosby 1992). Case example of Minneapolis Regional Planning from John Bryson and Barbara Crosby (1992).
      c. Advocacy planning. This approach focuses on efforts to link concerns for knowledge with issues of social justice

(Davidoff 1965; Heskin 1980). Cases from Norman Krumholz and John Forester (1990).

    d. Marxist critique. This approach criticizes popular forms of
planning rationality as efforts to reform and justify the
unjust inequalities of a capitalist society. Socialist planning
alternatives require serious attention to class relationships
and rational analysis that informs revolutionary social
movements organized to remedy class exploitation and associated injustices (Beauregard 1978; Fainstein and
Fainstein 1979; Roweis 1983). Case example on the U.S.
Department of Housing and Urban Development (HUD;
Friedmann et al. 1980).

D. Critiquing the rational approach using critical and interpretive
reasoning. Modern forms of instrumental rationality produce
uncertainties as they remove others. Furthermore, they treat
the emergence of various forms of modern rationality and their
institutionalization not only as a source of uncertainty but
injustice. Historical and experiential assessment of planning
uncovers systematic distortions and inequities in the organizational world and built environment:

    a. Interpretive approach using hermeneutic and phenomeno-
logical orientations to understanding that emphasizes the
social construction of concepts of rationality and planning
(Bolan 1980; De Neufville 1983, 1987; Krieger 1981). Empirical chapters from Martin Krieger (1981) or Peter Marris
(1987) as case examples.

    b. Critical pragmatism focusing on practical reason and demo-
cratic participation as guides for planning conduct. Two
sources of inspiration: the critical theory of Jürgen Habermas adopted by John Forester (1989, 1993) and pragmatic
philosophy adopted by myself (Hoch 1984a,b, 1988). Forester (1989) or Hoch (1992) as case examples.

    c. Postmodern critiques of modern rationality that reject ef-
forts to find foundations and unified theories (Boyer 1983;
Milroy 1991). Helen Liggett's (1991) article on the homeless
as a case.

    d. Feminist critiques of rational planning theory. Here I use
the article by Leonie Sandercock and Ann Forsyth (1992).
The article by Marsha Ritzdorf (1993) offers good case
material.

These topics get covered over a sixteen-week semester. I do not
expect students to learn the ideas of each author but urge them to use

the ideas associated with each approach to offer different interpretations of the same case material. I encourage students to apply and compare the concepts in assessing the meaning and merits of different planning cases. However, many students find attention to argument and critical thought difficult and seemingly irrelevant to their pressing worries about acquiring technical skills and knowledge that will enhance job prospects and career opportunities.

The Professional Development Seminar

This class comes midway in a regular two-year course sequence. Students attend either after or concurrent with an internship experience working as a planner. The course has a thematic structure with different class sessions dedicated to exploring common or especially difficult problems people encounter working as organizational professionals. These include the relation between expert argument and political objectives; the impacts of racial, national, ethnic, and/or sex discrimination; the relationship between public goods and private interests; and conflicts between maintaining organizational loyalty and serving the public good.

Students who come to planning schools at the graduate level usually exhibit a diverse variety of educational specialties. I try to treat this diversity as a resource and seek ways to use our cultural worship of the individual as an ally. For instance, I spend considerable time and effort urging and encouraging students to tell individual experiences. Of course, not every or any experience proves useful for learning, but giving time and attention to individual autobiographical stories tells students that this activity is important and valuable.

Since I take planning as an inherently normative enterprise, I probe, stimulate, and direct attention to the ethical issues that emerge as individual students tell their experiences. I purposely avoid taking the more formal and distinctly philosophical approach to the subject that I adopt in the theory course. Instead of reviewing the ethical arguments among moral philosophers, we focus on the ethical assessment of practical planning cases. Students need not learn how to argue for the relative moral superiority of one planning theory relative to another in order to improve their conduct as planners. I want students to get an intelligent feel for the comparative moral value of different ideas about planning by putting these ideas to use, first in the familiar context of their own experience and later extending such efforts to social contexts shaped by the actions and experience of other individuals, groups, and institutions.

I adopt a pragmatic pedagogy, introducing my comments and questions using the experiences students relate either orally or in written essays. There are three kinds of learning activities that I promote throughout the course: storytelling, critical interpretation, and creative design. Each draws on the tacit moral sensibility of the students and uses the practical moral experiences many have already had as the crucial point of departure for moral inquiry. (See Jerome Bruner [1990] for a psychological account of the use of narrative to grasp the meaning of moral experience and Peter Marris [1987] to see how the construction of meaning shapes planning activity.)

Storytelling

We all tell stories. There are all sorts of stories to tell: myths, fables, fairy tales, novels, arguments, reports, messages, and more. Yet students frequently expect that expert professional talk and writing respect only certain ones, namely, rational arguments. The professional planner speaks and writes good rational arguments. Students often expect to learn only one kind of rationality—one kind of argument—they can rely on for justification. This usually includes a comprehensive rationalism (universal truth), a skeptical empiricism (just the facts), and a common sense pragmatism (Does it work?). Their attachments are not so much philosophical as cultural.

THE RIGHT STORY

As I mentioned above, if students or practitioners think of knowledge as sunlight then they expect to act as professional transmitters or conduits of the light. The rational planning model provides the architecture for the conduit and individuals learn to build their own version. However, this specialized product taps only a portion of the narrative resources professionals and others use to make moral sense of the world, whether setting objectives, assessing alternatives, or justifying decisions. Furthermore, this connection tends to elevate the role of the detached, objective expert as the most worthy and desirable one. This frequently generates perverse consequences. For instance, experienced professionals with considerable practical wisdom will find themselves wanting when they compare the roles they have played to the moral persona of the servant of truth. Others, unwilling to diminish their ethical professional conduct, frequently discredit the role and with it the idea of planning. "Face it," they will complain. "It's all politics. This sort of planning exists nowhere except in the academy."

My purpose is to persuade students that this represents one kind of professional role and one form of narrative or storytelling that, while useful in certain contexts and for some purposes, may often prove an impediment. Other roles and stories might better be used in different circumstances. (See, for instance, *The Call of Stories* by Robert Coles [1989] and recent work by John Forester [1993].) In other words, the usefulness and moral significance of stories vary with context and purpose.

"But then it's all relative!" I hear a student cry out. "Yes," I reply (Rorty 1989). Formal theoretical accounts can explain or interpret some confusing and uncertain relationships making them clear and predictable, but we make a mistake when we place too much confidence in the rational model as the primary standard for inquiry and understanding. First of all, there are plenty of disagreements among those who use the model about its significance and scope. Social scientists and planning theorists engage in ongoing and fundamental disagreements about what it is they do and study. These analysts share a language and tradition but not a dogma or consensus about truth. Second, the pursuit of a complete and precise certainty defies the complexity and particularity of our world. The worry about moral relativism—that accepting multiple sources of moral good means accepting moral license (Anything goes!)—can be adequately addressed without appealing to a final transcendent source (either religious or rational).

To help make this distinction clear, I usually tell some of my own experience with religious belief. (I studied in a Roman Catholic seminary for five years and can draw on a plentiful supply of stories about the relationship between God and his creations, ranging from pastoral and scriptural tales of conversion, confession, and faith to theological arguments about the authority of natural law.) Most students have some form of experience with religious belief. The contrast between religious faith in a transcendent God and a secular commitment to rational inquiry reminds students of the historical and contingent quality of their own belief. I do not try and conduct a history lesson but seek to show students that the liberal secular culture of society in the United States is a historical product that is neither inevitable nor fixed. (I find selections from Martin Krieger [1981] useful here.)

The qualities we find most attractive about liberal culture—the respect for the individual and the protection of freedom—also create serious problems for us. The contingency and uncertainty necessary to make free choice meaningful also evoke fear. We want our choices to be

validated as the right ones, but the presence of competing and incompatible options makes this difficult. (Here I use selections from Howell
Baum [1983, 1987]; Robert Bellah and colleagues [1985]; and Richard
Sennet [1980]). Our desire to cope with the plurality, diversity, and
conflict that must accompany individual freedom in a liberal society
confronts us with ethical paradoxes. Following is one I pose for the
students to consider.

THE WISE AND THE RIGHTEOUS

While virtually everyone makes ethical judgments, in our liberal
culture we recognize and respect those individuals who make such
judgments based on their own initiative. Such people are different from
those who consistently follow the rules of proper conduct. Those good
at making practical ethical judgments, especially in liberal societies
where conflicting rules abound, we call wise. Those who excel at following the rules we call righteous. This is an important distinction to make
early on as I argue that people who try to practice planning in an
ethically proper way frequently confuse the two.

First, this confusion is fostered by middle-class culture in the
United States that emphasizes individual initiative and autonomy.
Hence, members of the middle class value the wise more than the
righteous. Most practical planning problems, however, deal with uncertainties that are produced by individuals or corporate entities pursuing
their own purposes without adequately responding to the purposes of
others. Planners develop policies and rules that seek to encourage rule-
responsive conduct—righteousness—but in a culture that does not value
this sort of behavior. Therefore, people worry a great deal more in our
culture about appearing foolish and feeling guilty than they do about
appearing shameful and feeling separated. This explains in part the
pervasive use of litigation to attempt to enforce conformity to rules.
Since individuals do not take the rules to heart, they do not experience
shame when they break the rules. The powers of the state must be
brought to bear upon them. Ironically, such regulation inspires even
stronger appeals to the integrity of individual judgment that the imposition of legal force threatens to subject. Planners, insofar as they support
such forms of state intervention, appear as bureaucratic agents seeking
to destroy the freedom necessary for individual development.

The planning profession also reinforces the confusion. The model
of professional practice presumes that planners will act as individual
professionals whose judgments flow from their own experience, knowl-

edge, and ethical beliefs. Yet the vast majority of planners work as employees in organizations and must conform to certain institutional rules and political demands or face serious sanctions. Individual planners can possess and act on ethical beliefs but they must do so in ways that take into account the desires and purposes not only of clients and colleagues but those who exercise authority over them as well. Institutional hierarchy and rules do not foster righteous conformity among most planners but ambivalence. Most want to offer ethical judgments about how to do things differently but find that the powerful reserve such action for themselves.

GOOD STORIES

The initial class opens with my definition and some questions. "Planning is applied reasoning that seeks to reduce the collective uncertainty that accompanies the reproduction of a diverse liberal society (in countries like the United States, anyway), but what counts as good planning and who are good planners? If we do not have some common or unified theory, what sort of rational justification do we use?"

Usually silence here.

"Well?" I ask. "What excuses or reasons do you give for your own actions as a planner and professional?"

Moving to the personal level usually works. The responses frequently include detailed narratives about a moral conflict or dilemma and what the student did to cope and how he or she made sense of it. The more detailed and graphic the account, the more evident it becomes that the definitions of good planning and good conduct are closely intertwined. Students get some feel for the tensions and conflicts their own moral commitments might provoke in doing planning. (I should note that many of my students are in their later twenties and early thirties. Most have already acquired a wealth of experiences in a variety of jobs.)

ANALYZING STORIES

It is tempting to sort and classify the accounts students give according to the fit with different ethical theories or planning theories. "Sheila assessed the benefits and costs to others in determining what to do. She is utilitarian. James stuck by the principle of fairness even when the costs were high. His ethics are rule governed." However, careful attention to details usually exposes combinations of reasons and the important influence of relationships (such as emotional, social, political, cultural, and so on) in any particular case. Besides, I do not want to nurture philosophical reflection but ethically informed practical judgment. So I avoid the terms of philosophical discourse.

Instead of treating stories as didactic examples, I urge students to listen to the stories much as they read a novel or watch a movie and then seek to reflect upon and interpret the stories as sources of moral and cultural meaning. Listen to one another not as scientific observers using detached analysis to classify without bias but as engaged colleagues seeking mutual understanding through compassionate and critical reflection.

There are two kinds of questions I ask when we read a case or listen to a story. One set probes the literal meaning of the story, the integrity of the narrative. What are the facts? Was anything missing? Did the story hang together? Was the account believable, plausible, coherent? These are the sorts of tests literary theorists use to judge good fiction (Kaplan 1986; Throgmorton 1990, 1992). The other set focuses on the figurative or rhetorical qualities of the tale. Critical to such reflection is the following question: "What feelings did the tale evoke in you?" What forms did the speaker use to direct the attention of the audience and shape response? I especially emphasize the close ties between the facts and the form of each story. Rhetoric in this sense shapes not only the appearance but the very integrity of the story. We use figures of speech not as a facade but a scaffolding to construct a meaningful account that will move our audience.

This practical exercise in storytelling illustrates the complex quality of even the most simple tale and the pervasive influence of moral concerns at the very core of how we make sense of our world. When we compose the stories we tell, we construct a meaningful moral order we expect listeners to recognize and respect. The listener may not get the point of the story. It may not make sense. In such a case, the narrative is in some way inadequate. More frequently, the listener understands the plot but may disagree with the interpretation or form of the story offered by the teller: "That wasn't funny." "Oh, yes, it was."

When we tell stories drawn from our own experience, and especially ones that tell about moral conflicts that we found troubling, we tend to treat our own versions as canonical. We tend to conflate the literal and the figurative in ways that we find pleasing, reassuring, convincing, and so on. Just as good stories can offer guidance and hope, though, bad ones can mislead and foster cynicism. This problem is intensified in a liberal society in which individuals are expected to take responsibility for their conduct and offer good reasons (stories) for what they do. Once students tell their stories, how can they learn from their listeners? How can students learn to revise their own stories based on what their audience heard?

Critical Interpretation of Stories

Listening to personal stories attentively and carefully does not flow naturally in the context of the university classroom. While students for the most part trust one another, many expect to receive knowledge from lectures and texts rather than engage in storytelling and interpretation. They feel betrayed. Others have made their commitments and find the fair-minded yet critical discussion of diverse individual stories trivial or perhaps threatening.

The purpose here is not so much to enhance the critical argumentative powers of students but to demonstrate ways in which students can explore different interpretations of the same narrative. Take, for example, someone telling about an episode in which her boss subjected her to unjust criticism. When the storyteller offers her account of what happened, she constructs the narrative using rhetorical choices that necessarily shape the meaning of the story for her audience. So, in the context of the seminar, a story may take the form of a confession in which the storyteller seeks the sympathy and support of the audience.

> "How did the storyteller evoke your sympathy?" I ask. "How did she portray the boss?"

If the storyteller skips over the details of what people did, said, and felt and offers stock characterizations—"He was a jerk."—then the audience gets the storyteller's interpretation and conclusions but little else. The audience may respond appropriately—"Oh, that was awful."—but ritually and superficially. Critical listening searches for narrative omissions or commissions in the story that substitute (versus complement) rhetoric for narrative. So the critical listener suspends the stock response and asks, "What did he do to you that made him a jerk?" Before you apply a conventional label, let me know more details of what went on. What did he say? How did you feel? Was anyone else there? What did you say in response? How did he appear? Show me. Don't explain and interpret yet. I need to hear more about what went on before and during the episode:

Storyteller:
"What! You don't trust my story?"
Critic:
"I haven't heard enough of the story. That's all. I believe you think you were the victim of injustice, but that's not evident from the actions and events you described."
Storyteller:
"You don't want to be here all night, do you?"
Critic:
"No, but I'm not expecting you to tell me everything. Just enough detail so I can form my own opinion about the fairness of the actions your boss took."

If the storyteller wants to learn from her experience and trusts the audience, she may tell the story again in greater detail. In retelling, she may include actions and events skipped over in the earlier version. As the audience learns her expectations and feelings, as well as those of others, including her boss, the outcome becomes less determined and more dramatic. The story of obvious betrayal gets reworked into a story of moral conflict. She appears less the innocent victim than an assertive and impatient idealist. The boss appears less a villain than an overworked and insecure middle manager. Including more details on the organizational context illustrates what was at stake for others as well as herself. For instance, she saw opportunity; he saw risk. The "unjust" criticism of the boss appears less an act of power than a defense against a threatening subordinate. This is a careful recrafting of the story—a craft that selects the narrative elements and rhetorically shapes them into a more complex account that will evoke an intelligent and curious sympathy in the audience. The good story still offers a particular interpretation, but instead of fostering a stereotypical response, it inspires reflective inquiry about the meaning of the narrator's own actions. The audience will probably agree that what the boss did was morally objectionable, an injustice, but they will also ask the narrator why she didn't consider her superior's fears. Might she have acted differently without compromising her own purposes? The narrator can now learn from her own experience in a way that solitary reflection seldom enables any of us to do. She can reconsider her conclusion and imagine taking different actions that could have avoided a painful event:

> Only very skilled analysts are capable of rich, congruent, consistent narratives that describe all relevant true stories, that allow readers to see themselves in stories yet also transform how readers see the stories,

and that integrate the many factors needing consideration. The transformational quality is especially hard to achieve. Much skill is required to tell a true story about past events or a rich story of hoped-for future events in a way that, simply through restrained descriptive power, has the ability to change the reader's mind (Kaplan 1986, p. 26).

Creative Design

We all know what it means to make up a story. We also can usually tell the difference between a good story and a bad one. However, what does it take to make good ones and to avoid bad ones, and how do we go about improving how we do it in planning? This is the theme I take up near the end of the class.

We use elements of narrative and rhetoric to compose our stories. In planning tales, we usually combine logic and rhetoric, argument and poetics. The readings and lectures in the class supply the arguments justifying different types of planning. These arguments incorporate different moral orientations, contrasting modes of reasoning and competing rhetorical forms, not to mention the influence and impediments of emotional attachments, power relations, organizational context, and other sources of institutional and cultural conflict (Bailey 1983).

Students are expected to craft their own planning theory story. Take up one of the flashlights and use it to explore a dimly lit tunnel of collective uncertainty. Here I turn to written stories from fiction and literature to stimulate the imagination. To focus efforts in a class setting, though, I break the class into small groups and have them engage in different conflict resolution simulations (Susskind and Ozawa 1984). I ask them to pay special attention to the relationship between different ethical issues and power relations. After the simulation is complete, I ask each member to write a story about the planning that occurred among the participants—a story that would advise future participants about what they might consider and how they might act to improve their effectiveness and serve the public good.

Conclusion

These classes presume a basic attachment to liberalism in its North American (mainly United States) cultural form. Many foreign students find the classes especially difficult because they do not share the cultural expectations and problems common among graduate students who grew up in the United States. However, instead of trying to offer formal concepts of moral right and good in an analytic style that draws on the abstract or thin forms of technical and scientific English usage more commonly used abroad, I stick with thick cultural description. In the "Professional Development Seminar," I encourage foreign students to draw comparisons and talk about the difficult passage from one culture to another. The experience of storytelling is pervasive and robust enough to enable them to speak about their own problems and concerns, but usually in ways that embody different cultural and ethical values. The contrast often proves useful to the other students, who recognize the contingent quality of their own beliefs and, less frequently, discover some promising possibilities for mutual understanding and accommodation across deep cultural differences.

Contrasts, comparisons, differences, and conflict about what should be done are for me the proper subject for discovering our ethical beliefs and fostering moral improvement in our practical activity. In the United States, the problems of individualism are foremost, and I take those as a point of departure for introducing students to theoretical conversations about coping with the problems of our collective life. I try to introduce students to traditions of thought and forms of reflection that challenge liberal institutions and practices that subject, exploit, or dominate others at public expense. I am neither unbiased nor detached about my observations and beliefs. Still, I try to be a fair-minded liberal, tolerant and, above all, playful.

Most students find the Professional Development Seminar interesting and a few find it quite useful, but students want skills and techniques they can use to advance their careers and find a desirable niche in the hierarchy of planning occupations and specializations. Although most exhibit a basic desire to do good, they do not expect to spend time reconsidering their moral convictions as part of getting a graduate degree in planning. Since students usually have greater confidence in their own moral and conceptual outlooks than they do in their knowledge of GIS (geographic information systems), statistics, economic development policy, and land use control, they spend more time and effort on such specialized course work than on a professional development seminar. I don't blame them for this; the curriculum favors such a strategy, not to mention the job market. I try to use my limited contact to raise questions, and perhaps doubts, about the moral complexity of professional practice. Doing more would require significant revisions to the entire curriculum—revisions that other faculty would not willingly embrace.

Bibliography

Altshuler, A. A. 1965. *The city planning process.* Ithaca, NY: Cornell University Press.

Bailey, F. G. 1983. *The tactical uses of passion.* Ithaca, NY: Cornell University Press.

Baum, H. S. 1983. *Planners and public expectations.* Cambridge: Schenkman Publishing.

————. 1987. *The invisible bureaucracy.* New York: Oxford University Press.

Beauregard, R. A. 1978. Planning in an advanced capitalist state. In Burchell, R. W. and Sternlieb, G., eds. *Planning theory in the 1980's.* New Brunswick, NJ: Center for Urban Policy Research, Rutgers—The State University of New Jersey. 235–254.

Bellah, R., Madsen, R., Sullivan, W., Swidler, A., and Tipton, S. 1985. *Habits of the heart: individualism and commitment in American life.* Berkeley: University of California Press.

Benveniste, G. 1989. *Mastering the politics of planning.* San Francisco: Jossey-Bass.

Bolan, R. 1980. The practitioner as theorist: the phenomenology of the professional episode. *Journal of the American Planning Association* 46, 261–274.

Boyer, C. 1983. *Dreaming the rational city.* Cambridge: MIT Press.

Branch, M. 1983. *Comprehensive planning: general theory and principles.* Pacific Palisades, CA: Palisades Publishers.

————. 1990. *Planning: universal process.* New York: Praeger.

————. 1992. *Planning and human survival.* New York: Praeger.

Bruner, J. 1990. *Acts of meaning.* Cambridge: Harvard University Press.

Bryson, J. 1988. *Strategic planning for public and nonprofit organizations.* San Francisco: Jossey-Bass.

Bryson, J. and Crosby, B. 1992. *Leadership for the common good.* San Francisco: Jossey-Bass.

Christensen, K. 1985. Coping with uncertainty in planning. *Journal of the American Planning Association* 51, 63–73.

Coles, R. 1989. *The call of stories.* Boston: Houghton Mifflin.

Conkin, P. 1975. *The new deal.* New York: Thomas Y. Crowell.

Davidoff, P. 1965. Advocacy and pluralism in planning. *Journal of the American Institute of Planners* 31, 596–615.

De Neufville, J. 1983. Planning theory and practice: bridging the gap. *Journal of Planning Education and Research* 3, 35–45.

————. 1987. Knowledge and action, making the link. *Journal of Planning Education and Research* 6, 86–92.

Fainstein, S. and Fainstein, N. 1979. New debates in urban planning: the impact of Marxist theory within the United States. *International Journal of Urban and Regional Research* 3, 381–403.

Faludi, A. 1973. *Planning theory.* Oxford: Pergamon Press.

————. 1987. *A decision-centered view of environmental planning.* Oxford: Pergamon Press.

Fogelsong, R. 1986. *Planning and the capitalist city.* Princeton, NJ: Princeton University Press.

Forester, J. 1989. *Planning in the face of power*. Berkeley: University of California Press.

———. 1993. *Critical theory, public policy, and planning practice*. Albany, NY: State University of New York Press.

Friedman, J., Kossy, J. and Regan, M. 1980. Working within the state: the role of the progressive planner. In Clavel, P., Forester, J. and Goldsmith, W., eds. *Urban and regional planning in an age of austerity*. New York: Pergamon Press, 251–278.

Friedmann, J. 1973. *Retracking America*. Garden City, NY: Anchor Press.

———. 1987. *Planning in the public domain: from knowledge to action*. Princeton, NJ: Princeton University Press.

Friedmann, J. and Weaver, C. 1980. *Territory and function: the evolution of regional planning*. Berkeley: University of California Press.

Gellen, M. 1984. Institutionalist economics and the intellectual origins of national planning in the United States. *Journal of Planning Education and Research* 4, 75–85.

Gerckens, L. 1988. Historical development of American city planning. In So, F., and Getzels, J., eds. *The practice of local government planning*. Washington, DC: International City Managers Association, 20–59.

Hall, P. 1988. *Cities of tomorrow*. Cambridge: Blackwell.

Hays, S. P. 1959. *Conservation and the gospel of efficiency*. Cambridge: Harvard University Press.

Heskin, A. 1980. Crisis and response: an historical perspective on advocacy planning. *Journal of the American Planning Association* 46, 50–63.

Hoch, C. 1984a. Doing good and being right. *Journal of the American Planning Association* 50, 335–344.

———. 1984b. Pragmatism, planning and power. *Journal of Planning Education and Research* 4, 86–95.

———. 1985. Make no large plans. *Plan Canada* 25, 80–87.

———. 1988. A pragmatic inquiry. *Society* 26, 27–34.

———. 1992. The paradox of power in planning practice. *Journal of Planning Education and Research* 11, 206–215.

Kaplan, T. 1986. The narrative structure of policy analysis. *Journal of Policy Analysis and Management* 5, 761–778.

Krieger, M. 1981. *Advice and planning*. Philadelphia: Temple University Press.

Krueckeberg, D. 1983. *Introduction to planning history in the United States*. New Brunswick, NJ: Center for Urban Policy Research, Rutgers—The State University of New Jersey.

Krumholz, N. and Forester, J. 1990. *Making equity planning work: leadership in the private sector*. Philadelphia: Temple University Press.

Liggett, H. 1991. Where they don't have to take you in: the representation of homelessness in public policy. *Journal of Planning Education and Research* 10, 201–208.

Lindblom, C. 1959. The science of muddling through. *Public Administration Review* 19, 79–88.

Lubove, R. 1967. *The urban community.* Englewood Cliffs, NJ: Prentice Hall.

McKelvey, B. 1982. The emergence of industrial cities. In Callow, A., ed. *American urban history.* New York: Oxford University Press, 117–128.

Mandelbaum, S. 1979. A complete general theory of planning is impossible. *Policy Sciences* 11, 59–71.

Manieri-Elia, M. 1979. The marvels of the fair and the Plan of Chicago. Translated from the Italian by Barbara Luigia La Penta. In Ciucci, G.; Dal Co, F.; Manieri-Elia, M.; and Taturi, M. *The American city.* Cambridge: MIT Press.

Marris, P. 1982. *Community planning and conceptions of change.* London: Routledge and Kegan Paul.

———. 1987. *Meaning and action.* London: Routledge and Kegan Paul.

Merriam, C. 1944. The National Resources Planning Board. *American Political Science Review* 38, 1075–1088.

Meyerson, M. and Banfield, E. C. 1955. *Politics, planning and the public interest.* New York: The Free Press.

Michael, D. 1973. *On learning to plan—and planning to learn.* San Francisco: Jossey-Bass.

Milroy, B. 1991. Into Postmodern weightlessness. *Journal of Planning Education and Research* 10, 181–188.

Needlman, M. and Needlman, C. 1974. *Guerrillas in the bureaucracy.* New York: Wiley and Sons.

Nolen, J., ed. 1929. *City planning.* New York: Appleton.

Perloff, H. 1957. *Education for planning: city, state and regional.* Baltimore: Johns Hopkins Press.

Rittel, H. and Webber, M. 1973. Dilemmas in a general theory of planning. *Policy Sciences* 4, 155–169.

Ritzdorf, M. 1993. The fairy's tale: teaching planning and public policy in a different voice. *Journal of Planning Education and Research* 12, 99–106.

Rorty, R. 1989. *Contingency, irony and solidarity.* Cambridge: Cambridge University Press.

Roweis, S. 1983. Urban planning as professional mediation of territorial politics. *Environment and Planning D* 1, 139–162.

Sandercock, L. and Forsyth, A. 1992. A gender agenda: new directions for planning theory. *Journal of the American Planning Association* 58, 49–59.

Schön, D. 1983. *The reflective practitioner.* New York: Basic Books.

Scott, M. 1969. *American city planning since 1890.* Berkeley: University of California Press.

Selznick, P. 1953. *TVA and the grass roots.* Berkeley: University of California Press.

Sennet, R. 1980. *Authority.* New York: Alfred A. Knopf.

Simon, H. 1957. *Administrative behavior.* New York: The Free Press.

Susskind, L. and Ozawa, C. 1984. Mediated negotiation in the public sector: the planner as mediator. *Journal of Planning Education and Research* 4, 5–15.

Sussman, C., ed. 1976. *Planning the fourth migration: the neglected vision of the Regional Planning Association of America.* Cambridge: MIT Press.

Throgmorton, J. 1990. Passion, reason, and power: the rhetorics of electric power planning in Chicago. *Journal of Architectural and Planning Research* 7, 330–350.

––––––. 1992. Planning as persuasive storytelling about the future: negotiating an electric power rate settlement in Illinois. *Journal of Planning Education and Research* 12, 17–31.

Tugwell, R. [1939] 1975. The fourth power. In Salvador, Padilla M., *Tugwell's thoughts on planning.* San Juan: University of Puerto Rico Press.

Weber, A. F. 1967. *The growth of cities in the nineteenth century.* Ithaca, NY: Cornell University Press.

Wildavsky, A. and Pressman, J. L. 1973. *Implementation.* Berkeley: University of California Press.

JONATHAN E. D. RICHMOND

14   *Introducing Philosophical Theories to Urban Transportation Planning*

Introduction—Life Inside a Bubble

Planners inhabit bubbles. The bubble provides a womblike sense of comfort and security, an uncertainty-controlled environment in which the planner can work, using the repertory of procedures on the list of problems contained within the bubble's walls. The planner may peer out to glance at the outside world; it is seen, however, only from the perspective afforded by the individual's particular bubble. Because the bubble has invisible walls, the planner is not even aware of being in a bubble.

Martin Heidegger (1966, p. 45) was surely observing the retreat into bubbles when he wrote that "Man today is in *flight from thinking*. . . . Part of this flight is that man will neither see nor admit it. . . . He will say—and quite rightly—that there was at no time such far-reaching plans, so many inquiries in so many areas, research carried on as

This chapter is a revised version of the author's article originally published as "Introducing philosophical theories to urban transportation planning," *Systems Research* 7, 1 (1990), 47–56. It is included here with permission of Pergamon Press PLC.

301

passionately as today." According to Heidegger, though, such work revolves around "calculative thinking," which takes place within "conditions that are given." The conditions are taken into account "with the calculated intent of their serving specific purposes. Thus we can count on specific results. Calculative thinking computes. It computes ever new, ever more promising and at the same time more economical possibilities. . . . Calculative thinking never stops, never collects itself. Calculative thinking is not meditative thinking, not thinking which contemplates the meaning which reigns in everything that is" (Heidegger 1966, p. 46).

Meditative thinking is about identifying, questioning, and moving beyond assumptions. It is about bursting bubbles to discover that few planning problems may be productively tackled with a limited set of technical procedures and without an understanding of how those problems relate to other questions.

At the core of meditative thinking is the asking of what to C. West Churchman (1982, p. 132)—following his teacher, Edgar Singer—is the most crucial ethical question: Should a particular question be investigated at all? Asking one question, rather than another, is an ethical act in that the answers to different questions imply the implementation of alternative sets of possible outcomes with divergent impacts on the lives of different people. Social systems and therefore social problems are necessarily interconnected. If we forget this and unquestioningly concentrate work on one part of the cloth while ignoring the complex patterns of the fabric as a whole, the result is likely to be unharmonious and unaesthetic.

Teaching in substantive areas of planning has become increasingly calculative. As Donald A. Schön (1983, p. 39) puts it, attention to problem "solving" has been at the expense of problem "setting"— students have been taught how to put real-world problems into the models of techniques that appear to render them soluble but have not been taught how to inquire into whether they are asking the right question in the first place.

A course taught at the University of North Carolina, Chapel Hill, during the 1987 spring semester attempted instead to emphasize a meditative approach to transportation planning. A theme of exposing and criticizing assumptions—bubble bursting—lies at the heart of the course. Philosophical theories were employed to help accomplish this. Problem setting was shown to be essentially a question of ethics, and students were encouraged to see alternative ways of looking at problems and the ethical implications of doing so. The interrelationships between transportation and related social systems—such as land use and urban form, housing, employment, education, equity, race, and so on—were stressed throughout.

This chapter discusses the need for such a course, describes the course and the experience of teaching it, and suggests that the approach it took could be useful in other substantive areas of planning.

In the following, a discussion of the limitations of narrowly defined approaches to transportation planning is first presented. Problems resulting from the increasing emphasis put on computer techniques in planning practice and education are highlighted, with illustrations drawn from transportation demand modeling. The need for a more meditative form of thinking is argued, and philosophical argumentation is put forward as a path to greater critical awareness. The remainder of the chapter describes how such an approach was embodied in the new course in urban transportation planning taught at Chapel Hill. Details of the nature of existing transportation curricula, as well as of the rationale of the new course—and the structuring of its classes and assignments—are provided before the conclusion is reached.

The Need to Broaden the Scope of Transportation Planning

For too long, transportation planning—especially in the United States—was regarded as an essentially engineering activity. Roads were to be built wherever needed to allow cars to flow quickly and efficiently. How easy it was to overlook the reality that more roads would simply intensify the anarchic Brownian motion of vehicular traffic, bringing with it pollution, congestion, and unforeseen autopian urban forms.

Major limited-access arterials were often put through low-income areas, disrupting communities but rarely providing transportation benefits to the people living there. Looked at from this angle, a question of transportation policy becomes not only one of providing transportation facilities but of providing *access* to them and also of equity. What use are freeways—which provide *vehicles* with "free" access—to *people* who don't own cars?

Access needs to be defined more broadly than the potential ability of an individual to use a particular transportation facility. Well-meaning attempts to provide "access" have floundered when the concept has been narrowly defined. Take the case of the new light rail line from downtown Los Angeles to Long Beach, California. It is supposed, among other things, to provide access to new employment opportunities for the residents of poverty-torn areas, including Watts and Compton. Yet, if employers will not hire people from these areas because they lack skills or because they were born with the wrong color of skin, what sort of access is thereby provided?

Questions of education and race must therefore be raised to properly probe what superficially appears to be a problem of mere physical movement. However, these issues are locked away in other bubbles, not generally thought by transportation planners to be in their realm of responsibility; it is easier to let them float by on the outer horizon than to break the intellectual and bureaucratic barriers that must be traversed to engage them directly.

The question of bureaucratic barriers is one that requires several shelf loads of treatises to itself. Suffice it to say that if—with a Federal Highway Administration separate from an Urban Mass Transportation Administration—it is a rare enough event for one agency to reflectively consider roads and transit in the same breath, how much less likely it is that such an agency will simultaneously look at transportation, education, race, and urban form. The intellectual barriers are briefly considered below.

Intellectual Barriers

As Donald Schön (1987, p. 8–9) has pointed out:

> The professional schools of the modern research university are premised on technical rationality. Their normative curriculum, first adopted in the early decades of the twentieth century as the professions sought to gain prestige by establishing their schools in universities, still embodies the idea that practical competence becomes professional when its instrumental problem solving is grounded in systematic, preferably scientific knowledge. . . . The greater one's proximity to basic science, as a rule, the higher one's academic status.

Departments such as city planning, "yearning for the rigor of science-based knowledge and the power of science-based technique" (Schön 1988, p. 9), have brought in scholars from social science departments. "And the relative status of the various professions is largely correlated with the extent to which they are able to present themselves as rigorous practitioners of a science-based professional knowledge and embody in their schools a version of the normative professional curriculum" (Schön 1983, p. 4).

The desirability of quasi-scientific approaches is intensified by their apparent ability to provide simple and clear-cut answers to complex problems. We have a basic intolerance for uncertainty, and it is reassuring to have "hard numbers" that we may presume were "rigorously" obtained to tell us in which direction to go. As Schön remarks, though, "formal modeling has become increasingly divergent from the real-world problems of practice."

The teaching of techniques for forecasting demand—exemplary of such formal modeling—nonetheless plays a central role in many current transportation planning curricula, equipping students to apply the principles of UTPS (Urban Transportation Planning System) modeling. Such methods form the core of the textbook *Urban Transportation Modelling and Planning* by Peter Stopher and Arnim Meyburg (1975, p. 60). The text describes the "transportation-planning process" as a series of seven technocratic steps. An inventory is to be taken of existing travel and land use, socioeconomic population characteristics, and existing transportation facilities. A series of forecasts follow: "of land uses that should occur in the forecast period, and then of the demand that may be anticipated and the way this will occur throughout the region" (Stopher and Meyburg 1975, p. 60). Four models are used: to gauge total demand; allocate it between origins and destinations; between competing modes of transportation; and among the set of available network paths. Finally, alternative strategies for providing transportation are evaluated in the light of the above, and policy choices for planning are made:

> The conduct of these transportation studies and their general structure is [*sic*] based on the premise that the demand for travel is repetitive and predictable, and that future transportation systems should be designed to meet a specific, predicted travel demand. This demand is itself based on an analysis and extrapolation of current travel, and an investigation of its relationship to the patterns of population, employment and socioeconomic activity (Stopher and Meyburg 1975, p. 60).

Martin Wachs (1985a) provides an account of the pitfalls of forecasting of the type central to the UTPS process outlined above. The assumptions upon which the forecast is based and which influence its outcome are necessarily subjective, not objective. They can be politically shaped, nullifying the claims to rigor of the modeling process. Past data must be relied upon: it may not be an indication of the future, especially as actions taken as a result of the forecast may change that future. It might be added that the UTPS process assumes that patterns of the past form a desirable program for the future. We may not want a future in which we simply provide transportation capacity to meet an extrapolation of current trends.

As Wachs (1985a, p. 253) says:

> Sophistication in the technique of forecasting is . . . more apparent
> than real. Computers are used because there is often a great deal of
> data: many variables, many units of analysis for each, several time
> periods. These conditions lead to the requirement for training and
> experience in mathematics, statistics, data manipulation, and computer
> programming. But together, such skills ensure no special perspective
> on the future, and there is relatively little theory derivable from the
> social sciences to help one arrive at reasonable core assumptions.

The computer has itself taken on a magic aura, especially with
developments in the microcomputer and its almost universal availability
for planning students to use. When, as operations researcher John
Mulvey (1983) suggests, "many educated people treat computers and
the ensuing recommendations as objective fact," it is easy to appreciate
the seductive appeal of a machine that so readily seems to deliver the
truth. Besides, the virtuosity of the machine is seen to reflect favorably
on its operator.

The importance of the computer's role to educators is signified by
the fact that while there was no special "Brain User's Group" meeting to
deliberate during the 1987 conference of the Association of Collegiate
Schools of Planning in Los Angeles, there was a special day set aside for a
"Micro-Computer User's Group One-Day Conference." The fascination
with computers is becoming ever greater, as is the tendency to formulate
planning problems around what a personal computer can do rather
than based on the essence of the problems themselves.

Employers are partly to blame, for it has become a standard part
of interviewing nascent planning professionals to ask if they know
computer software, such as Lotus or Symphony, as if they could not
quickly pick up the essentials of either tool while holding an entry-level
position. Students, knowing that these "skills" will be demanded of
them, thus ask for courses making use of them. Planning problems, in
turn, are modeled to give the appearance of being soluble by such
devices. The need for "computer literacy" is being stressed while too
many students are illiterate in their own language and unable to use it
effectively to structure thought. The apparent elegance of the computer
model makes for an easy way out.

Let us probe some of the dangers. Transportation demand models
can often be run on spreadsheet software, such as Lotus or Symphony.
The spreadsheet can display varying levels of detail—different columns
can be assigned to display each step in the operation or whole algorithms
may be programmed into just one cell. Such setups can be used to make

forecasts; and variables, such as costs, trip time, and the frequency of departures of particular modes of transportation, can be paired to see the projected impact on demand.

Rarely is every step displayed, and it is much easier to play with the model as supplied than to attempt to dismember it. It is the assumptions the model makes—on matters such as car ownership, willingness to transfer from one vehicle to another, population, and elasticities of demand with respect to both dollar cost and time cost—that play the most important role in shaping the model's output, but these are hidden behind the scenes.

I recently forced myself to run through the algorithms of such a model on a pocket calculator to give myself the feel of what was going on—something denied by the instant recalculation of the spreadsheet. While it may not be practical to hand-calculate the projected demand for a particular transportation mode between all origins and destinations on a complex network, it does not take excessively long to run through the model with a small number of examples of origins and destinations, and this is frequently helpful in revealing the model's structure. It was only through this strategy that I discovered a glaring error in the spreadsheet model itself. Even then it was not possible to fully determine the basis of model assumptions since this rested on the validity of sample surveys, the quality of which could not be determined by the information supplied, and on a series of judgment calls not clearly spelled out.

The graceful flow of the model, as it effortlessly produces numbers with the solid appearance of truth, does not invite such worries. Quite to the contrary, the user can be readily allured into an uncritical belief that the model is a reliable representation of the real world. If this gullibility does not seem alarming to you at the level of the graduate student, let me say that I have met too many professionals who have used computer models without proper awareness of the assumptions driving them. One modeler, for example, was unaware that the cookie-cutter relationship between commercial floor space and the number of work trips made to a particular employment site was producing substantially more work trips to a proposed new development than the number of people expected to work there (which was specified elsewhere in the plan).

Other potential model users have been unaware of unreasonable assumptions about people's willingness to transfer (some models assume people would be willing to change vehicles five or six times during a single trip) or the applicability of the database upon which the model they are using is calibrated or the myriad of other details that go into determining output.

Even fewer users have paused to identify and evaluate the structure and sources of a model's mathematical architecture. The "trip distribution" model in UTPS demand modeling, which allocates trips between origins and destinations in a network, for example, is derived from the Newtonian gravity model of physics, which states that:

$$f_{12} = \frac{GM_1M_2}{d_{12}^2}$$

where

f_{12} = Force of attraction between bodies 1 and 2
M_1 = Mass of body 1
M_2 = Mass of body 2
d_{12} = Distance between the bodies

and

G = The gravitational constant.

In the transportation application, the body masses are replaced by the total volume of trips sent out from or attracted to each zone on the network. This volume, calculated in a previous "trip generation" model, is a function of factors, such as population and employment, that, therefore, indirectly constitutes the "masses" under study. The trip distribution model distributes this total volume between the different origins and destinations. As in the Newtonian model, distance (generally specified primarily in terms of travel time) acts as a form of "friction," which constrains attraction (see the discussion in Stopher and Meyburg [1975, pp. 140–158]).
We end with:

$$T_{i,j} = \frac{P_i A_j (F_{i,j})}{\sum_j A_j (F_{i,j})}$$

where

$T_{i,j}$ = Number of trips generated by zone i and attracted to zone j
P_i = Total number of trips produced (generated) by zone i
A_j = Total number of trips attracted to zone j

and

$F_{i,j}$ = A measure of the spatial separation of zones i and j, generally an inverse function of travel time.

The gravity model provides a metaphorical representation of complex problems of social science in vivid, easily understandable terms. Such simplification and clarification is a hallmark of metaphor (Lakoff and Johnson 1980). This borrowing from physics also gives the impression of scientific rigor for which planners yearn. Yet the mapping from physical bodies interacting in space to human bodies commuting across cities lacks theoretical grounding. People do not interact across space in the same way as objects, no matter how tantalizing it may be to pretend that they do.

It is not surprising, therefore, that gravity models in transportation planning have performed poorly. In response, ad hoc adjustments have sometimes been made to try to make them do better (that is, produce the expected results) under particular circumstances. The use of such patchwork devices serves only to highlight the inadequacy of the overall theoretical conception.

In some cases, use of such models leads to the justification of poor planning. In the modeling done for the Los Angeles–Long Beach light rail project (Southern California Association of Governments [SCAG] 1984), for example, an unrealistically large number of passengers was forecast to travel between the midsection of that corridor and downtown Los Angeles because many people live in the midcorridor, because there is a substantial employment base in downtown Los Angeles, and because they are not geographically far apart. Midcorridor residents, however, unfortunately lack the skills that would get them jobs in downtown Los Angeles, even if the "friction" of distance separating them from those jobs is relatively low. The "friction" of inadequate education and other deprivation simply is not accounted for by the model. By predicting trips that are unlikely to materialize, the model has, nonetheless, helped justify a new transit system ill-suited to the needs of area residents.

There are certainly applications where computers can be helpful if their use is properly taught. The extreme confidence placed in computer virtuosity is, though, misplaced. It too often provides an excuse to avoid confronting the more troublesome wider issues of planning, where there are no easy answers and where neither faculty nor students can feel the instant glow of success that is delivered along with the neatly printed computer output. Too often students and planners are provided with a set of computational procedures but without a corresponding knowledge of their limitations. Too little emphasis, meanwhile, is put on providing an understanding and critique of the goals that such techniques are supposedly there to serve. A mechanistic view is taken of what are essentially social and human problems, and the core problems remain unattended to and unresolved.

What is most lacking is an exposure to different modes of thinking, an awareness of the existence and fragility of the assumptions of planning applications, and an inculcated predisposition to seek out such assumptions, critically evaluate them, and move beyond them. We need to seek an alternative educational approach that throws calculative thinking in perspective and that emphasizes relevance rather than technique in planning. The following provides a discussion of ways of possibly arriving at such an approach.

Exploring Alternative Modes of Inquiry

We need to emphasize a more meditative form of thinking to planning students, and philosophical argumentation provides an important path to greater critical awareness. No single author has made a more important contribution to a philosophical critique of planning than C. West Churchman in his volumes on *The Design of Inquiring Systems* (1971), *The Systems Approach and Its Enemies* (1979), and *Thought and Wisdom* (1982). In the second of these, he includes a "Historical Debate" between Immanuel Kant and Jeremy Bentham that provides the framework for a critique of utilitarianism (see also chapters by Steven Kelman [1985] and Alasdair MacIntyre [1985] in Wachs [1985b]).

Such study reveals, first, that our quantitative planning tools are essentially utilitarian in nature and, second, that exposing only the technical assumptions of one particular model is merely to emerge from one deeply recessed bubble into another, perhaps slightly larger, bubble. The performance of UMTA (Urban Mass Transportation Administration) "Alternative Analysis" using transportation demand modeling and estimates of costs in itself implies adoption of the following utilitarian formulation: that we have a set of alternative transportation systems from which to choose; that each one has associated with it a series of benefits ("pleasures" in Bentham's language), in terms of numbers of passengers carried, and costs ("pains" to Bentham)—in both dollars and travel time; and that we are to choose the one that provides the greatest net benefits over costs.

A major failing of such an approach to a Kantian critic is its refusal to confront issues of distributional justice; of who gets to benefit from the new service provided; and who gets to pay. It is not that issues of distribution are excluded: it is that "optimal" distribution is determined as a by-product of the technical attempt at efficiency maximization. Kantians explicitly confront ethical choices by asking what "ought" to be done up front. Utilitarians allow such allocations to be made behind mathematical closed doors, allowing values to be automatically allocated by models that they will insist are value-free.

Asking what we ought to do in a direct way allows us to pop

another bubble. Applying another Kantian-rooted idea allows us to pop one more. That idea is that data do not come to us theory-free but that there is necessarily an a priori framework through which information is filtered. Awareness that a filter exists can lead us to try to examine its presuppositions and to inquire whether some other filter might not be better. Of course, if the nature of the filter is determined by the knowledge, skills, and beliefs contained within our particular bubble, and if alternative perspectives lie outside that bubble, coming to a critical awareness is no easy matter; we have to use tools available within the scope of our current bubble to hack our way out of it. Hegelian dialectic provides one possible heuristic. Making yourself argue as forcibly as possible against what you believe most deeply may—if done sincerely—lead you to a totally new conception of what you previously believed. If you believed in your model and your model told you to build more roads or more rapid transit, you might seek out the reasons not to do that. These, in turn, might then lead you to ask questions about the model.

Churchman (1982, p. 8) leads us a vital step further when he calls for "an 'unbounded' systems approach which must include a study of humanity, not within a problem area, but universally." This leads to some disturbing questions, one of which is: How can we pour dollars into designing better bombs while half the world is starving? However, to return to my more mundane subject, something that starts out as a transportation problem cannot, from this view, be adequately investigated in purely transportation terms. How can you start using a technique to choose between buses and trains on the basis of how many people they might carry before you have asked what good it would do to carry them in the first place? It is by this realization that planners may pop themselves outside the transportation bubble and come to grips with issues of race and education, poverty and discrimination, land use and urban structure. "The problems of human society," Churchman says, "are not like exercises at the end of a chapter of a textbook, where all information is given for you to deduce a perfect answer. But you can make some progress if you can begin to 'sweep-in' to your inquiry the broader issues" (Churchman 1982, p. 126).

It would be glib to say that more enlightened thought will instantly produce a better world, but a critical view of the conceptual foundations on which our planning takes place and an understanding of the limitations of any one framework provide the groundwork for a career of seeing that there are other possibilities. Moving out of intellectual bubbles provides a path for coping with more practical bubbles, too. Even the planner who leaves graduate school and goes to work in a traditional bureaucratic bubble might then be equipped to see its walls and perhaps thereby be drawn to transcend them.

A case is not made here to abandon teaching all quantitative techniques. A case is made to dispel the myth that such methods are appropriate, unbiased arbiters in prescribing proper planning action to be taken and for taking them away from center stage in favor of a broader, more critically oriented approach than is currently taken in many transportation planning courses.

Quantitative techniques can make a useful contribution when they perform an informative rather than prescriptive function and when they are based on theories with proven relationships between cause and effect that can withstand empirical test. Once a given level of service has been determined, transit operations planning can be effectively and efficiently accomplished with algorithms for scheduling vehicles and crews, for example. There is also a known relationship between highway loading and rate of flow of vehicles on a highway. We can determine quite accurately how many vehicles an hour can be accommodated on a highway before the facility breaks down with congestion. We cannot, though, precisely determine when that is going to happen; nor can we technically determine whether we should restrict access to the road to promote efficiency, build another highway, or do something else. To invoke the textbook prescription (Stokey and Zeckhauser 1978) of cost-benefit analysis to make such a determination is to be drawn into its utilitarian orientation toward supposed efficiency at the price of more fundamental issues, such as justice.

Bubble Bursting in the Planning Curriculum

It would be wrong to assume that all courses in transportation planning restrict themselves to a narrow technocratic approach to the subject. While the uncritical development of technical skills does play too great a role in many courses, others do reflect the realization in the planning profession of the need for a broader perspective.

Alan Altshuler's 1979 pathbreaking book, *The Urban Transportation System*, recognized the narrowness of analysis of policy alternatives that, he said, tended to focus on "preselected solutions, rather than on laying bare the character of the problems generating demands for public action or on searching with a fresh eye for effective remedial strategies"; that "policy practice frequently races ahead of policy analysis"; and, of particular significance in influencing educational approaches, that "The urban transportation literature is characterized . . . by a paucity of serious political analysis. The vast preponderance of scholarship in the field has been by engineers and economists who have tended to ignore political variables or merely note their relevance as contextual constraints" (Altshuler 1979, pp. ix–x).

Altshuler's work has set the path for a more thoughtful consideration of many issues in transportation and for introducing political and institutional analysis into many transportation planning courses in a more sophisticated way.

It is still rare in such courses, nonetheless, to stress the interrelationship of transportation systems with other social systems or to systematically evaluate the assumptions of techniques rather than merely teach them. It is not current practice to directly use philosophical theories for this purpose or to make ethical analysis the central theme of the course.

One approach to the art of philosophical bubble bursting is the increased appearance of courses devoted to ethics and its application to planning. The danger, however, is that it will remain business as usual in other courses. I am reminded here of the evident influence of his marketing course on a student in Harvard Business School's ethics class who, two-thirds of the way into the term, looked at the professor with a puzzled but sincere expression and asked, "Well, how can I recognize a moral good when I see one on the shelf?"

Since ethics affects all areas of planning, all planning courses should encourage students to probe the ethical foundations of what they are doing, to not merely acquire skills but to inquire into the wider implications of those skills and consider alternatives. The course on urban transportation planning taught during the 1987 spring term at the University of North Carolina made a preliminary effort to do that.

A constant theme of the course was one of assumptions: recognizing them, criticizing them, and moving beyond them. The curriculum was designed to provide students with the capacity for criticism, and philosophical theories were taught and employed through the course to further that end. The theories were applied, however, to real-world problems, and an emphasis was placed on showing how such approaches have important practical applications.

The course started by introducing themes in transportation planning. It continued with several sessions that introduced the philosophical material and discussed perspectives for understanding, critiquing, and attempting to cope with transportation problems. These perspectives were used in subsequent classes to examine specific transportation issues. The course required completion of three assignments designed to both develop students' critical abilities and to have them apply them to actual problems.

The Classes

The first class provided an overview of transportation institutions and recent policy developments, looked at how transportation problems have been defined at different times, and introduced themes of political and cognitive constraints to effective planning. A psychological experiment (Wason 1960)—using students as guinea pigs—was conducted to demonstrate our tendency to go for the set of assumptions that seem to be most obviously correct, even when it actually gets in the way of finding a solution to the problem at hand.

The next session included a subject too often ignored in an age when a paper more than a couple of years old is said to be dated—history. The class traced the evolution of the urban transportation system from the nineteenth century; examined the growth and decline of transit and the development of a public sector role; and showed how historical developments were relevant to current transportation problems. Showing the historical origins of current practices can be revealing. When it is understood that current transit pricing practices—to give one example—derive from the fare-charging traditions of horse omnibuses from the last century, the need for criticizing the assumptions of what is currently done is underlined. David W. Jones (1985) provided a well-researched, fascinating text for this session.

A major case study—on the case for building new rail rapid transit systems as against developing existing bus networks—was covered in two classes. The first included some down-to-earth consumer preference theory and a discussion of the physical and operating characteristics of the different modes. But it also looked at the assumptions of city form tacitly imposed by the different approaches (such as the fact that rail systems suggest development toward a central place–oriented city while bus systems are often associated more with dispersion) and at the presuppositions of advocates for different systems. Some of the questions asked were: Can rail systems really lead to focused urban growth? Is it desirable that they do so? Will people transfer between different modes in order to use a rail system? Why does the Automobile Club of Southern California advocate the development of a system of express buses on freeways?

The second session of the case continued discussion on these themes several weeks later, after the first assignment had been completed.

In between these classes, four lectures (each followed by a discussion) were given to introduce students to major philosophical issues and to demonstrate how they might be applied in real-world planning contexts.

Utilitarianism took up one class. Two texts—Edith Stokey and Richard Zeckhauser (1978) and Peter Stopher and Arnim Meyburg (1975)—were used to argue the case for cost-benefit analysis and UTPS modeling transportation, respectively. Kelman (1985) and MacIntyre (1985), among others, were used to present the case against. Stokey and Zeckhauser (1978) maintain that cost-benefit analysis promotes systematic, clear thinking. Kelman (1985) and MacIntyre (1985) both show how cost-benefit analysis is governed by utilitarian principles and discuss their flaws. As Kelman (1985, p. 235) puts it, "It is indeed amazing that economists can proceed in unanimous endorsement of cost-benefit analysis as if unaware that in the discipline from which the conceptual framework of cost-benefit analysis arose, namely moral philosophy, this framework is, to put it mildly, highly controversial." He shows why "there are a number of reasons to oppose efforts to put dollar values on nonmarketed benefits and costs, beyond the technical difficulties of doing so."

This material was used to critique utilitarianism in practice in two case studies: of planning for a commuter rail line in Los Angeles and planning for a third airport in London. In the latter case, for example, the elaborate cost-benefit analysis conducted was shown not to have accounted for—and to be unable to account for—certain principles that populations living near the proposed airport sites did not want bridged.

Session 5 was entitled "Barriers of Complexity." Using the classic article by Christopher Alexander (1965), which shows how "complexity defeats us unless we find a simpler way of writing it down," the class introduced theory on the mind's tendency to reject complexity and discussed the implications for planning of our tendency to opt for simple, evocative actions that may not prove to provide solutions at all. Martin Wachs and Joseph Schofer's 1969 article on "Abstract Values and Concrete Highways" provided a provocative illustration of this theory in a transportation setting, showing the pitfalls of our inclination to focus on concrete phenomena, such as highways, while glossing over the harder to conceptualize and handle but more important abstract values that should be considered to decide on whether the highways should be there in the first place.

Mark Johnson (1987), George Lakoff (1987), Lakoff and Johnson (1980), and Donald Schön (1979) have done important work on the role metaphor plays in everyday as well as planning life, and this was covered in the sixth class. These authors show how concepts are understood in terms of other concepts, often tacitly, and how bringing metaphorical understanding to the surface can be a significant tool of criticism. There are many rich examples of metaphor operating in transportation (to add interest, the Greek word for metaphor actually means "transport"). Our tendency to see highways as blood-circulating systems—terms such as "arterial," "circulator," and "bypass" and references to the "heart" of the city in the surface language provide vital clues—makes for one vivid case in point. Showing that metaphor is an instrument of thought—not just a display of colorful language—brings home the importance of the concept.

One example of the circulation metaphor at work lies in the suggestion that bringing a major new transportation facility through a depressed area will stimulate revitalization. Its inhabitants will supposedly benefit from the freer-flowing interaction thereby made possible, just as a human organ is brought back to health after a blocked artery is unclogged. Unfortunately, the rejuvenation of depressed areas requires far more than the simple installation of physical transportation links; but to those constrained to the partial view governed by the assumptions of the circulation metaphor, this may not be apparent. Metaphor, along with related issues of symbolism, imagery, and myth, was covered in the sixth class.

The seventh class considered a number of alternative systems of inquiry, including Kantian, Hegelian, and Singerian approaches (as discussed in Churchman 1971). William Hyman's 1983 creative paper on "Constructive Uses of Contradictory Thinking in Transportation" provided one source of real-world applications. Other classes discussed issues of equity, the disabled, suburbia, and management of existing infrastructure using the theoretical approaches to surfacing and critiquing assumptions taught earlier. Students gave in-class presentations of research projects before a final wrap-up class.

Assignments

The three major assignments were designed to encourage the surfacing and criticism of assumptions in transportation planning, using theory introduced during classes.

The first assignment had two parts. The first part required students to critically evaluate and compare books by authors whose different modes of argumentation led to very different recommendations on transit system development. They had to identify the different assumptions of John R. Meyer, John F. Kain, and Martin Wohl (1965; who favor highway-based and express bus transportation improvements over rail for low-density Western cities) and Boris Pushkarev, Jeffrey M. Zupan, and Robert S. Cumella (1982; whose findings suggest that rail systems are justifiable in many such cities) and show how the different assumptions had led to different conclusions.

The second part invited students to read between the lines of a transcript of a debate on transportation policy at SCAG (1983) in Los Angeles. The positions of the different parties were to be characterized with descriptions of how they each supported their positions. Students were asked to once more compare different sets of assumptions and show how they led to different conclusions.

The second assignment required the writing of an essay on a choice of topics, such as on setting boundaries to inquiry; the case for forecasting future transportation demands; a critique of the underpinnings of cost-benefit analysis; or a study of competing philosophical modes of inquiry. Each essay demanded both the use of theory and its application to practical examples.

The final assignment consisted of the cooperative preparation by groups of students of presentations to be given in class in which the assumptions of the planning process were to be unearthed and critiqued. "Roads in London," for example, required students to elucidate the development of thinking about transportation planning in London since World War II: examining the assumptions behind plans for an urban motorway system; how forecasting had been employed; and the involvement of grass-roots interests. A case on BART (San Francisco's Bay Area Rapid Transit) asked students to analyze the assumptions behind competing explanations of the rail system's creation.

How the Course Went

Students were quite surprised by the content of the course, and there was some concern before it had even started that it did not emphasize the practical side of transportation planning or provide the type of preparation employers were looking for. The concern was still evident among some students at the end of the course, but there was also a positive response to the new perspectives for criticism that were introduced and an appreciation that there was more than one way to do planning. One student complained in a course evaluation that there was "too much philosophical study"; another wrote that the course had "little practical use in the real world." A third student, however, said that the "extensive reading list will remain very useful for years," while a fourth declared that "I genuinely carried many of the course teachings in preparing my final project, and doubtless I'll carry them in practice."

It was often difficult to get effective discussion going on the more theoretical issues since the approach was rather different from that of other planning courses in the department. Still, while some students produced only mediocre homework assignments, others used the theoretical concepts of the course to produce insightful work.

In many ways, the third assignment provided the "proof of the pudding," for it required the application of what the course had taught to the interpretation of real planning issues. One presentation was outstanding and showed a highly effective use of the critical concepts taught earlier on. At the other end of the scale was a rather superficial presentation that showed little understanding or sympathy for these concepts. In the middle terrain were two moderately good presentations that showed a greater critical awareness on the part of the students than they had appeared to possess at the start of the course. They might not have burst out of many bubbles yet but at least they were now equipped with sharp-enough needles if they wanted to use them later on.

Conclusion

The course on urban transportation planning made an attempt to introduce subjects in a substantive area of planning with an emphasis on the use of philosophical modes of inquiry: to equip students to surface the assumptions of planning processes that so often lie hidden but are equally often at the core of problems of inadequate planning. It showed that proposed solutions to problems would be futile if the assumptions that defined the problems were inadequate; and it encouraged broader based thinking about planning methods. It did not teach students how to use Lotus software but prepared them to watch out for the pitfalls of using such tools unreflectively.

Teaching the course demonstrated that there is a useful role for courses that expose and criticize assumptions, rather than merely teach techniques, and that reveal the essentially ethical nature of all planning—not just transportation planning—and, indeed, all social inquiry. The experience underlined the point that if we want future generations of thinking planners, we need to teach them how to think.

In the end, it seems that we can never escape from some sort of bubble. We must always interpret the world through the artifacts of our culture and lifetime's experience. However, we do have the ability to burst at least the smaller bubbles that constrain our effectiveness as planners; the habit of deliberately seeking to do so can only result in increased freedom of movement. Planning has become too calculating, too unthinking. Planners should endeavor to seek out a meditative way of thinking. That is why all planners should practice bursting bubbles.[1]

Notes

1. This revised chapter discusses a course developed and taught while the author was a Visiting Lecturer at the Department of City and Regional Planning, University of North Carolina, Chapel Hill. The author thanks the university for the opportunity to do this work. The course has since been given in the Department of Civil Engineering at MIT, and gratitude is extended for the department's support of this author's attempts to bring new approaches to the graduate curriculum.

The idea that any area of planning should be taught from a perspective of ethics germinated during "West's Seminar" at the University of California, Berkeley. The author was a student in C. West Churchman's class during the 1981 fall term and acknowledges with gratitude the continuous inspiration which that encounter with fundamental issues of morality has provided. The ideas contained here owe much to other sources, too, including the work of Donald Schön, Martin Wachs, and Joseph Wezenbaum, all of which have had a particularly significant impact. While retaining full responsibility for the inevitable errors and omissions, the author would like to thank all of the above for their criticism and support over the past several years. Thanks are also extended to the anonymous referees of *Systems Research,* whose suggestions have, it is to be hoped, resulted in improvements to this discussion.

The Center for Transportation Studies at MIT provided assistance with the expenses of attending the 1987 conference of the Association of Collegiate Schools of Planning in Los Angeles, at which an earlier version of this chapter was presented, and has also provided funding for the author's research on the interface of ethics and transportation planning. Its contribution is gratefully acknowledged.

Bibliography

Alexander, C. 1965. A city is not a tree. *Architectural Forum* 122, No. 1, 58–61, and 122, No. 2, 58–62.
Altshuler, A. 1979. *The urban transportation system: politics and policy innovation.* Cambridge: MIT Press.
Churchman, C. W. 1971. *The design of inquiring systems.* New York: Basic Books.
———. 1979. *The systems approach and its enemies.* New York: Basic Books.
———. 1982. *Thought and wisdom.* Seaside, CA: Intersystems Publications.
Heidegger, M. 1966. *Discourse on thinking.* Translated by John M. Anderson and E. Hans Freund. New York: Harper and Row.
Hyman, W. A. 1983. Constructive uses of contradictory thinking in transportation. Paper delivered at the Transportation Research Forum, 24th Annual Meeting, Washington, DC.
Johnson, M. 1987. *The body in the mind: the bodily basis of meaning, imagination and reason.* Chicago: University of Chicago Press.

Jones, D. W. 1985. *Urban transit policy: an economic and political history.* Englewood Cliffs, NJ: Prentice Hall.

Kelman, S. 1985. Cost-benefit analysis and environmental, safety, and health regulation: ethical and philosophical considerations. In Wachs, M., ed. 1985. *Ethics in planning.* New Brunswick, NJ: Center for Urban Policy Research, Rutgers—The State University of New Jersey, 223–245.

Lakoff, G. 1987. *Women, fire, and dangerous things: what categories reveal about the mind.* Chicago: University of Chicago Press.

Lakoff, G. and Johnson, M. 1980. *Metaphors we live by.* Chicago: University of Chicago Press.

MacIntyre, A. 1985. Utilitarianism and the presuppositions of cost-benefit analysis: an essay on the relevance of moral philosophy to the theory of bureaucracy. In Wachs, M., ed. 1985. *Ethics in planning.* New Brunswick, NJ: Center for Urban Policy Research, Rutgers—The State University of New Jersey, 216–232.

Meyer, J. R., Kain, J. F., and Wohl, M. 1965. *The urban transportation problem.* Cambridge: Harvard University Press.

Mulvey, J. M. 1983. Computer modelling for state use: implications for professional responsibility. Paper delivered at the meeting of the American Academy for the Advancement of Science, Detroit.

Pushkarev, B. S., Zupan, J. M., and Cumella, R. S. 1982. *Urban rail in America: an exploration of criteria for fixed-guideway transit.* Bloomington: Indiana University Press.

Schön, D. A. 1979. Generative metaphor—a case of frame conflict in our language about languages. In Ortony, A., ed. *Metaphor and thought.* Cambridge: Cambridge University Press, 254–283.

———. 1983. *The reflective practitioner.* New York: Basic Books.

———. 1987. *Educating the reflective practitioner.* San Francisco: Jossey-Bass.

Southern California Association of Governments. 1983. *Transcript of Executive Committee Regional Transportation Plan Workshop.* Los Angeles: Southern California Association of Governments.

———. 1984. *Los Angeles–Long Beach light rail transit project, patronage estimation and impacts.* Los Angeles: Southern California Association of Governments.

Stokey, E. and Zeckhauser, R. 1978. *A primer for policy analysis.* New York: W. W. Norton.

Stopher, P. R. and Meyburg, A. H. 1975. *Urban transportation modelling and planning.* Lexington, MA: Lexington Books.

Wachs, M. 1985a. Ethical dilemmas in forecasting for public policy. In Wachs, M., ed. 1985. *Ethics in planning.* New Brunswick, NJ: Center for Urban Policy Research, Rutgers—The State University of New Jersey, 246–258.

———, ed. 1985b. *Ethics in planning.* New Brunswick, NJ: Center for Urban Policy Research, Rutgers—The State University of New Jersey.

Wachs, M. and Schofer, J. 1969. Abstract values and concrete highways. *Traffic Quarterly* 91, 135–155.

Wason, P. C. 1960. On the failure to eliminate hypotheses in a conceptual task. *Quarterly Journal of Experimental Psychology* 12, 129–140.

TIMOTHY BEATLEY

15 *Teaching Environmental Philosophy to Graduate Planning Students*

The Role of Environmental Ethics in Planning Programs

There is little doubt that we are in the midst of a period of environmental crisis—indeed, a constellation of crises at local, regional, and global levels. The role for environmental planning and management, then, has become ever important, and we are increasingly forced to confront the finiteness and natural limits of the planet, as well as the competing views about its appropriate use of and our relationship with it. Planners, as a professional group, are increasingly involved in the management and planning of environmental resources, from national forests to coastal wetlands to air and water quality. The myriad of policy and planning decisions, moreover, made by planning bodies at federal, state, and local levels invariably and inextricably involves ethical choices. An understanding of environmental values and ethics is, I would argue, an essential underpinning for environmental planners (and, indeed, all planners) and an especially important component of any environmental planning curriculum or concentration.

Environmental ethics as an explicit subject of academic or scholarly focus, or of popular discussion, for that matter, is a relatively recent development. Certainly, strong statements of environmental ethics can be traced to the deeds and writings of important figures in the American conservation movement, such as John Muir and Gifford Pinchot, and to the literary works of writers such as Ralph Waldo Emerson, Henry David Thoreau, and others. However, it was the work of Aldo Leopold, most notably in his seminal essay "The Land Ethic" (published widely in *A Sand County Almanac*, 1949[1]), that in many ways marks the modern beginnings of environmental ethics as a subject of major scholarly, as well as popular, attention. Leopold sought to redefine our ethical relationship to land and to the earth, arguing in support of a posture that would view ourselves (*Homo sapiens*) as "members and plain citizens" of this larger biotic community of which we are a part rather than as conquerors of it. In many ways, Leopold set in motion the modern debate about our ethical obligation to, or relative to, the environment, a debate that, I believe, planning students and planning programs must begin to join in a more significant way.

There has been a considerable ballooning of attention in academic circles in recent years to the subject of environmental ethics. There is now a growing subfield of environmental ethics within moral philosophy, for example, along with a growing number of journals, such as *Environmental Ethics*, devoted exclusively to the topic. There has been, moreover, an explosion of published materials on the subject (Attfield 1983; Callicott 1989; Hargrove 1989; Nash 1989; Oelschlaeger 1991; Regan 1984; Rolston 1988; VanDeVeer and Pierce 1986; see my article [Beatley 1989] for a review of much of this literature).

Despite the clear and direct connections between the field of planning—with its focus on the use and management of land and environment—and the subject of environmental ethics (see chapter 5), it is surprising that more attention is not paid to the topic in graduate planning curricula. Recent surveys of planning curricula confirm this. Evelyn Martin and I (Martin and Beatley 1993), for instance, found that among eighty-seven responding programs in North America, only three schools reported the existence of a separate course in environmental ethics.[2] Furthermore, little or no attention appears to be given to the subject in planning theory classes (Klosterman 1992). It is surprising that planning theory students are not given some exposure to at least Leopold's thinking, which has direct relevance to virtually all subfields in planning.

One program where an environmental ethics course has been taught is at the Department of Urban and Environmental Planning at the University of Virginia (UVa), Charlottesville. What follows is a discussion of this course and how environmental ethics has been taught, over a number of years, in this program. Of particular interest is the role this course plays in the planning curriculum; its structure, content, and pedagogy; and thoughts about the applicability of similar courses to other departments.

Ethics in the Environmental Planning Concentration

Environmental planning represents a major curricular concentration of UVa's planning program. The department offers a variety of environmental planning courses (beyond the courses mandatory for all students in the program), with three constituting an informational environmental core: "Environmental Policy and Planning" (an overview of key environmental programs and policies, such as the National Environmental Policy Act, the Clean Air and Clean Water Acts, the Endangered Species Act, Coastal Zone Management Act, and so on, including a discussion of how these programs function, their success, and their effectiveness, along with a discussion of political and other factors that impinge upon their implementation); "Natural Systems and Environmental Planning" (emphasizing the physical sciences, including coverage of natural carrying capacity, hydrology, soils, air quality modelling, and so on); and "Environmental Values and Ethics." While these courses are not required, most environmental planning students are strongly encouraged to take them. They also serve as a foundation for a number of more specialized environmental and land use planning courses offered, including "Environmental Impact Assessment," "Natural Resources Planning," "Third World Environmental Planning," "Growth Management," as well as project- and fieldwork-oriented courses (all students must take two so-called "Application Courses," offered in the different concentrations[3]). The ethics course, then, is taught in combination with a broader environmental curriculum intended to impart a fairly comprehensive understanding of physical and natural systems, environmental policy and planning, as well as ethics and values.

"Environmental Values and Ethics" has been taught on a yearly basis since 1987, including being taught occasionally at the satellite northern Virginia campus. It is explicitly structured as a seminar, though the class size has at times been quite large, ranging from about ten to thirty students. The primary objectives of the course are:

1. Sensitizing environmental planning students to the (inevitable and pervasive) ethical and value dimensions of environmental policy and planning issues;

2. Exposing environmental planning students to the variety of
    ethical positions, theories, principles, and points of view that
    can, or could, serve to guide environmental decisions and that
    they will likely encounter in future practice; and
3. Helping students to develop and/or clarify their own particular
    environmental ethic or set of ethics.

While each of these objectives is important, providing an opportunity to develop and clarify students' own values has, in my mind,
been especially critical. Much of the class is oriented around personal
reflection and clarification of what appropriate ethical standards ought
to be, and it is my belief that such a seminar can help to establish
a clearer sense of professional purpose and normative direction to
environmental planning students that will later serve as a source of
strength in difficult professional times.

The course tends to draw heavily from students in the planning
program but has attracted students from a variety of different departments around the university. In recent years, students have been drawn
heavily from law (there is a large and growing contingent of environmental law students at UVa), environmental sciences, marine affairs,
and engineering, among other places. Again, it is important to note that
the course is not aimed simply at environmental planning students
but has direct relevance to planning students in other concentrations,
especially land use planning (and a number of such students have taken
the course).

Course Pedagogy

As the review of the topical coverage indicates, this course focuses
heavily on the teaching of environmental philosophy—on the examination and study of values and the normative theories, concepts, and
principles relevant in guiding personal and societal decisions about the
environment. It assumes that as human beings (and specifically as
planning students), the selection of the values that guide our actions is,
to some degree, under our control and subject to reflection, discourse,
and deliberation. I assume human beings have the capacity to act
on principle and to contemplate, conceptualize, and choose among
alternative courses of action. The course is about values and about how
environmental ethics and philosophy can inform us about how we ought
to act in relation to the environment and its human and nonhuman
inhabitants.

This course, then, in its focus on philosophy and philosophical theory, is *not* a number of things. It is not an environmental politics course or a course that examines in much detail past or contemporary environmental movements and the dynamics or ideological underpinnings of such movements (for example, the Green movement in Europe and elsewhere). It is also not an environmental history course and focuses relatively little attention, for instance, on the evolution of the conservation movement in the United States or on the writings and thinking of major luminaries in this history. It is also not an environmental economics or resource economics course or an environmental law course, though it does draw to some extent from the philosophy and values found in these areas.

The course's focus on environmental philosophy, however, does not translate into a course disconnected from policy, politics, and the realities of contemporary environmental planning. Rather, the course takes an applied-philosophical approach (as the discussion below indicates), examining ethical concepts and theories in a policy context and with an eye to their ability to resolve or help decide tangible policy conflicts and dilemmas.

"Environmental Values and Ethics" is taught very much in a seminar format, with heavy responsibility given to the students in the class to come prepared each week to critically analyze and discuss course topics. The class is usually taught in a three-hour block of time once a week. Half of each session is devoted to a discussion of ethical theories, concepts, and principles, with the second half organized around applying them to specific tangible environmental policy quandaries or conflicts. Specifically, extensive use is made of a combination of hypothetical scenarios developed by the instructor and a set of recent newspaper clippings. For each class meeting, students are assigned a combination of scholarly (and often theoretical) articles and book excerpts, newspaper clippings, and hypothetical scenarios that effectively illustrate the types of ethical issues or topics to be addressed that week.

The reading assignments for the course are extensive by usual planning course standards. Scholarly readings are drawn from several required books (Nash 1989; Rolston 1988; Taylor 1986; VanDeVeer and Pierce 1986), and additional journal and book excerpts of classics not included in the required books are also assigned (for example, Hardin 1968). Leopold's *A Sand County Almanac* (1949) is also typically ordered as a required book, though "The Land Ethic" essay is also contained in Donald VanDeVeer and Christine Pierce (1986). While the reading load is at times quite heavy, students are generally able to keep up; because of the discussion orientation of the course, most students feel compelled

to come to class adequately prepared. For several of the more philosophically complex (and lengthy) works, such as Paul W. Taylor's *Respect for
Nature* (1986), students are given detailed outlines.

Incorporating an applied dimension to the course has worked
quite well. Students are forced to confront the realities of environmental
policy and see how abstract theories and concepts can (or cannot) help
to guide planning and decision making. Something on the order of
seventy-five clippings are assigned over the course of the semester, with
about four or five discussed each week. For example, when discussing
obligations to sentient forms of life, the students are assigned a clipping
that describes the gassing by a developer of a colony of prairie dogs in
Colorado and the controversy over why the developer could not wait for
a planned relocation of the colony. When considering the issue of
paternalism, students are assigned an article describing efforts to build
vacation housing on a remote and bridgeless barrier island and the
conflict surrounding (among other things) whether property owners
there ought to be allowed to place themselves at risk to hurricanes,
erosion, and other coastal hazards. In considering obligations for future
generations, students are asked to read clippings about recent conflicts
over protecting Civil War battlefields and to consider whether such
potential obligations require saving these kinds of historic landscapes.
Each clipping or scenario, then, is selected to highlight a particular
type of environmental conflict or dilemma, calling into play certain
competing values and ethical perspectives.

The course pedagogy depends heavily on free and open dialogue,
both about competing theories and how they are applied in resolving
particular ethical dilemmas. I have found it extremely important to set
the tone early in the class that all points of view are legitimate and are
to be respected. Students may be pressed to explain and defend their
point of view, but participants must be made to feel comfortable and
secure in expressing their ideas even where the majority of the class may
disagree with them. Thus, an ethic of respect and tolerance is critical.
While my own personal views tend to emerge over the course of the
semester, it is important to avoid "imposing" upon students, intentionally
or unintentionally, some sense that there is an official right or wrong
position. I have tended to view the role of the instructor as primarily
one of ethical facilitator and certainly not lecturer.

An important element of the course's pedagogy is the final paper
required of each student. Specifically, students are asked to develop and
put forth their own environmental ethic or set of ethics. A set of paper
guidelines is provided that asks students to consider and address certain
key questions. Students can (and have) taken many different ap-

proaches, from developing unified, comprehensive frameworks (for example, individuals may embrace a biocentric or ecocentric outlook and seek to apply it in a grand and overarching fashion) to more discrete and disjointed approaches (such as answering one by one the questions posed by the instructor). Students are free to develop a very personal ethic (that is, what they feel their own personal ethical obligations are) and/or a more collective or public ethic (that is, what they feel the environmental responsibilities of the collective or society are, as expressed through the decisions and policies of governmental bodies, ranging from local planning commissions to state legislatures to the United Nations). Students are asked to, where possible, provide examples that illustrate how their ethic would apply in resolving tangible environmental conflicts and what its implications for public policy would be (for instance, if one believes that all human beings are entitled to certain environmental goods and services, exactly how do we define these and how will they be provided or protected? If we believe that future generations are entitled to a certain level of environmental quality, what are the policy implications for managing population growth, controlling depletion of nonrenewable resources, and so on).

Presentation and discussion of the final paper is also an important part of the course. Each student is assigned an anonymous paper that she or he must present to the class as well as critique—for example, which arguments were convincing, which were not; logical inconsistencies in the arguments or principles; whether the policy implications flow from the ethical standards presented; and so on. The author has a chance to rebut and then general discussion by the class is encouraged. Through this final paper, students are forced to sharpen and clarify their ethical views sufficient to make them understandable to others. Over the course of the semester, students are exposed to a variety of ethical concepts and theories, and by the end of the semester, these have clearly and directly fed into the development of the students' own ethical positions. (Though, again, no particular position or view is advocated.[4])

Topical Coverage

The environmental ethics seminar covers a tremendous amount of substantive ground and begins with a relatively narrow view of what our ethical obligations relative to the environment are, gradually expanding this over the course of the semester. The initial few classes focus on developing a theoretical framework and on understanding what environmental ethics is and how it might be helpful in environmental planning and policy-making. I present one particular approach (there are undoubtedly numerous other ways to do this) to classify the different theories we cover, which employs two primary ethical dimensions: (1) the extent to which a perspective is teleological (ends-based) or deontological (duty-based or nonconsequentialist); and (2) the extent to which a perspective is anthropocentric (human-centered) or nonanthropocentric (life-centered or ecosystem-centered; Figure 15-1). While this is a simple classification, and some theories and concepts do not fit nicely within one of these four quadrants, it is at least an initial and useful construct for students to start thinking about organizing alternative ethical perspectives. There are numerous other dimensions, of course, on which theories and concepts could be classified, and students are encouraged to, over the course of the semester, add to and expand upon their own organizing framework.

The initial class or two also covers certain preliminary issues, including discussions of: (1) basic terminology, such as ethics versus values versus attitudes; (2) the alternative sources of ethics and values, such as the role of religion, family or political culture in shaping ethical views; (3) differences (and connections) between environmental ethics and professional ethics; and (4) the primary ethical questions to be addressed over the semester. A number of key ethical questions are identified early on and these include:

1. *How shall we define the relevant "moral community"?* A central question involves how we go about defining the category or categories of people or things in the environment to which ethical obligations are owed. There are at least three key dimensions to this question that are examined in some detail over the course of the semester: the biological dimension (for example, is it just *Homo sapiens* who fall within the moral community or does it include other forms of life, perhaps sentient creatures or perhaps all living organisms?); the temporal dimension (for instance, do obligations extend to future generations and posterity and, if so, how far into the future does this temporal community extend?); and the geographical dimension (for example, do obligations extend beyond one's own neighborhood or community to people and jurisdictions many hundreds or thousands of miles away?).

2. *What ethical standards, concepts, or principles should define obligations to the moral community?* Once the moral community is defined, what are the specific ethical duties and responsibilities that attach to them? If sentient organisms are indeed part of our moral community, what level of respect or protection must we

FIGURE 15-1

Categorizing Ethical Theories about Planning and the Environment*

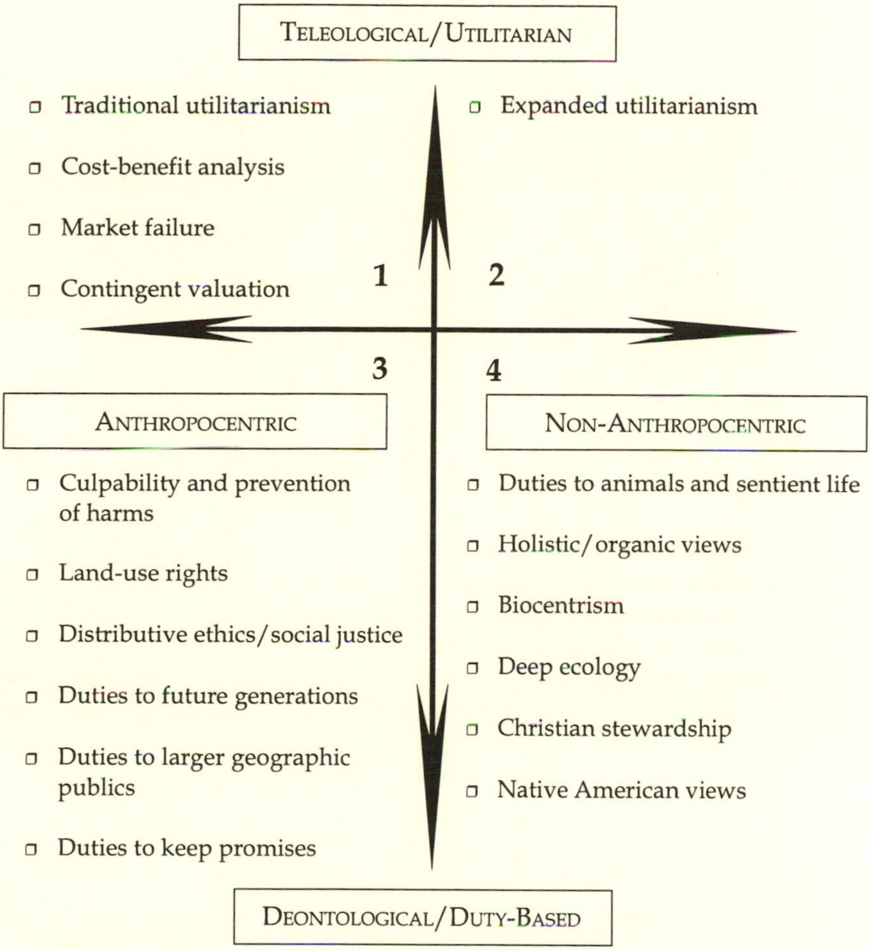

TELEOLOGICAL/UTILITARIAN

- Traditional utilitarianism
- Cost-benefit analysis
- Market failure
- Contingent valuation

1

- Expanded utilitarianism

2

3

4

ANTHROPOCENTRIC

- Culpability and prevention of harms
- Land-use rights
- Distributive ethics/social justice
- Duties to future generations
- Duties to larger geographic publics
- Duties to keep promises

NON-ANTHROPOCENTRIC

- Duties to animals and sentient life
- Holistic/organic views
- Biocentrism
- Deep ecology
- Christian stewardship
- Native American views

DEONTOLOGICAL/DUTY-BASED

* It should be noted that the concepts and theories contained in each quadrant are meant to be illustrative, not exhaustive. Moreover, no attempt is made within each quadrant to array the theories along the two axes.

accord them? If our environmental obligations extend into the future, what specifically do we owe to those people and creatures who follow us in time? In many ways, these first and second questions are inextricably connected, as part of the same broader question of what our environmental duties actually are.

3. *On what ethical grounds or bases can we defend or justify these ethical standards, concepts, and principles?* It is also important to understand how we derive and defend the ethical positions arrived at in answering the above questions. Sometimes referred to as critical ethics or metaethics, they are concerned with the question of whether there is a rational basis for the ethical positions we embrace. Can we refer to some Archimedean point—such as John Rawls's (1971) "original position"—from which to support a particular environmental ethic or ethics? Are the moral grounds, conversely, intuitive or spiritual? The issue of the moral grounds or bases of ethical positions is introduced to students in the seminar, but relatively little time is devoted to it.

Anthropocentric Perspectives

A number of specific ethical perspectives are discussed over the course of the semester, including most of those shown in Figure 15-1. As the semester progresses, students are gradually exposed to an ever-broadening moral community, moving sequentially from quadrants 1 to 4. What follows is a cursory introduction to some of the major ethical theories and points of view covered, roughly in the order they are addressed. The key ethical perspectives are identified and discussed below.

UTILITARIANISM, COST-BENEFIT ANALYSIS, AND MARKET FAILURE

The course begins its review of anthropocentric ethical perspectives on the environment in quadrant 1: teleological/anthropocentric positions. Within this framework, ethical decisions about the environment are determined through reference to the relative quantity of goods and bads produced or those actions, policies, and decisions that serve to maximize overall social utility. I typically have the students read portions of William F. Baxter's classic *People or Penguins* (1974), in which he puts forth one of the strongest statements in support of an anthropocentric decision framework (and is usually very effective for generating student discussion).

The utilitarian view is presented as the dominant ethical paradigm, and students consider how it has been institutionalized, for instance, through such procedures as cost-benefit analysis (such as Executive Order 12291, imposed by President Ronald W. Reagan in the United States, which requires that the benefits of environmental regulation explicitly be shown to exceed their costs; mandated cost-benefit for flood control projects and other public works; and so on). Students look at examples of cost-benefit analysis and techniques, such as contingent valuation. Examples reviewed in class include efforts to use cost-benefit in making project decisions (for example, Tellico dam) and in setting pollution control standards (for instance, setting lead standards for drinking water). Students also consider the practice of discounting and its effect of devaluing the future (Jacobs 1991). A number of examples of efforts to place dollar values on environmental goods and services are also reviewed, including efforts to attach values to visibility in national parks (Schulze et al. 1983), on the environmental services provided by coastal wetlands (Gosselink et al. 1974), and environmental damage from oil spills (Lancaster 1991), among others.

Students are asked to consider whether a utilitarian standard is morally defensible, whether dollar values can and should be attached to such things as endangered species and views in national parks, and whether society's ethical obligations to, and relations to, the environment should be determined through reference to consumer wants.

Because the free market system is usually the theoretical basis on which cost-benefit is based, some time is spent discussing its assumptions. Students consider arguments for public environmental policy based on market failure, including the existence of externalities, high transaction costs, information problems, and other factors that limit the ability to achieve Pareto efficiency. Public goods theory and problems associated with common pool resources (for example, the tragedy of the commons) are also considered.

Many students typically react to utilitarian approaches in a negative way, offended by the overly anthropocentric orientation and skeptical of the ability, and morality, of treating the environment solely as a narrow economic good. These discussions are often effective in setting students in search of other, more encompassing, ethical points of view. Though students often react negatively to utilitarian points of view, they are also, at least in the initial weeks of the course, uncertain about what more acceptable frameworks should or could include. I should note that even later in the semester, students acknowledge the practical value of utilitarian and economic arguments, believing that at least in this day and age, these arguments may continue to hold the greatest weight with the average citizen or public official. A constant source of personal anxiety for students in the course is how to balance and reconcile their own ideas of ethical treatment of the environment with what they feel will be "effective" or "feasible," that is, what will resonate well with the broader public. (This is, I would argue, a common dynamic they will face later in their careers and will be useful for them to contemplate in graduate school.)

ENVIRONMENTAL RIGHTS

Several key concepts are considered in quadrant 2, which expand the moral framework to include deontological ethical perspectives. Students are first asked to consider, in contrast to utilitarianism, a rights-based ethical standard. Still in the anthropocentric side of Figure 15-1, students are asked to consider whether human beings qua human beings are entitled to certain environmental rights—rights to certain environmental things (for instance, access to shorelines, natural wonders, scenic landscapes), as well as perhaps rights to be free from certain environmental harms (for example, air and water pollution or toxic waste). Examples of current policy or legal doctrine reflecting these values are provided. As an example of the first type of right, students consider several common law doctrines that protect rights of public access to shorelines and navigable waters, including the public trust doctrine and the doctrine of customary use (Sax 1971). As an example of the latter type of right, students consider national pollution standards (such as the National Ambient Air Quality Standards) as a reflection, to a large extent, of the view that all U.S. citizens regardless of where they live are entitled to be free from a certain level of environmental harm or risk. Students are also asked to consider the fairness of historic patterns of exposure to hazardous and toxic wastes (such as the placement of dumps or disposal and treatment facilities) and the disproportionate levels of risk experienced by poor and minority communities (Bullard 1990). Do such patterns represent the violation of individuals' basic environmental rights? Students are also asked to consider the extent to which they are entitled to procedural environmental rights and the extent of these potential rights (for instance, the right to know if one's home is built on a hazardous waste site or the right to have full knowledge about the likely environmental impacts of a proposed project, such as a highway). Students consider the extent to which existing laws represent expressions of these kinds of public environmental rights.

During this segment, a number of expressions of, and possible sources for, such rights are considered, including the United Nations' Declaration of Human Rights, state constitutions, and common law, among others. At a more philosophical level, students consider the ultimate moral grounds for such rights, including, for example, social contract theory.

FUTURE GENERATIONS

Consistent with exploring different ways of defining the relevant moral community, considerable time is also spent considering obligations to future generations and to posterity and the implications for environmental planning and management. Students are first asked to consider the ways in which actions and policies today influence the quality and nature of future existence, such as the destruction of scenic landscapes, loss of biodiversity, impacts of global warming, and upper atmospheric ozone depletion. Through readings and discussions, students then confront the question of whether future generations (again, primarily within the anthropocentric framework) have any moral rights and interests that may place certain duties and responsibilities on present generations (Partridge 1981; Sikora and Barry 1978). Students are subjected to a variety of points of view, including views skeptical of claims based on future generations (for example, arguments that future generations, because of a lack of reciprocity and mutual benefit, cannot be said to be part of our moral community; Golding 1972) and those that strongly argue in support of them. Much of the discussion focuses on the appropriate time frame of our moral duties (that is, how far into the future must we be concerned with) and the actual extent and nature of our duties to future inhabitants. Among the potential duties discussed are obligations to pass along a planet no more degraded than the current one; obligations to, wherever possible, keep options open (for future inhabitants); obligations to promote sustainability and to move to patterns of human consumption and life-style that are sustainable (that is, to the extent possible, living off the interest of our natural capital); and others. Contemporary concepts of stewardship, sustainable communities, and the planetary trust are also discussed (Berry 1981; Van der Ryn and Calthorpe 1991; and Weiss 1990, respectively).

DISTRIBUTIVE OBLIGATIONS

Students also consider decisions about the use and management of the environment in terms of their distributive obligations. Specifically, students are presented with several competing theories about what constitutes a fair and socially just society and how environmental goods and resources fit into this distribution. Among the distributive concepts reviewed are libertarian perspectives; equality and equal shares approaches; compensatory equality; and Rawlsian principles of justice (especially the "difference principle"; Rawls 1971).

Students are asked to apply these concepts in considering several contemporary environmental dilemmas. One issue discussed extensively is the major social inequalities that currently exist in the distribution of both environmental bads—pollution and toxic waste—and goods— scenic views, beaches, and recreational lands. Is it fundamentally unjust, for instance, that poor and minority communities experience a higher probability of exposure to hazardous waste dumps, incinerators, landfills, and other "NIMBYs" ("Not in my backyard")? Another issue extensively discussed is the conflict (at least perceived) between the goals of social justice and economic opportunity and the goals of environmental protection and conservation (for example, jobs versus owls).

PATERNALISM AND RISK-TAKING

Many environmental conflicts revolve around attempts by the collective or society to place constraints on certain kinds of risky behavior, raising charges of paternalism and questions about the extent to which individuals ought to be allowed to place themselves at risk to environmental hazards. Environmental planning may result in a regulation that prevents an individual from building a home and living along a seismic fault line, for instance, or in a dangerous riverine floodway. It may prevent a developer from building a housing project on an isolated barrier island subject to hurricane and coastal storm risks (at least without constructing bridges and other improvements to allow timely evacuation). The federal government, as a further example, may shut down a polluting factory based on public health concerns, even though the community in which it is located may be willing to accept the health risks in exchange for the jobs and economic activity the industry provides.

Students are asked to consider the extent to which government has moral obligations to protect the health and safety of individuals, and the general public, even when this runs counter to their own perceived interests and preferences. A number of possible theoretical positions justifying and supporting such restrictions are reviewed (for example, retrospective rationality—or the idea that individuals will later be thankful that the government prevented them from placing themselves at risk to a hurricane, earthquake, or other catastrophic event). Students also discuss the extent to which many forms of environmental regulation that are labeled "paternalistic" actually represent attempts to prevent or minimize the creation of public harms (that is, cases where the individual's decision to live on the barrier island has clear public implications, such as the expenditure of disaster assistance monies in the future, placing emergency rescue personnel at risk, and so on) or to ensure a certain level of consumer protection.

Nonanthropocentric Perspectives: Further Expanding the Moral Community

Much of the course is also devoted to nonanthropocentric ethical theories, and students are challenged to think about the extent that other things in the world—other creatures, natural objects, the environment as a whole—have value irrespective of their value to *Homo sapiens*. This is a major theoretical issue and is hotly contested in the environmental ethics literature. It also typically excites students and generates considerable in-class discussion. Can it be said that nature or elements in nature have intrinsic worth or inherent value? Students in the class are asked to consider whether the nature and magnitude of our environmental condition argues for the need for a new relationship to the earth (as some of us have suggested; see Beatley 1994 and Martin and Beatley 1993, for instance) and one that directs the moral framework away from narrow anthropocentrism.

To start the debate, I present several of Roderick Nash's diagrams that depict the gradual evolution of ethics to encompass an ever-larger set of people and things to which moral consideration is given (Nash 1985, 1989). This is a starting point from which the class then considers a number of different positions, including obligations to sentient life-forms; obligations to species; biocentrism; ecocentrism; and deep ecology, among others. Each of these is briefly described below.

DUTIES TO SENTIENT LIFE-FORMS

Consistent again with the overall strategy of the course, we begin to review nonanthropocentric theories in a narrow way and gradually

expand their moral coverage. We begin consideration of nonanthropocentric perspectives by examining positions that argue primarily on
behalf of intrinsic value as a certain category of "nonhuman" things,
namely, other forms of sentient life. These are life-forms that, similar to
humans, are thinking and feeling and are subject to sensations of
pleasure and pain. A well-developed literature has emerged from the
animal welfare and animal rights movements, and the students consider
a number of the more important works. Students consider both utilitarian rationales, principally the writings of Peter Singer (1975), and the
rights-based views of Tom Regan (1983). Students also consider other
more moderate views, such as that of Donald VanDeVeer, who constructs
a framework for balancing conflicts between human and nonhuman life-
forms (that is, his "two-factor egalitarianism"; VanDeVeer 1979). This
position, then, stresses the inherent worth essentially of animals, especially those that are most similar to human beings.

In considering examples, emphasis is given to conflicts between
human populations and sentient life-forms in nature (for example,
conflicts between deer populations and expanding suburban communities in the eastern United States; between mountain lions and resort
housing in the West; or between populations of wild buffalo and ranch-
ing) rather than many of the usual topics on the animal rights agenda
with less direct relevance to land and environmental management, such
as laboratory testing or factory farming.

DUTIES TO SPECIES AND BIODIVERSITY

A different ethical point of view is one that sees the primary ethical
duty to protect species and the diversity of life-forms on earth. Many of
our most contentious environmental planning issues in recent years
have involved conflicts between endangered species and some desired
human use of activity (for instance, logging versus the northern spotted
owl; resort development versus the key deer; or groundwater extraction
versus the fountain darter). Students are asked to consider a number of
questions, including: Must we protect every species of life on earth, even
when the social and economic costs are extremely high? Is it not the case
that the loss of a few species will have no discernible environmental
ripple effects (an anthropocentric perspective admittedly)? Is not extinction itself a natural process, with *Homo sapiens* simply excelling at what
every other species seeks to do (that is, expanding its ecological niche:
Darwinian "survival of the fittest")?

A number of ethical positions are considered, including the views of David Ehrenfeld and others who see current levels of human-caused extinction as unnatural and believe there exists a strong ethical duty to prevent the extinction of other forms of life. Ehrenfeld, for instance, introduces the concept of the "Noah Principle" and the position that species and communities ". . . should be conserved because they exist and because this existence is itself but the present expression of a continuing historical process of immense antiquity and majesty. Long-standing existence in nature is deemed to carry with it the unimpeach-able right to continued existence" (Ehrenfeld 1981, pp. 207–208).

The broader and more inclusive concept of biodiversity is introduced here and further reinforced in later sessions.

BIOCENTRISM

Gradually, the course expands its focus to consider even more inclusive nonanthropocentric perspectives. Philosophical biocentrism holds that it is all life that has inherent worth and thus ought to be the center of the moral framework. One of the most detailed and comprehensive developments of the "biocentric outlook" is that of philosopher Paul W. Taylor, and students in the seminar read his seminal work, *Respect for Nature* (1986). Though a philosophical treatise, Taylor translates the underlying assumptions of his biocentric position (that is, a belief that all organisms are "teleological centers of life" and thus can be said to have "a good of their own") into a series of very detailed "Basic Rules of Conduct" and a set of "Priority Rules" for working out conflicts between human and nonhuman life (Taylor, in fact, uses a number of planning-related examples). Therefore, what is said to have inherent worth is expanded further—it is not just sentient life-forms nor just species that have intrinsic worth but all life (that is, plants as well as animals, individual organisms as well as species).

ECOCENTRISM

Ethical holism, as it is sometimes referred to, is yet another ethical paradigm, again much more encompassing. In contrast to Taylor's biocentrism, ecocentrists point not to the intrinsic value of life but to the inherent worth of the larger ecosystem itself. The ecosystem, it is argued, has moral value because of its complexity, interconnectedness, and persistence (Rolston 1988).

Students compare and contrast the biocentric and ecocentric positions and explore the implications for policy and planning. Though the moral grounding of each is somewhat different, both positions argue strongly for the need to protect ecosystems and ecosystemic functions (the biocentrists because this is the most effective and efficient way to protect living organisms). A number of other questions about the implications of these positions are considered, including: At what ecosystem level does inherent worth apply (for example, do we have duties to protect a ten-acre wetland ecosystem . . . a watershed ecosystem . . . global ecosystem)? What alteration of ecosystems and ecosystem functions, if any, is permissible while still respecting their inherent moral worth?

DEEP ECOLOGY, ECOFEMINISM, AND BIOREGIONALISM

The biocentric and ecocentric positions, while compelling to many students in their prescriptions, also strike many as overly philosophical in their approach. Deep ecology is, in many ways, a much more intuitive position and another receiving considerable attention in the course. Coined by Norwegian philosopher Arne Naess, deep ecology refers to the development of a deeper ecological consciousness and of our overcoming the artificial separation between human beings and the rest of nature (Devall and Sessions 1985; Naess 1973). Deep ecology advocates argue that much of our contemporary environmental planning and management is "shallow" in its orientation—seeking to make changes at the margins but not seeking to fundamentally readjust human-nature relationships. Deep ecology argues for the need to develop a more fundamental identification with nature and the developing of an ecological self. As Bill Devall notes: "if we experience the world as an extension of ourselves, if we have a broader and deep identification, then we feel hurt when other beings, including non-human beings are hurt. . . . The integrity of the biosphere is seen as the integrity of our own persons." (Manes 1990, p. 148). Achieving such identification and connectedness, in turn, makes obsolete the need to speak in terms of "rights" and "duties" in the Western sense.

Ecofeminism shares many of the same underlying perspectives as deep ecology and is a theoretical perspective that has been added to the course's topical coverage in the last several years. Ecofeminism points to androcentric values as an important explanation for our current destructive and exploitative relationship to the earth and draws parallels between the domination of men over women and the domination of nature by the human species. It suggests that an important response to our current environmental crisis is the adoption of a more feminist perspective—one that stresses a nurturing and respective posture toward nature.

The deep ecology and ecofeminist outlooks are frequently controversial among students, and they are pressed to think about the extent to which such radical reorientations toward the environment are feasible and how they might be brought about. In this vein, the concept of bioregionalism is introduced and discussed. It suggests the importance of focusing on certain biologically distinct areas—bioregions—to which individuals would be able to develop personal (and political) connection and a sense of attachment and commitment. In considering bioregionalism, students discuss (and frequently argue) about whether such an approach would indeed promote identification and how in a practical and planning sense such a strategy could be implemented (for example, how do we go about defining bioregions and what institutional and government changes would be necessary to organize our lives around this concept?). One of the most contentious topics is the possible role physical mobility plays in discouraging bioregionalism. Some argue that a major reason why Americans are unable to develop bioregional attachments is the fact that they move too often (Andruss et al. 1990). Students in the seminar are asked to consider this and other reasons why bioregionalism may be difficult to achieve in contemporary American culture.

Other nonanthropocentric positions are also considered in the course, but not to the same extent as those cited above. These include, among others, Native American perspectives, Eastern religious views, and Christian stewardship. Greater attention probably should be paid to each of these topics, but the shortness of time prevents a truly comprehensive coverage of relevant ethical positions.

In addition to the above review of alternative ethical theories and perspectives, at least two class sessions at the end are devoted to more specific and specialized environmental topics. These have tended to change from year to year, reflecting different student interests, but have included corporate environmental ethics; the ethics of environmental activism (for example, tree spiking, monkey wrenching, or "ecoterrorism"); the professional ethics of environmental planners (for instance, revolving-door issues or conflicts of interest); and changing conceptions of private property (and the need for such changes), among others.

Conclusions

"Environmental Values and Ethics" provides an important opportunity for planning students (and others) to critically examine the question of our ethical responsibilities to, or relative to, the environment. Students are exposed to a range of ethical positions, are required to read and discuss the leading philosophical works in each, and are forced to apply them to tangible environmental planning issues and conflicts. While the course is not required, it is strongly encouraged as an important component of the environmental planning concentration in the master of planning degree. It is our belief at the University of Virginia that it is essential for environmental planners to understand the inherent value dimensions of decisions about how we use land and the environment. Moreover, graduate planning school is perhaps one of the last opportunities students have to engage in this kind of moral reflection and to clarify and critically assess their own values about the environment. It is an opportunity to take stock of their moral convictions before being thrust into the world of political and economic expedience.

In this regard, student response to the course has been very good. Planning students, especially those in the environmental planning concentration, find that it is useful in helping them to develop a personal ethical framework in which to view planning and policy issues and to provide a sharper sense of professional purpose. Students from other disciplines, such as law and environmental sciences, find that it fills an important void in their own curricula, where there are few opportunities to discuss ethics or the larger value issues in their professions. Even those students who are skeptical in the beginning of the semester about the usefulness of ethical theory almost universally praise the experience at the end. The course is critical and challenging and asks students to confront issues and ideas they have usually not considered. In most cases, students appear to come away from the experience with the feeling that their horizons have been expanded and that the process of having to look at the world through a number of different ethical lenses was very rewarding.

It is important to keep in mind that, despite the success of the ethics seminar, environment values and ethics should not be relegated to a single course. Rather, curricula should seek to inject consideration of ethics wherever possible, including within more specialized environmental policy and planning courses and in planning theory courses common to all planning students. At UVa, for instance, environmental ethics is discussed as an initial subject in our introductory graduate-level environmental policy overview course, "Environmental Policy and Planning." It is also a key component of a large schoolwide course entitled "Environmental Choices," intended to introduce all design students (whether planners, architects, or landscape architects) to the nature of contemporary environmental problems and the potential roles of these professions in helping to solve these problems. Ideally, then, there will be multiple and overlapping opportunities to expose planning students to the subject of environmental ethics and the inherent value dimensions present in environmental conflicts today.

Notes

1. This essay was originally published in the *Journal of Forestry* in 1933.

2. It should be observed, however, that while only three planning programs were found to offer entire courses in environmental ethics, a much larger number—64 percent—indicated that the subject was covered to some degree as a component of another course. It is difficult to determine what the actual coverage is in these other courses, though, and a review of syllabi by Evelyn Martin and myself (Martin and Beatley, 1993) uncovered few specific references to the topic.

3. In addition to environmental planning, three other formal concentrations are offered in the Department of Urban and Environmental Planning: land use planning, urban development planning, and policy planning. As well, students also have the freedom to craft their own more individualized concentrations if they wish. Concentrations must include fifteen credit hours, and one of the two planning applications courses must be taken in the concentration area.

4. Nevertheless, it could be argued that the very organization of course, and the order in which the topics are presented, reflects a clear bias. By beginning with anthropocentric/utilitarian perspectives and ending with biocentric and deep ecology views, this may well convey the impression that the latter are more appropriate or defensible than the former. There is probably some truth to this, but I would contend that there is considerable logic to starting with the current narrow construct and moving to one that is broader in moral scope and perhaps more visionary.

Bibliography

Andruss, V., Plant, C., Plant, J., and Wright, E., eds. 1990. *Home! A bioregional reader.* Philadelphia: New Society Publishers.

Attfield, R. 1983. *The ethics of environmental concern.* New York: Columbia University Press.

Baxter, W. F. 1974. *People or penguins: the case for optimal pollution.* New York: Columbia University Press.

Beatley, T. 1989. Environmental ethics and planning theory. *Journal of Planning Literature* 4, 1–32.

Beatley, T. 1994. *Ethical land use: principles of policy and planning.* Baltimore: Johns Hopkins University Press.

Berry, W. 1981. *The gift of good land*. San Francisco: North Point.

Bullard, R. D. 1990. *Dumping in Dixie: race, class and environmental quality*. Boulder, CO: Westview Press.

Callicott, J. B. 1989. *In defense of the land ethic: essays in environmental philosophy*. Albany: State University of New York Press.

Devall, B. and Sessions, G. 1985. *Deep ecology: living as if nature mattered*. Salt Lake City: Gibbs M. Smith.

Ehrenfeld, D. 1981. *The arrogance of humanism*. Oxford: Oxford University Press.

Golding, M. P. 1972. Obligations to future generations. *The Monist* 56, 85–99.

Gosselink, J. G., Odum, E. P., and Pope, R. M. 1974. *The value of the tidal marsh*. Baton Rouge: Center for Wetlands Resources, Louisiana State University.

Hardin, G. 1968. The tragedy of the commons. *Science* 162, 1243–1248.

Hargrove, E. C. 1989. *Fundamentals of environmental ethics*. Englewood Cliffs, NJ: Prentice Hall.

Jacobs, M. 1991. *The green economy: environment, sustainable development and the politics of the future*. London: Pluto Press.

Klosterman, R. E. 1992. Planning theory education in the 1980s: results of a second course survey. *Journal of Planning Education and Research* 11, 130–140.

Lancaster, J. 1991. Value of intangible losses from Exxon Valley spill put at $3 billion. *Washington Post* March 20.

Leopold, A. 1949. *A Sand County almanac*. Oxford: Oxford University Press.

Manes, C. 1990. *Green rage: radical environmentalism and the unmaking of civilization*. Boston: Little, Brown.

Martin, E. and Beatley, T. 1993. Our relationship with the earth: environmental ethics in planning education. *Journal of Planning Education and Research* 12, 117–126.

Naess, A. 1973. The shallow and the deep, long range ecology movement, summary. *Inquiry* 16, 95–100.

Nash, R. 1985. Rounding out the American revolution: ethical extension and the new environmentalism. In Tobias, M., ed. *Deep ecology*. San Diego: Avant.

———. 1989. *The rights of nature: a history of environmental ethics*. Madison: University of Wisconsin Press.

Oelschlaeger, M. 1991. *The idea of wilderness*. New Haven, CT: Yale University Press.

Partridge, E., ed. 1981. *Responsibilities to future generations: environmental ethics*. Buffalo: Prometheus.

Rawls, J. 1971. *A theory of justice*. Cambridge: Harvard University Press.

Regan, T. 1983. *The case for animal rights*. Berkeley: University of California Press.

———, ed. 1984. *Earthbound: new introductory essays in environmental ethics*. Philadelphia: Temple University Press.

Rolston, Holmes, III. 1988. *Environmental ethics: duties to and values in the natural world*. Philadelphia: Temple University Press.

Sax, J. L. 1971. *Defending the environment: a strategy for citizen action*. New York: Alfred A. Knopf.

Schulze, W. D. *et al.* 1983. The economic benefits of preserving visibility in the national parklands of the Southwest. *Natural Resources Journal* 23, 149–174.

Sikora, R. J. and Barry, B. M., eds. 1978. *Obligations to future generations.* Philadelphia: Temple University Press.

Singer, P. 1975. *Animal liberation.* New York: Random House.

Taylor, P. W. 1986. *Respect for nature: a theory of environmental ethics.* Princeton, NJ: Princeton University Press.

Van der Ryn, S. and Calthorpe, P. 1991. *Sustainable communities.* San Francisco: Sierra Club Books.

VanDeVeer, D. 1979. Interspecific justice. *Inquiry* 22, 55–79.

VanDeVeer, D. and Pierce, C., eds. 1986. *People, penguins and plastic trees: basic issues in environmental ethics.* Belmont, CA: Wadsworth.

Weiss, E. B. 1990. In fairness to future generations. *Environment* 32, 7–11 and 30–31.

Selected Bibliography

This bibliography is necessarily selective. It does not include unpublished conference papers or works that are forthcoming or in progress. Substantively, it lists books, reports, articles, and some graduate theses on planning ethics—not planning values, not planning theory, and not professional ethics. Its purpose is to provide a starting point for academics, planners, and students interested in this area of inquiry. References in Elizabeth Howe (1990) and Marta Escuin-Rubio and Jerome Kaufman (1993), as well as my own work, provided the basis for the following snapshot of the current state of the art of planning ethics, primarily in North America.

Allor, D. 1970–71. Normative ethics in community planning. *Maxwell Review* 7, 113–137.

Alterman, R. and Page, J. 1973. The ubiquity of values and the planning process. *Plan* 13, 13–26.

Amy, D. 1984. Why policy analysis and ethics are incompatible. *Journal of Policy Analysis and Management* 3, 573–591.

Arkes, H. 1981. *The philosopher in the city.* Princeton, NJ: Princeton University Press.

Balkus, K. 1987. Commentary on "Hamlethics in planning." *Business and Professional Ethics Journal* 6, 79–82.

Barrett, C. 1984. Ethics in planning: you be the judge. *Planning* 50, 22–25.

———. 1986. Does she or doesn't she? What do planners think are ethical issues? *Student Planner* 7, 1 and 4.

Barrett, C. and Meck, S. 1989. From the board: a heated response on ethics. *Journal of the American Planning Association* Summer, 362–363.

Bayles, M. 1987. Commentary on "The worm and the juggernaut." *Business and Professional Ethics Journal* 6, 61–65.

Beatley, T. 1984. Applying moral principles to growth management. *Journal of the American Planning Association* 50, 459–469.

———. 1985. Paternalism and land use planning: ethical bases and practical applications. In Ahig, T., Callen, D., and Gray, J., eds. *Restraint of liberty.* Bowling Green, OH: Bowling Green State University, 53–70.

———. 1987. Planners and political philosophy. *Journal of the American Planning Association* 53, 235–236.

———. 1988a. Equity and distributional issues in infrastructure planning: a theoretical perspective. In Stein, J., ed. *Public infrastructure planning and management.* Urban Affairs Annual Reviews, Vol. 33. Sage Publications, 208–226.

———. 1988b. Ethical dilemmas in hazard management. *Natural Hazards Observer* May.

———. 1988c. Ethical issues in the use of impact fees to finance community growth. In Nelson, A., ed. *Development impact fees: policy rationale, practice, theory, and issues.* Chicago: Planners Press (American Planning Association), 339–61.

———. 1989a. Environmental ethics and planning theory. *Journal of Planning Literature* 4, 1–32.

———. 1989b. The role of expectations and promises in land use decision making. *Policy Sciences* 22, 27–50.

———. 1989c. Towards a moral philosophy of natural disaster mitigation. *International Journal of Mass Emergencies and Disasters* 7, 5–32.

———. 1991. A set of ethical principles to guide land use policy. *Land Use Policy* 3, 3–8.

———. 1992. Environmental ethics and hazardous waste management. In *Hazardous materials/wastes: social aspects of facility planning and management.* Conference proceedings of the Institute for Social Impact Assessment, Winnipeg, Manitoba, Canada, 228–236.

Berry, D. and Steiker, G. 1974. The concept of justice in regional planning: justice as fairness. *Journal of the American Institute of Planners* 40, 414–421.

Bolan, R. 1983. The structure of ethical choice in planning practice. *Journal of Planning Education and Research* 3, 23–34.

Camhis, M. 1979. *Planning theory and philosophy.* New York: Tavistock Publications.

Campbell, M. 1986. *Ethics and professionalism in planning.* Columbus, OH: Department of City and Regional Planning, Ohio State University.

Escuin-Rubio, M., and Kaufman, J. 1993. *Ethics in planning: an annotated bibliography.* CPL Bibliography 290. Chicago: Council of Planning Librarians.

Euston, A. 1986. Ethics and the planner's vision. *Student Planner* 7, 4–5.

Fainstein, S. and Fainstein, N. 1971. City planning and political values. *Urban Affairs Quarterly* 6, 341–362.

Forester, J. 1986. Politics, power, ethics and practice: abiding problems for the future of planning. *Plan Canada* 26, 224–27.

Fotian, N. 1987. Simmons and the concept of consent: commentary on "consent and fairness in planning land use." *Business and Professional Ethics Journal* 6, 21–24.

Gertel, S. 1990. *Ethics for planners amidst political conflict.* Master's research thesis, the Technion-Israel Institute of Technology, Haifa, Israel.

Goldstein, A. 1987. The expert and the public: local values and national choice. *Business and Professional Ethics Journal* 6, 25–40.

Gowdy, A. 1993. *The environmental values of Ottawa planners and the role of these values in a professional code.* Master's of Planning thesis, Queen's University, Kingston, Ontario, Canada.

Grant, J. 1990. Ethical problems in planning for development. *Plan Canada* 30, 30–32.

Hare, R. M. 1987. Commentary on "Hamlethics in planning." *Business and Professional Ethics Journal* 6, 83–87.

Harper, T. L. and Stein, S. M. 1983. The justification of urban intervention: a moral framework. *Environments* 15, 39–47.

———. 1992. The centrality of normative ethical theory to contemporary planning theory. *Journal of Planning Education and Research* 11, 105–116.

Haworth, L. 1963. *The good city.* Bloomington: Indiana University Press.

———. 1984. Orwell, the planning profession, and autonomy. *Environments* 16, 10–15.

Hendler, S. 1990a. Moral theories in professional practice: do they make a difference? *Environments* 20, 20–30.

———. 1990b. Professional codes as bridges between planning and ethics: a case study. *Plan Canada* 30, 22–29.

———. 1991a. Do professional codes legitimate planners' values? In Thomas H. and Healey, P., eds. *Dilemmas of planning practice.* Aldershot, U.K.: Avebury Technical, 156–167.

———. 1991b. Ethics in planning: the views of students and practitioners. *Journal of Planning Education and Research* 10, 99–105.

Hendler, S. and Kinley, J. 1990. Ethics and the planning consultant: a play in one act. *Plan Canada* 30, 29–32.

Hoch, C. 1984. Doing good and being right: the pragmatic connection in planning theory. *Journal of the American Planning Association* 50, 335–344.

Hoover, R. 1961. A view of ethics and planning. *Journal of the American Institute of Planners* 27, 293–304.

Howe, E. 1980. Role choices of urban planners. *Journal of the American Planning Association* 46, 398–409.

———. 1990. Normative ethics in planning. *Journal of Planning Literature* 5, 123–150.

———. 1992. Professional roles and the public interest in planning. *Journal of Planning Literature* 6, 230–248.

———. 1994. *Acting on ethics in city planning*. New Brunswick, NJ: Center for Urban Policy Research, Rutgers—The State University.

Howe, E. and Kaufman, J. 1979. The ethics of contemporary American planners. *Journal of the American Planning Association* 45, 243–255.

———. 1981. The values of contemporary American planners. *Journal of the American Planning Association* 47, 266–278.

———. 1983. Ethics and professional practice. In Dunn, W., ed. *Values, ethics, and the practice of policy analysis*. Lexington, MA: Lexington Books, 9–31.

Kaufman, J. L. 1980. Land planning in an ethical perspective. *Journal of Soil and Water Conservation* 35, 255–258.

———. 1981a. Ethics and planning: some insights from the outside. *Journal of the American Planning Association* April, 196–199.

———. 1981b. Teaching planning ethics. *Journal of Planning Education and Research* 1, 29–35.

———. 1985. American and Israeli planners: a cross-cultural comparison. *Journal of the American Planning Association* 51, 352–364.

———. 1987a. Hamlethics in planning: to do or not to do. *Business and Professional Ethics Journal* 6, 67–77.

———. 1987b. Teaching planning students about strategizing, boundary spanning and ethics. *Journal of Planning Education and Research* 6, 108–115.

———. 1990. American codes of planning ethics: content, development and after-effects. *Plan Canada* 30, 29–34.

Khakee, A. and Dahlgren, L. 1986. Values in futures studies and long-term planning: two Swedish case studies. *Futures* 18 (1), 52–67.

———. 1990. Ethics and values of Swedish planners: a replication and comparison with an American study. *Scandinavian Housing and Planning Research* 7, 65–81.

Klosterman, R. G. 1978. Foundations for normative planning. *Journal of the American Institute of Planners* 44, 37–46.

———. 1983. Fact and value in planning. *Journal of the American Planning Association* 49, 216–225.

Krieger, M. 1987. Commentary on "The expert and the public." *Business and Professional Ethics Journal* 6, 47–50.

Lake, R. 1993. Planning and applied geography: positivism, ethics and geographic information systems. *Progress in Human Geography* 17, 404–413.

Lang, R. and Hendler, S. 1986a. Ethics: drawing the boundaries for professionals. *Ontario Planning Journal* 1, 15–16.

———. 1986b. Planning and ethics: making the link. *Ontario Planning Journal* 1, 14–15.

———. 1986c. Right or wrong: planners respond. *Ontario Planning Journal* 1, 13–15.

———. 1987. Towards a new ethical code. *Ontario Planning Journal* 2, 7–10.

———. 1990. Ethics and professional planners. In MacNiven, D., ed. *Moral expertise.* New York: Routledge, 52–70.

Lucas, J. 1987. The worm and the juggernaut: justice and the public interest. *Business and Professional Ethics Journal* 6, 51–59.

Lucy, W. 1988. American Planning Association's ethical principles include simplistic planning theories. *Journal of the American Planning Association* 54, 147–149.

Mandelbaum, S. 1988. Open moral communities. *Society* 26, 20–27.

McConnell, S. 1981. *Theories for planning: an introduction.* London: Heinemann.

Marcuse, P. 1976. Professional ethics and beyond: values in planning. *Journal of the American Institute of Planners* 42, 264–275.

Marlin, R. 1989. Rawlsian justice and community planning. *International Journal of Applied Philosophy* 4, 36–44.

Martin, E. and Beatley, T. 1993. Our relationship with the earth: environmental ethics in planning education. *Journal of Planning Education and Research* 12, 117–126.

Muller, R. 1991. Ethics: theory and practice in South African planning. *Town and Regional Planning* 31, 17–25.

Pirie, G. 1983. On spatial justice. *Environment and Planning A* 15, 465–473.

Richardson, N. 1990. Four constituencies revisited: some thoughts on planners, politicians and principles. *Plan Canada* 30, 14–17.

Richmond, J. 1986. Review of *Ethics in planning. Journal of the American Planning Association* 52, 370–371.

Shrader-Frechette, K. 1987. Land use planning and analytic methods of policy analysis: comments on Goldstein's essay. *Business and Professional Ethics Journal* 6, 41–46.

Simmons, A. 1987. Consent and fairness in planning land use. *Business and Professional Ethics Journal* 6, 5–20.

Sorensen, A. 1982. Planning comes of age: a liberal perspective. *The Planner* 68, 184–188.

———. 1983. Towards a market theory of planning. *The Planner* 69, 78–84.

Starnes, E. 1987. General commentary. *Business and Professional Ethics Journal* 6, 89–93.

Stegman, M. 1989. Ethical implications of the HUD scandals. *Journal of the American Planning Association* 55, 481–483.

Timmerman, P. 1984a. *Ethics and hazardous waste facility siting.* Solid and Hazardous Waste Management Series, Department of Civil Engineering and the Institute for Environmental Studies. Toronto: University of Toronto.

———. 1984b. *Ethics and the problem of hazardous waste management: an inquiry into methods and approaches.* Solid and Hazardous Waste Management Series, Department of Civil Engineering and the Institute for Environmental Studies. Toronto: University of Toronto.

———. 1992. The ethical sphere. In *Hazardous materials/wastes: social aspects of facility planning and management.* Conference Proceedings. The Institute for Social Impact Assessment, Winnipeg, Manitoba, Canada, 243–248.

Udy, J. 1980. Why plan? Planning and the eternal values. *Plan Canada* 20, 176–183.

Virtanen, P. 1987. Unethical land use. *Planning and Administration* 2, 7–13.

Wachs, M. 1982. Ethical dilemmas in forecasting for public policy. *Public Administration Review* November/December, 246–256.

———. 1989. When planners lie with numbers. *Journal of the American Planning Association* 55, 476–479.

———, ed. 1985. *Ethics in planning.* New Brunswick, NJ: Center for Urban Policy Research, Rutgers—The State University.

Walker, B. 1980. Urban planning and social welfare. *Environment and Planning A* 12, 217–225.

Wood, M. 1982. Planning, justice, and the public good. In Healey, P., McDougall, G., and Thomas, M., eds. *Planning theory: prospects for the 1980s.* Toronto: Pergamon Press, 68–80.

About the Contributors

Timothy Beatley is an Associate Professor and Chair of the Department of Urban and Environmental Planning, University of Virginia, Charlottesville, Virginia.

Hilda Blanco is an Assistant Professor in the Graduate Program in Urban Planning at Hunter College of the City University of New York, New York, New York.

Marcia Marker Feld is a Professor and Director of the Graduate Program in Community Planning and Area Development, University of Rhode Island, Kingston, Rhode Island.

Thomas L. Harper is an Associate Professor in the Faculty of Environmental Design, University of Calgary, Calgary, Alberta, Canada.

Sue Hendler is an Associate Professor in the School of Urban and Regional Planning, Queen's University, Kingston, Ontario, Canada.

Charles Hoch is an Associate Professor in the School of Urban Planning and Policy at the University of Illinois, Chicago, Illinois.

Elizabeth Howe is a Professor in the Department of Urban and Regional Planning, University of Wisconsin–Madison, Wisconsin.

Harvey M. Jacobs is an Associate Professor in the Department of Urban and Regional Planning, University of Wisconsin–Madison, Wisconsin.

Jerome L. Kaufman is a Professor in the Department of Urban and Regional Planning, University of Wisconsin–Madison, Wisconsin.

Richard E. Klosterman is a Professor of Geography and Planning at the University of Akron, Akron, Ohio.

Reg Lang is a Professor in the Faculty of Environmental Studies, York University, North York, Ontario, Canada.

Shean McConnell is an Associate Senior Lecturer in the School of Land and Construction Management at Greenwich University, Dartford (Kent), England.

Randal Marlin is an Associate Professor in the Department of Philosophy at Carleton University, Ottawa, Ontario, Canada.

Jonathan E. D. Richmond is a Lecturer in Economics at the University of Reading in England and will shortly be New South Wales Department of Transport Visiting Professor in Transport Planning at the University of Sydney.

Marsha Ritzdorf is an Associate Professor in Urban Affairs and Planning at the Virginia Polytechnic Institute and State University, Blacksburg, Virginia.

Stanley M. Stein is a Senior Instructor in the Faculty of Environmental Design, University of Calgary, Calgary, Alberta, Canada.

James A. Throgmorton is an Associate Professor in the Graduate Program in Urban and Regional Planning, University of Iowa, Iowa City, Iowa.

Martin Wachs is a Professor of Urban Planning and Director of the Institute of Transportation Studies at the University of California, Los Angeles.

Index